SUPERVISION

SUPERVISION

An Applied Behavioral Science Approach to Managing People

Jerry L. Gray, Ph.D.
Faculty of Administrative Studies
University of Manitoba

KENT PUBLISHING COMPANY
Boston, Massachusetts
A Division of Wadsworth, Inc.

Kent Publishing Company
A Division of Wadsworth, Inc.

Senior Editor: Jack McHugh
Production Editor: Nancy Phinney and Pamela Rockwell
Text Designers: Nancy Phinney and Carol Rose
Cover Designer: Armen Kojoyian
Production Coordinator: Linda Siegrist

Printed in the United States of America

1 2 3 4 5 6 7 8 9 — 87 86 85 84

Library of Congress Cataloging in Publication Data

Gray, Jerry L.
    Supervision: an applied behavioral science approach to managing people.
    Includes index.
    1. Supervision of employees.   I. Title.

HF5549.G676   1984   658.3'02   83-22224
ISBN 0-534-03129-3

To the supervisor who trained me,

FREMONT A. SHULL, JR.

Preface

Any author who takes the time to write a textbook no doubt does so for a variety of reasons. There are two reasons, however, that are probably common to all authors. The author believes, first, that he or she has a unique contribution to make to the field, and second, that existing texts have shortcomings that the author proposes to correct. Decidedly egoistic in nature, these two reasons nevertheless describe my reasons for writing this text on supervision.

My unique contribution consists of the learning I have had firsthand in dealing with supervisors and their problems. In my teaching, training, and consulting activities, I have learned from others a series of concepts and principles that seem (to me at least) to be worth passing on. In some cases, the concepts are not new, but I have attempted to package them in a way that is relevant for first-line supervisors. I firmly believe that supervisors occupy a unique role in organizations, and that much of the management theory taught to them cannot be effectively used simply because it does not consider the uniqueness of the supervisor's position and is not presented in a manner that supervisors can relate to.

This brings me to the second reason. Many textbooks on supervision are available. Unfortunately, there seems to be a perception that supervisors lack the conceptual skills to understand sophisticated management concepts. Consequently, many supervisors are written to as if they cannot think for themselves and must be told what to do. In my experience, most supervisors are quite capable of thinking in analytical terms and, given a clear explanation of the principles, are able to apply the concepts selectively to their own situations. What they need most is a presentation that considers the specifics of the supervisory role and describes the concepts in a language with which they are familiar.

This is what I have tried to achieve in *Supervision: An Applied Behavioral Science Approach to Managing People.* One of the best compliments ever paid to me by a supervisor was, "You sure don't talk like a professor!" and in this book I have tried my hardest not to write like one.

The value of science in any field of inquiry is inestimable. In management particularly, the use of science in developing useful principles of managing people has helped us make great strides in improving the effectiveness of our management systems. But the best scientific findings in the world are of little value if they cannot be understood and applied by those who face managerial problems on a daily basis. In this text, most of the concepts and ideas presented can be backed by scientific evidence, though I have chosen not to clutter the writing with detailed references except in those instances in which specific credit was due. For those ideas that are not purely scientific, I have had to rely on my gut feelings — which are based upon my observations of supervisory practice. In writing about these ideas, I have tried to be more cautious and point out that each supervisor must test them in the work situation to see how they operate.

Examples

I have found in teaching supervisors about managing people that using extreme examples helps make the principles stand out more clearly. I have followed that practice in the text by interspersing examples throughout the chapters. Some of these will be hard to believe, but I assure you that each one is true. In all cases, I have used the examples to illustrate a point, not to prove it.

Orientation of Book

It is difficult to write a supervision text that contains topics of interest and value to everyone. Supervisors' jobs have a wide range of responsibilities and activities. My selection of topics is based solely upon my experiences, both in practicing supervision and in interacting with other supervisors. I have attempted to cover all the topics that relate to the general area of managing people, and to present the material in a manner relevant to practicing supervisors. Rather than write a general management text and adapt it to supervisors, my first consideration has been the supervisor and what he or she needs to succeed in the job. I have always been wary of texts that present and discuss theories and concepts that supervisors cannot use because of their usually limited authority. So my focus starts with the supervisor and the unique properties of that role, and then develops those concepts that can improve supervisory effectiveness.

The Audience

The primary audience for this book is practicing supervisors who are studying supervision for the first time, or students who have no supervisory experience but are taking a first course in supervision. It is designed for junior and community colleges, supervisory training programs, and other educational institutions in which the training of supervisors is the primary focus. No background is assumed, although like any book on management, some organizational experience will be helpful in understanding the concepts.

Student Aids

THE EXERCISES.   Each chapter contains two exercises designed to get the student to internalize the learning up to that point. The nature of the exercises varies widely, but they generally require the student to engage in some type of activity with others. This might be a group discussion, interview, problem-solving session, or role-playing exercise.

THE CASES.   Each chapter contains a case at the end with discussion questions. All cases have been written especially for this text and are based upon real incidents. Suggested case analyses are contained in the Instructor's Manual.

OPENING INCIDENTS.   To assist in getting the student into the topic as early as possible, each chapter begins with an incident. The incident sets the stage for the chapter content by ending with a problem or unanswered question. At the end of the chapter, the incident is analyzed for the students so they can see how the chapter content might be applied.

OTHER STUDENT AIDS.   Each chapter also contains a set of behavioral learning objectives, a list of key terms covered in the chapter, and a glossary of terms and definitions for easy reference.

Ancillaries

STUDENT STUDY GUIDE.   A Student Study Guide is available to assist the student in understanding the text. The book contains sample test questions, terminology questions, and review questions. The primary purpose of the book is to reinforce what the student has learned in the text and in class.

INSTRUCTOR'S MANUAL.   An accompanying Instructor's Manual contains true-false questions, multiple-choice questions, suggested teaching aids, case analysis suggestions, and transparency masters. A computerized test bank is also available.

Acknowledgments

I wish to thank Don Miller of Emporia, Kansas State College and Robert Redick of Lincoln Land Community College, who read part of the initial manuscript. I owe special thanks to the following people, who read the final manuscript and made many constructive suggestions for improvement. They are Harry Schneider of Longwood College, Fred Sutton of Cuyahoga Community College, Ralph Todd of American River College, and Tom Von der Embse of Wright State University.

Special thanks goes to Harry Schneider, who wrote Chapter 17, "Safety Management." Harry's experience in the safety field has added significantly to the text.

As I noted earlier, much of the material in the text is not footnoted. However, I would like to recognize the source of many of the ideas, particularly the material on minimal managerial authority, prescribed and discretionary tasks, and the general properties of supervisory roles. Much of my earlier training was with the Glacier Project in London, England, and many useful and innovative ideas were generated by Elliott Jaques and Wilfred Brown. I have used their ideas freely. Some of the material has been adapted from Fred Starke's and my other book, *Organizational Behavior: Concepts and Applications*, 3rd edition (Merrill Publishing Company). Chapter 15 in particular relied heavily on Fred's work.

I would also like to thank Irene Rabb for her preparation of the accompanying student Study Guide.

Thanks are also due to my manager and friend, Dean Roland Grandpre, for his understanding and support during the writing of this book. It cost him half an associate dean for more than a year, and I intend to pay him back.

Finally, my wife and son, Lynda and Derek, deserve untold gratitude for putting up with half a husband and probably less of a father for far too long. Yes, son, the book is done and we can go play now.

Jerry L. Gray, Ph.D.
Winnipeg, Manitoba, Canada
December, 1983

Contents

I

Understanding the Role of the Supervisor

Introduction to the Behavioral Science Approach

1

Chapter Learning Objectives

After reading and studying this chapter you should be able to:
1. Define the term *supervisor*.
2. Describe the scientific approach to the study of behavior.
3. Describe the applied behavioral science approach to supervision.
4. Compare and contrast theory and experience as methods of learning about supervision.
5. Describe the major advantages of the applied behavioral science approach to supervision.
6. List the basic principles of behavioral science.

Key Terms

Supervisor
Behavioral science
Scientific method
Model

Theory
Applied behavioral
science

The Newspaper Ad

John Coznowski read the ad over carefully for the second time. He never saw an ad like this before and it aroused his curiosity. Also, the job sounded appealing. The ad read:

We are looking for a first-level supervisor who knows how to manage people. Our firm is in a very competitive industry and we depend upon our people to maintain an edge on the competition. Ideally, the successful applicant will have 3–5 years experience in supervision and have a good track record of motivating people. Prior experience in our industry is not required. If you think you are good enough, complete the following quiz and mail it in with a summary of your background.

Mark the following questions either true or false.

1. Money is a good motivator for people. (T   F)
2. Participative supervisory styles are best. (T   F)
3. People appreciate improvements in working conditions. (T   F)
4. People like to work towards challenging goals. (T   F)
5. A supervisor should be the natural leader of the work group. (T   F)

John then began thinking about the answers to the questions.

This book is about supervision and managing people. Although their responsibilities differ considerably, all supervisors have the responsibility for managing the people that work for them. It is often said that people are the most important asset in any organization, and supervisors are the first level of management responsible for this asset.

Supervisors manage first-level workers (as shown in Figure 1.1) and supervision is often referred to as getting things done through people. If we assume for the moment that the *people* part of this definition is true, then our need to understand people and their behavior becomes obvious. Unless a supervisor can work with people and get the best from them, efficiency and productivity will suffer.

There are many ways of studying supervision. We can study what supervisors do, how they spend their time, whom they interact with, the kinds of decisions they make, and the kinds of problems they have. Each way reveals something different about the concept of supervision and this book will examine them all in detail. But, over the years a specific approach—one based on the scientific method of research and termed **behavioral science**—has proved to be of great practical value to supervisors. Perhaps it is because supervisors must spend so much of their time managing people that they have found it so useful. In any case, behavioral science is the approach adopted by this book, so it is important to

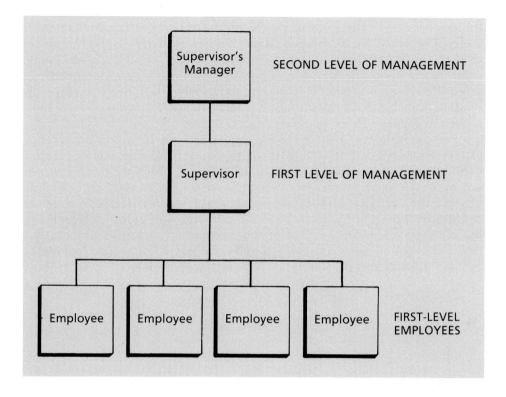

Figure 1.1. Position of Supervisor.

understand the role of science and the study of behavior as it relates to learning about supervision.

This chapter introduces the behavioral science approach: what it is, and how it can be used to make you a better supervisor. It sets the stage for the rest of the book, which applies the behavioral science principles to supervision.

Supervision and Science

The Scientific Approach

Generally speaking, the purpose of science (and the methods of science) is to help us understand things. We usually associate science with the physical part of our world, that is, biology, chemistry, or physics, but it applies to the behavior of people as well. A greater understanding of human behavior can be gained by applying the **scientific method** to its study. The scientific method consists of controlled and detailed examination of the subject, precise measurement of the variables, and conclusions based upon the analysis of the information. The outcome of the scientific research is referred to as a **model,** which attempts to show the relationships between the variables under study. A sample of a model is shown in Figure 1.2.

For example, suppose we wish to understand how communication affects motivation. The scientific approach requires that we first define explicitly the two concepts communication and motivation. Once these are defined, we must devise a method of measurement; then we can observe the changes in motivation that occur when there is a change in communication. On the basis of the information we gain, we would formulate a model of cause-and-effect between communication and motivation. We could then use this model in other situations involving communication and motivation to manage people more effectively.

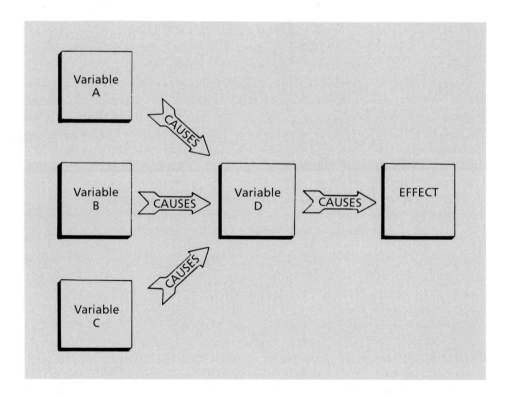

Figure 1.2. Sample Model Showing Cause and Effect.

While the example above is most simplified, it does give a flavor of the scientific approach to human behavior. Behavioral science principles have been reasonably well tested both in theory and in practice. The principles that have proved to be the most useful constitute the foundation of this book.

The Purpose of the Scientific Approach

The primary objectives of any science are *understanding, prediction*, and *control.* Examples of this are most obvious in the physical sciences, such as physics, chemistry, and mathematics. For example, in the case of weather, our understanding of how weather systems operate allows us to predict—to a reasonable degree—what the weather will be. More research into weather systems may someday allow us greater control over the weather, although it is unlikely that we will ever have total control.

To illustrate how understanding, prediction, and control operate in real life, let's use an example we are all familiar with. Assume that we are the senior managers of a utility company and we wish to control the use of electric power in our city. Our first step is to measure the usage of electricity with a reliable device, in this case a meter that measures kilowatt hours of usage. After repeated observations, we discover that more electricity is used between the hours of 6:00 A.M. and 9:00 A.M., and 4:00 P.M. and 7:00 P.M. This constitutes the pattern that shows us how the system behaves, so we can now predict fairly accurately when electricity will be consumed, and at what levels. Now, if we wish to control the usage (which, you will recall, was our original objective), the answer is pretty obvious. If we increase the rates during the peak hours, consumption of electricity is likely to decrease as people begin to postpone usage until a time when the rates are lower. Therefore, we have exerted a degree of control over the system.

The Behavioral Science Approach

The scientific approach to studying people, called behavioral science, has the same objectives. Supervisors and managers would like to exercise better control over the behavior of employees. To accomplish this, they must first understand why people behave as they do. This understanding makes it more possible to predict what people will do in certain situations. The next step, control, is based upon the level of knowledge of the first two steps.

While the scientific approach and the behavioral science approach have much in common, there are some differences. For one thing, it is much easier to measure things in the physical sciences than in the behavioral area. Unfortunately, we have no meters that can measure how people feel, what their level of motivation is, or what their goals are. Supervisors, therefore, are left with a lot more guesswork than is typically the case in other areas.

Another difference between the two approaches is that behavioral systems tend to be more complex than many physical systems. In the electricity example, we faced a relatively simple system: demand for electricity was a function of price and we could control that system by changing the price of electricity. Rare is the case in the behavioral sciences in which a single factor could have such an impact on people's behavior. Only in the case of *major* changes in something might a single factor produce a measurable, long-term change in behavior.

What Good Is Behavioral Science?

In view of what has been said so far this is certainly a legitimate question. There is no doubt that the ability of behavioral science to understand, predict, and control is significantly less than that of the physical sciences. However, to appreciate its value, an understanding of the alternatives is needed. Without the scientific approach to studying people at work, managing people would be even more difficult than it is. Every time a manager or supervisor approached a people problem, it would be like encountering fire or rain for the first time. We would have no theory to use until we tried a solution and created our own. In fact, in the early days of management this was largely the case. However, as various managers and researchers began to discuss their experiences with others to find common patterns, some general principles emerged that proved use-

Money As a Motivator

As an example of how complex behavioral systems can be, consider the question of money as a motivator. Is it or isn't it? The question has been studied for years and, as you might expect, the answer is not clear. Sometimes it is and sometimes it isn't. It's also easy to understand why the answer isn't clear. If you just received a pay increase of 5%, this increase may be thrown in with the fact that (a) your house payment is due, (b) you just received a substantial increase in your insurance bill, (c) your grandmother died and just left you a $2,000 inheritance, (d) the stock market just took a nosedive and cut the value of your portfolio by 25%, (e) your income tax refund just came in the mail, (f) the average salary increase in your company was 10%, and (g) you expected an 8% increase. It is not difficult to see that all these factors in the system will make it difficult to tell if the money motivated you. However, if you received a pay increase in the area of 50%, there is a very good chance that your motivation would increase. This is because the size of the increase overwhelms all the other factors that normally affect your behavior.

ful. Over time, these experiences accumulated to the extent that we now have a useful body of knowledge that can be applied to the management of people. As the content of this book will illustrate, we still have much to learn about managing people, but we have also made some significant progress towards understanding, prediction, and control in the behavioral sciences.

Behavioral Science Theories

As we have suggested, the use of the scientific approach to managing people provides us with theories. These theories, many of which are discussed in this book, can be used to improve effectiveness in managing people once the role of theories is understood.

The Role of Theory in Supervision

A **theory** is designed to give a basic understanding of what causes what by describing the relationships between the variables in a system. In our electricity example, the scientific approach allowed us to create a theory of electricity consumption, which we could then use to achieve our objective. This theory would not, however, allow us to predict what any specific household would do regarding consumption of electricity. As the pay increase example shows, other factors would probably affect the use of electricity, such as number of people in the household, their lifestyle, level of wealth, and so forth. If we apply our theory to any single household, we stand a good chance of being wrong.

The same is true of theories in the behavioral sciences. They are not normally designed to predict individual behavior. Those that do attempt it are very complex. It is wise therefore to be wary of any theory that proposes that all people are this way, or all people do such and such in this situation. In this book you will find some qualification, such as, most people *tend* to do such and such, and even this is a pretty strong statement given the complexity of individuals.

Sources of Behavioral Science Theories

Where do our behavioral science theories come from? They come from many sources. The scientific origins lie in the fields of psychology, sociology, anthropology, economics, and political science (see Fig. 1.3). Many of the principles contained in this book originated, not in studies of supervision, but in research involving people in a variety of situations. It is only relatively recently that management and supervision have received the full attention of behavioral scientists.

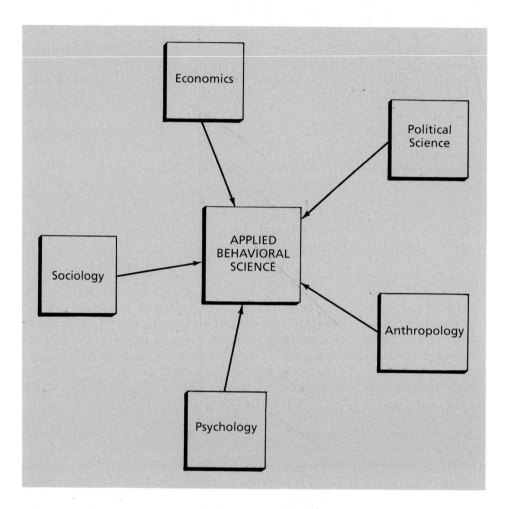

Figure 1.3. The Applied Behavioral Science Approach.

Most frequently managers and supervisors themselves are the source of theories. A problem may occur in the work situation, and the supervisor attempts to solve it. The solution works, so that decision now becomes a theory in the mind of the supervisor. The next time that situation occurs, the solution is applied again. When this happens to many supervisors over a long period of time, an accepted theory of managing people is created. At some point in the process, someone (here referred to as a behavioral scientist) will apply a more scientific approach to the problem, but its origins will often be from the practical side of the problem.

Theory and Practice

The argument about theory versus practice is well known to us all. But since this book is based upon behavioral science *theories*, you will want to understand how these theories can help you in practicing supervision. Can you learn to be a good supervisor by reading a book?

Can Supervision Be Studied?

Since you are now reading a text on supervision, the answer is apparently yes, but an explanation and qualification is in order. A comment often heard from experienced supervisors (who proudly claim they graduated from the school of hard knocks) is that good supervision cannot be learned from a book, but can only come from the experience of actually being a supervisor. Furthermore, there is no doubt that some very effective supervisors have never studied the theory of managing people, and some very ineffective supervisors know a lot about behavioral science theories. If this is true, why should you study a behavioral science approach to supervision?

The answer has to do with probabilities. Despite the fact that some good supervisors know little theory and some bad ones know a lot of theory, these are in the minority. Most people fall somewhere in between the extremes and for them, studying behavioral science principles can help. Also, it is worth remembering that good supervisors who have not studied any theory are still operating using theoretical principles. It's just that they haven't formally studied them. But if you ask them what they do to be effective with people, they will give you their personal collection of behavioral science theories.

The other factor to consider is that the school of hard knocks can teach some very expensive lessons. Since there are no theories available, each lesson must be learned from experience, and although experience is an excellent teacher, it is also relatively inefficient. In this book you will study theories that will help you avoid at least the more expensive lessons. Something that might take you years to learn on the job can be learned relatively quickly by studying the theory.

Finally, it should be noted that learning from experience can also be very painful. Supervisors will constantly encounter new and different situations and will have no choice but to experiment with solutions. It is unlikely that all of these experiments will turn out right, so many errors are likely to be made along the path of learning. Unfortunately, this process has turned many potentially good supervisors into unhappy people because they could not take the pain of learning. All too often, companies practice poor selection and training practices that stack the odds against the new supervisor.

Exercise 1.1

Driving and Supervising

Have you ever thought about the fact that it is often more difficult to get a driver's license than it is to become a supervisor? To obtain a driver's license the applicant has to read a book (usually describing principles or laws), then take a test on his or her knowledge about driving, and finally get behind the wheel for a driving test. If the principles are mastered and put into practice, a driver's license is granted.

Interview at least two supervisors and compare their preparation for supervision to the driver's license example. Are they similar or different? Why?

Is Experience of Any Value?

Of course it is. Imagine trying to learn to ride a bicycle by reading a book! You might read every book written and still fall flat on your face the first time you tried actually to ride one. In fact, experience is so important in learning to ride a bicycle that most of us don't even bother to read a book about it at all and we function quite well.

How can this be? Doesn't this negate the value of theory? Not really when you think back as to *how* most of us gained experience in riding the bicycle. Usually, we started with a small bicycle, probably with training wheels. Someone helped us on, showed us the basics, and walked beside us as we took our first spin down the driveway. Eventually, we could do all this by ourselves, so we followed our parents on their bicycles and learned the principles and problems associated with riding a bicycle: traffic patterns, street signs, and exuberant dogs. After we proved our abilities to our parents' satisfaction, the training wheels came off and the whole process began again. Eventually, we mastered the bicycle and were on our own, an occasion that can take up to two years for some. Compare this with how many supervisors learn their supervisory skills; in some cases the training program consists of a set of keys to the office and a backlog of work.

The moral of the bicycle example is that experience can be a good teacher, provided that we receive an adequate amount of training, support, and guidance in the experience.

Organizations clearly place a very high value on experience. When is the last time you saw an advertisement stating, "Wanted: A Supervisor With a Strong Theoretical Background"? Most advertisements specify that they want a supervisor with *experience.* The reason for this is that theories are general in nature and it is experience that improves the supervisor's skill in applying them properly.

The other reason why organizations prefer experienced supervisors is that it takes less time to learn *about* theories than how to apply them. Given a choice, most organizations would prefer someone who already has the most difficult part (i.e., experience) behind him or her, even though it does mean putting the cart before the horse.

How to Learn from Experience

To get the maximum benefit from your experiences you have to learn the correct lessons from them. The lessons, coupled with the theories you will learn from this book, will assist you in becoming a more effective supervisor.

The best way to learn from your experiences is to examine them as scientifically as possible. This means doing two things: trying to find a cause-and-effect relationship in the experience, and being as objective as possible. If you cannot be objective, you will have difficulty tracing cause and effect. Objectivity is critical in the scientific approach. Without it, your analysis will be distorted by biases, perceptions, stereotypes, and other emotional factors, as Figure 1.4 illustrates.

The Applied Behavioral Science Approach

The integration of the theory and the practice of supervision results in the **applied behavioral science** approach, which uses accepted principles to understand, predict, and control people's behavior. This book de-

A Supervisor Learns from Experience

I encountered a man once who was very unhappy with his progress as a supervisor. It seemed that he consistently lost his best employees. This became quite frustrating to him because he was always having to hire new people and train them. The company was concerned because he had the highest training costs and turnover rate of any supervisor. When asked why these people kept leaving, he generally answered, "We don't pay them enough. If we paid more, I wouldn't lose as many." He said this in spite of the fact that pay rates were the same for employees under other supervisors who had much lower turnover.

He began some individual counselling sessions with a person in the personnel department who had been trained in problem solving. During their discussions, it came out that perhaps the major reason for his high turnover was the way he managed his people. It seemed that he was a very critical supervisor who seldom praised his good people, but was always there to point out their mistakes. It was only after a lot of help from others that he was able to become objective about the problem and begin to improve his situation.

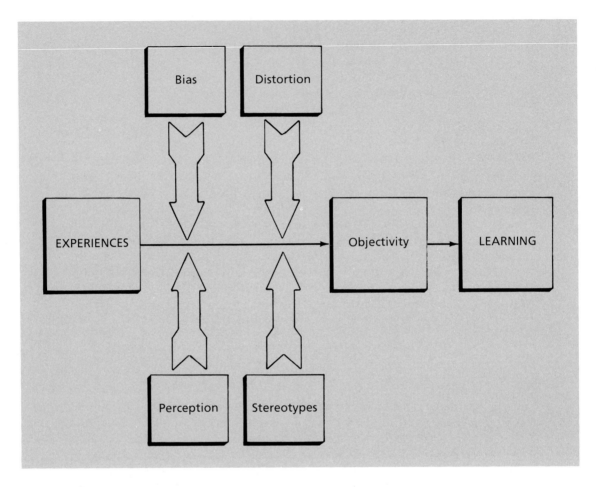

Figure 1.4. Factors Affecting How We Learn from Our Experiences.

scribes what we know about people at work, and how this knowledge can be applied. To illustrate the principles, there are numerous examples sprinkled throughout each chapter (you have already seen two in this chapter) to show how the theory or concept might be applied. It is probably obvious by now why there are many more theories and concepts than there are examples.

Each chapter also contains exercises that allow you the opportunity actually to experience the theories firsthand. Most will require you to engage in an activity that utilizes the theories presented. The final part of each exercise is usually a discussion, which offers you an opportunity to examine cause-and-effect relationships in your experience. The objective is not only to give you the experience of using the theory, but also to assist you in learning from your experiences.

Basic Behavioral Science Principles

The following chapters present many theories and concepts that are relevant to specific supervision topics. All have been subjected, in varying degrees, to the test of behavioral science. However, on a more fundamental level, there are accepted behavioral science principles that provide a foundation for learning about supervision and how to put theories into practice. These foundation principles not only provide a base for the theories that follow, but also serve as a useful guide in the daily practice of supervision on the job.

For many reasons, no proof of these principles is offered. They are the culmination of research, experience, and wisdom, tempered with common sense. Their application is wide, their uses are many. Any supervisor would be well advised to etch these principles in memory and make them a permanent part of his or her philosophy of supervision.

1. *All people are different.* While people are similar in many ways, each person is different. No two people have the same values, attitudes, feelings, goals, or abilities. It is primarily because of this principle that a supervisor's job can be so difficult.

2. *There is no one best way.* The fact that all people are different prevents the development of principles that can have universal application. Although it may appear that a particular supervisory strategy works all the time, beware of the exceptions.

3. *Personalities cannot be changed.* Part of managing people is dealing with a variety of personalities. Occasionally, you will find personality clashes that affect performance and are difficult to handle. However, behavior—not personality—*can* be changed, and much of this book deals with strategies appropriate for changing behavior.

4. *Perfection with people is impossible.* You will not be able to solve all people problems, nor should you try. If you expect people to behave perfectly, you will continually be disappointed.

5. *Natural motivations are more powerful than artificial ones.* This is another way of saying that you will find it easier to accept people for what they are, rather than trying to make them into something they aren't.

Although they are not always mentioned specifically, these five principles are basic to applying all the theories and concepts in this book. They are the essence of the applied behavioral science approach to supervision.

Practical Theories of Supervision

It was noted in this chapter that all supervisors operate according to theories. This exercise requires that you find out what these theories are. Interview anyone who manages other people, preferably one who has the title of supervisor. Ask the question: "What principles of managing people do you use in your job?" Make a list of as many principles as the supervisor can provide. In class, compare your list with those of others, and discuss the following questions:

1. Are any of the principles similar? Which ones?
2. Which principles, according to your experience, are the most valid?
3. Which principles, if any, reflect the basic behavioral science principles discussed in this chapter?

Key to Success

Although the benefits of the scientific approach are widely recognized with regard to the hard sciences, this approach is often neglected in areas such as supervision and management. However, the benefits from using the scientific approach in supervision are no less significant than those gained in other areas of scientific research. The applied behavioral science approach to supervision is the best method of acquiring knowledge, attitudes, and skills about managing people at work.

The theories and concepts in this book are based on behavioral science principles. These principles have been tested in a variety of work situations and have proven to produce predictable effects on most people. You will find that occasionally a theory or principle will not work as proposed, or that an individual employee does not behave as the theory says he or she should. However, instead of rejecting all you have learned about behavioral science, these "exceptions" should be analyzed objectively to find out WHY the situation has happened. Other behavioral science techniques, such as good communication and observation, will help you understand the behavior of others, which in turn will add to your understanding of people and further sharpen your skills. Although you must remember that behavioral science is not as precise as the physical sciences, you will add to the body of knowledge known as supervision by analyzing as scientifically as possible the behavior of those working around you.

Some years ago a teacher of mine gave me a paper about successful supervision. In that paper, the author stated that all managers should "think like doctors." By that he meant that managers should analyze problems in the same way that doctors examine patients. Doctors try to learn as much about the symptoms of the patient as possible, analyze the causes of the symptoms, and then prescribe a solution based upon principles of medical science. Throughout the process, they remain objective and rational; i.e., at no time should they form an emotional feeling about the patient or the disease. This objectivity is universally characteristic of the scientific approach in both medicine and other sciences. It is also the characteristic that often separates good supervisors from poor ones. Supervisors who learn from their experiences grow and develop as supervisors. They are able to overcome their mistakes by objectively analyzing cause-and-effect processes in their own behavior. Although we do not expect supervisors to be as objective as the pure scientist, it is an ideal to shoot for.

There will always be some things that cannot be learned scientifically. Sometimes personal traits, hereditary factors, or just plain luck, help or hinder our success as supervisors. There is no way of eliminating these factors from supervision, nor would we want to. What you should do, however, is distinguish between scientific and nonscientific aspects of supervision, for only the scientific part can be taught to others. Therefore, you should not attempt to acquire supervisory behaviors that are not reasonably scientific in their basis.

Summary

This chapter has described the behavioral science approach and how it can be used to study supervision. The application of the scientific method to behavioral situations produces theories of human behavior that can be used in supervising people. Although these theories do not provide exact answers, they are useful in analyzing problems and suggesting possible alternative solutions. Experience in supervision is a valuable teacher, but it has its limits; having to learn everything by doing is inefficient. Theories result from the combining of scientifically controlled experiences and can therefore be used by other supervisors. The chapter concluded with five basic behavioral science principles that are used in the remainder of the book.

Opening Incident Revisited

John Coznowski's situation can be analyzed from two perspectives. First, how he should answer the questions, and second, the company's purpose in placing this type of advertisement. Let's take the second one first since that will help John decide what to do.

The company is obviously attempting to devise a selection tool that will help it select a supervisor who is good with people. Nothing wrong with that, of course, but how is it doing it? First, it is assuming that there are correct answers to the questions. But the complex nature of people (which has been described by behavioral science research) suggests that there are no single right answers about supervising people. Therefore, a supervisor who believed that money is a good motivator would be unsuccessful at motivating someone who didn't care about money. A similar conclusion could be reached for all the questions.

Second, the company is apparently assuming that knowing the right answers to the questions means one would also be able to supervise people effectively. As this chapter explains, the science of knowing something about people, and skill at implementing that knowledge are two different things.

This presents an interesting dilemma for John. Is the company really looking for a true or false answer, or does it want people to question the validity of the test? If it believes that there are right and wrong answers to the questions, then if John points out that behavioral science would not support cut-and-dried answers, he would probably never get an interview. However, maybe the company wants applicants to point out that the statements are too general to be of any use, and this is its measure of a person's ability to manage people. In either case, John has no choice. He must answer the questions in a manner consistent with his knowledge about behavioral science because to do otherwise would jeopardize not only his personal integrity, but also his chances of succeeding in the job if he were to get it.

Review Questions

1. What is the applied behavioral science approach to supervision?
2. What is the purpose of the scientific approach to supervision?
3. Where do behavioral science theories come from?
4. What is the major difference between theory (learning about supervision) and experience (actually being a supervisor)?
5. What are the basic behavioral science principles?

Chapter Glossary

Supervisor.   The first level of management in an organization that must get work done through others.

Behavioral science.   An approach to studying behavior based upon the scientific method of research.

Scientific method.   A method of research which requires repeated and controlled observation of a system to determine the cause-and-effect relationship between the variables in the system.

Model.	A diagram of the relationship between variables in a system.
Theory.	A proposed description of relationships between variables in a system.
Applied behavioral science.	The use of accepted behavioral science principles to understand, predict, and control the behavior of people.

Case Problem

Charter Manufacturing Company

Marion Schmidt, personnel manager of Charter Manufacturing Company, just had her third meeting in as many weeks with Tom Dodd, the section head in the accounting department. Tom has been having difficulty with Frank McCreary, one of his supervisors. He has received several complaints from McCreary's staff and the turnover in his department was higher than in other units in the section. Their discussions usually center around what to do about McCreary. This recent conversation is typical:

TOM: I just don't think he has it. He's been supervisor now for over a year and things just don't seem to be getting any better.

MARION: Do you think he knows he's been having trouble?

TOM: Sure he knows. I've told him on several occasions that he'd better shape up, but there's been no change.

MARION: Why is he having problems?

TOM: I think it's his personality. He just rubs people the wrong way.

MARION: Has he ever had any training in supervising?

TOM: No, but we've got a lot of good supervisors around here who have never had any training.

MARION: Why don't we send him to a supervision course. Maybe that would help.

TOM: I think it would be a waste of time. He just can't get along with his people. I think we should just fire him and start with someone else.

Questions for Discussion

1. What are the merits of Marion's proposal?
2. What are the merits of Tom's position?
3. Should McCreary be fired? Why or why not?

Understanding the Role of the Supervisor

2

Chapter Learning Objectives

After studying this chapter you should be able to:

1. Describe why managing people is an important skill for supervisors.

2. Describe the unique characteristics of the supervisor's role.

3. Define the concept of role.

4. Define and explain the relationship among authority, responsibility, and accountability.

5. List the areas of authority a supervisor needs to have in order to be accountable for the performance of others.

6. Describe the common limits to authority.

7. Explain the relationship between the supervisor's job and technical tasks.

8. Explain why the best worker does not necessarily make the best supervisor.

Key Terms

Role
Supervisory role
Authority
Responsibility
Accountability

Supervisor
Minimal supervisory
   authority
Veto Authority

21

To Supervise or Not To Supervise

Mary Bradford has worked for the Atlas Paper Company for three years as a clerk and secretary. During that time, she has always received good performance ratings from her supervisors and has been told that advancement is possible if she maintains her good record.

Just before she was leaving for the weekend last Friday, the general manager called her in her office and told her that a supervisor's position has opened up and the management group has selected her for the position. If she wants the job, she will be in charge of a small office that handles shipping invoices and employs seven clerks and typists. She will report to the manager of the shipping department.

Mary is concerned about the new position because she has never worked in the shipping department before. She wonders why the company did not choose someone who has already worked there and knows the jobs well.

Since the previous supervisor quit without giving any advance notice, the company needs to know Mary's answer by Monday morning.

The Need for Understanding

I once saw a cartoon that pictured two senior newspaper people talking after what had obviously been a hectic day at the paper. One said to the other, "Just think! Hundreds of highly paid people have stayed up all night to write, edit, and print the most important news of the day, and in the final analysis the success of our work lies in the hands of a ten-year-old newspaper delivery boy!" Interestingly, the same situation also occurs in oganizations; success lies in the hands of a supervisor. This is not to mean that supervisors have no more skill than a ten-year old, but it does emphasize the fact that all of the planning, developing, financing, and creating typically done at the higher levels of the organization ultimately depends upon a first-line supervisor for its success. It would not be too presumptuous, therefore, to suggest that the supervisor is the most important element of the managerial hierarchy, or is at least no less important than any other manager.

The Importance of Managing People

As its title indicates, this book is about supervisors managing people. This is not to say that managing people is the only responsibility of a supervisor, or even the most important one. That will vary from situation to situation. Supervisors also have responsibility for financial management, technical supervision, cost control, production (or service) management, and materials management, for example.

The one thing that tends to be common to most supervisors, however, is the large amount of time they spend dealing with people. Studies consistently show that managers spend a majority of their time (sometimes as high as ninety percent) interacting with other people. These may be subordinates, other supervisors, union officials, or higher management, as Figure 2.1 illustrates. Of these groups, most of the time is typically spent with employees, depending, of course, upon the size of the work group.

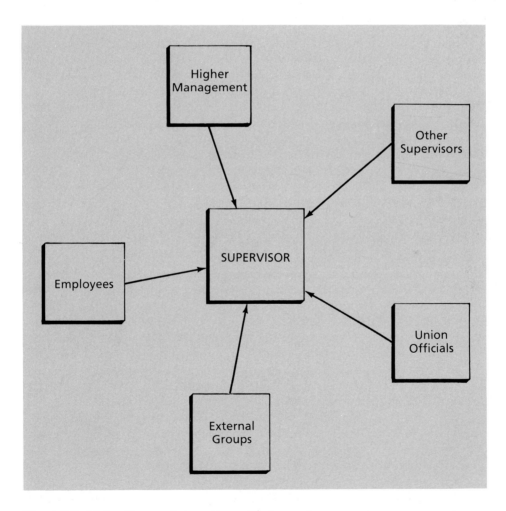

Figure 2.1. Major Groups Interacting with Supervisors.

This book will concentrate on the people side of the supervisor's job, with emphasis upon managing employees. The general opinion is that people are the most underutilized asset in most organizations and that greater increases in productivity can be achieved in this area than in any other, and that supervisors play a key role in these potential increases.

It is because of this importance that supervision is a major area of study today. When we stop and realize that for the majority of employees in an organization the only manager they will have any significant contact with is their supervisor, the importance of improving the quality of supervision in industry, government, and nonprofit organizations is apparent.

The Nature of the Role

In this chapter the major emphasis is upon understanding the basic nature of the supervisory role. Rather than merely describing typical supervisory roles, however, we shall develop a description of the ideal role, and then show how this role is modified in the real world. The reason for this approach is that often the failure of newly appointed first-line supervisors is due not to inadequacies of the individual, but rather to problems in how the supervisory role was designed. Understanding how the role *should* be designed will help you avoid these problems.

What Is a Supervisor?

In Chapter 1 a definition of *supervisor* was given, so the question "What is a supervisor?" may seem strange. Doesn't everyone know what a supervisor is? The evidence suggests that they probably do not. A few examples will illustrate what we mean. Try an experiment sometime. Post a memo addressed to all supervisors announcing a meeting and see who shows up. You will probably get everyone from middle managers to the person in charge of a one-person department. Or, you might get no one! If you did the same thing in another organization you would probably get a totally different response. Another method is simply to ask people to name all the supervisors in the organization or a given area of the organization. Odds are you will never get the same list twice.

Why does this happen? How is it that something as common as a supervisor is so difficult to identify? The major reason is something that has always been a millstone around the neck of management and will, unfortunately, continue to be so in the foreseeable future: the lack of scientifically determined concepts in the study of organization and management. Compare, for example, how precisely terms are defined in the physical sciences. When we speak of basic concepts like gravity, atmosphere, calorie, or horsepower, we can always refer to a specific set of constructs that universally define the concept so that everyone knows what we are talking about. The lay person usually relies heavily on generally accepted definitions; so when we buy a car with one hundred horsepower we know what we are getting.

Of course one of the major reasons for these differences lies in the more precise measurements available in the physical sciences. It is much easier to measure horsepower than a supervisor's duties. But measurement is only incidental to the problem. It is still possible — and necessary — to identify concepts by their unique properties, that is, to enumerate the specific characteristics of something that differentiate it from other things. This, then, is the method we shall use to identify supervisors: not to list the behaviors and skills that are common to all managers, but the ones that are peculiar to the role we call *supervisor*. Later in this book we shall deal with managing people in the more general sense and show how these concepts and principles can be applied to anyone engaged in supervision, including supervisors. After all, presidents must still supervise vice-presidents even though they are not normally thought of as being supervisors.

The Concept of a Role

Before getting to a more precise definition of a supervisor, we must first understand the concept of role. The term is often mistakenly used as a synonym for job. The job (or **job description**) is the official statement of the responsibilities for a position. It describes the formal expectations of the organization, and deals with duties, responsibilities, reporting relationships, and so forth. The **role,** on the other hand, is the total of *all* expectations from others who must interact with the person in the job. Figure 2.2 contrasts an organizational job description with a role. Note that the notion of role recognizes many different expectations coming from various sources. The number of expectations alone suggests that the role is more complicated than the formal job description. Assuming that some of these expectations are in conflict with each other (for example, the boss wants the supervisor to press for more productivity and the employees want the opposite), we gain some appreciation for what real life is like.

In this book the term supervisory role will be used to describe what supervisors do, that is, what they are formally required to do *and* what is expected of them. Not only is this consistent with our applied behavioral science approach, but it also recognizes the realities of the supervisor's position.

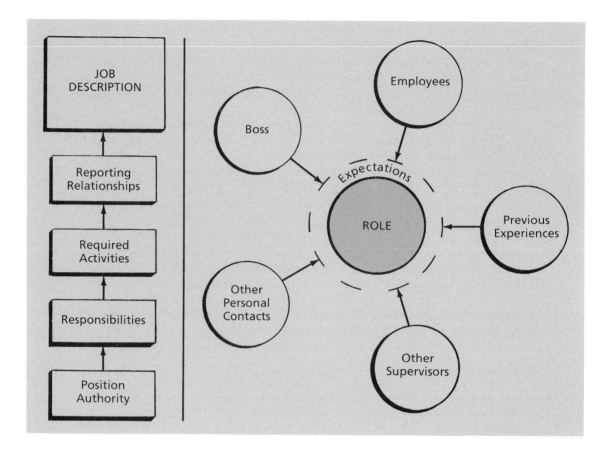

Figure 2.2. Comparison of the Job Description with the Concept of Role.

The Basic Building Blocks

There are three concepts that constitute the basic building blocks of any managerial role, including the supervisory one. They are authority, responsibility, and accountability. We deal with these in detail in Chapter 4, but definitions are needed here to develop the concept of supervisory authority.

Because *role* is a behavioral science concept, it is, by definition, devoid of value judgments. In other words, roles are described with regard to their properties, not the people in them. For example, some people object to use of the terms *subordinate* and *superior*, thinking that they are an affront to individual dignity. Scientifically speaking, however, these terms describe role relationships, not the individuals in the roles. If we have two roles, one of which is accountable to the other, then one role is subordinate to the superior role. So while reading these terms throughout the text, remember that we are describing roles and role relationships, not people.

1. **Authority** is the right to make decisions. Taken literally, all jobs have some authority in them since everyone makes decisions about something. As used here, authority is a formal concept not necessarily associated with the individual or role expectations. Another concept (power), which is developed later in this book, is that part of authority associated with the individual.

2. **Responsibility** is the obligation to make decisions. Likewise a formal concept, it describes the types of activities attached to a job. For example, a supervisor might be responsible for maintaining a safe work environment for employees.

3. **Accountability,** being answerable for the exercise of authority and responsibility, is the process that ties these first two concepts together. Without accountability, there would be no evaluation as to how well a manager performed his or her duties.

With these three basic concepts, we can now develop a specific definition of the supervisory role.

Defining the Formal Supervisory Role

There are three properties of supervisory roles that distinguish them from other managerial roles in the organization: (a) their place in the organizational hierarchy, (b) the people they supervise, and (c) the amount of authority they have.

In our context, supervisors are those individuals who occupy the first level of management in the organization. In other words, they perform the managerial functions — planning, organizing, directing, and controlling — at the first level above the operative employees. Below this level such functions may be performed, but not by one person for another.

The people they supervise are rank-and-file employees who have no managerial authority themselves. The size of the work group is not important for our definition since the managerial functions must be performed regardless of the number of employees supervised.

Authority is difficult to measure objectively since it is a relative concept. While the specifics of each supervisory position will vary considerably, all should have in common accountability for the performance of employees. Therefore, supervisors should have the authority necessary to direct and control their subordinates. The specifics of this authority will be developed shortly.

So, having set forth the unique properties of the supervisor's role, our definition of a **supervisor** is *a first-level manager who is accountable*

Defining the Supervisory Role

The text has noted that the concept of a role is defined by the expectations of others. A general picture of the supervisory role can therefore be constructed by learning what expectations others have of supervisors. This exercise requires that you interview a manager who has supervisors reporting to him or her. The question you are to ask is, "What do you expect of your supervisors?" Make a list of these expectations and share them with the rest of your class. What expectations are common to all of the roles analyzed? Which ones were mentioned only once? Can the class integrate all these expectations into a common perception of a supervisory role?

---

for the performance of operative employees. It should be noted that this definition describes the unique characteristics of the supervisory role. In other words, no other role in the organization will have these same properties. Because it is unique, supervisors tend to have problems unlike those of other managers, and the thrust of this book is to address these problems from the point of view of the supervisor.

As we have just noted, one of the unique properties of the supervisory role is the concept of authority. In order to carry out their responsibilities effectively, supervisors need certain types of authority.

The Supervisor's Authority

One of the most frequent complaints heard from many supervisors is, "I just don't have the authority I need to do my job." This is important because authority is the backbone of the supervisory role. Without it, the supervisor is reduced to little more than a cheerleader who has to rely totally on interpersonal skills to get the job done. Without a doubt, the authority of supervisors has been eroded in recent years as other groups, particularly unions and government organizations, have achieved control over many aspects of organizational life that used to be the supervisor's prerogative. Whether one is pleased or displeased with this phenomenon is not the issue here. The fact remains that it has happened and supervisors must learn to adapt to the changing conditions. Traditional supervisors may have difficulty adjusting since they are used to a system in which the supervisor's word was law.

The Difficult Position of the Supervisor

As we noted in our earlier discussion of the definition of supervision, authority and accountability go hand in hand. If authority is given to a supervisor, then that person is held accountable for using that authority to achieve certain results. The problem that many supervisors face is that although their authority has been reduced over the years, their accountability has not. They may still be held fully accountable even though they lack the necessary authority to make decisions.

Supervisors who survive this untenable situation may find that they must rely heavily on their interpersonal skills in the supervision process, and this is often the area in which they receive the least training. So again, the people-managing part of the supervisor's job looms more important than ever.

It would be easy to suggest that supervisors should deal with this problem by reducing their accountability to match their authority. Unfortunately, this decision is not theirs. Accountability is determined by higher level managers and they tend still to expect results. The next best alternative is for the supervisor to understand what the *minimal* limits of authority should be and work within those limits.

Minimal Supervisory Authority

The myth of total authority is just that — a myth. No one, not even the president of the organization, has total authority over the organization's resources. Each individual has limits placed on his or her authority, although different limits are imposed on different managers within the hierarchy. After first examining in what areas of the supervisory role authority should be present, we shall discuss the practical limits.

We begin with the ideal situation. In order for a supervisor to be fully accountable for the performance of others, he or she must have certain rights that comprise **minimal supervisory authority** (see Figure 2.3):

1. the right to select (hire) and deselect (dismiss) subordinates,
2. the right to assign work to the subordinates,
3. the right to assess the performance of subordinates,
4. the right to select and assign resources to subordinates to do their jobs, and
5. the right to reward subordinates differentially.

SELECTION AND DESELECTION OF SUBORDINATES. This should be the basic right of all supervisors. To be accountable for the performance of employees foisted upon one makes for a very difficult situation. This does not mean, however, that new supervisors should

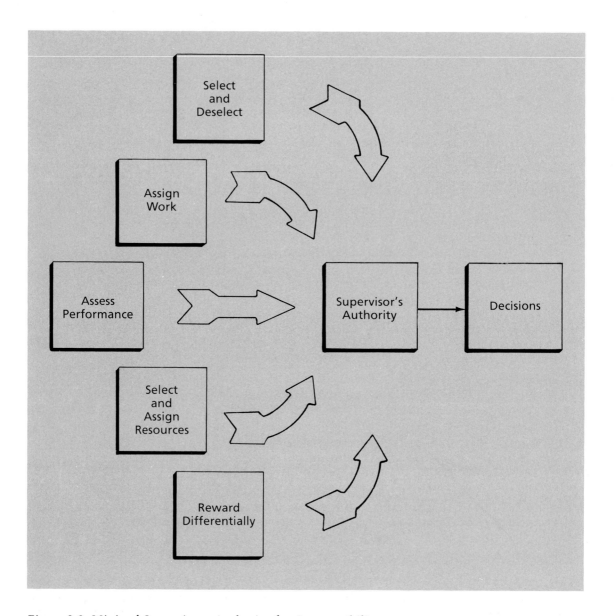

Figure 2.3. Minimal Supervisory Authority for Accountability.

have the right to dismiss all subordinates and hire new ones. In fact, to accept a supervisory position under existing conditions is implicitly to accept the present staff. It does suggest, however, that supervisors should have a role in selecting new appointments to their unit as well as deselecting those whose performance is consistently substandard.

The right to select and deselect is limited by several factors. Government regulations such as equal opportunity laws and human rights legislation reduce discretion in selecting employees. Company policies regarding selection processes and standards also impose limits on the authority of the supervisor. So while the supervisor cannot expect to have *total* authority in the selection process, it is reasonable — and necessary — to have a minimum amount. This minimum amount necessary for accountability is **veto authority,** the right to reject other people's appointments and decisions pertaining to the work unit for which the supervisor is responsible.

ASSIGNMENT OF WORK. Employees bring different skills and abilities to the workplace and the supervisor must be in a position to use these as effectively as possible. Often short-term crises develop and the supervisor must have the authority to reassign tasks as necessary. Also, the supervisor is usually the person who knows the employees best and is therefore the most qualified to assign tasks to individuals. If job assignments are made by someone else, not only will the supervisor's management of people be inefficient, but accountability for performance will be affected.

Again, there are practical limits to how much authority in this area a supervisor can have. Union contracts, for example, sometimes define specific jobs for specific workers, thus reducing the supervisor's flexibil-

Implementing the Veto Process

In my experience of working with supervisors, I find that comparatively few have the right to select their own subordinates. I have even seen cases in which new people were hired for a department and the supervisor did not know about it until the first day the employee showed up for work. Others have found out by noticing a new name on the payroll sheet, and in one extreme case, through a neighbor.

If this happens to you in your role as a supervisor, prepare to take action. Many times companies think they are doing their supervisors a favor by selecting their subordinates, so it may be just a case of informing higher management about the problem. The most common way of involving the supervisor is this: the supervisor initiates the process by requesting and getting approval from management to hire new personnel. The request, along with relevant job descriptions, skill and experience requirements, and other details, is then sent to the personnel department (or whoever conducts the external search). The search is conducted and the personnel department does the initial screening. Depending upon the number of qualified applicants, the best of those meeting the minimum selection criteria are then sent to the supervisor for a final selection decision. This system allows for the best of both worlds because it takes advantage of the personnel department's expertise in the search process, but retains the veto authority of the first-line supervisor.

ity. Health and safety regulations can prevent assignment of some types of people to certain jobs. But within these externally imposed constraints, the supervisor should have authority to assign tasks within the objectives set for the work unit. The supervisor can then be held accountable for achieving those objectives.

ASSESSMENT OF PERFORMANCE.   This form of authority tends to differ from the others because sometimes it is not a matter of the company usurping the authority from the supervisor, but rather is a case of the supervisor's not using the authority delegated to him or her. Few organizations actually prevent supervisors from conducting performance appraisals. More likely, they are not explicitly required; so supervisors often avoid the responsibility completely.

It should be apparent that the right to assess performance is closely related to the deselection process. Prior to dismissal, demotion, or transfer, an employee must know about any performance deficiencies. If the supervisor does not have the authority to assess performance, then it will be even more difficult to deselect an employee. The right to assess performance is also crucial to the authority relationship between supervisor and employee. If a worker knows that his or her performance is assessed by someone other than the supervisor, the potential influence of the supervisor will be correspondingly reduced.

The minimum amount of authority in this area should be at least the right to assess performance and forward that assessment to upper management for review. The specifics of how to conduct the appraisal are covered in Chapter 18.

Unwanted Interference

A common example of the violation of a supervisor's right to assign work became obvious recently while we were conducting a supervisory training program for a large amusement park. We began the session by discussing the role of the supervisor and one of the participants told us, ''My job is to supervise a cleanup crew of about fifteen people. Since there are several crews, we have to coordinate our activities before we begin work. We supervisors divided up the park and I sent my crew on their way, which was about a fifteen-minute walk from my office. About an hour later I went to their assigned area to see how they were doing. They were nowhere in sight. After searching for almost an hour, I found them in a completely different area of the park. They explained that between my office and their assigned area, they encountered three of the bosses, each of whom gave them a different assignment. They simply did what the last guy told them to do. Now how am I to be a good supervisor when that happens?''

SELECTION AND ASSIGNMENT OF RESOURCES. Every employee needs some form of physical resource to perform the allotted tasks. These could be tools, equipment, physical space, books, or technical support. The supervisor must have the necessary authority to determine what the resource needs are, and assign them to individuals who have the skills to use them. Without this authority, the supervisor has diminished control over one of the major determinants of productivity.

The major limiting factor in this area is financial. It would be impractical to expect a supervisor to purchase whatever equipment was necessary to get the work done. There are many other considerations, often beyond the supervisor's knowledge, that must influence purchase decisions. The common method of dealing with this situation is the budget. To place limits on the supervisor's authority, higher management sets a budget that is usually determined with the supervisor's input. Once the budget is fixed, however, the supervisor should have complete authority within its limits. Accountability is then based upon how effectively the supervisor uses the allocated budget.

DIFFERENTIAL REWARD. This area of authority refers to a supervisor's right to recognize differences in performance. The most common instance is where a supervisor has the right to pay some employees more than others because their performance is better. This type of authority gives the supervisor more potential influence over employees. If no pay differentials for performance are allowed (e.g., if pay is based solely on seniority) or if the decisions regarding pay differentials are made by someone other than the supervisor, the supervisor's accountability for performance should be reduced correspondingly.

The limits placed on this authority come from budgetary considerations as well as organizational pay policies. Supervisors should not be able to pay employees whatever they want but they still must have discretion within limits. What usually happens is that company pay policies set the pay ranges for a job category (these might even be negotiated ranges) and the supervisor decides who gets what within these ranges.

Conclusions

What has been outlined here is the concept of the ideal supervisory role as well as how this role actually exists in the real world. You will find many variations of the ideal situation because different organizations expect different things from their supervisors. However, the position is taken here that in order for first-line supervisors to be effective in their role, they must be held accountable for the performance of their subordinates, and if accountability is to exist, supervisors must have minimal

Exercise 2.2

Frustration and Supervision

This exercise can be done in one of two ways, depending upon whether you are a supervisor now or not. If you are presently in a supervisory position, review your job and rate it in each of the five authority areas described according to how much authority you have. Compare your rating with that of other supervisors. If you are not a supervisor, interview someone who is (or at least has the title). See how much actual authority he or she has in the job. Your final task is to get a measure of the frustration he or she feels in the job.

Do you find any relationship between the amount of authority in the role and the amount of frustration experienced?

authority in the five areas discussed. The less the authority, the less effective the supervisor can be.

There are important lessons here for potential supervisors as well. Before you agree to take a supervisory position, be sure you are clear on what authority you will have. It might even be advisable to use this list as a starting point and go over the areas with your future manager. If it seems that you will have practically no authority but the manager will still hold you accountable for performance, think twice before you say yes.

Clarifying the Supervisory Role

With the previous discussion as our foundation, we can now proceed to clarify some common misconceptions about the supervisory role.

Job Titles

Anyone who has spent any time at all at the supervisory ranks in a sizeable organization knows that the job titles used can be confusing. Some common job titles encountered at this level are leadhand, charge-hand, assistant manager, assistant supervisor, and, of course, supervisor. Even the term supervisor has no commonly held meaning and can be found at any level in the organization. For example, in the city government of San Francisco, the senior administrative body is called the Board of Supervisors.

As far as this book is concerned, the term supervisor *should* describe individuals who possess the minimal levels of authority in the areas discussed in the previous section, and who are managing first-level employees. What *should* happen is that any role that has less than the minimal level should be given a different title, such as leadhand or assistant supervisor. The problems that may arise with these assistant roles will be discussed in detail in Chapter 3.

Is a Supervisor a Manager?

This may seem like a strange question to ask but it is an important one. In the light of what has just been discussed regarding the authority of supervisors the answer is an unqualified yes. But in real life, the issue is not always that clear. In some organizations, for example, first-line supervisors are members of the union; legally, at least, this means they cannot be considered management. In others, the supervisor may be called a manager but still be expected to perform operative duties. This requires constant shifting back and forth between two different roles and makes it difficult to be an effective supervisor.

This identity problem becomes even worse when we look at the behavioral (i.e., perceptual) problems that can occur. Traditionally, particularly in manufacturing organizations, supervisors are blue-collar people and this conflicts with the common perception that all managers wear white shirts and never get their hands dirty. Supervisors, therefore, are often excluded from many management activities. It is no surprise that many supervisors identify more with their subordinates than with the management of the organization. So if managers complain that their supervisors don't act like managers, perhaps the question should be asked, "Do you treat them like managers?"

Should Supervisors Perform Technical Tasks?

To answer this question we need to examine the types of skills managers need in their jobs. Figure 2.4 presents the three-skill approach to management and identifies the three different types of skills that managers need to have.[1] These are:

1. technical skills: skills pertaining to doing a task, such as typing, computer programming, machining, nursing, accounting, or welding;
2. human skills: skills in dealing with people, such as leadership, communications, interpersonal relations, or motivation;
3. conceptual skills: skills involving the ability to think in abstract terms, such as planning, forecasting, and decision making.

1. Robert L. Katz, "Skills of an Effective Administrator," in *Business Classics: Fifteen Key Concepts for Managerial Success (Harvard Business Review*, 1975), pp. 23–35.

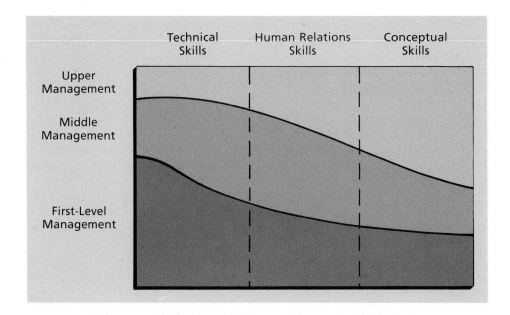

Figure 2.4. Skills Required at Different Levels of Management.

For our purposes, we can label the human and conceptual skills as managerial in nature, and the technical skills as primarily characteristic of operative employees.

In general, then, there is nothing wrong with a supervisor doing operative work. In some cases it is even required because of staff shortages. The only danger is that sometimes the technical tasks can detract from the more managerial tasks that the supervisor should be doing. It is possible, for example, that a supervisor may purposely do technical tasks as a means of avoiding supervisory duties. This happens because most of us are better qualified in the technical area than the managerial one, so we tend to gravitate toward those activities that we do best. Better training of supervisors and clear-cut expectations as to what comes first are two methods of dealing with this problem.

Does the Best Worker Make the Best Supervisor?

This is a problem constantly encountered by organizations. A supervisory position opens up and likely candidates are reviewed. Do you make the best typist the supervisor of the typing pool? The answer is, not necessarily. As our three-skill approach suggests, the qualities necessary to be a good typist (technical skills) are different than the qualities necessary to be a good supervisor (human relations and conceptual skills).

Unfortunately, many supervisors have been promoted on the basis of their technical qualifications which, although important, are not sufficient in themselves to assure that they will be good supervisors. At a minimum, supervisors should have sufficient technical expertise to make good decisions regarding technical matters, but they need not be the best at performing the technical task itself. In fact, if the best employee is chosen to be the supervisor, there is a risk that he or she will spend too much time on technical matters since they will continue to be more attractive and therefore more rewarding than supervisory duties.

Key to Success

It is difficult to imagine a supervisor being successful in a poorly defined role. Since a role tells us what is expected of us, how could we do a good job if we didn't know what we should be doing? Although any role requires clear definition, it is particularly important for supervisors because of their unique position in the organization. Supervisors are in constant danger of being caught in the middle unless their roles are fully clarified.

It should be obvious that your first task as a supervisor is to find out how much authority you have. A job description is useful, but should be supplemented by an in-depth discussion with the other managers who influence your role. This will let you know what decisions you can make and the limits to your authority within those decisions. Supervisors who should be making decisions but are not, and supervisors who make decisions but should not, make for nervous bosses.

If you still doubt the value of clarifying the supervisory role, consider this analogy. Imagine no speed limits on public roads. Drivers could drive at any speed they wanted, and you and I would be very nervous pedestrians. To avoid this dangerous situation, we do not tell drivers at what speed they must drive, but what the LIMIT is. This way we can be reasonably sure that most people will not go faster than the stated limit, although many may go slower.

The same is true for supervisors. You should always find out the limits of your role so that you do not exceed them. Remember that just as it is easier for pedestrians to tolerate drivers who go slower than the speed limit than those who exceed it, it is easier for managers to tolerate supervisors who do not fully use their authority than those who exceed it.

Another key to your success is constant self-analysis of your own behavior. As this chapter explained, supervisors are not just glorified workers. The supervisory role is significantly different with different expectations. Your self-analysis simply requires that you examine your own behavior to see if you are behaving like a supervisor. Are you engaging in supervisory duties? Are you doing tasks different from those of your subordinates? Are you simply doing more of what you were doing before you were a supervisor? These and similar questions should be constantly on your mind as you make the transition from operative employee to manager.

Most people have a tendency to do those things they do best and avoid those things that they do poorly or with which they are unfamiliar. It is easy, therefore, to unconsciously lapse back into the tasks that made you famous, rather than plunge into the more unfamiliar ground of supervision. Unfortunately, there is no hard and fast rule about how much time supervisors should actually spend on supervision. For this reason you must constantly engage in analyzing your role behavior before someone else does it for you.

Summary

This chapter has described the uniqueness of the supervisory role in organizations. Because it is unique, it presents some special problems that must be solved if individuals are to be effective in their roles as supervisors. It has been pointed out that managing people is an important function for supervisors, who spend so much of their time dealing with other people.

It was also noted that authority, responsibility, and accountability are major building blocks for a supervisor. The supervisor must have a minimal amount of authority to perform the role properly and be held accountable legitimately for the performance of his or her unit.

This chapter also pointed out that although supervisors are managers, they still must have a reasonable level of technical skills. Moreover, when a new supervisor is selected, the best worker in the group may not be the best choice.

Opening Incident Revisited

It may seem that Mary does not have a problem. After all, she has been offered a promotion, quite likely a raise in salary, and more responsibility. Should she be concerned? Yes, and there are several reasons.

The most important concern Mary should have is the amount of authority in this new job. While the job has the title of supervisor, that alone does not mean that she will have sufficient authority to perform adequately her supervisory duties. Her first task should be to meet with the manager of the shipping department to get a clear understanding of the responsibilities and authority that manager is willing to delegate. Without the proper authority, Mary would have difficulty managing the work group.

Mary's second concern should be over the technical side of the jobs she would be supervising. Never having worked in the shipping department, she is not familiar with the specific tasks they do. However, since she has performed clerical and secretarial duties before, she will have some basic knowledge of the jobs. She will have to allow herself some learning time on the job, since a clear understanding of the technical side of the department will be necessary for her to be an effective supervisor.

Mary should also find out why she has been chosen for this job. What qualities did management think she had that made her their choice? Does she think she has those qualities?

Finally, Mary may be apprehensive because she has no supervisory experience. If she does poorly at the job, she may ruin her chances for further advancement. While there is no particular reason why this should cause her to refuse the position, she will have to recognize that her lack of experience can cause difficulties. It would be wise for her to get a head start by reading about supervision and what it entails and comparing her experiences with what she reads. Conversations with other supervisors can help, too, as can advice from higher management. In any event, Mary is a good candidate for a course in supervision. Even if she decides not to take the job, she should begin preparing herself for another opportunity rather than using only on-the-job training.

Review Questions

1. Why is the supervisor a key manager in the organization?
2. Why is it difficult to have a precise definition of a supervisor?
3. What is an organizational role?
4. How are authority, responsibility, and accountability related?
5. What are the three major properties that distinguish the supervisory role from other roles in the organization?
6. What are limits to supervisory authority?
7. What is minimal supervisory authority?
8. How can the concept of veto authority assist the supervisor?
9. In what areas should a supervisor have authority?
10. Is a supervisor a manager? Why?
11. Should supervisors perform technical tasks?
12. Does the best employee make the best supervisor? Why or why not?

Chapter Glossary

Role.	The complete set of expectations, formal and informal, that define the behavior in a job.
Supervisory role.	The set of behavioral expectations associated with the supervisor's job.
Authority.	A right to make decisions.

Responsibility.	The duty or obligation to make decisions.
Accountability.	Being judged on how authority and responsibility are used, or a review of how effective decisions have been.
Supervisor.	A first-level manager who is accountable for the performance of operative employees.
Minimal supervisory authority.	The minimum amount of authority a supervisor must have to be held accountable for the performance of others.
Veto authority.	The right to reject the decision of another person which impacts upon the supervisor's area of responsibility.

Case Problem

Mid-West Newspapers, Inc.

Mid-West Newspapers, Inc., was started by John Mills at the turn of the century. After his death, the family took over the paper and put Charlie Mills in as President. The Board of Directors consists mostly of family members, only a few of whom have had actual experience in the newspaper business. Second in command is Charlie's brother Sam, who serves as the paper's editor.

The steady growth of the newspaper has placed considerable strain upon its management system. The family makes it very clear that they want to keep tight control over what goes on at the paper, and most of them make a habit of dropping in during working hours from time to time. The family also prides itself in caring about its employees. It is not uncommon to see one of the family members in the coffee lounge talking with employees. Both Charlie and Sam make it a practice to walk through the office and plant at least once a day.

The major problem now facing the company is poor quality supervision of the noneditorial staff. Much of Charlie's day is spent sorting out problems created by one or more first-line supervisors. Union shop stewards are constantly calling Charlie about a problem they have, and they usually blame it on the supervisors. It is also not uncommon for one of the family to phone Charlie or Sam about a problem picked up in conversation with the employees.

A more recent event, however, was quite disturbing to the family. One of the foremen in the composing room quit to start his own printing business. Charlie posted a notice on the bulletin board in the composing room announcing the vacancy and asking interested employees to apply. The notice has been up for a week, and no one has applied for the job.

Questions for Discussion

1. Why would you think no one has applied for the job?
2. What kinds of authority would you imagine the supervisors in Mid-West have?
3. What special problems would a family-owned business present for a first-line supervisor?
4. Based upon the information in the case, what changes would you recommend be implemented?

Organizational
Relationships
and the Supervisor

3

Chapter Learning Objectives

After reading and studying this chapter you should be able to:

1. Diagram the major organizational relationships that supervisors have with other roles in the organization.

2. Describe why a clear organizational structure can help a supervisor be more effective.

3. Show the ideal placement of the assistant role in an organization.

4. Describe the difference between an assistant supervisor and an assistant to the supervisor.

5. Describe why the part-time assistant's role causes problems in the organization.

6. Describe the problems that can occur if the accountability upward principle is not practiced.

7. Describe under what circumstances a subordinate should question the decision of his or her manager.

8. Define line and staff roles.

9. Describe the difference between power and authority as it relates to line and staff relationships.

10. Describe generally how staff roles affect the supervisor's job.

Key Terms

Organization chart
Assistant supervisor
Chain of command
Accountability upward
Judgment
Limits on authority

Line functions
Staff Functions
Command authority
Staff advice
Power

43

Great Northern Gas and Electric Company

Juanita Romero, a supervisor in the billing department of Great Northern Gas and Electric Company has become increasingly frustrated. It seems that every time she gets her department running smoothly, someone from upstairs comes down and starts changing things again. The most recent visit was from John Washington, a systems analyst with the Data Processing Department. John was on one of his annual streamlining visits, in which he examined the work done in a department and recommended improvements that would increase productivity. Last year as a result of his visit, it took Juanita three months to train her staff to adapt to the new system. Not only that, but Juanita could not see that the new system had improved anything at all.

On this visit, John spent most of his time reviewing the department's filing system. Although he was in the department for more than a week, he said little to Juanita; so she assumed he was having difficulty in finding a way to improve the filing system. It was only this morning that she received a copy of his report and saw that he was recommending a major reorganization of the files.

In order to do their jobs effectively, supervisors must interact with other people in the organization: subordinates, managers, and other supervisors at the same level in the hierarchy. Each of these relationships is unique. Depending upon the organizational relationship, the supervisor will have to behave in different ways. The purpose of this chapter is to show how the role of the supervisor fits into the rest of the organization, by exploring the various types of relationships that can exist between supervisors and subordinates, between supervisors and other supervisory roles, and between supervisors and their managers. Finally, we shall describe the line and staff functions and their impact upon the supervisor.

The Supervisor and Subordinates

Basic Relationships

Chapter 2 established that the supervisor is the manager of operative employees, and that being the manager means that the supervisor is accountable for the performance of the subordinates in his or her unit. The supervisor must have the necessary authority to manage effectively, and will be held accountable by his or her manager for using that authority properly.

It is often useful to use **organization charts**—diagrams of the formal reporting relationships in the organization—to show the managerial hi-

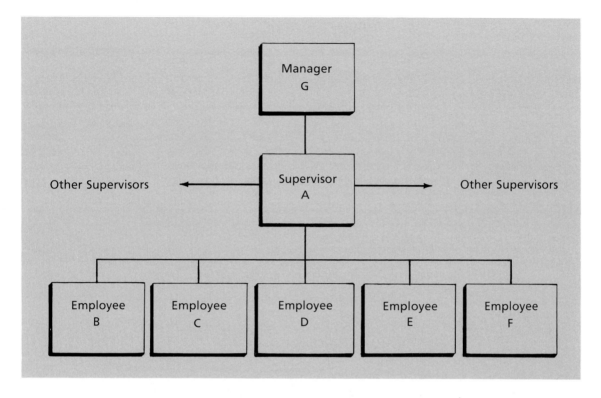

Figure 3.1. Organization Chart of First-Line Supervisor and Work Group.

erarchy. Figure 3.1 is an organization chart illustrating a typical first-line supervisor and work group. This chart indicates that:

1. Supervisor A is the manager of subordinates B through F.

2. Supervisor A is only one of the supervisors reporting to manager G.

3. Subordinates B through F receive their direction only from supervisor A.

4. If subordinates B through F wish to communicate with manager G, they should do so through supervisor A.

5. Manager G holds supervisor A individually accountable for the performance of Subordinates B through F.

6. If manager G wishes to give direction to any of Subordinates B through F he or she should do so through supervisor A or with A's knowledge and permission.

This, of course, is the way things *should* happen in this organization. If the supervisor is to maintain full control over his or her area of responsibility, then these basic principles must be followed. This is often

Who's on First . . . ?

For those with little or no organizational experience, it may seem hard to believe that something as simple as the supervisor-subordinate relationship can be complicated. But it can. While doing research in a municipal organization I had to examine some supervisory roles. Many problems were present (most to do with reporting relationships and supervisors' authority), but one case in particular still stands out. The following chart shows how the reporting relationships were *supposed* to be.

However, my interviews with those involved revealed that, "A does not see B as his subordinate, but rather as a coworker. B sees A as his manager and says he gets instructions from him. C, who organizationally reports to B, receives instructions from others in the section, most often from A. A does not see C as subordinate to B, but to himself, that is, on an equal level with B. C sees himself as reporting to B (as shown on the organization chart) but acknowledges that he receives instructions from A, B, and also D, who is subordinate to B's manager." Would you care to try to hold someone accountable in this group?

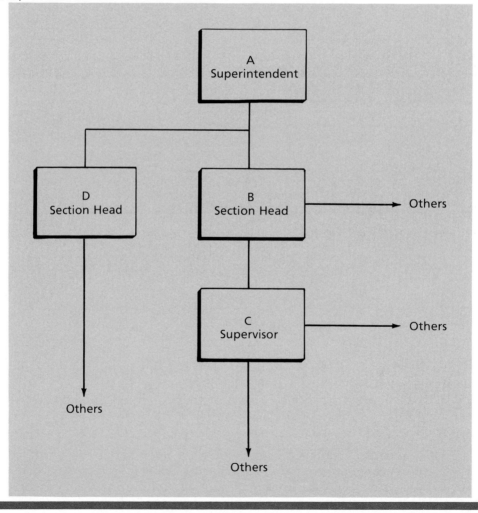

not the case, however, and when the lines of authority are not respected the confusion that results in reporting relationships can breed inefficiency, frustration, and poor performance. Since the supervisor's job is difficult enough at the best of times, sloppy organizational arrangements only make things worse.

The Role of Assistants

One of the common ways of complicating the neat relationships portrayed in Figure 3.1 is the appointment of **assistant supervisors,** whose authority is necessarily less than that of the supervisor. Regardless of the job title, most organizations of any size create positions designed to assist supervisors in their duties. These might be called leadhands, chargehands, assistant supervisors, section heads, assistant foremen, or some other general term. These roles are obviously useful since they relieve supervisors of some of the managerial duties. However, unless they are clarified they can cause confusion in the lower ranks. Most often this confusion takes the form of either unclear lines of authority or communication problems. If we begin with the organization chart in Figure 3.1 and add an assistant (in this case a leadhand) the chart might then look like that pictured in Figure 3.2. A level has been added between the operative employees and their immediate manager. But the new level is not really a managerial level at all because the assistant supervisor A_1 (leadhand) does not necessarily have full managerial authority over the subordinates, but over only one of the areas, most likely the assignment of work. However, if this chart describes how employees *should* relate to management, then they would have to go through assistant supervisor A_1, the leadhand, to communicate with their manager.

This creates several problems. If a subordinate comes to the assistant with a problem outside of the latter's regular duties the problem must be then transmitted to the supervisor. This takes time and the added link in the communications channel increases the chances that the message will be communicated inaccurately. Also the positioning of the leadhand in this manner separates the supervisor from those for whom he or she is accountable, thus causing problems because the supervisor will not have first-hand knowledge of the problems at the operative level. Furthermore, the assistant position can create a psychological barrier between operative employees and the supervisor, who may be seen as aloof and distant from them. Finally, it can create frustration for the leadhand, who is in an ambiguous position, being caught in the middle.

A much better arrangement is depicted in Figure 3.3. In this situation, the leadhand has been removed from the *direct* **chain of command** (the line of authority, responsibility, and accountability) and placed outside the regular supervisor-subordinate relationship. The subordinates now have direct access to their immediate supervisor and therefore the flow of communication and authority is improved. The supervisor can

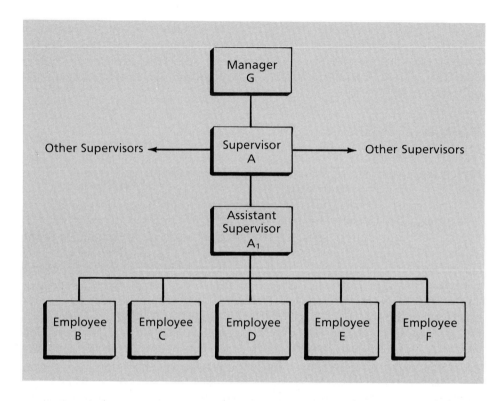

Figure 3.2. How Adding an Assistant Creates Another Level of Supervision.

now be fully accountable for all subordinates, including the assistant/ leadhand, and the role of the leadhand has now been clarified as being outside the regular line of authority. This method of clarifying relationships can be used regardless of the number of assistants involved.

Whether the organization system depicted in Figure 3.2 or that in Figure 3.3 is better depends upon the authority of the first-level manager, not the job title. For example, the first-level supervisor could be called assistant manager and be pictured as in Figure 3.4, providing that this person has full managerial authority over the subordinates. The fact that the title supervisor lies with the next level of management is unimportant. The organizational relationships must depend upon authority in roles, not the titles of those roles.

Relationships Between Assistants and Supervisors

If this system is to function as it should, the role of the assistants has to be clarified. This is the responsibility of the supervisor. If it is not done,

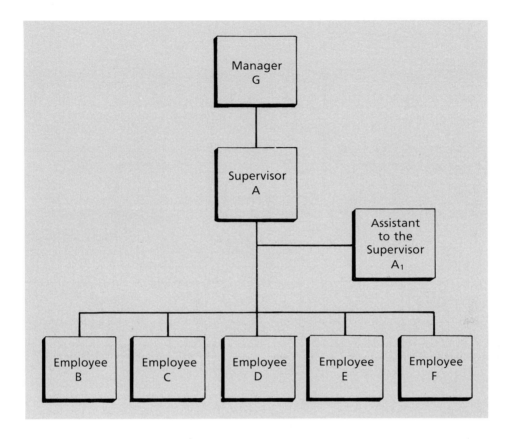

Figure 3.3. Organization Chart Showing Proper Placement of an Assistant Role.

then the assistants never know where they stand and will experience considerable frustration as they try to weave their way through a system of ambiguous relationships.

First, the supervisor should clarify whether the assistant has authority only in selected areas of responsibility (the assistant to the supervisor), or assists the supervisor in *all* areas of authority (the assistant supervisor). If the latter is the case, this is tantamount to declaring that the assistant is authorized to make decisions in all areas of responsibility on the superior's behalf. There is nothing inherently wrong with this, although it is advisable to be clear as to this intention. Sooner or later the assistant will make a decision that the supervisor disagrees with and this can present difficulties. For example, to abide by the assistant's decision will probably cause difficulty somewhere (or else the supervisor would not have disagreed with the decision in the first place). Conversely, to reverse the assistant's decision, is to undermine the latter's authority.

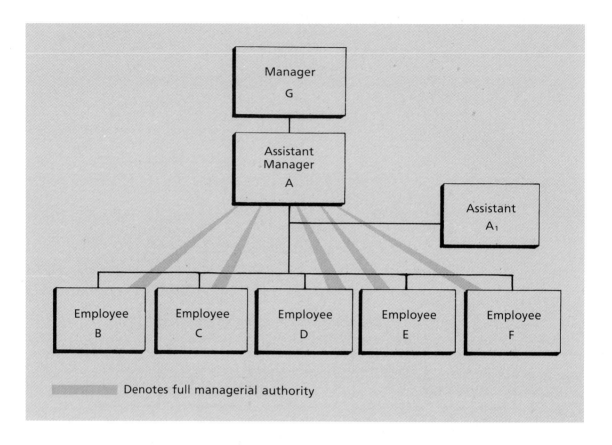

Figure 3.4. Assistant Supervisor with Full Managerial Authority.

Besides causing morale problems for the assistant, this implicitly communicates to the subordinates that the assistant's decisions are not final until the supervisor has approved of the decisions. Since the subordinates will now realize that the supervisor is the *real* authority, they will probably start bypassing the assistant, thus rendering him or her ineffective.

The assistant supervisor role in which the assistant is authorized to act for the supervisor is not an impossible one, but it is difficult. This difficulty is due primarily to the fact that two individuals—the supervisor and the assistant—are both accountable for the same thing, thus creating duplication and potential communication problems. In many cases, the same purposes can be accomplished without all the headaches by using the "assistant to" role.

The alternative is to use the assistant for a specific purpose. The example given so far, that of assigning tasks to operative employees, has been used because it seems to be the most common in practice. But the supervisor is free to assign virtually any part of his or her supervisory duties to the assistant, provided that others know that the assistant has complete authority (within limits set by the supervisor) in that area. Other examples might be: assigning someone to do all the training of new employees, giving one person responsibility for procurement of all materials needed by employees, or making a specific assignment of scheduling the sequence of work activities for a period of time. Whatever the assignment, all employees should be told that this is the organizational relationship.

Once the task has been delegated, the supervisor, the assistant, and the subordinates are aware of the assistant's accountability. Provided that the job has been delegated properly (Chapter 14 explains how to do this) the supervisor is able to hold the assistant fully accountable for the performance of this specific managerial task. If subordinates are not used to this type of arrangement they will quickly adapt if the supervisor, when asked a question about a task that has been delegated to an assistant, replies, for example, "See Jane. She's in charge of that area." The advantages here should be obvious: the supervisor frees time that can be more profitably spent on other matters and the assistant remains an important role in the system, without interference from others when making decisions.

The Part-Time Assistant

Without a doubt, one of the most difficult roles in any organization is the part-time assistant (whatever the title may be). These unfortunate creatures truly are neither fish nor fowl because they must change hats as the need arises. These roles are usually created because the unit cannot justify the need for a full-time assistant, or because the nature of the work requires the supervisor to be away a lot and needs someone to fill in in his or her absence. Regardless of the reason, I have yet to see one function effectively, although this is not to say that it cannot be done. But to make it work, the person would have to have the hide of an elephant, the human skills of a psychotherapist, and the patience of Job. Unfortunately, people with these qualities rarely spend much time at the supervisory level; they are usually whisked away into positions of higher authority, such as president.

The reason that these roles are so difficult is that they require the individual to shift back and forth intermittently between subordinate and supervisory duties. Unfortunately, getting results through people is not something that can be accomplished simply because you have the title, especially if it is a temporary title. Supervisors must often make decisions that are unpopular, but they can do so because they know the decision is best for the unit and their own personal accountability. Knowing that he or she will soon be back in the work group as a subordinate, a part-time supervisor will be reluctant to make difficult decisions. Moreover, for the same reasons the subordinates tend not to perceive the part-time assistant as the real supervisor and this adds to everyone's frustration. They often exhibit the "Who does he think he is?" attitude, which puts the part-time assistant uncomfortably in the middle.

Chapter 5 describes at length the significance of the roles we occupy and how they are related to our behavior. Suffice it to say here that all of us have difficulty in occupying roles that are either poorly defined, or that provide little support for the tasks we must undertake. The part-time assistant's role suffers from both of these problems, and is therefore to be pitied.

The Supervisor and Management

Although the major responsibility of supervisors is to manage subordinates effectively, their relationship with their own manager is also important. In particular, the relationship between the two roles is critical since the supervisor will bear the brunt of any deficiencies in this relationship. Authority limits must be specified by the superior so that the supervisor can get on with the work at hand, but this requires that the

The Life of a Part-Time Supervisor

In one of my supervisor training courses I encountered a situation much like that described above. After a morning session on roles and role relationships, I was eating lunch with a foreman and his assistant. The discussion that morning had them both thinking and they were open about their thoughts during lunch (and in my view, their openness with each other was probably the only thing that made the following situation tolerable). The subordinate's main task was driving a forklift truck, but during the supervisor's lunch hour he changed roles to be assistant foreman. He expressed mixed feelings about the assignment. On the one hand, he was glad that the supervisor had confidence in his ability to supervise the other employees and was pleased that he had been chosen. On the other hand, he felt uncomfortable having to supervise his colleagues during the one-hour lunch period. His feelings ranged from helplessness to frustration, depending upon the mood of the other employees that day. He believed that every morning the other employees got together and decided how much trouble they would give him during that one hour. His supervisor was surprised at his reaction and had no idea he felt that way, but understood his feelings. He agreed to speak with his own manager about the problem, with the possibility of upgrading the job to full-time assistant with appropriate responsibilities.

Exercise 3.1

The Real-Life Relationships of the Supervisor

Your task in this exercise is an interesting and useful one designed to illustrate the points mentioned in the previous discussion. Arrange to interview any nonsupervisory employee in any type of organization. Your task is to understand and describe the organizational relationships that he or she faces on the job. First, gather the information necessary to draw an organizational chart much like those in Figure 3.1 or 3.2. Having obtained this information, ask the person, "Who is your boss?" Some people may have trouble with this question (for reasons you should now understand) so you might rephrase it something like this: "Suppose you really had a serious problem that you wanted resolved. Whom would you go to?" The person named is the first level of *real* management in that work unit. The others in your diagram are hybrids of various sorts. Your last task is to redraw the diagram as you think it ought to be. Compare the results of your interview with those of others and see just how frequently problems of organizational role relationships occur.

---

superior manage the supervisor properly so that accountability can be maintained. This and other potential problems will be explored in this section. For our purposes, the term superior will be used to describe the supervisor's manager.

Accountability Upward

If superiors seem reluctant to delegate proper authority to supervisors, as we have suggested thus far, they have good reason: they themselves are held accountable for the decisions taken by the supervisors. Since mistakes at the operative and supervisory level tend to be very visible, superiors often guard their areas of delegated authority very closely lest they look bad when a wrong decision is made.

It has been our position so far that the supervisor must occupy a clearly defined role and possess the minimal managerial authority to be effective. This does not mean, however, that supervisors should be given full rein to run their departments or units as they please. But it is possible for superiors to delegate and still have control if proper management principles are followed up and down the line. What is often missing in many superior-supervisor relationships is the accountability upward.

Accountability upward means that the superior, while delegating authority to the supervisor to make necessary decisions, will ultimately hold the supervisor accountable for making good decisions and producing results. If the authority is misused or used poorly, the supervisor should perhaps be removed from the role, or some other action taken to prevent the same thing from happening again.

As an example, consider the authority to select and deselect subordinates, a decision we said earlier was crucial to the supervisor's accountability. If the supervisor decides to hire an individual, and later it turns out that the person is not satisfactory, accountability upward means that the supervisor cannot now use this person as an excuse for not meeting unit objectives. When it comes time to appraise the supervisor's performance, the superior will consider that the supervisor did not use good judgment in selection. Whether or not the superior would dismiss the supervisor for this alone depends, of course, upon many other factors. Nevertheless, the supervisor must bear the responsibility for having made a substandard decision.

Effect upon Subordinates

Failure to follow the principle of accountability upward can have a devastating effect upon the subordinates who work for the supervisor. They may see the supervisor as incompetent in certain areas and, because there is no accountability upward in effect, they will find little hope for improvement in the future. But there still remains a possible remedy to the situation, because the *manager of the superior* should hold that person accountable for the accountability of the supervisor. Therefore, this manager might see that his or her subordinate is not holding the supervisor accountable and would take action.

The ideal situation, then, is for accountability to go up and down the line, in such a way that each level holds the level beneath it accountable for the authority delegated to it. If at any level the accountability breaks down, then it is the responsibility of the next higher manager to deal with it. This constitutes a system of checks and balances against the improper use of authority.

Should a Subordinate Question a Manager's Decision?

No matter how good the system of checks and balances, managers and supervisors will eventually make decisions that others do not agree with. This could happen either in the case of subordinates disagreeing with the decision of a supervisor, or a supervisor disagreeing with one of his or her manager's decisions.

How should this situation be handled? Is it proper for a subordinate to question the decision of the superior? It all depends. Figure 3.5 presents a diagram of the authority in any managerial role. Inside the brackets is the sphere of authority in which the manager is free to make

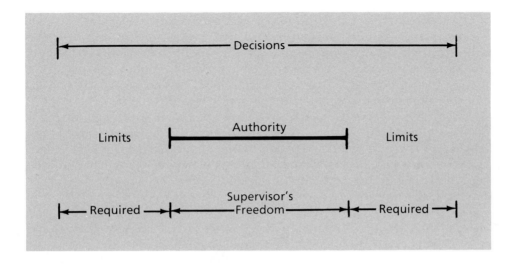

Figure 3.5. Limits to Managerial Authority.

decisions. The brackets themselves indicate the **limits** to the authority; this means that the manager may not make a decision that is outside those limits. For example, a typical hiring policy in most organizations is that the company will not discriminate with regard to race, creed, sex, color, religion, or national origin in its hiring practices. These are limits on the manager's authority. If a manager did not hire someone because of color, this would be a violation of company policy and of the limits of the role. The manager would also be held accountable for this decision. However, provided that a manager stays within the limits prescribed by the organization, he or she is free to take whatever decision is judged to be best. The key term here is **judgment.** All manager roles require that judgment be exercised, and the organization holds managers accountable for exercising sound judgment, as well as for staying within the limits of their authority.

We can now return to the original question: should a subordinate question the decision of the superior? The answer is an unequivocal "yes" *if the decision made is beyond the limits of the role.* However, if it is a matter of the manager's judgment within those limits the subordinate would be out of line in questioning the decision (although he or she could still do so). In the first instance, the superior would welcome information that one of his supervisors has made a decision that is against company policy (i.e., outside the limits of his or her authority). Courtesy would dictate that the subordinate first inform the supervisor of the concern, but if no action is taken he or she should feel free to bypass the supervisor and go (possibly with the supervisor) to the superior.

In the second instance, in which the supervisor has exercised judgment (albeit poor judgment) within the limits of his or her authority, the subordinate is in a more difficult position. Anyone who constantly questions the judgment of his or her supervisor will no doubt cause a strain in the relationship. It is up to the individual to choose whether to do this, but organizationally he or she would be out of line. It is the responsibility of the superior to question the supervisor's judgment, if indeed it need be questioned, because the supervisor is exercising authority that has been delegated by the superior. If the superior performs his or her responsibility properly, substandard judgment will be recognized and the supervisor will be held accountable accordingly.

If all this appears to be excessively belaboring a very basic point, it is a fact that many problems at the supervisor level would disappear if these organizational relationships were more often taken into consideration. A supervisor should be concerned if subordinates are by-passing him or her to complain to the manager about matters of judgment, and should be even more concerned if the manager takes action on the basis of those complaints. A thorough discussion between supervisor and superior regarding authority, accountability, and decisions taken within limits would be helpful in clarifying the precarious relationship that often exists. Of course, the same principles apply to the supervisor in a subordinate role. He or she should feel free to approach the manager's manager regarding decisions made outside the limits of the manager's authority, and should be wary of questioning decisions taken within those limits. It goes without saying that questioning a manager's judgment is a delicate matter and should be handled with discretion. Much

Protecting the Supervisor's Authority

Perhaps a real-life example will show how these principles should operate in practice. A particular company had a policy that supervisors could instruct any employee to work up to ten hours of overtime per week provided that (a) the employee was given at least three days notice, and (b) the seniority list was used to give more senior employees first chance at the overtime if they wanted it and if job skills were appropriate. Items (a) and (b) are therefore the limits on the supervisor's authority. A situation arose in which a junior employee was instructed by his supervisor on Monday that he was to work three hours overtime on Friday. He complained to the manager of the supervisor that this was unfair, that others should be asked before him, and that he had already made plans for that Friday evening. The superior (without even communicating with the supervisor) replied, "From what you have told me the supervisor is operating within company policy on overtime. I am sorry that you do not like his decision, but I trust his judgment that he knows what is best for his department. You will have to do as your supervisor requests."

depends upon the relationship between supervisor and manager. In some situations, the two individuals find it easy to talk about areas of disagreement; in others, it would be organizational suicide for the supervisor.

If the example above bothers you, it's probably because you are saying, "But what if the supervisor is wrong?" Well, let us assume for the moment that he is. The superior would probably not be aware of it right then, so he might talk with the supervisor to find out why he made the decision. If, after the conversation, he believed it was a poor decision he could reverse it. But what would this do to the supervisor's credibility with his subordinates? They would now think that every time the supervisor made a decision they didn't like, they could go to his manager and have it overturned. The superior would quickly find that he, not the supervisor, was managing the work group, and the supervisor would become increasingly frustrated at losing control of the group. Barring decisions that would seriously damage the productivity of the group (which, incidentally, would probably be outside the limits of the supervisor's authority), the superior might be better off letting the decision stand, regardless of his or her personal opinion. First, the superior, who would not have the same information the supervisor had, would probably be in a poor position to judge the decision. Second, the cost of overturning the decision would likely outweigh any benefits derived from improving it. Moreover, if the superior has selected a competent supervisor, he or she should have confidence in the supervisor's judgment. Finally, the superior will still be able to hold the supervisor accountable for his or her total supervisory responsibilities, and should not judge the supervisor's competence by this single decision.

In summary, the relationship between supervisors and their managers is a crucial one. It requires a thorough understanding of the authority and accountability of each, and the practice of principles described here. Although they are seldom practiced to perfection, knowledge about how the relationship *should* be is a useful starting point for both supervisor and superior.

Line and Staff Relationships

In addition to their subordinates and superiors, supervisors must also interface with other supervisors and higher managers in the organization. None of these, of course, will be in the supervisor's chain of command, so the relationship with these other roles will be different from the managerial relationships just discussed. All of the roles interfacing with the supervisor can be classified as either line or staff. Staff roles particularly can present some interesting problems for supervisors, so in this section we explore the nature of staff roles and how these can affect the supervisor's job.

Definition of Line and Staff

The terms line and staff have traditionally been used to designate functional areas having different relationships to organizational goals. There are some functions that have a *primary* relationship to organizational goals and these are referred to as **line functions**. Examples would be the production department in a manufacturing organization, the nursing function in a hospital, the credit function in a bank, or the teaching function in a school. These functions are primary because their normal activities relate directly to the major purpose of the organization.

Staff functions have only a secondary relationship to the organization's goals. Some typical staff functions would be: quality control in the manufacturing organization, the laboratory in a hospital, the computer programming department in the bank, and the custodial function in the school. Therefore, any function in the organization that is not directly related to the organization's major purpose is a staff function.

Line and Staff Authority

This distinction is made between the functions because although both are working toward the same *general* goals, their functional and day-to-day goals can be different. Therefore, conflicts can arise that could eventually jeopardize the operation of the entire organization. Imagine, for example, the difficulty that would arise if a custodian (staff function) began cleaning a classroom while the instructor (line function) was teaching a class. To prevent this, the relationship between line and staff functions is specified clearly so that conflicts in authority and responsibility will be minimized.

Because of their primary relationship to organizational goals, line functions are given **command authority,** that is, line managers have final authority over what happens in their operational units. This is necessary, not only because of this relationship, but also because line managers could not be held accountable for the performance of their units if others were making decisions that affected their operations. In contrast, staff functions are given the right to give **advice** to line managers in how to manage their units, but, theoretically at least, the line manager has the right to reject the advice. The advisory role of staff functions takes many forms in organizations. They can be supportive (e.g., personnel), technical (e.g., production planning), or control (e.g., quality control).

Staff supervisors and managers have command authority within their own units, as Figure 3.6 illustrates, while retaining an advisory relationship to the line functions.

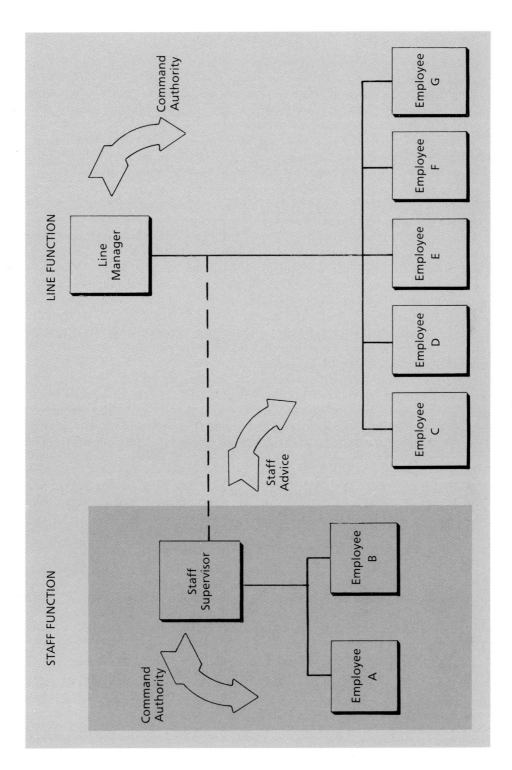

Figure 3.6. Major Role Relationships Between Line and Staff Functions.

Power and Authority in Line and Staff Roles

Line and staff are convenient categories for classifying the authority attached to organizational functions. Unfortunately, things are not so neat in real life. It is common, for example, to find staff functions exercising command authority, line functions that ignore staff advice, and, in general, a lot of conflict between the two.

The primary cause is the difference between authority and power. Authority is the *right* of a manager to use discretion in making decisions, a right that is built into the job description. **Power** is more of an interpersonal concept and is based upon a person's *ability* to use influence, irrespective of the job description. Therefore, two managers can be in conflict because one has authority and the other has power.

Power can have many sources, but the most common are knowledge (i.e., expertise), and the ability to inflict punishment, either real or imagined. A staff function often acquires power because of specialized knowledge in a relatively narrow functional area. If a line manager needs that expertise, the staff person will have power over the manager, even though no formal authority relationship exists. Staff may also be perceived as able to inflict punishment on line managers, partly because they have a needed expertise, but also because they tend to be attached to higher line managers in the organization.

Staff roles can acquire an immense amount of power. For example, even though the company legal department is theoretically a staff function, its expertise and the possible consequences of not heeding its advice make it appear to have command authority. The same is true of quality control in pharmaceuticals, auditing in finance, and safety in mining.

Supervisors and Staff Roles

Staff roles can either complicate the life of a supervisor or make it easier. Also, supervisors may be managing staff functions themselves and this

Utilizing Staff Functions

In Chapter 2 an example, "Implementing the Veto Process," illustrated how the supervisor should have the right to select employees. This same example can be rephrased to show how the line and staff functions should interrelate. The personnel department performs a staff function. As such, its major responsibility is to support line managers in matters pertaining to personnel management. The supervisor, therefore, can utilize the expertise of the personnel department to assist in selecting new employees. In its supportive role, the personnel department will advertise positions, conduct initial testing and screening, and make an initial selection of qualified applicants. The personnel department can advise the supervisor as to which applicant it believes to be the best, but the final decision must rest with the supervisor so that accountability can be maintained.

requires yet another perspective. If you are a supervisor of a line department you will probably have staff people trying to help you. This is their job and they usually have expertise or advice that is useful. In fact, you should actively seek the advice of staff. The danger comes about when (a) staff advice is foisted upon you by either your superior or a superior staff manager, or (b) the staff person attempts to exert command authority in your areas of responsibility.

In the first situation, if the advice comes through your own manager, then it is the same as command authority. Therefore, you will follow the instructions of the staff person. However, this reduces your accountability since your manager has, in effect, made decisions that affect your areas of responsibility. This is all right, providing that the accountability issue is fully understood by all. If there is any doubt, you should clarify it. If the advice is given through a superior staff manager (which makes it difficult to reject), the situation becomes more complicated because there technically is no command authority present. Your difficulty is caused by the power of the superior staff manager. Your best alternative is to communicate your feelings to your manager (especially if you do not think the advice is in the best interests of your department) so that either your manager can handle the situation at his or her level, or, if that cannot be done, at least you will have clarified your accountability.

Let us reverse the situation and assume that you are the supervisor of a staff department. You now face the problem of getting the ideas of your subordinates implemented in the line organization. Since you do not have the authority to do so, the best way of accomplishing this is through power. In other words, you can increase the effectiveness of your unit if you can acquire the power necessary to exert influence. Although there are many ways of accomplishing this (and some can be quite underhanded), the best long-run strategy is to acquire so much expertise that people will see you and your department as being able to contribute to the effectiveness of line departments. A good track record of achieving results will improve your credibility immensely.

Exercise 3.2

Working Through Line-Staff Conflicts

What would you do in the following situation? You are the supervisor in the quality control department of a firm that manufactures garden hose. You report to the Manager, Quality Control, and you have five inspectors who report to you but work in the production area of the plant. One morning an inspector comes to you and reports that the molding department is consistently turning out substandard work. Your subordinate informed the supervisor of the molding department of the problem last week but to date no changes have been made. This morning he told the supervisor once again and the response was, "Thanks." Role-play this situation with one person as the supervisor of quality control, and the other playing the role of the supervisor in the molding department.

Your major temptation will be to push your ideas too hard, because as an expert you think you know what is best for the other department. However, as a staff person you tend to see only your narrow area, whereas the line manager must consider the entire operation. What may appear to be a good idea to you may be totally unrealistic in the eyes of the line personnel. For staff supervisors, good interpersonal skills are a must because the potential for conflict with the line people is built into the system. Your employees should be trained well so that they are seen as competent by line managers.

As a staff supervisor, you always have the alternative of going over the head of the line department to get your ideas implemented. You may get your idea through, but it will be at a very high price. When you go over their heads to force decisions, especially unpopular ones, upon line supervisors, you severely jeopardize your credibility with them.

Key to Success

Because of the supervisor's unique position in the organization, relationships with other managers and supervisors are quite fragile. The clarification of the supervisor's role and its relationship to other roles, both managers and subordinates, is perhaps the most important determinant of effectiveness. Chapters 2 and 3 have shown how supervisors can have serious problems if their authority is not defined, understood, and respected by all.

Supervisors are in a difficult situation because they are usually the victims of ill-defined roles, not the cause of them. The responsibility for specifying authority relationships lies with higher management, but by recognizing the problems likely to be encountered, supervisors can take the initiative in getting relationships clarified.

Some supervisors have difficulty and are never quite sure why. A better understanding of roles and role relationships is a first step towards diagnosing and solving their problem.

Finally, what you have learned thus far can help you to plan your advancement strategies carefully. If in your first advancement in the organization you do not perform well, it very well may be your last. So why accept a position in which the chances for failure are high? Before accepting you should be clear on (a) the limits to your authority, (b) the nature of your accountability, and (c) the objectives of the unit you will supervise. This will not guarantee success, but it will certainly make the path to it much more enjoyable.

Summary

The major role relationships that characterize most supervisory roles are with subordinates and it is important that specific lines of authority between subordinates and their manager be made clear. Without well-defined and well-understood lines of authority, communication and accountability suffer.

A potential problem is the assistant to the supervisor. If the assistant does not have full authority, the role should be removed from the direct chain of command so that subordinates can have direct access to their supervisor. Similar difficulties can be encountered by part-time assistants, whose roles are usually more difficult because of the temporary nature of their authority.

It is up to higher management to specify authority relationships. Once the supervisor's authority is defined, it must be preserved. The manager must respect the supervisor's right to make decisions regarding his or her work group, provided that they are within the limits of the supervisor's authority. Similarly, the supervisor should question a manager's decisions only if they exceed the limits of the manager's authority.

Supervisors must work with others in the organization, some of whom are staff. Although they can exert considerable power at times, ideally, staff functions have the right only to advise, so that the accountability of supervisors can be preserved. Dealing with staff roles can be a difficult challenge for a supervisor because some important staff roles appear to have command authority.

Opening Incident Revisited

Juanita's problem is common to many supervisors. Changes implemented at the supervisory level are often designed by individuals at higher levels who have little firsthand knowledge of the unit. This can be very frustrating to the supervisor on the receiving end of these changes.

Juanita's problem is also typical of the conflicts that occur between line and staff functions. John Washington is in a staff function. His department supports the rest of the organization through its services. Technically, therefore, Juanita can refuse to implement his new system on the grounds that his role is only an advisory one.

However, the problem is not as simple as that. Staff people do not like to have their advice rejected; John would likely apply pressure on Juanita to implement his new system. Not only is this going to create interpersonal conflict between John and Juanita, but it will probably jeopardize the success of the new system.

So what should Juanita do? Her first step should be to discuss the problem with her manager. If her manager believes she should accept the new system she would be violating the requirements of her position if she did not do so. If her manager agrees to abide by Juanita's judgment, then the ball is back in her court and she must then deal with John Washington.

This means that the ultimate decision is hers. As a staff function, John can only advise Juanita what to do. If she decides to implement the change, she automatically becomes accountable for seeing that it works. If she refuses to change, she is still accountable for refusing staff advice and, on the assumption that she did reject an improvement, should be held accountable for doing so.

It should be noted that John is not a very effective staff person. His success as a staff advisor will be determined by how influential he is with his clients. If he had worked with Juanita and kept her involved in his study, Juanita might have been much more cooperative.

Review Questions

1. What problems are created by a sloppy organizational situation?
2. What problems do assistants usually have when their roles are not properly defined?
3. Why is accountability upward important in an organization?
4. When may a subordinate question the decision of a higher manager?
5. What are line and staff functions?
6. What types of authority do line and staff functions have?
7. What is command authority?
8. What is the difference between power and authority?
9. Why is power important for staff functions?

Chapter Glossary

Organization chart.	The diagram of the formal reporting relationships in an organization.
Assistant supervisor role.	A role that has less than full authority over others in the work unit.
Chain of command.	The system of authority, responsibility, and accountability relationships in an organization.
Accountability upward.	The process of holding the supervisor accountable for his or her performance as a supervisor.
Judgment.	What a manager uses when making a decision in which there is not perfect information.
Limits on authority.	The constraints placed upon any manager which limit the kinds of decision which can be taken.
Line function.	The primary function in an organization, with command authority.

Staff function.	The secondary function in an organization, has the right to advise line managers.
Command authority.	The right of line managers to make final decisions in their area of responsibility.
Staff advice.	The advice given to line managers by staff persons, which may be refused by line managers.
Power.	The ability to influence the behavior of another without having command authority.

Case Problem

Bruce Harvey's Assistant

Since Bruce Harvey became supervisor three years ago in the automobile service department at Washington Auto Parts, the business has grown every year. When he began the job, Bruce had four clerks reporting to him and now he has twelve. He has found that the clerks, most of whom take orders over the counter, require more and more of his time, especially as the company has taken on more and more product lines to better service the customers. The training time now required has consumed practically his whole working day.

In a discussion of the problem with the store manager, Eileen Post, she suggested he promote one of the clerks to the role of Assistant Supervisor. This seemed like a good idea to Harvey, so after reviewing all possible candidates, he chose Brian Heaton as his assistant. Heaton has been with the company almost as long as he, and is probably the most knowledgeable clerk in the group.

He reviewed the position with Heaton and explained why he needed an assistant. He made it clear that he (Harvey) has to spend more time in other areas of the department and cannot devote as much time to training the other clerks in the many new products that were being handled. In the future, Heaton's primary responsibility would be to train the other clerks and, if time permitted, to assist the clerks in their activities.

After several weeks, Harvey felt things were going well. Now that he was free from the training responsibilities, he could devote more time to the customers and his other management duties. Also, he noticed that Heaton seemed to enjoy his new position and appeared to be doing a good job.

One afternoon recently, upon returning from a two-hour management meeting, he entered the shop and heard the following exchange between Heaton and Bob Morris, one of the clerks:

MORRIS: I don't care who you are! You aren't telling me what to do!
HEATON: Yes I am! I'm the assistant supervisor around here and you'll do as you're told! I need you back in the stockroom now, so get back there!
MORRIS: Stuff it! I do what Harvey tells me, not you.

Questions for Discussion

1. Should Morris do what Heaton asks? Why or why not?
2. Why has this situation developed?
3. What should Harvey do now?

Supervision and the Management Process

4

Chapter Learning Objectives

After reading and studying this chapter you should be able to:

1. List and define the four major management processes.

2. Describe the general nature of the planning process.

3. Describe how the planning horizon relates to the supervisor's job.

4. Explain the relationship between planning and accountability.

5. Define objectives, policies, procedures, and rules.

6. Describe the major characteristics of good objectives.

7. Describe the relationship between planning and control.

8. Describe the basic elements of organizational structure.

9. Define span of control.

10. Describe the two major supervisory styles.

11. Describe how information and control relate to the supervisor's job.

Key Terms

Planning
Planning horizon
Objectives
Policies
Procedures
Rules
Management by objectives
Organizing

Job description
Job analysis
Span of control
Directing
Autocratic style
Democratic style
Control
Information systems

67

The Overworked Supervisor

Charlie Simpson was promoted to supervisor of the data processing department over a year ago. Because of company expansion, this department has grown quickly over the past several years and Charlie now has twenty-five employees reporting directly to him. The company has been quite unhappy with Charlie's performance as a supervisor. Other units have complained as well that they can never depend on Charlie's department to meet deadlines.

When Charlie was first promoted, he complained constantly of not having enough staff to carry the workload. His own manager noted that he still spent a lot of time doing basic programming tasks; according to Charlie, he had to because there was no one qualified to do those jobs.

Many bottlenecks have developed because Charlie refuses to send a job out until he has inspected it to make sure it was done right. Several times, the night shift has had to shut down the entire system until Charlie could come in and solve whatever problem has occurred. More recently, he has been the target of a lot of criticism from the financial department for overspending his budget on supplies and personnel costs. Charlie shrugs these criticisms off, saying he has better things to do than count paperclips.

The preceding chapters have been concerned with the fundamental nature of the supervisory role and how it fits into the rest of the organization. In this chapter we consider the supervisor as a manager, exploring those types of activities supervisors must perform in order to fulfill the managerial portion of their role. Oddly enough, many organizations do not refer to their first-level supervisors as managers (probably partly because of some of the role problems noted in Chapters 2 and 3) but yet expect them to perform all the usual managerial functions. It will be no surprise that the position taken here is that first-level supervisors should be managers in every sense of the word. The only characteristic that should distinguish the supervisor's role from that of other managers is the level of employee managed.

The management process consists of the functions that managers perform in order to carry out their responsibilities. These functions are managerial in nature in that they are unique to roles that have accountability for the performance of others. Various authors propose different processes (or functions) as fundamental to the managerial role. There is no correct list since different managers are required to perform different functions, depending upon a variety of factors. The basic functions—planning, organizing, directing, staffing, and controlling—are probably common (to various degrees) to all managerial positions. Each of these functions includes other processes such as decision making, communicating, delegating, and training. This chapter presents the basics of the management functions, particularly as they relate to the supervisory role. The other processes will be noted briefly since separate chapters on these topics are contained later in this book.

Planning

It has been said that to be against planning is like being against motherhood (or fatherhood). It is generally agreed that planning is necessary and that all managers should plan. Yet, all of us can think of an example in which poor planning resulted in disaster. Perhaps it is because the need for good planning is so obvious that many people take it for granted, or at least do not give it the attention that it deserves.

One theory about planning from the behavioral sciences is that poor planning is often the result of subconscious motivation to create crises. It is proposed that poor planning knowingly causes crises to develop, thus requiring the manager to make immediate decisions. This creates an artificial feeling of importance for managers who might otherwise feel unneeded. Not surprisingly, this tendency is most frequently encountered in managers who feel insecure in their positions. Their insecurities prevent them from planning and delegating responsibilities under a plan, thus creating a strong dependent relationship between themselves and their subordinates.

Without planning, the organization (or department) has no sense of direction. Poor planning can result in crisis management and frustration of employees. Not planning is akin to beginning an automobile trip to a strange place with no road map; a lot of energy is spent and some progress is made (after all, you do know the general direction), but arrival at the destination will be delayed by unproductive and expensive side trips.

What is Planning?

Planning is the anticipation of future events and the decision making based upon those events. Planning would be easy were it not for the decision making that commits resources to future action. Without decision making, planning becomes little more than wishful thinking or crystal ball gazing. Once a manager creates a plan, all future actions and decisions are based upon that plan; if the plan is incorrect or poorly thought out the future actions and decisions will be ineffective.

Planning is also an ongoing process. Rarely is a plan created that is not changed at some point in the future. Anticipation of future events cannot always be precise because of changes in the environment in which the planning is done. For example, a plan for staffing a department will likely have to be changed if economic conditions deteriorate. This means that plans always have to be reviewed and revised to keep them current.

Planning is also vital to the control process. Since plans deal with future events and decisions, follow-up is necessary to see that the plans have achieved their objective. This follow-up is called the *control* process, and is used to monitor the effectiveness of planning and to suggest ways of improving the original plan. If no control system is used, the organization will not be able to measure the effectiveness of the planning process.

Planning also occurs at every level. Ideally, of course, the plans at each level should coincide with those of every other level. Later in this section we describe one method—referred to as management by objectives—of attempting to have plans that coincide. But whether or not these plans coincide, each level must still engage in the planning process.

Supervisors may feel that planning is not necessary at their level, but closer inspection will reveal many opportunities for planning. Some examples might be:

- daily planning of work schedules,
- planning for vacation schedules,
- planning for future manpower requirements,
- planning for an upcoming meeting,
- planning of budgets and finances
- planning training programs for subordinates, and
- planning for monthly or year-end reports.

The general nature of these plans suggests that the planning process permeates the entire job of the supervisor. It is not something that is done for an hour each day, or at a certain time during the week. Rather,

No Surprises

During an interview with a supervisor I noticed on his desk a large sign bearing the words, "No Surprises." Of course I asked him its meaning, and he replied, "This sign represents my managerial philosophy. It means that if we do things right around here, there should never by any surprises. I tell my subordinates never to surprise me and I promise in turn never to surprise them. A surprise to me means that someone hasn't been doing his job. If we plan, are well organized, and everyone is trained properly, then there should be no surprises."

At the time it seemed to me to be a pretty superficial description of the planning and management process. But upon deeper reflection, I would be hard-pressed to find a better working definition of planning.

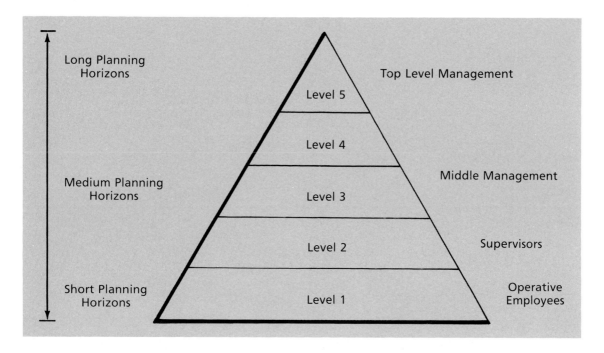

Figure 4.1. Comparison of Planning Horizons for Various Organizational Levels.

the supervisor will constantly be planning in order to carry out the responsibilities of the role. In fact, it has often been said that there is no such thing as not planning, since not having a plan is in itself a plan.

Planning—How Far Ahead?

One of the most important questions regarding planning is how far ahead should one plan? There is no single answer to the question, but there are some important principles that supervisors should understand. As Figure 4.1 illustrates, the length of time for planning ahead (known as the planning horizon) varies from level to level. The longest periods, the long-range plans, are at the top levels. In large organizations, senior managers must plan ahead for years at a time. Lower in the organization, the planning horizon decreases accordingly; middle levels engage in medium-range planning and the lowest levels typically plan only over relatively short periods.

As Figure 4.2 indicates, however, the process is much more complicated than simply long-, medium-, and short-range plans. Each of the levels will have its own set of plans which conform to the long, medium, and short ranges. At the highest level, for example, a large company

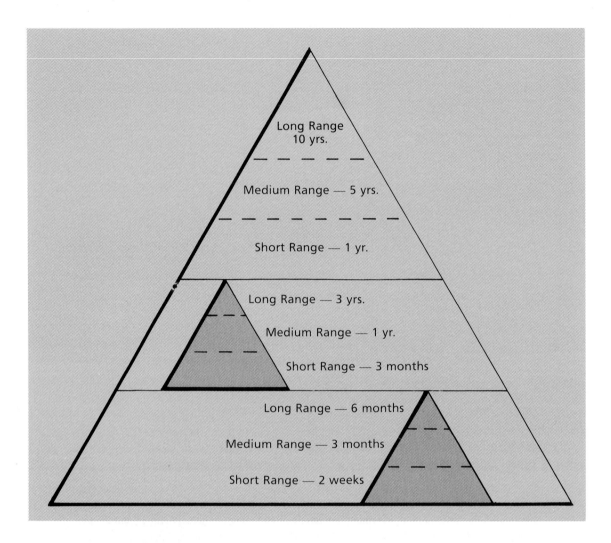

Long Range
10 yrs.

Medium Range — 5 yrs.

Short Range — 1 yr.

Long Range — 3 yrs.

Medium Range — 1 yr.

Short Range — 3 months

Long Range — 6 months

Medium Range — 3 months

Short Range — 2 weeks

Figure 4.2. Planning Horizons Within Various Organizational Levels.

might have a plan to open new markets in foreign countries that could have a time horizon of ten years, but it would also have a short-term plan over a year to improve its cash position. So at that level, the phrase short-term plan takes on a different meaning than it would for a supervisor. A supervisor's long-term plan might be to improve productivity over a six-month period; a short-term plan might be to keep costs within the monthly budget.

A supervisor's planning horizon is determined by the planning horizon of the next higher level. Planning horizon is the length of time a supervisor or manager must plan ahead in his or her work. A supervisor could not be planning two years ahead (using the definition of planning presented earlier) if the next level of management is only planning ahead for six months. This is a problem for supervisors who want to plan ahead but may find they cannot because of the lack of planning of those above them.

Planning and Accountability

The time horizon of the planning process also has important implications for the accountability function discussed in Chapters 2 and 3. It follows from the foregoing discussion that accountability for performance (and plans) should follow closely the time horizon of the plan itself. In other words, if a supervisor is embarking upon a three-month plan to improve quality control in a department, then the performance of the supervisor should not be reviewed until the end of the three months. This does not mean that the supervisor cannot discuss the plan with the manager before that time, but the actual judgment regarding how well the plan was implemented cannot be made until the plan has run its course. The control process, which involves monitoring the progress of the plan, provides both parties with feedback on how well the plan is going and can therefore occur at any useful time during the three-month period. Judging performance before the time of the plan is completed can discourage supervisors from attempting long-term planning.

The Structure of Plans

Plans are of many types and are created through many different processes. Some are created for special problems, others are more permanent and only revised when they clearly are not contributing to the organizaton's goals. The permanent ones can be described by the structure illustrated in Figure 4.3. The highest level plans are the organization's **objectives**. Objectives describe the general purpose of the organization and what it hopes to achieve. Objectives can be long-, medium-, or short-term. Once formulated, they provide the framework for all the plans at the lower levels.

The second level plans are **policies**. Policies can be defined as guidelines to action, meaning that they provide guidance to managers in the decision-making process. Policies are designed to implement objectives and should always be tested against them. As an example, an organization may have an objective of improving the quality of managerial talent in the company; if it also has a policy of promotion from within, this should be examined to ensure that the policy is consistent with the objective.

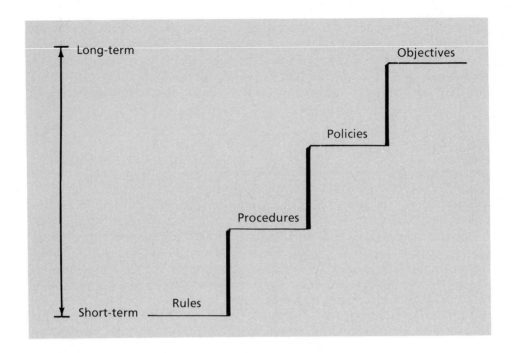

Figure 4.3. Structure of the Organizational Planning Process.

The plans on the third level, **procedures,** are methods designed to implement policies. Procedures usually involve a formalized process (or system) for ensuring that decisions made are consistent with policies. For example, policies on absenteeism usually have a system for reporting absentee cases.

The lowest levels of planning are **rules.** We may not think of rules as plans, but in fact they are the most common form of planning. Rules are standing plans that tell people what to do or what not to do. For example, in a plan to minimize on-the-job accidents, a rule might be formulated requiring employees to wear safety shoes while working. This rule, in effect, plans for the footwear of employees in the future. Rules have the unique characteristic that they are black-and-white in their implementation. They require no judgment or decision making, only understanding.

Rules and policies are frequently confused and the terms are used interchangeably. We often refer to the company policy pertaining to a situation, whereas a closer inspection reveals that it is a rule. For example, some companies have a policy on smoking on the job—they don't allow it. Obviously, this is not a policy but a rule.

The Planning Process

Like the other supervisory functions, the planning process does not occur in isolation. It is an integral part of the supervisor's job and involves coordinating, delegating, directing, and so on. Planning is the initial step upon which any actions the supervisor will take will be based.

Planning at the supervisory level is done within the overall plans established by higher management. Poor planning at these levels can adversely affect planning at the supervisory level. Consequently, the planning process for supervisors begins with clear objectives that are based upon or derived from organizational objectives. As noted above, the supervisor's objectives will have a shorter time horizon than those of higher levels. For example, if a supervisor's manager is formulating plans nine months in advance, then the supervisor will be planning approximately five or six months in the future.

SETTING OBJECTIVES.   Since the planning process is so heavily dependent upon objectives, it is important to know how to set objectives. The following four principles will serve as a useful guide.

1. *Objectives should be realistic.* Objectives are not wish lists. They should be reasonable expectations regarding what can be achieved over a given period of time. If objectives are too ambitious, the motivation of others can be adversely affected since they will foresee little chance of achieving the target.

Talent + abilities

Policies Versus Rules

The distinction between policies and rules may appear to be merely semantic, but the example of the supervisor and the overtime situation in Chapter 3 illustrates how the confusion can create problems for supervisors. Recall that the employee was complaining to his supervisor's manager about being asked to work overtime on a Friday evening. The company had formulated an overtime *policy* for supervisors to use and the supervisor was acting within the limits of the policy in that he was using it as a guideline in making his decision. A different situation would have occurred had there been a *rule* on overtime rather than a policy (note that the limits to the supervisor's authority are, in effect, rules). Had the supervisor violated a rule, then the subordinate would have been justified in questioning the supervisor's decision. As it was, the supervisor was acting within company policy.

Would the situation have been better if there was a rule instead of a policy? It is difficult to say, but a rule would have removed some of the supervisor's ability to plan because he would be more constrained on how he could use overtime work in his department.

2. *Objectives should be defined in specific terms.* Objectives that are vague and uncertain provide little guidance for those striving to reach them. To say that the objective is to improve the productivity of the department does not tell subordinates (a) in what way it is to be improved, (b) by how much it is to be improved, or (c) how much time the improvement is expected to take.

3. *Objectives should have a time horizon.* Setting time horizons provides specific targets for employees. It also provides a control mechanism through which plans can be reviewed and evaluated. If targets are not met by a specific time, objectives and plans can be reviewed to get things back on course.

4. *Objectives should involve participation.* There are some exceptions to this (to be discussed later in this book) but in most cases participation is necessary, as it tends to increase commitment to the objectives. Through the communication that occurs in participation, more information comes to bear on the objectives and there is a greater chance that those affected by the objectives will understand them.

MANAGEMENT BY OBJECTIVES. These four principles are often implemented through a formalized program known as **management by objectives** (MBO). MBO is a system designed to link the objectives of each operating level together so that everyone is ultimately working toward the same set of objectives. Figure 4.4 shows how the system links the objectives of the various levels together. The process begins at the top of the organization and objectives are set successively between each level and the one below. Important to the system is the communication that occurs between manager and subordinate at each level as objectives are set. This communication relates the levels to each other and also serves as the control process for reviewing the achievement of objectives at a subsequent time.

Even though a particular company may not practice MBO in a systematic way, supervisors can still use the concept. It would begin with the supervisor setting his or her own objectives for the unit for a specified time period. These objectives are then discussed with employees to gain their input, and some modifications may occur. Then the supervisor discusses with each employee his or her individual objectives in light of the unit's objectives. They reach an agreement which includes a review point at some time in the future when supervisor and employee will discuss the latter's progress toward the objectives. These objectives then constitute the major planning tool for the immediate future.

Although there are other factors that should be kept in mind when setting objectives, the four listed are basic ones necessary to plan effectively. In some situations, extremely short-term plans for example, not all of the steps may be possible or necessary.

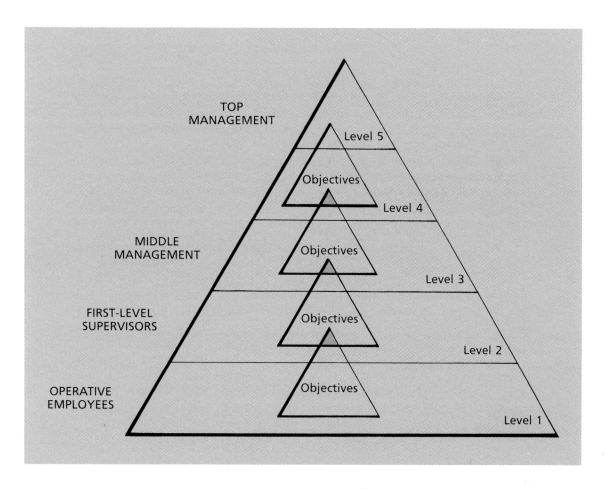

Figure 4.4 Management by Objectives, a Device Linking Different Organizational Levels.

IMPLEMENTING PLANS. Unfortunately, there is no list of generally accepted principles of how to implement a plan. This is probably because there are so many different types of plans that no single list would be satisfactory. There are, however, certain things that supervisors should always consider when implementing a plan.

First, *communication* is important. Everyone involved in the implementation must know who is doing what and when they are to do it. As noted above, participation in formulating the plan itself will do much to alleviate potential problems in this area. Second, the supervisor must make sure that the *resources* necessary to implement the plan are available. There is little point in going through the planning process if those

Exercise 4.1

Analyzing a Plan

This exercise requires that you analyze a supervisor's plan. If you are now a supervisor, it can be a plan of your own. If not, interview a supervisor to find out about a plan he or she designed and implemented. Your objective in this exercise is to find out how closely the planning process you are investigating followed the principles of planning described in this chapter so far. The steps in this exercise will be to: (1) analyze and describe the plan, (2) identify the principles of good planning presented in this chapter, and (3) compare the principles with the plan itself. Finally, was the plan successful? Why or why not?

---

responsible for its implementation are not properly equipped. Third, there must be some type of *schedule* for the plan. This provides direction to the people involved so that they know what is expected of them over the specified period of time. It also allows the supervisor to discover deviations from standard so that corrective action can be taken. Finally, implementation should not be left to chance. Constant follow-up on scheduling and overall effectiveness is the responsibility of the supervisor. Even though a plan may have a time horizon of six months, the supervisor should monitor its progress regularly. Frequent feedback and monitoring of the implementation will help keep the plan on course.

Planning and Control

As noted at the outset of this chapter, planning and control go hand in hand. Control is only meaningful if there is an objective or standard against which progress can be evaluated. Generally speaking, control involves the examination of information which communicates how effective the planning process has been. This information may take the form of productivity data, conformity to schedules, cost data, or other benchmarks of results. Effective control provides the planner with information that can be used to measure the effectiveness of plans and to take corrective action. More will be said about control later in this chapter.

Organizing

The organizing process is an obvious sequel to planning. Once the overall plans have been formulated, the unit must organize its resources to carry out the plan(s). Without proper organization, resources and efforts will not be coordinated and inefficiency will result. One of the important functions of a supervisor is to provide the organization necessary so that employees can work effectively toward the unit's objectives.

The term **organizing** can have a variety of connotations, depending upon the particular context. From the perspective of the broader organization, the term suggests an emphasis upon major organizing decisions such as which departments should be created, where authority should be concentrated, and how large departments or units should be. While the importance of these decisions is obvious, supervisors are generally not involved at this level. Therefore, this section concentrates on those aspects of organizing that can be influenced by the typical supervisor: specifically, job descriptions, job analysis, authority relationships, work-flow design, communication, measurement of organizational effectiveness, and span of control.

Job Descriptions

A fundamental determinant of good organization is adequate job descriptions. Regardless of how well planned a particular activity happens to be, if it is not clear who is to do what there is an excellent chance that something will go wrong. **Job descriptions** describe the specific activities and responsibilities of an individual. While most job descriptions cannot describe everything a person does, they attempt to cover the most frequent and most important activities.

Job descriptions should be reviewed periodically by the supervisor to make sure that all activities and responsibilities of the unit have been assigned. Departments are rarely static and unless job descriptions are updated, some responsibilities can fall between the cracks and not get the attention needed.

Most companies have formal programs to review job descriptions, but supervisors should not view this as someone else's responsibility. Those closest to the work are the best prepared to compare job descriptions to actual responsibilities and it is here that the supervisor must take the initiative. In point of fact, the actual job description is probably not as important as the process that occurs when a job is analyzed.

Job Analysis

The **job analysis** is an investigation into what people *are* doing as compared to what they *should be* doing. Analyzing jobs requires intimate knowledge of the entire work unit and how each individual job fits into the total system. Without it, effective organization is impossible.

Job analysis must be performed regularly so that the supervisor is current on who is doing what. In some cases, people take on duties that have never been formally assigned to them and unless these are integrated into the total system, inefficiency can result. In other cases, job analysis may show that several people are performing essentially the same task and productivity might be improved if their assignments were consolidated into a single job.

Authority, Responsibility, and Accountability

The result of proper job analysis and job descriptions is the specification of who is accountable for what. Chapter 2 dealt with these important concepts from the standpoint of the supervisory role, and the same principles should apply to employees. The classical approach to management principles states that subordinates should be delegated the proper authority to carry out a specific set of responsibilities, and they should be held accountable for using that authority.

Not only must authority, responsibility, and accountability be specified, but they must also be _equal_. If a person has more responsibility than authority he or she will not be able to make the decisions necessary to fulfill the responsibilities. If accountability matches responsibility (but not authority), then the employee is likely to feel unfairly treated at having to answer for results over which he or she has little control.

Although the concepts of authority, responsibility, and accountability are widely recognized and understood, many organizational problems can be traced back to areas as basic as these. Poor coordination and dupli-

The Case of the Personality Conflicts

As a new supervisor, I once had the occasion to deal with two individuals with a long history of what had been called a personality conflict. The two literally hated each other and each seemed to take joy in pointing out the other's mistakes. Talking with them seemed to improve things in the short run, but after a week or two things were back to normal. Probably more out of frustration than clear thinking, I decided to analyze their jobs and see if a clue to the solution might lie there. My analysis revealed that considerable opportunities for conflict arose from the way their jobs were organized. Each was responsible for essentially the same area, only at different levels. One was the supervisor of the other, although each did essentially the same work. The subordinate thought himself capable of carrying all the responsibility (which he was) and therefore resented his supervisor. The problem was solved by assigning other responsibilities to the supervisor and removing him as the supervisor of the subordinate. The subordinate was given all the responsibility for his area and assigned to a new, higher-level supervisor.

It is worth noting that this solution worked in that previous errors disappeared and the work began to get done more efficiently. The bad feelings between the two individuals did not change, but now responsibilities were such that their feelings could not affect their work. One can only wonder what the interpersonal situation could have been had their jobs been designed properly at the start.

caton of effort, for example, are often caused by unclear authority relationships. Often, responsibilities may receive either inadequate or no attention because organizational growth has outpaced the authority and responsibility relationships in place. One of the more common problems caused by poor authority relationships is the *personality conflict.* Closer inspection may reveal basic flaws in the organization itself which aggrevate the personality differences already present. The example on the opposite page illustrates one such case.

Workflow Arrangements

Most organizational units need a well-organized workflow arrangement whereby the activities of members are related in a systematic fashion. In some units, (usually those in which individuals perform a whole task themselves) workflow is of minimal importance and only overall coordination is needed. In others, however, the sequencing of work and work stations is a major determinant of effectiveness.

Workflow considerations have both technical and human aspects. On the technical side, it is important that work be sequenced properly so that the requisite attention is given to each aspect of the task and proper accountability is in place for each step in the workflow. Physical considerations are important in that people should be in reasonable physical proximity with others in the system. For example, copying equipment manufacturers often report that people spend more time travelling back and forth to the copying machine than they spend actually doing the copying.

Workflow design should also take into account the importance of various tasks in the sequence of operations. For example, the design should provide for a review of the product or operation before an important and expensive operation is performed. Otherwise, considerable time and effort may be wasted performing secondary tasks on a product or operation that was substandard to start.

On the social side, workflow problems can create stress and conflict within a work group. Poorly designed work procedures can aggravate personality differences within a group. Some part of a task may be perceived as more important or requiring more skill than others, and ignoring these factors when hiring new people or redesigning the workflow can cause behavioral problems. Generally speaking, the basic workflow arrangements in a unit should follow the informal hierarchy as closely as possible to minimize social disruptions of the work. However, the opposite situation could arise if there was too much social interaction on the job. In these cases, the supervisor should consider changing the workflow and thus breaking up the group. The implications for this strategy are discussed in greater detail in Chapter 9, Working With Groups.

Communication and Organization

It should be no surprise that communication plays an important role in organizing. First, a sound and clear organization is necessary for efficient communication. Clarification of responsibilities allows communication to flow directly and properly. Information flows to those who need it because everyone is aware of what information is important to whom.

Secondly, communication is important in that it is through communication that everyone knows how things are organized. Others cannot be expected to respect the organizational structure, procedures, and workflow if they are not aware of it. Changes in responsibilities, authority arrangements, and workflow should be communicated to all concerned.

And finally, it is through communication that we learn how our organizing strategy is functioning. Upward communication through both formal and informal channels allows the supervisor to decide when and how the organization should be changed.

Measurement of Organizing Effectiveness

It would be nice if we had a simple yardstick with which we could measure a supervisor's success at organizing. Unfortunately, life is not that simple. There are some supervisors who, though they are poorly organized, still reach their objectives, and there are others who are, by most standards, well organized but are relatively ineffective as supervisors. Given that these situations exist, it is clear that good organizing skills are only one determinant of supervisory effectiveness. It is also important to note that good organization is only a means to an end, not

Exercise 4.2

Signs of a Poorly Organized Supervisor

Everyone knows that to be well organized is good and to be poorly organized is bad. Fine. But how do you know which is which? This exercise requires you to reflect on your experience with supervisors and describe the evidence (signs) that tell you a supervisor and his or her unit is poorly organized. In other words, what things happen when there is poor organization?

Make a list of as many signs as you can, share them with a group and see how many are common to the whole group. If you are presently a supervisor, how many of these signs apply to you?

an end in itself. It is possible to spend so much time getting organized that the ultimate objective is forgotten.

The major purpose of this section has been to describe the importance of organizing for the supervisor and suggest a few areas in which organizational principles can directly affect a unit's performance. The specifics of how organization (or lack of it) would affect any particular unit or department will vary with the situation. The best judges of good or poor organization are the people who work under the supervisor since they will experience the effects.

Span of Control

Span of control refers to the number of subordinates reporting to a manager. Spans of control can be viewed as being narrow (i.e., relatively few employees reporting to a manager), or wide (i.e., a relatively large number of employees reporting to a manager). Figure 4.5 on page 84 compares narrow and wide spans of control.

For many years it was believed that there was an ideal span of control and a lot of research was conducted in the attempt to find what it was. It is now thought that there is no ideal span of control, that it depends upon several variables that affect the supervisor-subordinate relationship. Some of these variables are (a) type of tasks performed by subordinates, (b) skill, training, and maturity of subordinates, (c) geographical dispersion of subordinates, (d) required contact between supervisor and subordinates, (e) ability of the manager, and (f) degree of interdependence among the subordinates.

Each of these factors interacts to either reduce or expand the span of control. For example, complex tasks tend to require small spans of control since more supervision is needed; employees who are mature and well trained need comparatively less supervision, and this tends to broaden the span of control; employees who are widely dispersed tend to require more time to supervise, so this leads to a small span of control. Finally, certain tasks (for example, when the risk of making a wrong decision is high) require close contact between supervisor and subordinate, thus reducing the span of control. The determinants of span of control also serve to illustrate why it is impossible to find the ideal span of control. As each determinant changes, its interaction with the others becomes increasingly difficult to predict.

It is possible, however, to tell when a span of control is too large or too small. Symptoms that may indicate that a span of control is too narrow would be (a) poor motivation due to close supervision, (b) high turnover caused by close supervision, and (c) lack of advancement and growth of subordinates because of the lack of freedom on the job. Symptoms indicating too broad a span of control would be (a) poor communi-

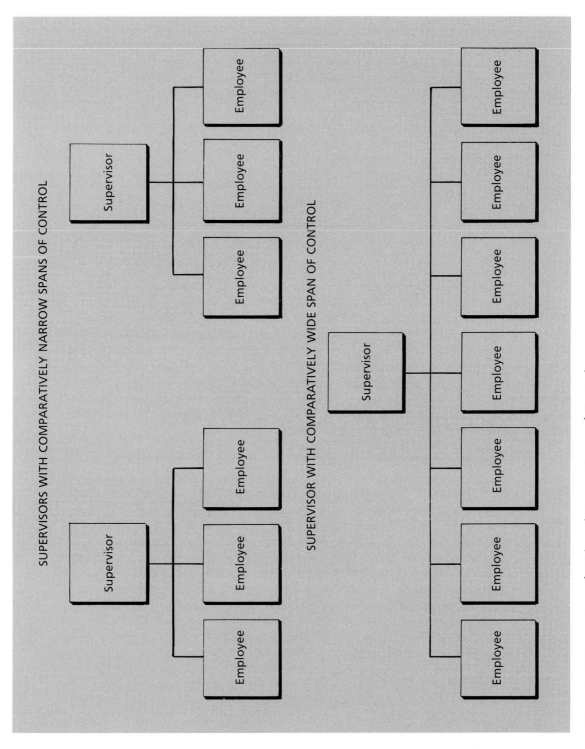

Figure 4.5. Comparison of Wide and Narrow Spans of Control.

cation between supervisor and subordinates, (b) inadequate control over performance, (c) failure by the supervisor to detect errors, and (d) performance problems resulting from lack of direction by the supervisor.

Supervisors who experience any of the above problems should examine their span of control. Possible solutions if the span of control is too small are to increase the number of subordinates or to eliminate the problem by reorganizing the department with another unit. A solution when a span of control is too large is illustrated in Figure 4.6 on page 86, in which new levels of supervision are created. As noted in Chapter 2, it is advisable not to create an additional half-level of supervision that would not have the proper authority to be effective.

Directing

Directing, the process of influencing subordinates toward organizational goals, involves the leadership role that the supervisor assumes in the management of the unit's activities. Only a brief discussion of the topic will be presented here since both Chapters 11 and 12 treat the subject in depth.

The directing function can be understood literally from the term itself; the supervisor *directs* the behavior of the work group. However, it does not follow that telling people what to do is the essence of the directing function. While instructing is certainly an important part of a supervisor's job, it is not necessarily true that employees will obey every instruction. In some cases, employees will not follow instructions because they do not understand them, but they also may consciously choose not to obey. Any supervisor who assumes that direct orders will automatically be followed is in for a surprise.

There are two aspects to giving instructions: the first is the technical, that is, whether or not the instruction is sound in relationship to the job to be done. For example, an instruction from a nursing supervisor to sterilize the operating equipment will be evaluated by the subordinate in terms of whether or not the equipment should be sterilized. The major requirement for good technical instructions is that the supervisor be familiar with the job requirements and how they should be accomplished.

The second aspect of giving instructions is the behavioral. Instructions can be given in a variety of ways, some of which will motivate employees and some of which will alienate them. An important part of being an effective supervisor is being able to give instructions properly without alienating the workers. An understanding of leadership styles will help in developing this skill.

Two leadership (or managerial) styles, the **autocratic** and **democratic styles,** are used to describe the behavior of supervisors while directing. Autocratic supervisors are characterized as telling employees what to do,

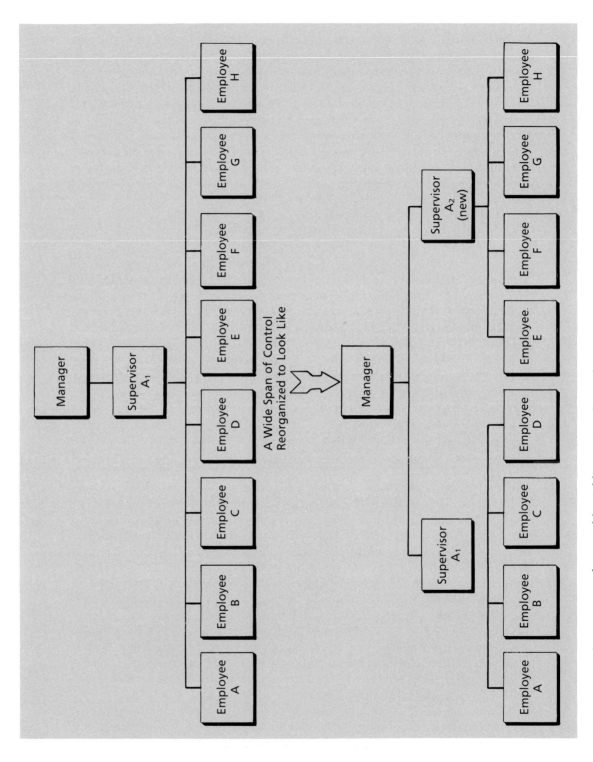

Figure 4.6. Reducing Span of Control by Adding a New Supervisor.

how to do it, when to do it, using one-way communication, and allowing little or no employee participation in the decision-making process. Autocratic supervisors gather the information necessary to make a decision, formulate the decision themselves, and then announce it to the group. They tend not to trust subordinates to make their own decisions and therefore exert tight control and close supervision over them.

Democratic supervisors tend to exhibit the opposite characteristics. They allow subordinates to participate in decision making, practice two-way communication, and allow subordinates comparatively more freedom on the job. Democratic supervisors tend to have a higher degree of trust in their subordinates and give them more responsibility.

The extremes of autocratic and democratic supervisors are just that —extremes. They can be compared as illustrated in Figure 4.7, which shows them as being at opposite ends of the style continuum. In practice, however, most leadership styles fall somewhere in between. A particular supervisor may lean towards being autocratic but occasionally exhibit more democratic tendencies. Others may be largely democratic but behave autocratically in certain situations. One would rarely find a supervisor operating at one extreme end of the contiuum.

One of the more common myths about leadership styles is that democratic supervisors are more effective than autocratic ones. While this could be true in many cases, it does not follow that autocratic supervisors will always be ineffective. Some situations, a crisis for example, require autocratic management and supervisors should be capable of utilizing this style if necessary.

Another misconception about leadership styles is the belief that democratic supervisors are nice and autocrats are obnoxious. This is not true

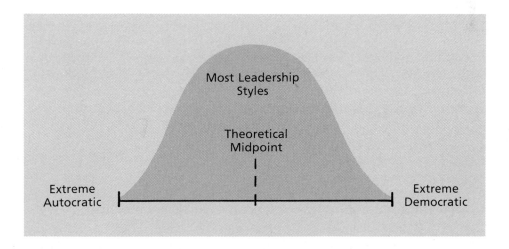

Figure 4.7. Comparison of Autocratic and Democratic Leadership Styles.

because leadership styles are not personality traits. In other words, leadership style describes how people are managed, not how they are treated. This suggests that it is possible for a supervisor to be nice, yet autocratic, or to be obnoxious yet democratic. If we remember that autocratic refers to the degree to which instructions are structured, then we can see that clear, unilateral instructions can be given very pleasantly. This is an important distinction for supervisory training since personalities cannot be changed but leadership styles can. More will be said about supervisory styles in Chapters 11 and 12.

Controlling

As we mentioned earlier in this chapter, controlling is closely related to the other functions of management. For example, it provides feedback on how effective the planning process has been; organizational factors such as structure and job design place controls on organizational performance; and the directing function is partly oriented toward controlling employee behavior. Control, therefore, is best viewed as an important ingredient of the other functions rather than a separate and distinct function of its own.

Control involves measurement of performance or a related result area of the organization. In its most basic form, it involves deciding which information is needed to monitor performance, how that information should be gathered, who should receive the information, and what action should be taken when the information is processed. We will deal with each of these as they relate to the supervisory role.

What Information?

Deciding what information is critical for control purposes is a fundamental step in the control process. Without correct information it is impossible to judge the effectiveness of the organization. The supervisor of a clerical group, for example, might be interested in the following information:

* number of days absent by employee,
* number of complaints received from other departments,
* turnover of employees in the department,
* numbers of items processed in a given period,
* dollars expended on equipment repairs,
* monthly status reports on all budgets, and
* amount of time spent by employees on particular projects.

The supervisor could then periodically examine the information and compare it with a previous estimate or some other standard of performance. In some situations the information forthcoming to a supervisor is determined by others in the organization. Large organizations in particular may have complete information systems which provide necessary data to each manager. In other situations, it would be up to the supervisor to decide which information would be useful for control purposes. The supervisor must therefore examine carefully all areas of performance and decide which information is needed on a systematic basis. Such systems may be highly formalized (such as computerized information systems) or very informal, such as a situation where employees routinely keep their supervisor informed about certain activities.

How Should It Be Reported?

The type of information reported as well as its format can affect the control process. Certain types of information, for example, are relatively useless to the supervisor if the factors that affect the result areas are not within the supervisor's authority to control. Receiving a report on allocation of capital expenditures to a department will have little meaning to a supervisor who cannot make decisions about capital expenditures. The best information for supervisors is that which allows them to effect change in areas of their responsibility and control.

The specific format of the information is also important to the supervisor. The data provided may be correct but if they are not organized properly supervisors will have difficulty understanding the information and will not be able to use it.

Useful Information

One of the most common conflict areas in organizations is the design and implementation of information systems for control purposes. On the one side are the computer jocks who delight in impressing everyone with their skill at getting the computer to produce reams of information, and on the other side are the user groups who frequently complain that the data processing people haven't a clue about what information the managers really need. One of the more amusing examples of this occurred once when I visited the manager of a grain elevator owned by a large grain company. This company had a centralized information system which sent monthly reports out to each elevator so the manager could monitor elevator performance. I asked the manager if he found the reports useful. His immediate answer was "yes," and then he asked if I could keep a secret. It seemed that one of his cars had a transmission leak and he didn't want the leaking fluid to stain his new garage floor at home. He discovered that if the monthly report (which was about three inches thick) was placed underneath the car, it soaked up the leaking fluid beautifully. The real bonus, he claimed, was that at just about the time the stack was soaked through, the home office sent him another month's reports and he could start all over again. His summary comment was, "These are the most useful reports I get."

This example may be an unusual one, but it does indicate a common problem many supervisors have with information systems. One way of combatting this problem is for supervisors to take the initiative and request specific information in a specific form.

Who Should Receive the Information?

Getting the correct information to the right person is obviously important. While many may receive information for review purposes, it is equally important that the information reach those who can influence results. For example, information on quality control should be reported to those who can affect quality control results. This could even be the employees themselves, in addition to the supervisor.

What Action Should Be Taken?

This managerial aspect of the information issue pertains to the action that should or should not be taken on the basis of the information provided. Results are compared to a standard or expectation and the supervisor then decides (a) whether the level of performance is acceptable, and if not, (b) what actions can be taken to improve performance. As we noted earlier, deviations from standard make it necessary to begin the planning process again.

Control in Perspective

Supervisors have to keep in mind that control expends resources and therefore must justify itself. Or, to put it another way, some deviations from standard or expectations are normal and to eliminate them would cost more than what is saved. A supervisor could easily spend the major-

Useless Information

Several years ago we encountered an example of a poorly used control system in our office. In a large university bureaucracy forms are a way of life and we tended to fill them out without giving much thought to their use. For several years, my secretary had been bringing in the "Attendance Report" form every two weeks for me to sign. The form reported the number of absences for the secretarial staff in the department for the period. Like a robot, I continued to sign these forms. For reasons I do not now remember, one day I asked her what happened to the forms after I signed them. She replied that she filed them in our own file and to her knowledge, they were never looked at again. Since we both knew who was absent and when, we stopped completing the form because no action had ever been taken (or likely would be taken) as a result of the form itself.

ity of a working day performing various types of control functions that are counter-productive. Existing control systems must be constantly reviewed to assure that they are providing useful information to the right people in the right form, and that decisions are being based upon that information. If this is not done, then the control system is not a wise economic decision.

Key to Success

On several occasions we have referred to the differences between supervisors and operative employees, and noted that supervisors engage in different activities as managers. This chapter has briefly described what those activities should be. Planning, organizing, directing, and controlling are characteristic of managerial roles. Therefore, one method of measuring your supervisory versus operative orientation is to determine how much of your time is spent in these activities. Some supervisors might find, for example, that although they do planning well, their execution of the control function is weak. Others might find that they can handle the technical aspects of planning and organizing, but their leadership style fails to direct employees' efforts toward departmental goals. Examining your own behavior in each of the functional areas can help spot any weak points.

Perhaps the most important thing to remember about management functions is that they are interrelated and ongoing. One does not, for example, plan on Monday, organize on Tuesday, direct on Wednesday, and so on. In fact, it is difficult to imagine a supervisor engaging in planning without considering the other functions as well. Plans must be made with regard to some type of organization scheme and with follow-up in mind. And all effort will be wasted if the supervisor cannot provide leadership behaviors that will direct subordinates toward planned goals.

Management functions are truly the key to any supervisor's success. Supervisors are evaluated on how well they perform the managerial, not the operative, functions of the role. Once you become a supervisor, fulfilling these managerial functions well will become the most important part of your work life.

Summary

This chapter has presented an overview of the major management processes: planning, organizing, directing, and controlling. Since every supervisor is also a manager, these processes constitute most of what supervisors do.

Planning involves looking ahead and attempting to anticipate future conditions. Organizations also plan in various ways; there is a structure of plans that includes objectives, policies, procedures, and rules, as well as a planning process that projects plans according to specific time periods in the future.

Organizing is the grouping of activities together so that they can contribute to attainment of the organization's objectives. This involves job design, job analysis, design of reporting relationships, and designation of line and staff functions. A well-organized body can channel effort toward objectives more efficiently by eliminating unproductive conflict.

The directing function pertains to the leadership style of the supervisor. Two styles, democratic and autocratic, are the most common. There is no one best style and the task of the supervisor is to select the right style for the right situation.

Control is the process that provides feedback to the organization on how well it is doing compared to its objectives. Control normally involves providing meaningful information to the right people so that corrective action can be taken as quickly as possible. Control also completes the feedback process so that plans can be revised if necessary.

Opening Incident Revisited

Charlie Simpson's problem is that he has never learned to be a manager. He apparently views himself as some sort of super-hero who deals with one crisis after another, while giving little thought as to why the crisis developed in the first place.

Although there is no hard and fast rule on span of control, twenty-five people are a lot to supervise. Imagine if Charlie spent only five minutes per day with each person—he has lost an hour each day as a result. However, if Charlie was a good supervisor, he could manage twenty-five employees with no difficulty. His present supervisory style—largely autocratic—means that he does not delegate responsibility, and therefore his employees require a lot of his time.

Charlie's remarks about his budget overexpenditure show his lack of understanding of what a manager should be doing. He should have a control system in place to keep him up to date on how much he is spending and for what purposes. So we see that his lack of organization affects his ability to control his operation as well.

Probably the saddest part of Charlie's story is that he feels it is the company's fault. Giving him more staff would only make his problem worse, because he doesn't know how to use his people well. He is trying to do everything himself because he doesn't understand how a real manager is supposed to function.

Review Questions

1. What are the major components of the management process?
2. Define planning.
3. How are planning and controlling related?
4. How are short-term, medium-term, and long-term planning related to organizational level?
5. What is the basic structure of plans in organizations?
6. What are the major characteristics of objectives?
7. What is management by objectives?
8. What are the major components of the organizing process?
9. How are communications and organizing related?
10. Define span of control.
11. Describe the two common supervisory styles.
12. What is the basic purpose of the control process?

Chapter Glossary

Planning.	The process of anticipating future events and making decisions based upon those events.
Planning horizon.	The length of time a supervisor or manager must plan ahead in his or her work. The higher the level of management is, the longer the time horizon.
Objectives.	The broadest type of planning which gives direction to the organization. They reflect the basic purpose of the organization.
Policies.	A type of plan that provides a guideline for decision making for those affected by it. Designed to achieve objectives.
Procedures.	The systems by which policies and objectives are implemented. Generally relate to work flow or information flow.
Rules.	Plans that place limits on people's behavior. Require no judgment on the part of decision maker.
Management by objectives.	A formal system used by many companies to translate broad corporate objectives down to the individual level. Successive levels jointly set objectives.
Organizing.	The process of defining the activities and jobs that must be performed to reach objectives, and then collecting them into a meaningful pattern of relationships.
Job description.	A formal document that describes the responsibilities allocated to a specific job.

Job analysis.   The process of analyzing jobs to see how work assign-
                       ments could be improved. Examines activities rather
                       than responsibilities.

Span of control.   The number of subordinates reporting to a manager.

Directing.   The process of influencing subordinates toward organi-
                       zational goals.

Autocratic style.   The style of leadership generally associated with one-
                       way communication, centralized decision making, and
                       order giving.

Democratic style.   The style of leadership generally associated with two-
                       way communication, participation in decision making,
                       and development of subordinates.

Control.   The process of collecting information regarding prog-
                       ress toward achievement of objectives.

Information system.   The formal system that develops and processes the in-
                       formation needed to make decisions. Involves getting
                       the right information to the right person at the right
                       time in understandable form.

Case Problem

Westman Memorial Hospital

The Westman Memorial Hospital is a small rural hospital containing one hundred beds plus an extended care unit for older patients who cannot be cared for at home. Most of the employees have been with the hospital for several years and feel a strong degree of loyalty toward it as a result of the community spirit that is often generated in smaller communities.

The board of directors has become increasingly concerned about the hospital, primarily as the result of increased complaints from patients and their relatives. Also, the hospital has had difficulty in retaining physicians recently, having lost four during the past year. They were replaced with other doctors, but many of the patients resent being treated by a stranger.

As a result of these problems, the board has requested the administrator to hire an external consultant to review the hospital's operations and make a fact-finding report back to the board. After several months of interviewing managers and employees, and examining relevant documents, the consultant has reported the following facts to the board.

1. Hospital expenses for food, medicine, and supplies are twenty percent above the average for hospitals of that size.

2. There is little control over job responsibilities. For example, the laundry manager often helps out in the kitchen and dietary area.

3. The board of directors often becomes involved in personnel matters.

4. The purchasing function is performed by all department heads, but there is no policy on suppliers, inventory levels, or pricing.

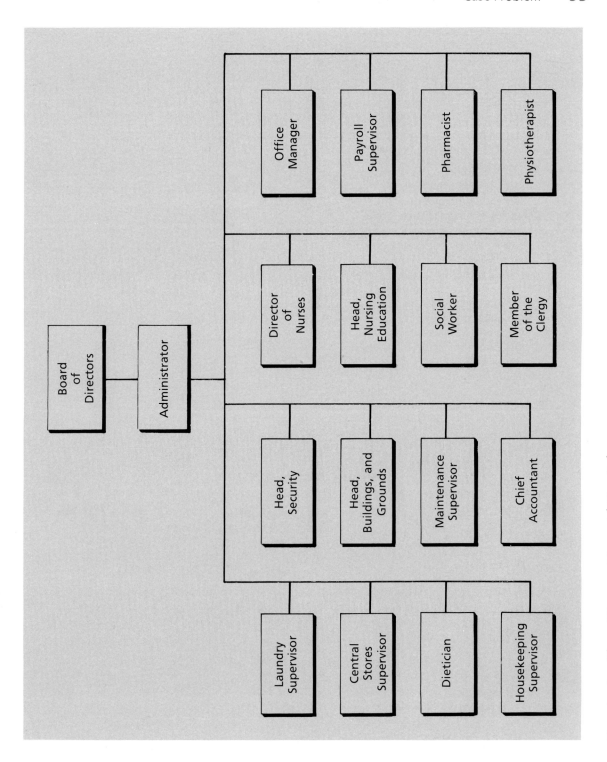

Organization Chart, Westman Memorial Hospital.

5. The student nurses receive little training on the job.

6. The director of nurses supervises all the nurses.

7. The consultant has also studied how the nurses typically spend their time and has presented the following data in the table.

Time study report of nurses.

Activity	Percentage
Accompanying doctors on rounds	10
Admitting and discharging	10
Instructing student nurses	3
Directing housekeeping staff	5
Cleaning rooms and making beds	10
Providing personal patient care	10
Serving food	5
Updating patients' charts	5
Leaving ward to get supplies	10
Working on patients' charts	5
Taking personal time	10
Developing professionally	1
Dealing with patients' relatives	4
Doing paperwork	7
Walking	5
	100

8. The consultant has also submitted the organization chart for the board's review.

Questions for Discussion

1. What are Westman Hospital's major management problems?
2. How should the board begin to solve these problems?
3. What organizational structure would you recommend to Westman?

II

Understanding and Working with People

Understanding
Causes of Behavior

5

Chapter Learning Objectives

After reading and studying this chapter you should be able to:

1. List and define the four major causes of behavior.

2. Describe how previous experiences affect present behavior.

3. Describe the appropriate strategies for changing behavior through the experiential method.

4. Define the concepts of a social and organizational role.

5. Describe the appropriate strategies for changing behavior through the social role method.

6. Explain how reward systems influence behavior on the job.

7. Explain how perception affects behavior.

Key Terms

Hereditary factors
Personality
Experiential learning
Significant emotional experiences
Perception
Social role

Role expectations
Organizational role
Role ambiguity
Role misfit
Pygmalion effect
Reward systems

George Hebert's First Day

George Hebert stood in the middle of the cafeteria and felt his heart sink and his throat go dry. He saw the situation he faced and almost panicked. Luckily, he got his thoughts together in time, turned and walked out the door with his lunch, and ate in his office. He wondered if he would ever be able to go back into the cafeteria again.

George Hebert's problem started because he is so good. He has worked as a machinist for Mid-West Manufacturing Company for ten years and has always received good performance ratings; he was promised that as soon as a supervisory position opened up he would probably get it. The previous foreman finally retired and George was asked by the plant manager if he would like the position of foreman. He agreed and was told that the following Monday he would be the new foreman.

On that Monday George was really feeling good. He was proud of the knee-length blue coat the company had provided (it even had his name sewn on the front), and this was the first day ever that he had occasion to wear a tie to work. The feeling didn't last long. When he entered the work area, the entire group gave him a mock salute and began razzing him about

his blue coat. Sam Johnson, who always was ready with a joke, went to his locker and got a shoe brush and began acting as if he was shining George's shoes. His good friend Joe Bovanni found some rope somewhere and made everyone a necktie, apologizing because they weren't as nice as the fancy one George had on. The razzing continued on through the morning until finally George went to his office and began sorting through the paperwork left over from the week before.

His first clue that something was different was when he noticed that when lunch time came, the group left without him. For ten years he has eaten with the group, but since he was busy in his office, he figured they didn't want to disturb him. After a few minutes he went to the cafeteria by himself, still thinking about the paperwork he had yet to do. When he purchased his food and paid the cashier, he realized that he was standing in the middle of the cafeteria and all eyes were upon him. On the right side of the room was his old group, waiting in eager anticipation. On the left side were the other foremen, all similarly dressed in blue coats and neckties. It was then that George decided to eat in his office.

The phrase "why is he doing that?" is one of the most frequently heard statements at work. Many people have a difficult time understanding the behavior of others and supervisors often find themselves in situations which require considerable understanding. Effective supervisors are those who have the skill, knowledge, and sensitivity to understand why people behave the way they do.

It is easy to confuse the terms *understand* and *agree,* and to believe that if you understand people, then it follows that you agree with them.

Not so. Understanding simply means that you know why they behave as they do; agreement is a separate and distinct step that involves a value judgment. In fact, one of the reasons we often have difficulty in managing people is that the value judgment process occurs with no understanding.

As Chapter 1 explained, applied behavioral science involves essentially three processes: understanding, prediction, and control (or change). All three are closely related and together they constitute a basic system for analyzing any type of behavior. For example, it has been said that if you really want to understand something, try to change it. Note that it is difficult to predict what some people will do if you do not understand *why* they are doing what they are doing now. Finally, your chances for changing someone's behavior are markedly increased if you can accurately predict what he or she will do in certain circumstances.

Our goal in this chapter is to get a better understanding of why people do what they do. Difficult as it may be, we will have to do just what supervisors must do everyday on the job: put our personal values aside and try to be objective in understanding the behavior of others.

Research on the behavior of people tells us there are four primary determinants of behavior: hereditary factors, experience, roles, and reward systems. We shall examine each of these in turn and show how the supervisor can use these four determinants to manage people more effectively.

Hereditary Factors

For several reasons, we will not spend much time on **hereditary factors,** the traits and behavioral characteristics that are genetically determined. First, research suggests that a relatively small portion of our total behavior is genetically determined, the remainder being learned (thus belonging to the other three categories). Second, we do not know with any accuracy which twenty percent of our behavior is hereditary in origin. Current research on genetic engineering holds some promise in this area but much is still to be learned. Finally—and most importantly—any behavior that is biologically determined is, by definition, beyond anyone's control. Therefore, it is pointless to dwell on this aspect of human behavior except to recognize that a certain (small) proportion of behavior cannot be understood or changed with any degree of accuracy. Perhaps the thing to remember is that this category is often used as a dumping ground for behavior that seemingly cannot be explained. Supervisors should always analyze the other three categories carefully before claiming that "Well, I guess he's just that way!"

It is tempting to attribute problems in managing people to personality problems. There is no doubt that **personality**—the manifestation of learned and hereditary traits, attributes, and behaviors—is a determinant of behavior, but in terms of use as a tool for supervisors it is of little value. Most psychologists agree that personality is formed at a very early age. There is also general agreement that part of personality is formed by environmental factors (e.g., treatment by parents and other experiences). Therefore, because of its complexity and early origin it is unlikely that a supervisor can change personality.

It is useful to understand that personality can be separated from behavior. This means that while personalities cannot be changed, behavior can. Oftentimes, what appear to be personality differences are actually conflicts caused by organizational problems that affect behavior. Chapter 4 presented an example illustrating how problems in organizational design caused differences between two employees that might wrongly have been attributed to personalities. It should always be remembered that no two personalities are alike, and therefore the *potential* for personality clashes among employees always exists. Since basic personalities do not change, it is wise to examine the other influences on behavior to prevent the natural differences in personality from hindering organizational performance.

★The Role of Experience

The phrase "we are a product of our experience" is a familiar one and has important lessons for managing people. Through our experiences we learn what is right and wrong, how other people react to us, and how our behavior affects them, both on and off the job. This is the process of **experiential learning.** The model is that people try to *avoid negative ex-*

Fishing for Experiences

Several years ago a friend and I went for a weekend's fishing at our favorite fishing hole (i.e., a place where we have had good experiences). For some reason the fishing was quite poor in our old spot so we began fishing new places. At one spot where a large rock protruded out from the shore down into the water we began to try our luck. Within thirty minutes, we had caught twenty nice fish, all weighing about three to five pounds each, and left only because of darkness. The next day we fished at the rock all day and caught nothing, and the weekend after that, and so on. That was seven years ago. We have not caught a fish at the rock since, but we still go back. An experience we had seven years ago is still a determinant of our behavior today.

periences and repeat positive ones, and is based on the environmental theory of learning, also referred to as behavior modification.[1]

Although all of our experiences teach us something, some are more important than others. These are referred to as **significant emotional experiences** because they have long-lasting effects on our behavior. Many of them occur at an early age and affect our behavior the rest of our lives. Some examples might be rejection by a loved one, extreme poverty during childhood, death of a close friend or loved one, separation of parents, or constant failure at an important task.

The cumulative effect of all our experiences influences our perception of our environment. **Perception** refers to how we screen our experiences and how we organize the information itself.[2] These two processes then influence how we see future experience. For example, if a supervisor severely criticizes an employee, that experience will influence the perception that employee has of the relationship between himself and the supervisor. The following morning when the supervisor says "Have a good day!" the subordinate may perceive that as an offhand reference to the criticism received the day before. It should be understood that in terms of the effect on behavior, it is perception that counts, not what the supervisor actually intended.

How Important Are Experiences on the Job?

It would be misleading to say that the experiences at work are the major determinants of behavior. For the vast majority of employees, their experiences earlier in life have already made a significant impression on their behavior patterns. Experiences at school, home, social activities, and other jobs have already established patterns of behavior that cannot be easily changed. In many cases, the supervisor inherits the good and bad behaviors and therefore must consider strategies for replacing these experiences with new ones. Some of these strategies will be discussed later in this chapter.

Returning for the moment to our task of attempting to understand employee behavior, let us use the experiential approach to look at some common employee types. Often we hear supervisors speak of bad or good employees. Although the analysis will be oversimplified to some extent, we could say that these are employees who have had good and bad experiences in life, and in some cases on the job. For example, if you encounter an employee who is negative, unenthusiastic, critical of man-

---

1. B. F. Skinner, *Science and Human Behavior* (New York: MacMillan, 1953).

2. Terrence R. Mitchell, *People in Organizations,* (New York: McGraw-Hill, 1978), pp. 45–46.

agement's decisions, and generally a pain-in-the-neck to manage, there is a good chance that he or she had either a significant negative experience with an organization, or a consistent series of smaller negative experiences some time in the past.

What Are Bad Experiences?

As we noted earlier, perceptions cause individuals to view experiences differently. Experiences are always colored by perceptions, which in turn are affected by values, attitudes, beliefs, and other experiences. Therefore, it is not always possible to label an experience as inherently bad or good. However, some common on-the-job experiences that tend to breed negative behavior are feeling left out of things, being passed over for promotion, not participating in decisions that affect oneself, being told one thing but having something else happen, feeling underpaid for the job, or generally feeling that one is being taken advantage of.

Supervisors can gain a better understanding of a employee's previous experiences through effective communication. Good communication processes help the supervisor learn how previous experiences are affecting behavior; this in turn provides valuable insight into what types of experiences might be useful in changing the undesirable behavior. Further information on how to accomplish this is presented in Chapter 10, Communication, and Chapter 18, Interviewing, Counselling, and Performance Appraisal.

You Just Can't Win

A welder in a manufacturing plant had been on the job for six months. During that time his foreman constantly harassed him about the poor quality of his work. The employee could not see that his performance was any different from that of his co-workers, but the foreman continued to closely supervise the quality of his work. The situation worsened to the point where it seemed to the employee that the foreman had it in for him and tried to find any fault possible with his work. Communication became so strained between the two that every conversation seemed to end in an argument.

Finally, the employee filed a formal grievance with the union, which eventually went to arbitration. The arbitrator ruled in the company's favor and denied the grievance. After discussing the situation with higher levels of management, the foreman decided it would be best for all if the employee were transferred to a different department and had a fresh start. When the transfer was announced to the employee, he promptly went to his shop steward and demanded that a grievance be filed to get his old job back.

Experiences: The Bad Get Worse

Failure to understand how experiences determine our behavior can lead to even more serious performance problems. Perception plays a key role in how employees might react to a supervisory decision and supervisors must always be on guard for this. Just as we often say that some people see the world through rose-colored glasses, people whose lives have been a series of negative experiences tend to see events through darker lenses. In the more serious situations, no matter what good things happen to these people, they still perceive them as negative. Needless to say, this can be extremely frustrating to a supervisor who constantly tries to change an employee's experiences from bad to good but continually encounters negative feelings.

Strategies for Changing Behavior

Since much of this book is concerned with strategies for changing behavior, this section will discuss it from a general point of view. Later, as you read about specific methods of changing employee behavior, you should relate them back to the concept of experience as a basic determinant of behavior. You will then see that the proposed strategies are simply different ways of providing employees with a new set of positive experiences.

As you can probably surmise, there are two ways of changing peoples' experiences: to provide a significant (positive) emotional experience, or to make available a series of lesser (positive) ones over an extended period of time. Given a choice, the significant experience is better since positive changes tend to occur more quickly. But, to be realistic, there aren't many opportunities to afford the really significant experiences that make drastic changes in behavior overnight (there is one possibility that will be discussed in the next section on roles). To provide a significant experience on the job requires that the supervisor have considerable control over the work environment—and that, unfortunately, is generally not the case. Chapter 2 pointed out that many times supervisors have little authority, and this is just one of the areas in which that creates problems for supervisors. Some examples that *might* be significant emotional experiences for employees would be:

- being promoted unexpectedly,
- being selected "Employee of the Year,"
- being put in charge of a major project,
- being formally reprimanded by a supervisor, or
- being demoted for poor performance.

Note that these are only examples of positive and negative significant emotional experiences. For some employees, none of these may be significant. It all depends upon individual perceptions.

Therefore, the alternative is to provide a series of smaller positive experiences over an extended period of time. Given the limitations noted above, this appears to be the most viable strategy for most supervisors. To do this effectively the supervisor must have a planned strategy for change. These experiences cannot be left to chance, for if they are, the bad is more likely to get worse.

One of the major problems many supervisors encounter in this strategy is that they fail to remember that experiences are *events*, not just words. Talk is cheap. Unless a supervisor can offer the employee genuine, positive experiences, satisfactory change will never occur. This requires that the supervisor understand what kinds of experiences are likely to be perceived as positive by the employee. Mistakes can be made here if the supervisor assumes that everyone sees the same events as being positive. Knowing that perceptions differ among people, the supervisor must make sure that the experiences are perceived as positive by the employee.

Finally, how much time should it take to make measurable changes in an employee's behavior using this method? That is difficult to say because much depends upon the employee, the supervisor, and the type of behavior that is being changed. One suggestion has been the one-half rule; that is, whatever time it has taken for experiences to determine the present behavior, one can expect that it will take approximately one-half that time to change it through a planned strategy of change. Obviously, behavioral science is not precise enough to make this type of prediction, but it does emphasize the fact that behavior generally does not change significantly over short periods of time. The one-half rule also underlines the importance of experiences as determinants of behavior; we simply cannot forget something that has happened to us just because someone tells us to.

Perry Mason: Behavioral Scientist

Some may recall the old Perry Mason television series that is still rerun today on many stations. In practically every episode there is a courtroom scene in which Perry Mason makes a statement in the presence of the jury which is contrary to legal procedure. The judge always responds in an angry voice, "The jury will disregard that remark!" and the camera slowly moves to a close-up of Mason's face showing the sly smile of a lawyer who is keenly aware of the importance of experience as a determinant of behavior, and knows the jury will do nothing of the kind.

Exercise 5.1

Reflecting on Your Experiences

This is an opportunity to examine the effects of your experiences upon your behavior. Reflect for a while on the significant experiences during your life. Make a list of these, describing each one briefly. Next to each experience, describe how this experience has affected your behavior; that is, what things do you do (or not do) because of the experience? Next make a similar list for experiences that have occurred at work and describe how these have affected your work behavior. To add to your learning, share these experiences in groups of three to five to see how other people's behavior has been affected by their experiences. A very challenging exercise is to listen only to the experiences of others, then see if you can predict how this experience has affected them.

Limitations of the Experiential Approach

From our discussion thus far, it follows that supervisors would have greater *potential* influence over employees who are relatively young since they have comparatively fewer negative experiences to overcome. It is generally the older, more experienced workers that seem the most difficult to change, and therefore tend to generate the most frustration in supervisors, although an older employee who has had many positive experiences on the job is not as likely to be affected by a poor supervisor. Later in this book we shall discuss how to induct a new employee into the organization. The point will be made that new employees always have the greatest potential for improvement because they have no experiences with the organization to overcome.

Of course, for this approach to work the basic requirement is for the supervisor to have a large amount of control over the workers' experiences. Supervisors who have little or no authority in their positions will predictably have difficulty in controlling their employees' experiences. As we noted earlier, it is unlikely that many supervisors will have the opportunity to provide the significant emotional experience that can have major effects upon behavior, so in most cases they will have to concentrate on the smaller positive experiences.

In a similar vein, supervisors must always recognize that they may be fighting something beyond their control. There are many examples of employees who receive their major sources of satisfaction (i.e., their most positive experiences) off the job. Activities such as hobbies, sports, families, or church activities can be extremely satisfying to many people. It is not so much that their jobs are bad, but rather that the external activities are so good! In these situations, the supervisor can only continue to provide as many opportunities as possible for good experiences on the job, but should not try to compete directly with the external activities or challenge their importance to the employee.

One of the best ways of understanding why people often find non-work activities more satisfying is to look at the decision-making process and compare leisure activities with job behaviors. Take the case of a typical assembly line worker in a manufacturing company. At work he is told what to do, when to do it, and what to do it with. He has very little control over his work life. His favorite leisure activity is hunting. Here he decides when to do it, what to hunt, where to go, what type of equipment to use, whom to go with, and so forth—all the decisions are his own. Is it any surprise that he enjoys hunting more than working?

How Roles Affect Behavior

Behavior is also partly determined by the roles we occupy in society, both in our personal lives and in organizations. Roles can be viewed as specific types of experiences, but it helps to examine them separately because this provides some important clues as to how behavior might be changed. In this section we shall examine the concept of the social role, how it is defined, and how managers and supervisors might use the concept to affect the behavior of employees.

The Concept of the Social Role

Chapter 2 outlined the fundamental framework of a social role in some detail, so in this section we shall review those ideas briefly. The concept of a **social role** is used by behavioral science to describe the set of behaviors that is expected of us by others. Depending upon the role in question, these **role expectations** change. For example, we expect clergymen to behave differently from college professors, young children to behave differently from mature adults, married people to behave differently from single people, and so on. When a significant number of people agree on a set of expectations for a specific role, then a definable role exists. Problems arise, of course, when there is little agreement on role expectations, or when the person occupying the role is not aware of all the expectations.

The Organizational Role

It is useful to view the organizational role in the same manner that we might view a role in a stage play or movie script. On the stage, the behavior of the actor or actress is determined by how the role is defined in the script and is communicated to the player by the director. The director can make immediate changes in the behavior of the player just by altering the script or the directions given. The changes can be so pronounced that a person can play the role of a hero in one movie and a villain in the next, simply because he or she is occupying a different role. Additional contrast is evident when we compare the behavior of the actor or actress on the stage with his or her behavior in another role—that of husband or wife. The villain during the day can easily change roles and be a loving parent at home.

To make the transition from the movie role to the **organizational role** we need only note that organizational roles tend to be less clearly defined because direction and expectations usually do not come from a single source. The social roles that exist in organizations are defined by many people: peers, subordinates, managers, friends—virtually anyone that has a reason to expect specific behaviors in the role. The general principle which determines our behavior is that if we wish to continue to occupy a particular role, we will attempt to engage in the behaviors which are expected of us. Not everyone, of course, adheres strictly to role expectations (the extremes are called deviates) but if the expectations are clear and enforceable, chances are we will not deviate significantly.

As we pointed out in Chapter 2, the concept of an organizational role and the job description have things in common, but there are also some

Understanding the Role of a Union President

While working with a company on ways of improving the quality of working life for its employees, I had considerable contact with the president of the local union. Never had I met a person so obnoxious and it became apparent that he would be one of my major problems in implementing needed changes. In addition to being personally difficult to get along with, he was against every suggestion I made, was totally negative toward the company, and was a very powerful influence with the rest of the workers. By accident, the two of us had an occasion to meet one evening off the job. His behavior was a complete contrast to what I had seen at work. He was warm, friendly, and had several positive comments about the company. After recovering from the shock of the contrast, I asked him about this drastic change in behavior. His reply was an educaton in organizational roles: "In our company, the workers expect the union president to make management's life difficult, and no one does that better than me. I've been told many times that I'm the best president they've ever had." It then occurred to me that I had failed to separate him from his role and that he was just like an actor on a stage. In our previous relationship, I had been treating him as a helper to the organization, something that was in direct conflict with his role as a union president. After I realized this, our relationship at work improved significantly because I began working with him and communicating with him in a manner consistent with his role.

important differences. The formal job description usually describes the duties, responsibilities, and reporting relationships of a position. The concept of role goes far beyond this. Although not on paper like the job description, the role is far more specific as to the behaviors required of the person occupying the role. For example, some common role expectations might be:

- Managers should wear suits and ties at work.
- All employees should call the President Mr. X.
- Employees should not socialize with their supervisors.
- Office employees should not wear jeans to work.
- Workers should not produce above the norm.
- Students should not wear suits and ties to school.
- All foremen should eat lunch together.
- Employees should be on time for meetings.
- Shop stewards should antagonize foremen.
- Managers should not take formal coffee breaks.

These, of course, are expectations of groups of roles; the expectations of individual roles are just as precise and generally more numerous.

Understanding How the Organizational Role Works

The key to using organizational roles for the more effective management of people is to understand the dynamics of how they operate. While no two roles are alike, all roles do exhibit certain characteristics in common. These will be explained here before we proceed with how to use role concepts to change behavior.

As we have just noted, roles are defined by the expectations of others. We learn of these expectations through direct communication and through more informal methods. We can tell, for example, when some individual or group disapproves of our behavior even though they may not say so directly. Just through observation we can tell when our behavior is different from that which is expected.

Of major importance to us in occupying our role is the clarity and consistency of expectations. When Chapter 2 pointed out the difficulties in being a supervisor, that was an example of conflicting expectations regarding appropriate behavior. Expectations can be clear, but they also can conflict. All of us occupy many roles simultaneously and it is not uncommon for expectations to conflict. For example, your manager may expect you to work Saturdays if necessary, but your family expects you to spend weekends with them. Severe and persistent conflicts in expectations can create unwanted stress that can negatively affect a person's performance on the job.

One of the most traumatic and difficult experiences you may ever have is the period immediately after you have been appointed to a supervisory position. Worse yet is if you have been made supervisor of the group you used to work with. The change of roles—and therefore of expectations—is sharp and many people have difficulty adapting. Although there can be many reasons for this (such as lack of adequate supervisory training) the conflict of expectations seems to cause the most problems. The old work group tends to resent your new behaviors and because you still identify with them (remember, you can't wipe all those fun years out of your mind!) you may find it difficult to engage in your new managerial behaviors This is why it often is a good idea to begin your supervisory career with a group you haven't worked with before.

Two additional concepts that are important are role ambiguity and role misfit. **Role ambiguity** exists when the expectations of the role are unclear. This causes the person to experiment with a series of behaviors to see which ones are most acceptable. The final outcome can be a suitable and well-defined role, but the process of getting there can be painful since the experimentation will undoubtedly lead to many mistakes along the way.

A **role misfit** problem is more serious. This occurs when all the other role problems have been solved, but it turns out that the person is not capable of exhibiting the expected behaviors, or at least that he or she is extremely uncomfortable doing so. For example, it has been found that many people cannot psychologically occupy the role of a police officer because it requires them to do things they don't like. Similarly, conscientious objectors refuse to occupy the role of a soldier because the behaviors required are contrary to their value system. Since most role misfit problems occur in relatively well-defined roles, the best solution to these problems is usually to remove the person from the role.

How to Use Role Concepts to Change Behavior

Since we have established that behavior on the job is partly a function of organizational roles, and roles are made up of expectations, then it follows that changes in behavior can be effected by changing either the role itself, or the expectations associated with a role. We will examine each of these in turn.

CHANGING EXPECTATIONS. For years social scientists have been aware of a phenomenon known as the pygmalion effect. The term, derived from Greek mythology, was later used by G. B. Shaw to title his play "Pygmalion," in which Professor Doolittle bets a friend that he can take a flower girl off the streets and through training, pass her off as royalty. He teaches her how to talk, walk, and dress in the manner expected of royalty and he wins his bet. So this highly entertaining story (more recently in a musical version, "My Fair Lady") illustrates how people can react to expectations and how expectations can be used to change behavior.

Pygmalion effect is also used to describe the phenomenon known as self-fulfilling prophecy. Taken literally, this means that people behave as they are expected to behave, or as the old saying goes, "treat a person like a child and he or she will act like a child." So if a supervisor expects an employee to be lazy or irresponsible and treats him that way, the pygmalion effect predicts that the subordinate will fulfill the supervisor's expectations.

Many studies have been done on the pygmalion effect in the field of education. A common one goes something like this: Second grade students are given a test that measures their reading ability and then the class is randomly divided into two groups. The students are told that the good readers have been put in one group and the slow readers in the other. The teacher then begins to teach them as if they were fast and slow readers, respectively. Within a short period of time, the slow group begins to read more slowly than the fast group.

The primary lesson to be learned from the pygmalion effect is that supervisors should have positive expectations of their employees. This will not guarantee, but will increase the chances that their behavior will be positive. However, there are other factors that affect a person's level of performance and these will be discussed in other portions of this book.

One of the difficult things for supervisors to grasp is how to turn the self-fulfilling prophecy from a negative one to a positive one. A common response is "When he changes his ways, then I'll change my expectations." But the cause-and-effect model implied by the pygmalion effect suggests that this is backwards. If we always view behavior as the *out-*

Fighting a Losing Battle

A supervisor once told me of a difficult problem she was trying to solve. One of her employees, a woman of about fifty, had no confidence in her own abilities. She needed continual direction and support and could not be depended upon to do anything on her own, despite the fact that she was quite capable of doing her job well. All of the supervisor's efforts at building up the woman's confidence were seemingly undermined by her husband, who treated her as though she could do nothing on her own. He called her at the office at least five times each day to ask her such things as, "Have you thawed the meat out for supper tonight?" or "Did you remember to put the garbage out?", or "Did you mail those letters I gave you?" We both agreed it would be very difficult to make changes in her job behavior when she was operating under such a negative set of expectations at home.

come of events, then the preceding events must be changed before the behavior can. In this example, it means that the onus lies on the supervisor to change his expectations (and his behavior!) first, thus increasing the chances that a change in the employee's behavior will follow.

How do you change expectations? Expectations by themselves are attitudinal in nature and therefore not obvious to others. Others learn of our expectations of them by the way we treat them (note that this is a change in their experience). So a supervisor may have to make some significant changes in the way he or she supervises employees to have the best chance of altering their behavior.

One of the limiting factors from the supervisor's point of view is that expectations are communicated by many different people. Some of these have more influence over the person than the supervisor does. So even though the supervisor may follow the proper change strategy, it will not work if it is being counteracted elsewhere.

CHANGING THE ROLE.   This strategy is often the most practical for supervisors because the process is more under the direct control of the supervisor. Moreover, since the change itself is clearer, the chances for behavioral change are greater. The major limiting factor is that in smaller organizations, the opportunities for a complete change of role are limited.

An old joke that is often bandied around management circles is that the best way of solving the problem of a dissident union member is to make that person a manager. Assuming that one would want to do this (and, of course, incur other problems as a result of the move), it can lead

Making Winners out of Losers

Some may find this difficult to believe, but it's true. One company (unnamed) has a meeting once each year with all its department managers. Each manager brings to the meeting (in name only) his or her worst employee. The purpose of the meeting? They trade! They use this process in recognition of the fact that only roles are unsuitable, not people, and that perhaps a more suitable role is available in another department. To make the transfer only two conditions must be met: the job skills must be reasonably transferable, and the employee must agree to the role change. Interestingly, almost all employees accept the change (after all, they aren't happy in a role where they can't meet expectations) and the program is successful (i.e., about one-third of those transferred improve their performance in the new role). Company policy also specifies that employees are allowed three role changes; if after that performance is still not satisfactory, they are urged to seek out a new role elsewhere (i.e., they are fired).

to effective behavior change. To the extent that a person's behavior is a function of his or her role, changing the role will go a long way toward changing the behavior. The reason this can work is because a change in role has the net effect of making clear changes in expectations, which we have already established as having an impact on behavior.

The most common examples of role changes in organizations would be promotion, transfer, and dismissal. Of these three, transfer is the most frequently used for making positive changes in a person's behavior. Transfers are useful strategies for change because they recognize that the individual is not necessarily bad, only his or her present behavior is not suitable for the role.

It would seem obvious that promotion must have a positive effect on an employee, since few would consider promotion to be a negative experience. However, there are some interesting wrinkles that should always be examined when considering individuals for promotion. The potential problems associated with promoting an employee to supervisor of the former work group have already been noted and can be reduced by providing the new supervisor with as much role support as possible. Also, recognizing the potential impact that a role change can have, management can look beyond the pool of talent that might normally be considered.

Reward Systems As Causes of Behavior

The final major cause of behavior is the **reward systems** that exist in our environment. Because Chapter 8 explains in detail how supervisors can use reward systems, this section will outline the basic concept.

Systematic analysis of the rewards and punishments that we experience as we go about our daily activities reveals that our behavior, both on and off the job, is rewarded, punished, or ignored. Behavior that is rewarded is more likely to occur again, and behavior that is punished or

The Union President—Again

The earlier example of the recalcitrant union president had an interesting conclusion. Some time later the company was looking for a candidate to fill a position of assistant plant manager. They chose the union president. Their logic? They were looking for managerial qualities and someone who was influential with the employees. Managing a 400-person union was a complex task and the president had proved his managerial capabilities. Knowing he had these important skills, the company was willing to let the role change do the rest.

Exercise 5.2

Exercise 5.2

Roles and Behaviors

First, make a list of the important roles you have occupied in your life. Beside each role, list the specific behaviors that were different in this role as compared to others. Decide whether these differences were caused by the role or other factors.

Then make a list of the organizational roles you have occupied during your work life. Beside each role, list the specific behaviors required in that role that were different from your other work roles. Decide whether these differences were caused by the role or other factors.

Finally, share your list with others to compare experiences.

---

ignored is less likely to occur again. Our behavior can therefore be changed by changing the reward and punishment systems that exist in our environment.

There are both formal and informal reward systems in organizations. Examples of the formal systems are performance evaluation systems, employee recognition plans, wage and salary systems, and promotion systems, to name just a few. Informal reward systems might include acceptance of the individual by the group, satisfaction with a particular job, or recognition by one's colleagues on the job. Each of these systems will have an effect on the employee's behavior. In some situations, supervisors do not have control over the reward system, so their potential influence is weakened.

One of the most common reward systems in organizations is the merit principle, that is, the better a person's performance, the more pay he or she receives. In this case, the organization desires better performance so it rewards that type of behavior. Disciplinary action is another example. If a firm wishes to prevent accidents on the job, it might implement a disciplinary system whereby employees caught violating a safety regulation would be punished. As Chapter 8 will explain, punishment should be used cautiously in organizations because of its potential negative side effects.

Depending upon how the reward system is designed and managed, organizations can exert significant influence upon employee behavior. Few people will purposely engage in behavior that will result in punishment, and most people will modify their behavior to maximize their rewards. In instances where this is not true, one or more of the following conditions will probably exist:

- It is not clear to employees which behaviors are rewarded and which are punished.

- Rewards and punishments are administered inconsistently.
- No rewards or punishments are administered.
- The rewards and punishments are not of sufficient magnitude to influence behavior.
- The wrong behaviors are rewarded.

The reward-punishment model is of considerable practical use to the supervisor. The analysis of behavior it involves can reveal possible solutions to performance problems. For example, the supervisor need only observe specific behaviors to begin the analysis. If an employee is goofing off on the job, it follows that the employee finds this behavior rewarding. If the supervisor wishes to stop this behavior, he or she must either reduce the rewards associated with goofing off, or establish a different behavior that is more rewarding to the employee. It frequently happens that the very reason an employee goofs off is to attract the attention of the supervisor, and employees consider supervisory attention to be rewarding. Therefore, if the supervisor ignores the goofing off and gives the employee the needed attention on other matters, the unwanted behavior may cease.

To a large extent, therefore, for a supervisor to understand the causes of behavior means that he or she must understand reward systems that affect workers. This frequently means looking beyond the immediate work environment because reward systems exist everywhere. In some cases, it will be impossible to overcome an external reward system, but at least a correct understanding of the reward system will allow the supervisor to concentrate on managing systems that can influence behavior.

Integrating the Causes of Behavior

This review of the major causes of behavior makes it clear that there is a strong relationship among them. Research has shown that personalities are partly formed through a series of experiences at an early age. Similarly, the experiential approach to managing people is based upon the types of experiences, both bad and good, that have an effect on behavior in later life. Role theory is based upon the idea that deviation from role expectations brings punishment and it is through rewards and punishments that the proper role behaviors are learned. Finally, reward systems are a specific way of creating good and bad experiences, or of enforcing role behaviors.

The common thread connecting all the causes of behavior, as far as supervisors are concerned, is that behavior on the job is largely caused by environmental factors. Whether the factors be experiences, role expectations, or reward systems is important only insofar as strategies for change are considered. In fact, the major reason for analyzing what is essentially a common cause from different perspectives is to provide a greater variety of strategies for changing behavior on the job. Some of these strategies have been discussed in this chapter, and others will be presented throughout the remainder of this book.

Key to Success

A supervisor's key to success in this area lies in understanding which behaviors can be changed and which cannot. The next decision is whether or not the behavior should be changed. Finally, the supervisor must decide how to change the undesirable behavior.

To help us with some approaches to these three important issues, let us examine some important principles of behavior change. First, major changes in behavior are difficult for any supervisor; they can happen, but it is the exception rather than the rule. Second, if important changes in behavior can be made, they usually occur over long periods, perhaps years for some behavior changes. And finally, the supervisor is only one determinant of an employee's behavior. Many other people impact on the employee's behavior.

One of the most practical strategies for dealing with undesirable behavior in the short run is *coping*, i.e., finding ways to minimize disruptive behaviors and using the positive ones. This does not mean that you should abandon the goal of major change, but recognizing the practicalities of the situation, coping may be the best short-run strategy. Attempting to force major change in a short time may cause more problems than it solves.

One method of coping is the adaptation strategy. The old saying "You can't make a silk purse out of a sow's ear" has particular relevance. Although you can't make the silk purse, perhaps you can use a sow's ear! This is adaptation, operating with actual rather than ideal conditions. Even though we may wish employees to be different, perhaps we can find a way to make them effective the way they are. This approach has two important advantages. First, it avoids the inevitable hassles encountered when attempting to change the way employees behave, and second, it uses natural rather than artificial motivations in employees.

Of course at some time, every supervisor is faced with an employee whose behavior must be changed. In these situations, a solid understanding of how behavior is learned and maintained is a good beginning point. The key here is patience. In most situations, people's behavior does not change quickly. Their previous behaviors served an important purpose and they won't be given up easily. In rare cases, major changes can be achieved almost overnight. But in the vast majority of instances, the supervisor will need understanding and patience as a necessary condition for achieving desired change.

Summary

This chapter has examined four major causes of behavior: hereditary factors, previous experiences, social roles, and reward systems. Hereditary factors play a relatively small part in determining behavior and cannot be influenced by the supervisor. Previous experiences affect behavior in that bad experiences are avoided and good experiences tend to be repeated. Significant emotional experiences have the greatest effect on behavior, and supervisors can bring about changes in behavior by providing a significant emotional experience that is contrary to previous experiences. They may also embark on a planned strategy for change over an extended period of time by providing employees with a series of smaller positive experiences. Roles determine behavior because individuals attempt to meet the behavioral expectations associated with the role. Behavior can be influenced either by changing the role, or by changing the expectations. Reward systems are the rewards and punishments that people encounter in their environment. Behavior can be shaped by changing the reward system to encourage the types of behavior desired by the supervisor.

Opening Incident Revisited

George Hebert is going through an experience that many new supervisors have to face. Since he had more important things to think about, it never occurred to George that his role would change when he moved from first-line employee to supervisor. This role change involves a very sharp modification in expectations. Interestingly, George was really aware of the necessity for change, for he came to work on Monday morning dressed differently than when he was an employee. Although no one told him specifically, it was very clear to him that supervisors dressed differently and he conformed to that role expectation. So even though it is often stated that behavior usually does not change significantly over a short period of time, this case is an exception because of the clear distinction between the two sets of expectations.

The part that really bothered George, of course, was the treatment he received from his former co-workers. But they were behaving in a manner entirely consistent with their roles and with the situation at hand. George obviously is not a member of their group any more. He works in a different place (his office), has a different title, and even dresses differently! From that point of view, the group is actually doing George a favor. Their behavior is their way of telling him that they recognize his role change and that he is no longer a member of their group. All this is to George's advantage since he cannot be an effective supervisor if he is still psychologically part of the group.

The lunchroom incident, of course, is one that George would have done better to avoid since it required a very major change in his behavior on the first day. Also, the openly conflicting expectations associated with the two groups made the situation even more awkward. To George's credit, he probably handled it the best way he could. When he ventures back into the lunchroom at some future date, he would be wise to come in with a group of foremen. This way he will receive the support of that group (which is his new group) and the break from his old group will be less severe.

Review Questions

1. What is the importance of understanding *why* a person is engaging in a particular behavior?
2. What is the general role that hereditary factors play in our behavior?
3. To what extent should supervisors be concerned with personalities?
4. How do experiences affect our behavior?
5. What kinds of experiences have the greatest effect on our behavior?
6. How can supervisors use the experiential approach to changing behavior?
7. What are the major problems in using the experiential approach to changing employees' behavior?
8. What is a social role and how does it affect behavior?
9. What is role ambiguity and how can it affect behavior?
10. What is role misfit and how can it affect behavior?
11. How can role theory be used to change behavior on the job?
12. How do reward systems affect behavior?
13. What are some common formal reward systems in organizations?
14. How can the supervisor use reward systems to influence behavior?
15. How are experiential learning, role theory, and reward systems related?

Chapter Glossary

Hereditary factors. Those traits and behavioral characteristics that are genetically determined.

Personality. The manifestation of learned and hereditary traits, attitudes, and behaviors.

Experiential learning. The process of learning from one's experiences.

Significant emotional experiences. The experiences that have a major impact on one's behavior.

Perception. The interpretive process by which individuals attach meaning to their experiences.

Social role.	The set of behaviors that is expected by others of an individual occupying a specific position in society.
Role expectations.	The events that communicate to an occupant of a role which behaviors are considered to be acceptable.
Organizational role.	The set of behaviors expected by others of an individual occupying a specific position in an organization.
Role ambiguity.	The situation in which role expectations are unclear or conflicting.
Role misfit.	The situation in which an individual is not capable of engaging in the behaviors expected of the role.
Pygmalion effect.	The phenomenon of self-fulfilling prophecy, that is, that behavior is a function of expectations; people will behave as they are expected to behave.
Reward systems.	The formal and informal reward and punishment systems that operate in organizations and influence behavior.

Case Problem

Juno Data Processing Company

The Juno Data Processing Company is a computer firm which contracts data processing services to companies that are usually too small to purchase their own computer. Juno performs basic services such as payroll, inventory, and accounts receivable. Most of the employees are technically trained and perform either programming tasks or general service work. Charley Drone is the supervisor of the Computer Services Department, and is particularly concerned about Bruce Simon, one of his service technicians. One day at lunch, he was describing his problem to Elaine Smith, one of the other supervisors.

CHARLEY: I just don't know what to do with Simon. I've tried everything I can to get him motivated but nothing seems to work.

ELAINE: What have you tried?

CHARLEY: Well, for example, I've told him that the only way to get ahead in this company is through hard work. I pointed out that that's how I got my promotion, but it doesn't seem to have much of an impact.

ELAINE: Has he ever applied for promotion?

CHARLEY: Yes, once about three years ago. But I just didn't think he was ready so we hired Paul Drake from outside. I told him why we hired Paul instead of promoting him, but he still took it kind of hard.

ELAINE: What happened then?

CHARLEY: Well, ever since then his motivation seems to have dropped. I can't figure out why he can't see that he's only hurting his chances. He'll never get promoted this way. Its gotten so lately I have to watch him like a hawk. He makes stupid mistakes and doesn't seem to really care.

ELAINE: What are you going to do now?

CHARLIE: I don't know. I just can't figure the guy out. He says he wants to be promoted, but he sure doesn't act like it.

Questions for Discussion

1. How might you account for Simon's behavior?
2. What role would perception play in this problem?
3. How might Simon view the reward system in this organization?
4. What strategies would you recommend that Charley use to try to change Simon's behavior?

Understanding Motivation

6

After reading and studying this chapter you should be able to:

1. Describe the general development of the morale-productivity controversy.

2. Define motivation.

3. Discuss why morale and productivity may not be causally related.

4. Explain how individual differences affect motivation theory.

5. Explain why happy workers are not necessarily productive workers.

6. Explain how the morale-productivity controversy affects the job of the supervisor.

7. Explain the importance of morale.

8. List the factors other than morale that affect productivity.

9. Describe the circular relationship between morale and productivity.

Key Terms

Morale
Productivity
Human relations school
Job satisfaction
Job enrichment
Job dissatisfaction

Motivation
Mutual causality
Task design
Technology
Group norms

Central Lumber Company

Central Lumber Company is a medium-sized firm that specializes in wholesale and retail lumber sales. They have four retail outlets throughout the city and together with the wholesale part of the company, employ a total of seventy-five people during peak season. The management of the company has lately been concerned about the increased labor cost over the past several years that has been eating into its profit margin. Since most of their other costs are largely beyond their control, the management has decided to review its labor costs to see if money can be saved there. In the past three years, although their total volume of sales has grown ten percent, their labor costs have increased twenty percent. Management has therefore concluded that if the motivation of the work force can be increased, labor costs can be reduced.

The General Manager organized a meeting of all supervisors and other managers to discuss the problem. After much discussion, it was decided that the morale of the employees was affecting their performance, and that the company should concentrate on improving morale. The General Manager opened up the discussion for ideas on how morale could be improved. The following suggestions were brought forward.

- Have an annual company picnic for all employees.
- Install piped-in music in all stores and offices.
- Give all store employees new and relatively expensive uniforms.
- Have the current fleet of trucks repainted.
- Raise everyone's pay by ten percent.
- Give longer coffee breaks.
- Cut the workweek by two hours.

The General Manager is now left with deciding which, if any, of the suggestions to implement.

As in the proverbial search for a better mousetrap, the world is always trying to find better ways of motivating workers. Since scientific research on management theory began, many different approaches to motivation have been proposed, each seeming to have the answer to motivation problems. Techniques such as job enrichment, human relations, participative management, and, more recently, the Japanese Theory Z have all received attention at various times as being the solution to motivational problems. However, it is seldom long before someone conducts a study that shows that the theory doesn't work as proposed, and new theories are devised to be tested once again. The problem for supervisors is that this smorgasbord of motivation theories can be quite confusing. There seems to be literally no end to the possibilities and many of them are contradictory. Every five or ten years, someone comes up with a new approach and everyone jumps on the bandwagon in the hope of finding a panacea for motivational problems. Most recently, for example, the Japanese method of motivation (called Theory Z) has been popularized, yet it is not clear whether this is really a new approach to motivation and, if it is, whether it can be applied effectively in North America.

One of the major limitations of all approaches to motivation is their lack of relevance to first-level supervisors. Even if a particular motivation theory offers promise, there may be little the supervisor can do because application of the theory requires decisions that are beyond the authority of the typical supervisor. For example, if money were a motivator (and we shall discuss the question in the next chapter), the fact would be of little value to many supervisors because pay rates are often determined by company policies or a union contract. Therefore, in this and the following chapter we concentrate on those aspects of motivation that are of immediate use to first-level supervisors, rather than those that require major organizational decisions to implement.

One of the reasons for the difficulty in applying motivation theories is lack of understanding of the basic concepts underlying the theories. In this chapter we review those concepts and give examples of how they affect the supervisor's job. In the following chapter we will review the more popular theories of motivation at work.

The Morale-Productivity Controversy

One of the thorniest issues in motivation theory is the morale-productivity controversy. Failure to comprehend this relationship complicates both the understanding and application of motivation theories. If this seems strange to you it is probably because you have always thought that **morale** (the state of mental and emotional well-being) and **productivity** (performance) go hand in hand, that high morale generates high productivity and low morale generates low productivity. As it happens, this can be true and is probably true to a degree in most situations, but in other situations it is not. In order to apply motivation theories effectively you must first understand when the relationship holds and when it does not, as well as how the concepts of morale and productivity differ.

Historical Perspective

Although it had always been generally believed that high morale led to high productivity, the earliest scientific investigation of the subject was the famous Hawthorne experiments conducted at the Western Electric

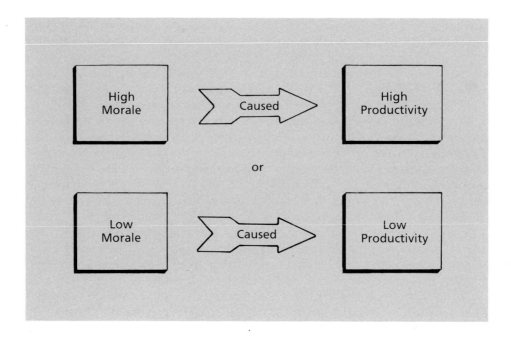

Figure 6.1. Basic Causal Relationships Between Morale and Productivity.

Company during the later 1920s and early 1930s.[1] These studies were thought to prove that when employees' morale increased their productivity also increased, and that this was a cause-and-effect relationship, as pictured in Figure 6.1.

The studies involved workers who fabricated and assembled various electronic components for the telephone industry. Several work groups were selected and isolated for a series of experiments. All of the experiments involved various changes in working conditions (e.g., lighting, group organization, payment methods) and, with some notable exceptions, suggested that improved working conditions (and therefore higher morale) led to measurable increases in productivity. This series of experiments was for many years taken as the gospel in morale-productivity research and still serves as the foundation for teaching and research into behavior in organizations today. The experiments and their aftermath led to application of the phrase *cow sociology* to the human relations philosophy because of its parallel to the belief that happy cows give more milk. Subsequently, an entire school of thought, known as the **human relations school,** became popular and proposed numerous human relations tech-

1. F. Roethlisberger and W. J. Dickson, *Management and the Worker,* (Cambridge: Harvard University Press, 1935).

niques designed to improve the morale of workers, such as participative management, loose supervision, better communications, counselling, and face-to-face work groups.

THE FIFTIES AND SIXTIES. After the Hawthorne experiments and up until the end of the war, research centered on better methods of improving morale. Productivity was not a serious problem during the war years, so new research centered on better methods of improving morale. Productivity was not a serious problem during the war years, so new research was not done until the late 1950s and early 1960s. At that time, more sophisticated research techniques were applied to the study of the accepted morale-productivity theory and to reexamination of the data from the Hawthorne experiments.

It became increasingly common to find situations in which workers with apparently high morale were not very productive, as well as situations in which employees with low morale were achieving high productivity levels. This lack of consistency between moral and productivity caused a major reconsideration of the theory and resulted in some new perspectives on **job satisfaction** (a new term used to replace *morale* and indicating the employee feelings and attitudes resulting from the job itself) and some innovative thoughts on the relationship between workers and their jobs.

The eventual outcome of this research was popularization of the **job enrichment** concept, which proposed that motivation and performance were directly related to the degree of satisfaction and challenge that workers experienced in their jobs.[2] The solution to motivation problems was said to be the redesign of jobs to give workers more responsibility, opportunity for growth, and a feeling of achievement. Morale was still presumed to be important but the job enrichment approach saw morale as independent of the job being performed and performance as primarily a function of how challenging the job was for the workers. Morale was important only insofar as poor morale was seen to inhibit the satisfaction that could have been received from the job itself. Thus, regardless of efforts to practice good human relations, workers would not have high productivity unless their jobs were intrinsically satisfying.

The weakness of the job enrichment approach was its universalist application, the belief that everyone aspired to a more challenging job. Research in the late 1960s and early 1970s found many workers employed in so-called dead-end jobs expressing considerable satisfaction with those jobs. Many companies found that some employees resisted the enriching experience of having more responsibility (after all, isn't

2. F. Herzberg, B. Mausner, and B. Snyderman, *The Motivation to Work* (New York: John Wiley, 1959).

that what gives executives ulcers?). Although there were many documented cases of companies improving productivity and quality through job enrichment programs it was by no means a magic cure for all motivation problems.

Another drawback of the job enrichment approach was that it was very difficult to apply at the supervisory level. The enrichment of jobs required major redesign of workflow and responsibilities, and this necessitated top management approval and involvement since such action generally affected areas beyond the supervisor's area of authority. Many supervisors attended training programs during this period to learn more about motivation, only to learn that the key to motivation was held by someone who wasn't at the program!

THE CURRENT VIEW. Perhaps more out of exasperation than anything else, researchers have concentrated more recently on something that other approaches consistently ignored: the concept (and fact) of individual differences. As we noted in Chapter 5, people have different experiences, needs, and goals, and this suggests that no single theory of motivation will be universally applicable. What works wonders for one employee may have no effect whatsoever on another. The modern approach, therefore, proposes motivation models that can be tailored to individual differences.

It is now believed that the concept of morale can be better understood if it is viewed as the *result* of satisfaction of employee needs, whatever those needs might be. In other words, an employee will be satisfied if the experiences on the job meet the need structure he or she has. So, in contrast to the historical view that morale causes productivity, it now appears equally plausible *that productivity causes morale.* Simply put, the statement "A happy worker is a productive worker" is also correct in the reverse, "A productive worker is a happy worker." Therefore, the model in Figure 6.1 changes to that shown in Figure 6.2.

If you find all this slightly confusing, you are beginning to grasp the complexity of motivation theory. One of the errors supervisors make is to assume that motivation is a simple process. Your confusion is the prelude to a better understanding of motivation, and will be cleared up later in this chapter. For the time being, consider the morale of winners.

Perhaps the best example of the productivity-causes-morale idea is with sports teams. One only has to examine the winner of the World Series to answer the question, "Who has the higher morale? The winner or the loser?" Obviously, the winners have the higher morale because they won (i.e., they were productive). Similarly, when a team fires a coach (which will happen not because of low team morale but because the team hasn't won any games) the management will invariably look for

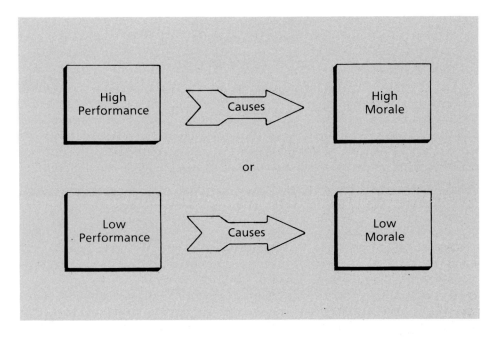

Figure 6.2. Revision of Historical Relationship Between Morale and Productivity (Performance).

a new coach who can turn the team into a winning one. Can you imagine seeing an editorial in the local sports page demanding that the team hire a coach who will raise the team's morale?

We will sort out this morale-productivity issue later in this chapter when we examine other factors that affect the motivation process. It is enough now to know that effective supervisors must be aware that the relationship is a complex one.

The first step toward clarification is to examine more closely the concept of motivation itself. The concept has many different meanings, such as "behavior above and beyond the call of duty" or "self-directed behavior," to name just two, so the first order of business will be to develop a definition of motivation.

Motivation: The Terminology Problem

Much of the confusion in trying to sort out the relationship between morale and productivity was directly due to problems of definition. The following terms have been used at various times in the literature of motivation: satisfaction, morale, job satisfaction, happy, effort, job attitudes,

Exercise 6.1

What Motivates You?

One of the more important advancements in understanding motivation theory was recognizing that different things motivate people—"different strokes for different folks," as the saying goes. Think about yourself for a few minutes and identify those things which seem to motivate you at work. Once you have a list of about ten items, rank them in order of importance. Compare your list with that of others. Why the differences?

---

and, of course, the basic term, motivation. Depending upon the circumstances, these terms have different meanings to different people and much of our confusion regarding the understanding of the motivation process stems directly from this terminology problem.

It is not the purpose of this chapter to establish a universal definition that would meet all purposes, but we can discuss the problems that may arise if we are not aware of the different meanings. Probably the loosest term is happy, normally used when referring to "happy workers." The danger with this term is that it is too general to be of any use to the supervisor. People can be happy for a variety of reasons; some might be happy because they are challenged at work and others might be happy because they are able to get by with a minimum of effort on the job. In the first instance, any supervisor would be gratified to have a crew of happy workers. In the second, serious problems would be present, although if the supervisor took a happiness survey the results would be positive.

The happy worker has been a problem for the human relations school. Its critics maintain that many human relations techniques serve only to improve the employee's happiness, a factor that may have little to do with his or her productivity. It certainly is not difficult to think of situations in which companies have done things to make workers happier (e.g., grant pay increases) with no measurable change in productivity. In fact, that very situation is common.

One step removed from happy is the term *morale*. Although slightly more precise, morale suffers from the same problem—it is too general. Morale has normally been used to describe the general attitude of employees without reference to specific attitudes such as feelings about pay, supervision, working conditions. So when general measures of morale are taken, the company has no way of knowing the individual attitudes toward these important factors. For example, if a company simultaneously gave employees a ten percent pay increase and reduced vacation time by one week, what would be the effect on morale? Complicating the situation is the fact that morale is not an absolute phenomenon, so measurement is always relative. When a company claims that its employees have high morale, one must ask, "as compared to what?" In summary, morale is a potentially dangerous concept since it has so many different meanings and measurement is so suspect.

What may appear to be only scientific and research-oriented questions actually have significant implications for supervisors. It should be apparent by now that any supervisor whose objective is improving morale may be embarking on the wrong strategy. In fact, it probably is reasonably easy to achieve an increase in morale. The difficult part is to achieve an improvement in morale *and* productivity.

A more precise (and therefore more useful) term is job satisfaction. This term is meant clearly to define satisfaction derived from the job, as opposed to any other source, and implies that changes can be made in a person's job and the degree of improvement that occurs can be measured. As will be seen in the following chapter, however, even this presented problems, for it was eventually discovered that two terms—job satisfaction and job dissatisfaction—were needed. Frederick Herzberg showed that rather than being opposites, job satisfaction and job dissatisfaction were different concepts, or apples and oranges if you like, and were influenced by different factors. Whereas the source of job satisfaction is the job itself, **job dissatisfaction** originates with the environment in which the job is performed. Herzberg's formulation of job satisfaction and job dissatisfaction is illustrated in Figure 6.3, which shows that the two aspects can be measured independently. In other words, it is possible for an employee to be both satisfied and dissatisfied at the same time. Herzberg's research explained why the single concept of satisfaction or morale failed to show a consistent relationship with performance. The specifics of how his analysis can be developed into a theory of motivation will be described in the next chapter.

Finally, there is the difficult task of arriving at a useful definition of motivation, one that will be helpful to supervisors. This is not easy since, in the most general sense, *all* behavior is motivated. For example, an employee who prefers to put forth as little as possible is motivated to avoid work under that definition. Also, we want to separate motivation from morale, happiness, or job satisfaction. Since motivation must be observed, our definition must also include something about behavior as opposed to attitudes. And finally, we must allow for positive as well as negative forms of motivation. For example, the prison inmate who is working on the rock pile under the watchful eye (and gun!) of the prison guard is motivated, albeit in a negative sense. This is an important point

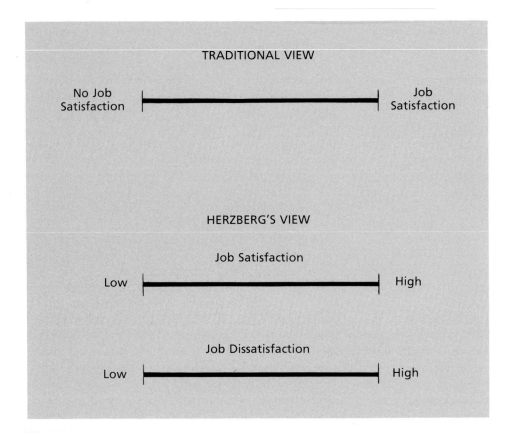

Figure 6.3. Comparison Between Traditional View of Job Satisfaction and Herzberg's View.

since supervisors will sometimes have to use negative methods of increasing motivation.

Given these conditions, a proposed definition of motivation is *behavior exhibited by an individual or group designed to reach a specific goal.* From the perspective of a supervisor, this definition warrants these four principles.

1. Motivation is defined in terms of observable behavior.
2. Efforts to motivate can be applied to individuals or groups.
3. Motivation can be increased if the supervisor can develop a relationship between organizational needs and employee goals.
4. Motivation is not something that a supervisor does *to* an employee, but instead is something that occurs within employees themselves.

So Is Morale Important?

The answer to this question is an unequivocal "yes," but it is imperative that you understand in what way it is important.

Morale is best seen as a necessary but not sufficient condition for motivation to occur. Regardless of what motivational approach a supervisor uses, if morale is extremely low it may preclude any positive effects of the supervisor's behavior. For example, a technique such as job enrichment would probably have little effect if the employees felt underpaid by say, thirty percent.

Morale can also be seen in a kind of preventive role, in that *good morale in the workplace helps prevent low productivity, though it may not cause high productivity.* Frederick Herzberg, whose two-factor theory of motivation will be explained in the next chapter, draws some interesting analogies to illustrate the preventive role of morale. Good dental hygiene, he states, does not cause our teeth to be healthy but it keeps them from becoming unhealthy. Similarly, public sanitation systems do not cause us to be healthy, but they keep us from becoming unhealthy. The equivalent of these examples in the organization is that good industrial hygiene (i.e., those factors that affect morale) doesn't cause workers to have high morale, but keeps them from having low morale.

Happiness and Productivity

Though not a typical case, this situation does illustrate the complicated relationship between morale and productivity. Several years ago I was doing a research project on job satisfaction and was allowed by a company to interview a sample of workers. One day I interviewed two workers who illustrated the extremes of the morale-productivity controversy. Worker #1 was a young male, about eighteen years of age, who had worked at the plant for about three months. Although I asked several questions, my bottom line was, "Are you happy here?" The young man talked for several minutes about how much he liked it, finally stating, "I've found a home here." When I asked him why, his reasons were (1) he worked nights and there was no foreman around to check on him, (2) the time-keeping system was so sloppy that his buddies could clock in for him if he was late, and (3) there were always stacks of boxes in the work area where he could go and nap if he had had a particularly hard night before. A check with his immediate supervisor indicated that his productivity record was dismal.

Later that same evening I interviewed a woman who was extremely distraught. She broke down and cried during the interview, mostly as the result of talking about her unpleasant personal life. Never had I met anyone with such low morale. I checked with her supervisor regarding her productivity. Her comment? "She's great! If I had two more like her I wouldn't need the other twenty-five." (My armchair diagnosis was that the only way she could maintain her sanity was to get totally involved in her job. It was the only escape she had from her problems).

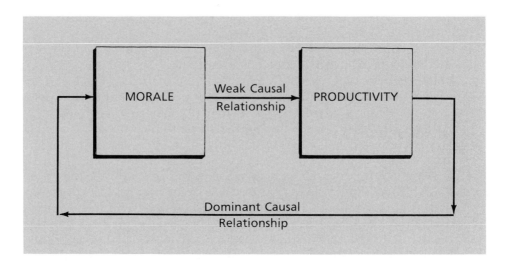

Figure 6.4. Current View of the Morale-Productivity Relationship.

To resolve the morale-productivity problem we have to borrow a page from social systems theory discussed in Chapter 1. This approach, you will remember proposes that all factors in any behavioral system are interrelated to some degree. This means that there will always be **mutual causality** present between the variables in the system. In the case of the morale-productivity system, the research evidence tends to conclude that productivity affects morale more than morale affects productivity. Or, to use the terms noted earlier, the model you should keep in mind is that performance affects satisfaction more than satisfaction affects performance. This circular relationship is illustrated in Figure 6.4.

The literal translation of Figure 6.4 is that, all things being equal, performance can be affected more by manipulating variables that affect what workers *do* in their jobs, than by how they are treated (in the human relations sense) while performing their jobs. Examples of factors affecting what people do are: personal ability, the kinds of equipment, tools, or technical assistance they have available, and the rewards they receive for performing the job properly. This last one is so important that an entire chapter is devoted to managing reward systems.

To take an example from the sports world, the concept of the hometown advantage is well known. In basketball, for example, some coaches believe that playing on the home court can mean as much as ten points in some cases. Assuming this is true, it is an example of morale causing productivity. The euphoria of the hometown crowd can improve average performance by a given amount, even though the other factors (e.g., players' skill, coaching, physical layout of the court, and game patterns)

Exercise 6.2

What Do Workers Want from Their Jobs?

Several years ago a survey was taken to find out what workers wanted from their jobs. They were asked to rank the items listed below in order of importance from 1 to 10, with item 1 being the most important, and so on. The questionnaire was also given to the supervisors of those workers to see if they knew what their own employees wanted from their jobs. See how much you know about what workers want from their jobs. Rank the same ten items in the order you think the workers ranked them. Your instructor will then give you both sets of rankings and you can compare your answers with theirs. Do you know what workers want from their jobs?

1. promotion and growth
2. good wages
3. job security
4. appreciation of work
5. feeling in on things
6. tactful discipline
7. interesting work
8. understanding and help with personal problems
9. personal loyalty to workers
10. working conditions[3]

remain the same. But notice also that it would be practically impossible for the hometown effect to generate enough improvement in productivity for a weak team to beat a team far superior in the other factors. Of course this is the exact analysis that the bookies do when deciding on the odds. They give the home team ten points for their home court, and then examine the technical factors such as players' skill, coaching, etc. In other words, they know these are the more important determinants of productivity.

Notice also the difficult role that cheerleaders have; their job is to improve productivity by raising morale *first*, a process I hope we have established as being fairly inefficient. (Incidentally, this is why cheerleaders are never held accountable when a team loses!) This illustrates that the morale-productivity relationship, though complicated to ex-

---

3. List from Leslie Matthies and Ellen Matthies, "How Important Are People?" *Journal of Systems Management* (July, 1975).

plain, is really something that most people understand intuitively. Yet, the fact remains that many organizations engage in considerable corporate cheerleading in hopes that it will pay off in increased motivation and productivity. Unfortunately, it is here that the analogy between the sports cheerleaders and the supervisor ends, because unlike the cheerleaders, the supervisor will be held accountable if the team loses. It is therefore important to understand all the factors that affect productivity and what this means for improving productivity and motivation.

Motivation, Productivity, and the Supervisor

If motivation was the only factor that determined productivity, the life of a supervisor would be comparatively easy. Unfortunately, this is not the case. Several other factors in addition to motivation have an effect on productivity and some of these are under the direct control of the supervisor. In one sense, we are now answering the question, "Is a motivated worker a productive one?" The answer is "yes," provided that (a) the task is designed properly, (b) proper technology is available, (c) the employee has the ability, (d) the group norm supports productive behavior, and (e) other organizational units do not hinder task accomplishment. By examining these factors in more detail we can show the role supervisors have in improving productivity, as well as its occasional limitations.

Task Design

Productivity will be limited if the job is poorly organized and work methods are not current with objectives to be accomplished. No matter how much motivation is present, working in a poorly designed system will hamper output. For example, airlines have separate locations in the baggage compartment for luggage headed for different destinations. In this way, baggage handlers do not need to sort through all the luggage at each stop to determine which bags should be removed. This is an element of task design that improves productivity but has little to do with motivation. The supervisor should be constantly reviewing work methods and how jobs are being performed. Often, workers themselves have excellent ideas on how task design can be improved and the supervisor must create a climate that will stimulate this kind of participation. A good rule of thumb is that if something has been done a certain way for a long time, there is probably a more efficient way of doing it.

Technological Factors

Employees' productivity is limited by the level and quality of technology available to them. An improvement in the technological factors sometimes can make significant improvement in the productivity even though motivational levels remain the same. Examples are replacing a secretary's electric typewriter with a word processor, or substituting a computerized dispatch system for a cab driver's radio. Although supervisors may not have much authority over major technological factors, it still is their responsibility to communicate such requests to those who do. On a lesser scale, often there are relatively minor technical improvements that can be made without the need for approval from above and the supervisor should constantly be on the lookout for these. Such efforts can have a dual impact; the technical improvement itself can enhance productivity, and morale can be affected since subordinates like to have supervisors who take an interest in their jobs.

3. Ability Factors

Although it is obvious that the ability of the employee is an important determinant of productivity, in practice the distinction between ability and motivation becomes clouded. Ability is composed primarily of aptitude, training, and experience. Motivation, on the other hand, is the *willingness* to achieve productivity. Although it is an oversimplification of reality, the relationship between these two factors and performance can be expressed as:

$$P = A \times M$$

This equation states that performance (P) is a function of two major variables, ability (A) and motivation (M). This distinction is important because, depending upon the source of the performance problem, different solutions should be used. The general principle is that *ability problems should not be solved with motivation solutions, and motivation problems should not be solved with ability solutions.*

It must again be stressed that the divison is not as precise as the

Motivated Incompetence

One of my hobbies is automobiles and my involvement is such that most people call me a car nut. I have a special affection for certain classic sports cars, and these types of cars tend to need a lot of attention (read: they don't run very often). I love to work on my cars. I thoroughly enjoy tinkering with them and getting my hands greasy while attempting to solve some mechanical problem. In other words, I am highly motivated. Unfortunately, I have practically no mechanical ability. My efforts generally result in causing more problems than I solve, even on the simplest of tasks. Even though this is quite frustrating, I continue to try because of my high motivation level. If you were my supervisor, you would be wasting your time trying to motivate me to improve my productivity. Better to try a good dose of training, although with my low aptitude level, you're still probably wasting your time. Some performance problems are beyond help.

equation implies, but this is a useful starting point for dealing with performance problems. If a supervisor is faced with a performance problem, the first question to be asked is, "Is this a skill (ability) problem or a motivation one?" If it is a skill problem then perhaps more training is in order. But if training makes no change in performance, perhaps motivation is the problem and different techniques must be used (some of these will be discussed in the next chapter). There is an interaction effect between ability and motivation, especially in the learning process, in that individuals with low motivation would be less likely to improve their skill, and people with low skill levels may lack motivation because of their skill problems. However, there are exceptions—as the example on the previous page illustrates.

Group Norms

People seldom work by themselves. The most common method of organizing tasks is around small groups, generally from five to fifteen people. These groups develop norms, that is, accepted ways of performing their jobs that do not threaten the group. If anyone violates these norms then pressure from the group increases to try to bring the deviate back into line. Each group has a production norm, which is the accepted level of output (or effort, productivity, results) that each member is supposed to attain. The norm could be either high or low, depending upon a host of factors that operate at the group level. Ideally, of course, supervisors would like to have work groups with high production norms since these groups tend to manage themselves in terms of motivation. Of much greater concern is the group with a low production norm. These groups can affect the productivity of a member who has the motivation to produce at a high level. The employee knows that unless he or she restricts production to the group norm, life will become difficult indeed. So even though the employee may be highly motivated, group factors can reduce productivity. Sometimes these norms are so powerful that the supervisor is unable to change them. There are, however, several strategies that are effective in working with groups and this is the subject of Chapter 9.

Other Organizational Units

As noted in Chapter 3, the supervisor is only one part of the total organization and therefore depends upon the rest of the organization to do its job. Disorganized, unreliable, and inefficient units in the rest of the organization will hinder the potential positive effects of motivation. If the situation persists, the disorganization may affect motivation itself because motivated people unable to use their motivation become frustrated. Unfortunately, there often is little the supervisor can do officially since the sources of the problems are outside his or her sphere of authority. On a more informal level, however, the supervisor can attempt to work with the offending departments, find out what their problems are, and offer to assist with a solution.

Performance Equation

We can now begin to develop a more comprehensive model of the motivation process which will prepare you for the trek through the specific motivation theories in the next chapter. The performance equation can now be shown as:

$$P = A \times M \times T \times TD \times G \times U$$

where A is ability, M is motivation, T is technology, TD is task design, G is group norms, and U is other organization units. This suggests that not only is improving performance a complicated phenomenon, but several of the contributing factors may be beyond the control of the supervisor. The equation also shows that although motivation is important, it is only one of the factors that affect performance. However, since it is one that can be significantly influenced by the supervisor (and in some cases may be the *only* one), it becomes more important than otherwise would be the case.

Despite the fact that motivation, morale, and productivity are complex topics, six specific conclusions can be drawn.

1. Morale may or may not have a predictable relationship with productivity.

2. Nevertheless, morale is important because it tends to be a prerequisite for productivity.

3. Morale can also be the result of productive behavior; thus, productivity is a source of morale.

4. There is a circular relationship between morale and productivity, with productivity having a greater effect on morale than morale has on productivity.

5. Motivation does not guarantee productivity. Other factors can intervene and reduce the effects of motivation.

6. Supervisors must examine all the factors within their sphere of influence that affect morale and productivity. The job of the supervisor is to stimulate factors that raise morale, motivation, and productivity, and reduce those factors that inhibit them.

These statements indicate that there are no easy answers to motivation. However, by understanding how the various factors interrelate to affect performance, the supervisor can be in a better position to deal effectively with performance problems. Applied behavioral science never promises answers, but it can help to avoid major mistakes.

Key to Success

In this chapter you learned that motivation is a complex topic. There is no simple way to motivate employees, although there are some general behavioral science principles that should be kept in mind.

The most important point for supervisors to remember is that winners—people who succeed on the job—are generally more productive than losers. Your task is to turn every employee into a winner. How do you do this? By creating an environment in which employees can attain goals that are important to them. Ideally, these goals are also important to the company, but it is of critical importance that they be important to the individual.

Contrary to popular belief, there need not be losers in order to have winners. Everyone can win, provided that the correct conditions are set by management. Winning includes employees' feeling good about themselves, what they have accomplished, and how they accomplished it. The supervisor can play an important role by recognizing winners and helping everyone to be a winner, by providing the resources necessary for winning, i.e., motivational support, training, proper equipment, etc.

It is important to note that supervisors cannot create winners. The most they can do is create the working environment in which winning can occur. This involves removing any existing barriers to motivation so that motivation can be channeled into the productive results that create winners.

It is easy for supervisors to be overly concerned with morale, especially if the relationship between morale and productivity is not understood. It is not difficult to create high morale in a work group. The key is to create the type of morale that produces meaningful results, from both the organization's and the employees' perspective. The specifics of how morale and productivity can be integrated are covered in the next chapter.

Summary

This chapter has developed the basic relationships among morale, motivation, and productivity. Historically, part of our problem in motivating employees has been a lack of understanding regarding the relationship between morale and performance. The present view proposes that morale is largely the result of performance, not the cause of it. Performance can be improved through raising morale, but this often is inefficient. It is also recognized that motivation is a very personal concept, meaning that not all employees will be motivated by the same thing.

It is also recognized that in addition to motivation, other factors such as ability, technology, task design, group norms, and other organizational units also affect performance. Sometimes supervisors have little or no control over these other factors. Supervisors should be concerned about morale because it is thought to be a prerequisite to performance, but high morale by itself will not necessarily result in high performance.

Opening Incident Revisited

The decision the General Manager makes could be an expensive one if he pursues the present course of action. While any of the proposed solutions could improve morale, the General Manager must realize that the improved morale may not lead to increased motivation. In fact, it is unlikely that any of these ideas will lead to a significant and sustained improvement in performance. Since all of the solutions will cost money, the General Manager had best reexamine the problem before embarking on any program.

As you now know from reading this chapter, the reasons for poor performance can be many, some of which have little to do with morale. For example, it could be that employees are not being trained properly and that with better training, their abilities (and therefore their performance) would improve. Not only would piped-in music not solve this problem, a live band could be hired to play all day long and it would not improve the skills of employees.

In general, management does not understand that morale is often the result of performance, not the cause of it. They should first examine any technical, organizational, or job-related causes to see if any barriers exist to performance. Once these have been sorted out, they can then deal with the more complex issue of morale. Even then, they must be careful, because morale is such a general term and can include many different factors. These types of problems usually cannot be solved with a quick-fix solution designed to make employees happier.

Review Questions

1. Why are many motivation theories of little use to supervisors?
2. Why is the relationship between morale and productivity confusing?
3. How did the human relations school view the relationship between morale and productivity?
4. What was the major limitation of the job enrichment approach to motivation?
5. How does the current approach to motivation differ from earlier approaches?
6. How can morale be the result of productivity?
7. Why is morale a difficult concept for supervisors to use?
8. What is the definition of motivation?

9. What role does morale generally play in productivity?
10. What are the major factors that affect motivation?

Morale.	A state of mental and emotional well-being which may or may not be related to behavior on the job.
Productivity.	The achievement of a work-related objective. Synonymous with the term *performance.*
Human relations school.	The school of thought that first investigated the relationship between morale and productivity. Generally credited with the conclusion that "A happy worker is a productive worker."
Job satisfaction.	The feeling or attitudes of employees resulting from the job itself.
Job enrichment.	Increasing the level of responsibility in a job in order to make it more challenging and satisfying.
Job dissatisfaction.	The feelings or attitudes of employees resulting from the job environment.
Motivation.	Behavior exhibited by an individual or group which is designed to reach a specific goal.
Mutual causality.	The systems concept that proposes that all variables in a behavioral system affect each other.
Task design.	One of the factors that affect motivation. Pertains to work methods, scope of authority in performing tasks, and degree of skill required for the task.
Technology.	One of the factors that affect motivation. Pertains to the type of technical methods, tools, and equipment used in performing tasks.
Group norms	A factor which affects motivation. The accepted behaviors of a group which group members must exhibit.

Case Problem

East End Public School

The East End Public School is one of several in the city that is experiencing severe problems with its teaching staff. Although the school system has been through several major changes in recent years, most administrators agree that the major problem affecting the performance of teachers is the lack of prospects for advancement. Since enrollments have been declining, some schools have been shut down and there are fewer opportunities for teachers to advance into the higher paying administrative positions.

Nadine Jones is the principal of East End Public School and is faced with a serious motivation problem in her teaching staff. It seems that within the last few years, it has become increasingly difficult to motivate the teachers to do anything other than their regular assigned duties. For example, this year she had to ask four different teachers before anyone would agree to take charge of the school science fair. Each week she dreads handing out the playground duties because of all the grumbling that occurs. Whereas ten years ago the teachers used to stay around after school hours and chat about students, classes, or other education-related topics, now most are gone within a few minutes of the end of classes. Worse yet, the attitudes and behaviors of the teachers seem to be affecting the students as well.

From time to time she gives a pep talk to the teachers at a staff meeting and these seem to have an effect for a day or two after. Eventually, motivation drops and performance goes back to its previous level.

Questions for Discussion

1. What problems does Nadine face in dealing with this problem?
2. What choices does she have in attempting to solve it?
3. What would you recommend she do to improve motivation?

Applying
Motivation Theories

7

After reading and studying this chapter you should be able to:

1. Explain why there is no best theory of motivation.

2. List and define the five levels of needs in Maslow's hierarchy of needs.

3. Explain the limitations of the Maslow model.

4. Give examples of how Maslow's theory might be applied by a supervisor.

5. Explain McClelland's achievement motivation theory.

6. Describe how a supervisor could use the achievement motivation theory.

7. Explain Herzberg's two-factor theory of motivation.

8. List the hygienes and motivators in Herzberg's theory.

9. Describe ways of applying Herzberg's theory.

10. Explain the limitations of the two-factor theory.

11. Explain the expectancy theory of motivation.

12. Diagram how the expectancy theory works.

13. Be able to compute the motivational potential of an employee.

Key Terms

Maslow's hierarchy of needs
Physiological needs
Security needs
Social needs
Ego or status needs
Self-actualization needs

Overcompensation principle
Achievement motivation theory
Achievement need
Affiliation need
Power need
Two-factor theory

Motivators
Hygienes
Job enrichment
Expectancy theory
Valence
Instrumentality
Motivational potential
Universalist approach

The Circle J Amusement Park

Tom Sanders is the supervisor of the sales staff at the Circle J Amusement Park. The job of his staff is to sell the park and its attractions to various groups, such as travel agents, tour guides, and other organizations likely to bring large groups to the park. One of his salesmen, George Irwin, has been a problem for him since he started three years ago. While George is one of the best salesmen, he lacks the team spirit that Sanders thinks is necessary for the department to function well. Irwin prefers to work alone and seldom works on any group projects. If Sanders specifically asks him to work on a project with another salesman, Irwin will do so but it is obvious that this bothers him.

On several occasions Sanders has told Irwin that he should work more with the other salesmen, and has pointed out how several of the other salesmen work well as a team. Irwin has agreed, but he still remains a loner. Sanders has been reluctant to come down hard on Irwin since he often has the best sales record in the department, but it annoys him that he can't motivate Irwin to work for the department as a whole rather than just for himself. The time is drawing near for the sales staff to mount its major campaign for the coming year and Sanders is trying to decide if he should have another talk with Irwin.

In the previous chapter we discussed some of the basics of the motivation process. We learned that morale and productivity may not always be related and that motivation itself does not guarantee performance. With these important qualifications in mind, we can proceed to specific theories of motivation and explore ways that supervisors can use them to improve motivation on the job.

But first a word about motivation theories in general. When we speak of motivation theories, the three aspects of human behavior mentioned in Chapter 1—understanding, prediction, and control—are important. Motivation theories attempt to understand why people are (or are not) motivated and this forms the basic premise of the theory. Given this understanding, theories then predict the behavior (or motivation) of people in given circumstances. The supervisor will be better able to control employees' behavior if the factors affecting motivation are understood.

Supervisors often ask, "Why take us through all these different theories? Why not just give us the best one and let it go at that?" If it were only that easy! In view of the complexity of human behavior it is unlikely that any single theory can account for all motivation. Also, theories are designed for the general case, not the specific one, so any

Is Money a Motivator?

The fallacy of the one best theory approach is easy to see if we examine what is commonly thought to be a motivator: money. Let us assume that as a supervisor you want to increase your subordinates' motivation so you give everybody a twenty percent increase in salary. Here are some possible effects of your action. First some, (but who knows how many?) will actually increase their productivity as a result of the raise in pay. Others, of course, may increase productivity but for entirely different reasons (e.g., they have found a better way to do the job, or they are thinking of quitting soon so want to make sure they get a good reference). For others,

motivation may decrease. Some may have felt they already deserved thirty percent more so your twenty percent serves as a kick in the teeth; some who were already highly motivated (and productive) may resent that the slackers are getting as much as they did; those who were previously slackers may now conclude that slacking is the best way to get more money; and yet others may feel that with this newfound wealth they can now afford to take off about one day a week (without pay), which decreases their overall productivity. Motivation is a complex topic, indeed!

individual can be an exception to the theory. Therefore, the more theories we have, the better our chances of understanding, predicting, and controlling behavior. At the end of this chapter a general system is presented which will give you a useful tool to apply to all motivation problems, but even this system must be used with a sensitivity for individual differences.

There are probably as many motivation theories around as there are supervisors and managers, since each learns through experience certain techniques that improve motivation. But we shall limit ourselves to a few widely accepted theories that have been scientifically tested and applied in work situations. If you have, through your experience, found something that works, it can probably be incorporated into one of the following theories of motivation.

Maslow's Hierarchy of Needs

The Theory

Probably the most basic theory of human motivation is the **hierarchy of needs** set forth by psychologist Abraham Maslow.[1] He has proposed that behavior is motivated by unsatisfied needs and that human needs occur in a predictable order. When a certain set of needs has been relatively

1. A. H. Maslow, *Motivation and Personality* (New York: Harper, 1954).

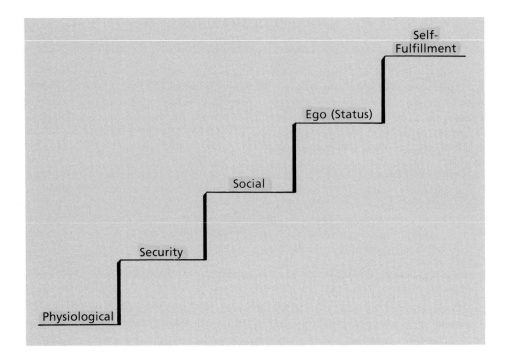

Figure 7.1. Maslow's Hierarchy of Needs.

satisfied, the individual is motivated to satisfy the next higher order of needs. The five levels of needs are illustrated in Figure 7.1.

The most basic needs, according to Maslow, are the survival or **physi-ological needs.** These needs are basic to human survival and consist of the need for food, water, sleep, and so forth. If these needs are not satis-fied, behavior is motivated towards attempting to obtain satisfaction. It is generally believed today that these needs are not major sources of motivation because, at least in the western world, the basic needs have been largely satisfied. The values in our western society are such that we believe everyone is entitled to the basic necessities of life, regardless of employment status. Therefore, these necessities are provided either through employment itself or through programs designed to maintain basic standards of living (e.g., welfare).

The next level of needs are the **security** or safety **needs.** Maslow maintains that when physiological needs have been satisfied, the source of motivation changes to begin providing both physical and psychologi-cal safety. In the physical sense, this could be a place to keep oneself safe from the elements or free from other types of physical harm. In psycho-logical terms, it means having a sense of personal security and freedom from anxiety. In the work situation this need is exemplified by job security clauses in union contracts. These clauses protect employees from arbitrary dismissal or layoffs. Though generally satisfied to a lesser degree than the physiological needs, the safety needs still tend not to be useful sources of motivation, again because of the relatively high levels of need satisfaction in our society. However, significant changes in the environment can temporarily affect need satisfaction. For example, when there is a serious downturn in the economy, the security needs tend to have a larger effect on motivation.

The **social** (or belonging) **needs** become important after the safety needs have been relatively satisfied. These are the needs to join informal and social groups and to form close interpersonal ties with some one person or group. It is often said that man is a social animal, but according to this theory, he is not until other needs have been satisfied. Social needs are satisfied by marriage, fraternal organizations, friendships, and the formation of cliques in work groups. Note, for example, that few people take coffee breaks by themselves.

As compared to the first two levels, the social needs present considerable opportunity for motivation at work. It is difficult to oversatisfy this need, which can be fulfilled in many different ways. Also, as we go up the hierarchy of needs, the relative satisfaction decreases, thus giving it more motivation potential. Chapter 9, Working with Groups, will discuss the possibilities for application of this need in greater detail.

The fourth level is the **ego** (or status) **need,** that is the need to differentiate oneself from others, to feel important, and to feel a sense of identity. The ego need, while comparatively less satisfied than the others, is manifested in a variety of ways: our individual manners of dress, and our desire to seek recognition from others, to have a feeling of importance and purpose to our lives, and to engage in activities that make us feel useful and competent. Status symbols, for example, illustrate the importance of the ego need in our society as well as our organizations. The ego level is often proposed as the level that offers the greatest practical potential for motivation. The redesign of jobs to allow for greater individual accomplishment, for example, is often proposed as one way of using the ego need to improve motivation.

And finally, the hierarchy is completed with the **self-actualization need.** Much more abstract than the previous levels, this is often described as becoming all one wants to be or achieving our ultimate goals in life. This is a very personal need in that different people will find a variety of experiences to be self-actualizing. The need was once explained to me as "When you get there you'll know it." From a practical point of view, this need is best viewed as an extension of the ego need, since distinguishing between them is a semantic exercise at best.

One of the best examples of how the hierarchy operates is the history of trade unions in North America. By tracing the development of union activities, it is possible to see how their motivations have changed. When unions were first organized, their major concern was with adequate pay levels for members (basic needs). When success was achieved at this level, unions began negotiating job security clauses in contracts (security needs). Following this, unions began to adopt more social activities, thus developing an organization that people could identify with and belong to. Unions also fulfill a need at the ego level. The power they wield no doubt instills some ego satisfaction in the membership, but the union managerial hierarchy itself offers opportunities for job satisfaction that often cannot be found in regular jobs. Self-actualization, being relatively abstract, is probably available to a few of the more senior union officials and is an extension of the ego need. Even these motivations can change as, for example, during periods of economic recession when unions become increasingly concerned with job security.

How the Theory Works

Within the general description given above, there are several operating principles that supervisors should be aware of.

1. *The satisfaction of needs, although occurring in a hierarchy, can occur simultaneously.* In theory, a person would never be motivated by a need until the previous level was completely satisfied. In fact, a given need level must only be satisfied to a *relative* degree before behavior is motivated by the next higher level. We are never totally satisfied in any given level. If we were to examine the motivational profile of a typical employee, it might look something like Figure 7.2, which is designed to show which need level has the highest motivation potential. Although the individual may not be totally satisfied at the social level, the ego level offers greater potential. However, the figure also suggests that no need level can be completely neglected in the motivation process. To understand how Figure 7.2 might influence motivation, let us look at money once again. If an individual had no need for status symbols (which can be purchased with money) or little need for increased social interaction (which money could also enhance), and was satisfied with his or her standard of living, then money would probably not be a very effective motivator.

2. *Blockage of need satisfaction causes overcompensation at a lower level.* Since it is natural for people to progress up the hierarchy, motivation will be affected if they are prevented by their environment from achieving this satisfaction. What tends to happen under these conditions is that the person will overcompensate at a lower level, that is, it will take proportionately more of a given item to produce motivation at the lower level than it would have at the higher level. A good example of this

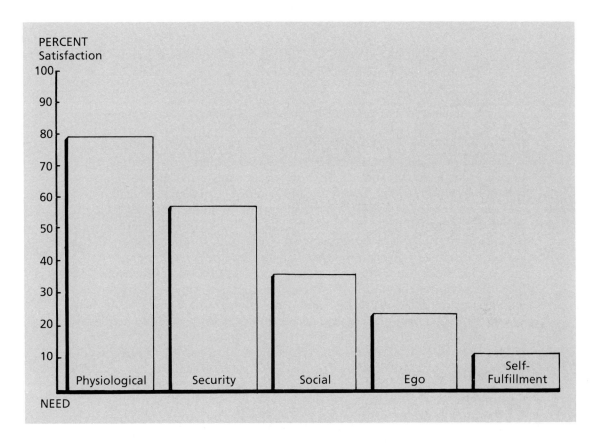

Figure 7.2. Possible Motivational Profile of Employee.

phenomenon is the wages paid for repetitive, boring jobs. Since it is difficult for workers to get any ego satisfaction from a repetitive task, they must be paid considerably more to stay on the job than the skill level would require. It is for this reason that a typical worker in an automobile assembly plant will earn more than, say, teachers, who have more intrinsically satisfying jobs.

3. *Relative satisfaction levels change over time.* The term *relative* is important when describing satisfaction levels. Not only is satisfaction of a need relative to each individual, but the perception of what is satisfaction changes as we mature and encounter new experiences. For example, on the physiological level, young people seem to find that hamburgers and french fries satisfy their basic hunger needs. As we grow older (and wealthier!), we would feel greatly deprived if this was our complete diet. This same princple operates at each level; jobs that are satisfying today bore us tomorrow because we have developed intellectually.

Some Cautions About the Hierarchy

Before proceeding to how the supervisor might apply Maslow's Need Hierarchy, some cautions about the theory should be understood. There are some important limitations to the theory of which a supervisor should be aware.

First, it should be made clear that the hierarchy, while reasonably valid on a general scale, was never designed to be a predictor of individual behavior. Because of individual differences (as described in Chapter 5) the hierarchy may not apply to specific individuals. For example, some people may have an abnormally low need for status and recognition, others may not be concerned with safety and security factors. Still others may have a low need for affiliation and group membership, and so forth. In short, the possibilities for individual variation within the hierarchy are literally infinite. So any supervisor who attempts to apply the model to an individual had better know that person extremely well.

Second, behavior rarely has only a single source of motivation. The hierarchy implies that at one level we engage in one type of behavior and when we progress to the next level our behavior then changes. In fact, however, a single act of behavior can be motivated by several need levels at the same time. For example, when an employee takes a coffee break, he or she is likely to be satisfying physiological needs (drinking the coffee), security needs (drinking from a clean cup), social needs (drinking coffee with friends), and ego needs (drinking coffee with a high-status person). So what appears to be a relatively simple model in theory becomes quite complex in practice. But given the previous analysis of the common coffee break, the supervisor could probably predict fairly accurately the effect on motivation if coffee breaks were taken away! A similar analysis could apply to any type of behavior observed on the job.

Finally, it should be noted that the hierarchy has not been fully supported in research studies attempting to verify its existence. Cultural differences have been found (not surprisingly since the theory was based upon research in North America) in addition to the individual differences noted earlier. This does not mean, however, that the hierarchy is not useful, but only serves to underscore the point that the model must be used selectively and with sensitivity to individual differences.

Applying the Theory

If the limitations of the theory are kept in mind, Maslow's Need Hierarchy has some useful applications for supervisors. First, the model tells us that in most instances, the basic needs are not strong motivators on the job and therefore supervisors should not rely too heavily on an appeal to them. Generally speaking, the more tangible motivators such as money, shorter working hours, cleaner work areas, longer vacations, better com-

Exercise 7.1

Are Coffee Breaks Productive?

The value of coffee breaks has been a subject of debate for years. Traditionally, managers have thought of them as time away from productive work while subordinates think of them as a necessary break from their jobs. Given your knowledge of human needs satisfaction, think of as many ways as you can to show how coffee breaks could have a positive effect upon motivation.

---

pany benefit plans, and air-conditioned offices, appeal primarily to the lower-order needs. As we noted in the previous chapter, not paying attention to these factors can cause morale problems, but improving them to the point of need satisfaction (or saturation) will not necessarily generate motivation.

This means that supervisors are more likely to improve motivation if attention is paid to the higher-order needs, particularly ego and self-actualization. Things the supervisor might do to appeal to these needs would be:

- delegating more authority to subordinates to make decisions;
- recognizing good performance;
- reducing supervision (control) over employees;
- assigning greater responsibility;
- assigning special projects in recognition of specific skills;
- using status symbols in recognition of individual skills and performance;
- letting a subordinate deal with external departments with regard to his or her area of expertise;
- assigning a whole task rather than just part of one; and
- consulting employees on how work should be done.

Any of the above could have a positive effect upon motivation, providing, of course, that the employee's ego needs are relatively unsatisfied.

Although the social needs are generally not thought of as part of the higher-level needs, they often do have motivational potential. One reason for this is that for some people, their jobs are also their primary source of social interaction. So to isolate these people from others (for example, assigning them to single-person work stations away from others) can have a demotivating affect. For such people, supervisors can improve motivation by taking advantage of group assignments whenever possible and generally encouraging interaction between subordinates.

In conclusion, then, Maslow's Need Hierarchy can be a useful tool to analyze sources of motivation problems and calculate at what need level the problems should be addressed. Supervisors should be careful, however, to consider the individual differences that will inevitably occur and to remember that solutions to lack of need satisfactions will vary between individuals. The hierarchy is a useful beginning point to study motivation and will become more helpful when used in conjunction with the other theories that follow.

The Achievement Motivation Theory

Although similar to the need hierarchy approach, the **achievement motivation theory** has some important differences that can improve a supervisor's ability to motivate employees. It is generally believed that unsatisfied needs are motivators of behavior, but the achievement motivation theory proposes a somewhat different need structure. Created by noted psychologist David McClelland, the theory has considerable scientific support and has been developed to the point where it is of practical value to supervisors.[2]

The Theory

McClelland believes that three needs—achievement, affiliation, and power—are the primary motivators of our behavior. In contrast to Maslow's hierarchy, these needs are said to occur in a *configuration*, that is, without a sequential relationship, and are present to various degrees in all of us. The needs are defined as follows:

- **Achievement**—the need to reach challenging goals;
- **Affiliation**—the need to form close interpersonal relationships with others; and
- **Power**—the need to control the behavior of others.

Most of the research on McClelland's theory has concentrated on the need to achieve since that is the one most often associated with economic wealth. From a supervisor's point of view, however, the needs for power and affiliation may be just as useful as motivators as the need to achieve, so we will analyze all three in some detail to show how supervisors might use these needs.

2. D. C. McClelland, *The Achieving Society* (Princeton, N.J.: Van Nostrand, 1961).

THE NEED TO ACHIEVE. From the name alone, it would seem that every supervisor would love to have a whole crew of high achievers. Actually, this would probably not make for a very good work group. High achievers are certainly highly motivated, but only under certain conditions and only toward certain objectives. They have some very specific characteristics that require that they be managed differently than other employees. McClelland's research has found that high achievers have the following five characteristics:

1. They like to set moderate, challenging goals for themselves;
2. They like to have control over the means of reaching those goals;
3. They prefer to work alone rather than in groups;
4. They like quick, concrete feedback on progress toward goals;
5. They can be motivated by money if the above conditions are satisfied.

Given the above description, you can imagine the motivation problems that would result if a high-achieving employee faced a situation in which the goals were set by the supervisor, much of the means by which the goals were to be attained were dictated by the organization (e.g., policies and procedures), working toward the goal required the cooperation of others, the task itself was nebulous (e.g., teaching new employees about the company's operation), and the pay system was straight salary. In this obviously contrived example, the achieving employee probably wouldn't stay very long.

As usual, we can learn from extreme situations such as the one described below. In practice, however, a supervisor is unlikely to encounter a really high achiever since (a) research has shown that only about five

A High Achiever in Action

A very close friend of mine—who happens to be an extremely high achiever—and I have a deal. He uses me for counselling whenever he feels the need, and I use him as my personal experimental rat. The following story is a result of that agreement.

One Sunday morning my friend, who sells insurance for a living, called me for a session. His problem could best be explained by his statement, "The old 'zip' is gone." (his term for lack of motivation). After engaging in the counselling routine (see Chapter 18), we agreed to take a drive that afternoon and look at a house he had seen advertised for sale. After examining the house and getting the general approval of his wife, he approached the salesman for the kill. "How much do you want?" he asked. "Eighty-nine thousand," replied the salesman. "I'll give you eight-five," said my high achieving friend, upon which the salesman called the owner and received a verbal acceptance of the offer. My friend, who at that time was living in a house worth about $27,000, turned to me and said, "The old 'zip' is back!"

percent of the population are extreme high achievers, and (b) high achievers gravitate towards situations that can satisfy their need to achieve (such as owning their own business or commisson sales work). Nevertheless, people who are employed have at least a minimum level of achievement need and for some of these achievement could be their dominant motivation (although it still may not be extreme).

High achievers are truly the self-motivated people in our society. They set their own goals based upon their perception of their own abilities. The challenge of meeting these goals is their source of motivation. The best a supervisor can do with a truly high achiever is to create the conditions in which the individual can satisfy the need to achieve.

THE AFFILIATION NEED. People with a dominant need for affiliation receive satisfaction from establishing deep and long-lasting interpersonal relationships. Their motivation is primarily determined by the effect that a particular behavior will have upon their relationships with others. They value friendship and are keenly concerned with other peoples' feelings about them. Given a choice of working companions, affiliative people tend to choose their friends and secondarily consider their skills in helping to accomplish the task. (In contrast, high achievers will choose those who can assist in achieving goals and those with high need for power will choose those whom they can influence and control.)

THE NEED FOR POWER. People with a strong need for power gain satisfaction from influencing and controlling others. Not surprisingly, studies have shown that managers tend to have a higher need for power than nonmanagers. This is to be expected (and desired!) since one of the major responsibilities of managers is to influence the behavior of others. These people will be motivated by positions of authority (such as police work) and the ability to control resources and information (such as politics). Providing, of course, that the use of power is not abused, these individuals can be valuable in the workplace because of their desire to influence others and to gain recognition for having power and influence.

How Do You Discover a Person's Needs?

There are basically two ways, the first of which is not very useful for supervisors. Tests have been constructed which claim to measure the level of need in each of the three areas. However, the administration and measurement of these tests require highly trained experts skilled in interpretation of psychological data. A better and more practical method for supervisors is observation of an individual's behavior over time to see which of the three patterns best fits him or her. This does not require specific training, although a degree of sensitivity and practice is necessary. Given your knowledge of the three motive patterns, careful observation over a period of time can give you a pretty good idea which of the three a person tends to respond to. Perhaps the affiliative person is the easiest to spot. This person likes to work in groups, is very concerned about how others feel, and is easily bothered by interpersonal concerns. In any case, understanding of the basic patterns and learning to interpret behavior are important steps toward applying this theory at the supervisory level.

Applying the Theory

The first step for the supervisor is to identify the dominant motives of subordinates as described above. Next, specific methods for using these motives must be designed and applied. The possibilities are unlimited, but below are some common methods of using the different needs.

ACHIEVEMENT

1. Provide as much concrete feedback as often as possible on progress toward goal;
2. Avoid having them depend upon others for doing their jobs;
3. Avoid placing them in group projects;
4. Let them set their own objectives;
5. Leave them alone.

AFFILIATION

1. Assign them to jobs in which they can interact with others;
2. Let them choose their co-workers whenever possible;
3. Support and show concern for interpersonal factors;
4. If productivity problems occur, solve them by showing how this would affect your feelings toward them;
5. Motivate by establishing a close personal relationship with them.

POWER

1. Place them in positions where they can control resources or information;
2. Deal with productivity problems by showing how lack of productivity will affect their power base;
3. Organize work groups in which these people can exert their influence;
4. Provide them with a special skill or knowledge which others need;
5. Use participative management so that they have an opportunity to influence you.

Any of the three motives can be harmful if it exists in the extreme. The supervisor should always be on guard for possible negative effects, particularly regarding the motivation of co-workers. But assuming that extremes can be kept in check, McClelland offers some practical ways that supervisors can influence behavior.

The Two-Factor Theory

One of the most popular (and controversial) theories of motivation in recent years is Frederick Herzberg's **two-factor theory,** also called the motivation-hygiene theory.[3] Herzberg's research provided some valuable insights into motivation problems and his solution to these problems— job enrichment—has been applied with considerable success in many organizations. As noted in the previous chapter, its major weakness is its universalist solution to motivation problems. Also, additional research has added some important reservations about the theory. Even though job enrichment is often something beyond the supervisor's authority, there are some aspects of Herzberg's theory that can benefit supervisors.

The Theory

Herzberg's major contribution to motivation theory was the analysis of the morale-productivity controversy discussed in the previous chapter. He began by noting that when individuals described the factors that caused them satisfaction on the job, they talked about one set of factors, which he called **motivators.** When referring to things that caused them dissatisfaction on the job, they talked about a different set of factors, and these Herzberg called **hygienes.** In general, the motivators consisted of items pertaining directly to the jobs people were doing, and the hygienes pertained to the environment in which the jobs were performed The specific list of motivators and hygienes is contained in Table 7.1.

Herzberg maintains that our inability to motivate workers in the past has been because companies have relied primarily on hygiene factors. These factors, while reducing job dissatisfaction (or improving morale) do not affect motivation. Because the motivators and hygienes are *different* factors (rather than opposites) it is theoretically possible for employees to be both satisfied and dissatisfied at the same time. Ideally, according to Herzberg, companies should have good hygiene factors as well as challenging jobs.

3. Frederick Herzberg, "One More Time: How Do You Motivate Employees?" *Harvard Business Review* 46 (January-Februrary, 1968), pp. 53–62.

Herzberg in the Backyard

It is often confusing to hear that employees can be both satisfied and dissatisfied at the same time. Perhaps the following analogy will help. Imagine yourself in your backyard on a hot summer day building a fence. While hard at work, you accidently hit your thumb with the hammer, which obviously produces pain. When the pain goes away, you will not feel pleasure but will feel a neutral feeling that is called "the absence of pain." Now, imagine the same situation, and while working at the fence you take a drink of cold water. Your feeling? Probably pleasure. And when that feeling goes away, you will again experience a neutral feeling called "the absence of pleasure." To appreciate Herzberg's analysis, simply put the two together: you hit your thumb with the hammer and at the same time take a drink of cold water. Surprisingly, you will feel both pain and pleasure at the same time! This happens because the sources of each are different. The same thing happens at work. You can feel satisfaction and dissatisfaction at the same time because the source of satisfaction is the nature of the work you do, the source of dissatisfaction is the environment in which you do it.

There is a close relationship between Herzberg's theory and Maslow's Need Hierarchy. Notice that the hygienes (which Herzberg maintains do not motivate) correspond closely to Maslow's physiological, safety, and social needs, which were earlier said to be poor motivators. Similarly, the motivators are closely related to the ego and self-actualization needs. In other words, the reason why Herzberg's motivators motivate is that they satisfy the unsatisfied higher-order needs on Maslow's hierarchy.

Given the nature of his motivators you can see why Herzberg viewed job enrichment as the solution to motivation problems. Job enrichment involves increasing the responsibility in jobs through redesign of the tasks. Increased responsibility will give greater opportunity for personal growth, achievement, and recognition. Herzberg believed that these were

Table 7.1. Herzberg's Motivators and Hygienes.

Motivators	*Hygienes*
achievement	company policies
recognition	technical supervision
advancement	interpersonal relations
work itself	salary
growth	personal life
responsibility	job security
	working conditions
	fringe benefits
	status

the major determinants of motivation, although good hygiene factors were a necessary condition for motivation to occur.

Some Cautions About the Theory

There are several technical and research-related issues about the two-factor theory, but our major concern here is how these problems might affect the application of the theory.

It is now believed that the motivation-hygiene theory is situation-specific, that is, it does not hold for all employees. Herzberg's original analysis was performed on data from scientific and professional people. Subsequent application to other types of workers has shown that the motivators and hygienes are not applicable to all workers. For example, money is a motivator for some employees; for others, interpersonal relations may be a motivator. It is probably safe to use Herzberg's basic formulation of motivators and hygienes as a general framework for motivation, but it is important to remember that individual differences can affect what is a motivator or hygiene for each employee.

Because of this, the solution of job enrichment must also be used with caution. If, for example, interpersonal relations is a major motivator for an employee, providing a more enriched job will have little effect upon motivation unless the increased responsibility is in some way related to interpersonal factors.

Applying the Theory

As we noted previously, job enrichment can be difficult for some supervisors to implement since it has consequences beyond the supervisor's sphere of authority. Redesigning jobs can be a major undertaking with company-wide implications. However, there are several actions that can normally be taken by most supervisors to provide a degree of job enrichment.

- Remove controls and checks on employees.
- Delegate more authority.
- Change work flows so individual workers have authority over a whole task.
- Assign special projects.
- Allow more discretion regarding quality and quantity of job performance.

Several of the motivators and hygienes listed in Table 7.1 can be directly affected by the supervisor, although the results would vary from employee to employee. These would be recognition, technical supervision, personal life, and to a degree, interpersonal relations.

Technical supervision refers to the degree of technical expertise a supervisor can provide for employees. Employees get frustrated if they discover their supervisor can provide them little technical assistance. This does not mean that the supervisor must be able to perform the job as well as the employee, but he or she should have at least an appreciation for the task so that assistance or support can be provided when necessary.

The supervisor clearly does not have control over an employee's personal life, but should have the skills necessary to deal with personal problems when they affect productivity. These skills, which are discussed in greater detail in Chapter 18, are important for assisting in the removal of this barrier to motivation.

The possible negative effects of interpersonal relations indicate that supervisors must also have good interpersonal skills in addition to the technical skills just noted. We do know that supervisors who aren't liked by subordinates can create productivity problems. Although we can't make major changes in personalities, good human relations skills can be taught and these can go a long way towards reducing this type of conflict.

Perhaps the most important motivator available to supervisors is recognition. Because it is so important, it is the subject of Exercise 7.2.

Conclusions

The primary use of the two-factor theory from the supervisor's point of view is the distinction between sources of motivation and sources of job dissatisfaction. This knowledge increases our understanding of motivation at work and provides some insights as to how motivation might be improved. But the limitations of the theory emphasize the importance of individual differences and in order to make the motivation-hygiene theory work, the supervisor has to know his or her employees well.

Exercise 7.2

Ways of Recognizing Employees

Recognition of employees is frequently believed to be the most powerful source of motivation a supervisor has. This is because many methods of recognition are totally within the discretion of the supervisor, and because recognition satisfies one of the most unsatisfied needs of many people—the ego need. The ability to provide ways of recognition is often limited only by the supervisor's imagination. Think for a few moments about this powerful motivation technique and make a list of as many different ways that a supervisor can recognize employees as you can.

Improved theories of motivation must be able to take into account the fact that all people are different. Thus, we come to the next and final motivation theory, expectancy theory.

Expectancy Theory

Expectancy theory differs from other theories of motivation in that it attempts to incorporate individual differences.[4] Since we know that all people are different, we could expect such a model to be quite complex, and it is. However, it can be explained in fairly straightforward terms; it is only when we apply it that it becomes complicated.

The Theory

As the name implies, **expectancy theory** proposes that employees will be motivated to exhibit behaviors that they expect will lead to desirable goals. Since goals will vary with each employee, the theory recognizes that employees will be motivated to exhibit different behaviors. Figure 7.3 shows how these behaviors are related to employee goals.

The model relates three important variables that determine employee motivation: the employee's goals, the alternative behaviors that lead (or do not lead) to those goals, and the expectancy of the employee that he or she is capable of exhibiting the alternative behaviors.

Two other terms in Figure 7.3 need explaining. **Valence** is used to describe the relative importance of the employee's goals. These have traditionally been measured on a scale of -1 to $+1$, with the positive end indicating desirable goals and the negative end indicating things the employee wishes to avoid. **Instrumentality** measures the relationship the employee sees between the alternative behaviors and his or her goals. Again, a $+1$ would mean that the employee sees a strong relationship between the behavior and a goal, a -1 would mean a negative relationship, and a 0 would indicate that no relationship is perceived. The final measure, *effort*, is the perception by the employee that he or she can affect the alternative behavior. A $+1$ indicates that the employee has total control over the behavior, a 0 indicates no control.

Figure 7.4 shows a simplified expectancy model of a hypothetical employee. Given the positive numbers for valence, instrumentality, and expectancy, this employee would be motivated to high productivity.

It has often been stated that one of the worst things a supervisor can

4. V. Vroom, *Work and Motivation* (New York: Wiley, 1964).

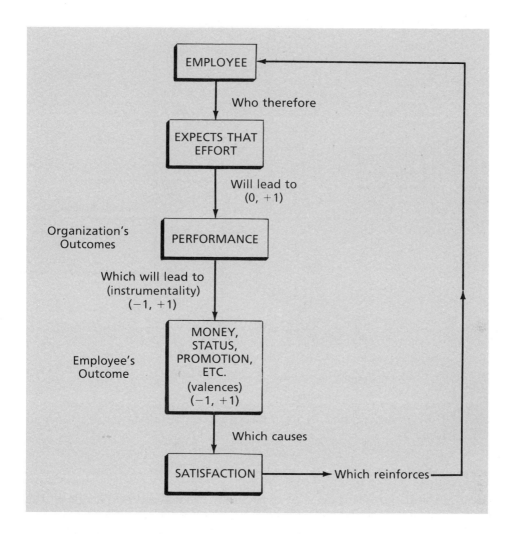

Figure 7.3. Diagram of Expectancy Theory of Motivation.

have is a motivated employee who has nowhere to go. Expectancy theory illustrates how this can happen. Assume an employee has a goal of advancing through the organization (high valence) and sees that the way to get promoted is to be a high producer (i.e., the instrumental relationship between productivity and promotion is high). Unfortunately, he is in a job where no matter how hard he works, he cannot affect productivity. An unusual situation? Not really. This is typical of the situation that many assembly line workers face. Because their work is so closely controlled by external factors (e.g., pace of the line, tools given to them, etc.),

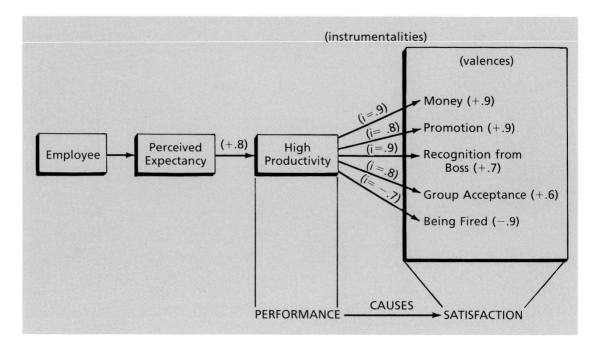

Figure 7.4. Sample Model of Expectancy Showing a Motivated Employee.

their effort is not related to productivity. The result is frustration and alienation.

Application of the Theory

One of the major advantages of expectancy theory is that the role of the supervisor in the motivation process is made very clear. First, the supervisor *must* know what the goals of employees are. What do they want from their jobs? What are they after? How can this job satisfy their needs? All these are questions that must be answered before the supervisor can be a good motivator.

Next, the supervisor must clarify the relationship between the behaviors desired by the supervisor and the employee's goals. In other words, if this is what the employee wants, what must he or she do to get them? If your employees do not see, for example, that being productive will lead to what they want, they will not be productive.

And finally, the supervisor must attempt to remove any barriers that may inhibit the employee's efforts from resulting in higher productivity. In some cases, this may mean additional training, or procuring tools or equipment the employee needs to do the job. In other cases (such as the assembly line situation described previously) there may be little the supervisor can do. If such is the case, the supervisor has no alternative except to emphasize the morale factors noted in the previous chapter to keep the employee happy, but with no expectation of increased productivity.

Computing Motivation Potential

We are now in a position to integrate all the motivation theories and show how a supervisor can actually compute the motivation potential of each employee. Supervisors are sometimes inefficient in their efforts at motivating employees because they emphasize things that are not important to the employee or that the supervisor cannot control. Effective motivation can only be accomplished if these two are properly integrated.

We can view motivation potential (MP) as a function of two major variables: (a) employee needs (or wants, drives, goals, etc.) and how important these needs are (NI), and (b) how much control the supervisor has over these needs (C). We can express this relationship mathematically as follows:

$$MP = (NI) \times (C)$$

The steps in computing the MP are as follows:

1. *Make a list for each employee of what he or she wants from the employment situation.* You may want to brainstorm this list, but there are two other ways of getting the information. First, you can always ask the employees (this may or may not generate honest information, depending upon your relationship with them). Secondly, you can deduce what their wants are through observation.

2. *Assign a relative value to each one.* Each item can be rated on a scale of 0–10, with zero meaning the item is of no importance, and 10 indicating that it is of crucial importance. Again, you can do this yourself or with the employee's assistance.

3. *Assign a relative value to each item showing how much control you have over it.* In one sense, this is a function of your job description and company policy. Using a scale again of 0–10, you would assign the appropriate number. For example, if an employee wanted more money but you have no authority over salaries, you would give this a low rating.

4. *Compute the motivation potential of each item.*

You now have a numerical figure that gives you the item(s) that have the highest motivation potential. This tells you how you should direct your efforts to get the most from them. Obviously, there is little value in

Table 7.2. Example of the Computational Approach to Motivation.

(EN) Employee Need	(NI)* Need Importance	(SC)* Supervisory Control	(MP) Motivational Potential
More Money	(7)	(4)	28
Promotion	(6)	(4)	24
Group Acceptance	(9)	(2)	18
Better Working Conditions	(4)	(6)	24
Longer Vacation	(7)	(0)	O
Less Supervision	(8)	(9)	(72)
More Responsibility	(8)	(7)	56
Better Pension Plan	(7)	(0)	O
More Power	(5)	(2)	10
Better Interpersonal Relations	(9)	(3)	27

*Items are measured on scale of zero (low) to 10 (high).
O indicates motivation source with greatest potential.

spending time attempting to motivate someone who is motivated by something beyond your control. Although every situation is relative, you should generally concentrate on items having a net value of about fifty or higher. Table 7.2 is an example of how this system is used in a hypothetical case.

Key to Success

In a sense, the motivation process is a paradox. On the one hand, it is simple and straightforward, as the MP index illustrates. On the other hand, human behavior is a complex phenomenon that resists simple formulas and universalist techniques. Our search for the better mousetrap continues today, despite the major advances that have been made in recent decades.

But even with these advances, one thing has not changed over the years: *the most important factor in the motivation process is for supervisors to know their employees well.* Regardless of which motivation theory is used, this basic principle is still the key to successful application. We cannot afford to assume that all people are alike, or that everyone is motivated by the same thing. Whether you prefer the Maslow, Herzberg, or McClelland approach, recognition of individual differences is the basis of effective motivation. The expectancy and motivation potential (MP) approach allows each of the theories to be used in an individual framework, thus increasing the effectiveness of all.

Summary

This chapter has presented the theories of motivation most widely accepted today. Maslow's Need Hierarchy is a general theory of motivation that attributes motivation to unsatisfied needs. The physiological, security, social, ego, and self-fulfillment needs motivate behavior when they are unsatisfied. Maslow proposes that they occur in a hierarchical arrangement, meaning that one level does not motivate behavior until the previous level has been satisfied. While useful as a general model of motivation, it is not helpful in predicting individual behavior.

The motivation theory of David McClelland proposes three needs as major motivators of behavior: achievement, affiliation, and control. Each need has different behavior patterns associated with it. Supervisors can use this theory of motivation by (a) diagnosing the employee's need structure, and (b) designing a work environment that utilizes the employee's personal needs. For example, high achievers need to be managed differently than employees with high affiliation needs.

Herzberg's two-factor theory proposes that motivation is a result of the content of the job itself. Factors such as responsibility, challenge, and growth cause motivation on the job. Factors pertaining to the job environment cause job dissatisfaction, and these are called hygiene factors. Hygiene factors include such things as pay, working conditions, and fringe benefits. Herzberg's prescription to solve motivation problems is to have a pleasant job environment and enriched jobs for employees. The major limitation of this approach is its universalist proposal that all employees desire more responsibility, and challenge.

Expectancy theory attempts to integrate the other theories by incorporating individual differences. It proposes that an individual's behavior is motivated by the desire to reach personal goals, and that organizations should relate personal goals to organizational goals. If an employee perceives that a certain behavior desired by the organization will lead to an important personal outcome, motivation will occur.

The computational approach to motivation provides a relatively structured approach to a complex problem. It can show the supervisor which factors in the motivational equation can be influenced to improve motivation.

Although Tom Sanders may not realize it, he does not have a motivation problem —at least in the sense that the term is generally used. George Irwin is a highly motivated employee. It's just that he's not motivated in the direction that Sanders wants. It could be that Irwin is a high achiever and prefers not to depend on others for his success. Or, he could be very low on affiliation or social needs, which would explain his desire to be a loner. In either case, Sanders would be wise to try to take advantage of Irwin's natural sources of motivation rather than to try to make him into something he isn't.

If Irwin's desire to work by himself is a strong one (and it appears that it is), then this can be a very powerful motivational force that Sanders can use. It would be possible to get Irwin to work more with others but the outcome would likely be unpleasant for all. Irwin would lose some of his motivation, and his annoyance at having to work with others would probably have an effect upon the group as well. So it would be a hollow victory, indeed, for Sanders if he forced Irwin to join the team and the performance of both Irwin and the team suffered as a result.

If Sanders does decide that joining the team is of critical importance, then it means that Irwin is not suitable for the role Sanders has for him. This is therefore a selection problem, not a motivational one.

This chapter concluded that it is important for supervisors to know their employees well. In this regard, Sanders has done his homework. His problem is that although he knows his employee's motivational needs, he doesn't know what to do with them.

Review Questions

1. Why is it important to learn about several different motivation theories?
2. List and define the five needs in Maslow's Need Hierarchy.
3. Why are the basic needs generally not strong motivators of behavior on the job?
4. How does the overcompensation principle operate in the need hierarchy?
5. Is the need hierarchy a good predictor of individual behavior? Why or why not?
6. What are the major limitations of the need hierarchy as an approach to motivation?
7. What are the primary needs in McClelland's achievement motivation theory?
8. What kinds of things motivate high achievers?
9. How might a supervisor determine an employee's need structure?
10. List some things a supervisor might do to motivate an employee whose dominant need is (a) achievement (b) affiliation, and (c) power.
11. What are Herzberg's motivators and hygiene factors?
12. How does Herzberg distinguish between job satisfaction and job dissatisfaction?

13. According to Herzberg's theory, what kinds of things should a supervisor do to motivate employees?
14. How does expectancy theory describe the motivation process?
15. What do the terms *instrumentality* and *valence* mean in expectancy theory?
16. According to expectancy theory, what things should a supervisor do to motivate employees?
17. How might the potential motivation for an employee be computed?

Chapter Glossary

Maslow's hierarchy of needs.	A general theory of motivation which proposes that physiological, security, social, ego, and self-fulfillment needs occur in a hierarchical sequence, and that unsatisfied needs motivate behavior.
Physiological needs.	The needs basic to human survival—food, water, and so on. The first level of needs in Maslow's Need Hierarchy.
Security needs.	The second level of needs in Maslow's Need Hierarchy. Primarily concerned with keeping the organism safe from harm (physical and mental) and arbitrary action. Exemplified on the job frequently as the need for job security.
Social needs.	The desire to belong to social groups and engage in social interaction. Becomes important only after basic needs have been relatively satisfied.
Ego (status) needs.	The desire to have an individual identity and to increase one's feeling of self-worth. Exemplified in organizations by status symbols and the personalizing of one's work space.
Self-actualization needs.	The highest level in Maslow's Need Hierarchy. Pertains to satisfying one's highest goals, becoming all one wants to be. A highly personalized need, seldom fully satisfied.
Overcompensation principle.	A principle operating in Maslow's Need Hierarchy which proposes that blockage at any need level causes overcompensation at a lower level. Frustration at satisfying a need causes an exaggeration of the importance of another need.
Achievement motivation theory.	Theory proposed by psychologist David McClelland describing three needs that motivate behavior: achievement, affiliation, and power. These occur in a configuration, not a hierarchy.
Achievement need.	The need to reach challenging goals, receive quick, concrete feedback, and have control over the outcome of one's efforts.

Affiliation need.

Similar to Maslow's social needs. Defined as the desire to form strong and long-lasting interpersonal relationships with others, and to be accepted by others.

Power need.

The need to influence and control others, to be in a position of exercising control.

Two-factor theory.

Theory proposed by Frederick Herzberg which states that two factors, motivators and hygienes, are major determinants of performance on the job. Motivators pertain to the job content, and hygienes to job context, that is, the job environment in which the job is performed. This theory proposes that job enrichment is the solution to motivation problems.

Motivators.

Herzberg's term for describing the sources of job satisfaction. They are: work itself, achievement, recognition, advancement, growth, and responsibility.

Hygiene factors.

Herzberg's term for the sources of job dissatisfaction. They are: company policies, technical supervision, interpersonal relations, salary, job security, personal life, working conditions, fringe benefits, and status.

Job enrichment.

Increasing the level of responsibility in a job. Usually involves a combination of increased delegation of authority, removing controls over employees, assigning special projects, or giving employees control over the complete task. The objective is to make the job more challenging and therefore more satisfying.

Expectancy theory.

The theory of motivation which proposes that employees are motivated by perceiving that behaviors desired by the organization will lead to satisfaction of the employees' personal goals.

Valence.

A measure of the relative importance of employee's goals in expectancy theory. The higher the valence, the more important the goal.

Instrumentality.

A measure of the relationship between behaviors desired by the organization and the goals of the employee. High instrumentality means that the employee sees a strong relationship between performance and personal goals; a weak relationship means the employee sees performance as not being instrumental in attaining personal goals.

Motivational potential.

A computational method of calculating the potential motivation of an employee. The system analyzes the interaction of (a) importance of employee goals and (b) the factors that the supervisor can influence which affect those goals.

| Universalist approach. | An approach to managing people which proposes that there is a single solution to motivation problems. Such approaches have generally been discredited. |

Case Problem

County Social Services Agency

County Social Services Agency is a government administered agency responsible for a variety of social services in the county. There are four different offices located throughout the county, each containing an office administrator, a staff of social workers, and a number of clerical employees. In most cases, the office administrator is a professional social worker and the majority of the professional staff are college graduates.

Because of the diverse nature of the services, professional employees are responsible for a variety of activities such as family services, community development, income security, counselling services, and other developmental programs. The busiest program is income security since all welfare and other financial assistance programs originate in the regional offices. The program is so designed that professional employees have the initial contact with the client, perform whatever diagnostic and counselling functions are needed, and then turn the case over to the clerical staff, who perform the necessary paperwork and administrative functions. The professional staff maintain contact with the client on an individual basis to continue the counselling and diagnostic functions as needed. Each professional staff employee maintains his or her own caseload in order to have closer personal contact with the clients.

Because of a recent reorganization of the entire social services function in the county, it was announced that one of the local offices would be phased out. The central administration decided that the level of service needed did not require four separate offices and that the services provided by one office would be slowly amalgamated with the other three. After considerable discussion and debate at senior levels, it was decided which office will be closed and where the employees would be transferred. It was made clear that no professional employees would lose their jobs, and that normal attrition would eventually reduce the workforce to the desired level.

The problems that have occurred at one of the three remaining offices are typical. When the professional staff were transferred, there were not a sufficient number of clients available to give each one a new caseload. Consequently, it was decided that until the reorganization had its full effect (estimated to be in about one year), the relocated employees would assist with some of the clerical activities that were created as a result of the move. There were many new files to be integrated into the system, and a considerable number of administrative tasks that needed to be performed. When informed of this, the social workers began to complain. They have complained about the new location, the inconvenience of having to drive so far to work (many of them purposely lived close to their old office), and the cramped quarters in which they have to work. The administrator of the office pointed out that they actually have more room in this new location than in the old, but the complaints have not stopped. Absenteeism has increased dramatically, and the administrator has noticed a number of violations of organizational policies and procedures that never occurred before.

The administrator keeps a record of how many clients are being serviced by examining the number of up-to-date files given to him each week. After two months in the new arrangement, he is surprised to note that fewer cases have been processed than before the change, and that the unit is at least a week behind on its filing system.

Questions for Discussion

1. What are the sources of the motivation problem?
2. What solutions are available to the administrator to solve this problem?

Using Reward Systems Effectively

8

After reading and studying this chapter you should be able to:

1. List and define the basic principles of applying reward systems.

2. Describe the differences between tangible and intangible rewards, and between internal and external rewards.

3. Describe the circumstances in which punishment should and should not be used.

4. List the basic principles of applying punishment properly.

5. Tell the difference between positive and negative strokes.

6. Describe the conditions under which money would be a motivator.

7. Explain why recognition is a potential motivator for supervisors.

8. Explain how performance appraisals can be adapted to the reward system principles.

Key Terms

Reward systems
Contingency principle
Awareness principle
Timing principle
Size principle
Type principle
Tangible rewards
Intangible rewards
Extrinsic rewards
Intrinsic rewards
Consistency principle
Control principle
Punishment
Strokes
Performance appraisal

175

Harvey Friesen

Harvey Friesen supervises twenty unionized service technicians for the Greater Westville Utilities Company. The technicians set up and service natural gas installations throughout the city. Harvey is particularly concerned about his newest technician, Bob Starke, who is approaching the end of his six-month probationary period. This period is crucial, Friesen thinks, because once an employee is past the probationary period, there is little a supervisor can do about poor performance. Friesen is concerned about Starke since he has had some negative feedback about the quality of his work and his relations with customers.

Yesterday, the day prior to the end of Starke's probationary period, Harvey called Starke into his office just before quitting time. The conversation went like this:

FRIESEN: Sit down, Bob. As you know, this is the last day before your probationary period is up and I wanted to talk with you about your performance so far. Quite frankly, I've got some concerns about you. I've had several complaints from customers that you were rude to them and these complaints have come down from top management. There's no excuse for that kind of behavior and it will have to stop. I've also noticed that you take longer than necessary on quite a few of your jobs. Things that most guys take an hour or so to do seem to take you twice that sometimes. Obviously, I can't be out on the job to check on you so I have to rely on a person's honesty to not goof off. When you started I told you that if you had any problems to come and see me, and since you haven't I assume that you know what you're doing. I think overall I'm concerned about your attitude. You don't seem to take an interest in your job. We can't have that around here since I depend on everyone to carry their weight. What I'm saying, Starke, is that I'm going to ask the personnel manager to extend your probationary period by another three months. If you don't improve your attitude in that time, I'm going to have to let you go. I don't want to do that, you understand, but we just can't have a person with your attitude around here.

STARKE: (slowly getting up) Fine! The next time we talk about this it'll be in a grievance hearing. (He slams the door and walks out.)

In recent years a new focus in the study of management and supervision has become popular. Sometimes called organizational behavior modification, performance management, or simply behavior management, it involves the study of how rewards and punishments should be applied to employees for maximum productivity and satisfaction. Recent research in the area has indicated that significant gains in productivity can be achieved with the scientific application of proper reward systems.

At first glance, it might seem that how to apply rewards properly is a simple topic: one simply rewards those who do perform and punishes those who do not. While that may be generally true, there are many other factors that determine whether or not the rewards and punishments will have the desired effect. It is not until we examine reward systems in detail that we can understand how rewards and punishments actually affect behavior.

One of the best (and commonest) examples of how lack of understanding of reward systems causes performance problems is the typical sick leave policy of many organizations. Most companies have a policy that allows for so many paid sick days per year. If this is the extent of the policy, the company is essentially rewarding sick people and punishing healthy people. If what the company wants is healthy people coming to work, then why do they create a reward system that rewards sick people who stay at home? Most systems accomplish just what they are designed to do; thus many employees take their full allotment of paid sick days. Isn't it amazing how sickness strikes people regularly for a certain number of days each year? It's not so amazing once you understand how reward systems work. This problem can easily be solved by reversing the reward system, that is, by rewarding people who come to work regularly (but not punishing those who take their sick days). For example, some companies are using programs that trade sick days not used for vacation days or other rewards. Others use lotteries in which eligibility is determined by level of absenteeism.

Understanding how rewards and punishments affect behavior is a valuable tool for supervisors. As noted in earlier chapters, often the supervisor is left with too few rewards to give employees. For example, pay and promotion policies are usually controlled by forces outside the supervisor's authority, so these are rewards that are *potentially* effective, but in fact may be useless for the supervisor. Because there are so few rewards available to supervisors, it becomes even more important to use the ones available as effectively as possible.

In this discussion we shall analyze the basic principles of effective reward systems, what types of rewards can be used, and how effective use of punishment can establish a climate of positive discipline. Additional applications of the principles will be illustrated in a discussion of rewards that most supervisors have available, as well as how one of the most important reward systems in organizations — performance appraisals — can be made a more satisfying experience.

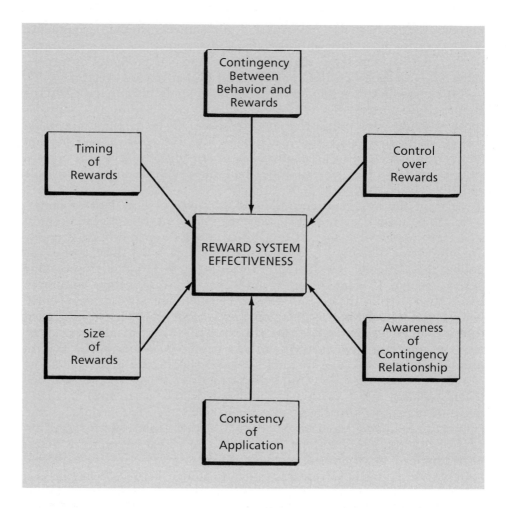

Figure 8.1. Factors Affecting the Effectiveness of Rewards Systems.

Basic Concepts

The study of how to apply rewards properly has generated several useful principles that will form the basis for our analysis. Once the basic principles are understood, they can then be tailored to individual circumstances. These basic reward concepts pertain to: contingency, awareness, timing, size, consistency, and control. Figure 8.1 illustrates the general principles, and the following sections discuss them in detail.

The Contingency Principle

The most important principle is the **contingency principle.** It states that rewards and punishments should be *contingent* (dependent) upon desired behavior. For example, if an employee receives a pay raise because he or she performed above a certain level, then the pay is said to be contingent upon the behavior or performance. If, however, an employee receives a raise in pay because of a normal annual salary increment, then the reward is not contingent upon any specific behavior or level of performance. The contingency relationship is critical for applying rewards effectively since we know that people seek out rewarding experiences and avoid unrewarding ones. The implementation of the contingency principle allows employees to engage in behaviors which they know will be rewarding. The significant aspect of the contingency principle is that the reward *follows* the behavior rather than precedes it.

The Awareness Principle

The **awareness principle** simply means that in order for the contingency principle to operate, people must be aware of what the contingency relationship is. To use the above example, if the employee does not know that a raise in pay will follow increased performance, then for all intents and purposes, the contingency relationship doesn't exist.

The lesson for supervisors here should be obvious. When you want to establish a contingency relationship between a reward and a desired behavior, you have to communicate this relationship to employees. Otherwise, the latter are left on their own and must try to figure

The Attraction of Games

One type of activity that has almost universal appeal is games, such as card games, sports games, and hundreds of entertainment games such as Monopoly, and Risk. One of the reasons why games have such a wide appeal is that they adhere to both the contingency and awareness principles. In games, the players know them as rules. When we play one of these games we always know the outcome of our behavior. If there ever is any doubt, we simply refer to the rule book. Notice that it's not nearly as much fun playing a game in which you don't know the rules because you don't know which behaviors will be rewarded and which ones will be punished. We would probably refuse to play a game in which the rules are made up as we go along. Yet, these very conditions exist in many organizations. Employees don't know the rules because they haven't been told or, worse yet, the rules appear to keep changing. Supervisors can have considerable impact on this problem by telling subordinates exactly which behaviors will be rewarded and by maintaining a consistent system.

out what types of behaviors the supervisor is rewarding. Not only is this inefficient, but it defeats the purpose of establishing the contingency relationship in the first place.

The Timing Principle

The effectiveness of giving rewards is also related to the **timing,** that is, how soon after the behavior the reward occurs. All things being equal, rewards applied quickly are more effective than rewards that occur long after the behavior. For example, one of the reasons why pension plans do not have a significant impact on our everyday behavior is because we have to wait so long for the reward. Not many people would increase performance today and wait twenty-five years for their payoff.

People generally are quite short-run in their thinking and in their behavior, even though they may dream about the future and engage in a lot of wishful thinking. Probably for administrative convenience more than anything else, many of the reward systems in organizations tend to be on an annual basis. We have annual performance appraisals, annual pay increases, and annual profit-sharing plans. Budgets tend to be timed for once a year, as are audits and company picnics. Outside the organizations, the situation is much the same: Christmas comes once a year, as do all the holidays, we have a birthday once a year, and we take our annual vacation. The effect upon behavior is obvious, as illustrated by the significant improvement in children's behavior as Christmas draws near.

Despite all these annual events, the behavior of most people on the job is determined by much shorter time horizons. The reason is that the longer the period of time between behavior and reward, the greater the chance that the contingency principle will be violated. If a subordinate does something today and is rewarded for it one year later, the relationship between that behavior and the reward is obscured. Our emphasis in this chapter is therefore upon how supervisors can effectively utilize relatively short-term rewards.

The Size Principle

The **size principle** relates to whether rewards should be large or small. Obviously, large rewards tend to be more effective than small ones, but there are several wrinkles that should be kept in mind.

First, *large* and *small* are relative terms. The same reward could be perceived as large or small, depending upon the effort required to obtain the reward. For example, a reward system that requires 50 percent more effort by the employee to obtain 25 percent more reward would probably violate the size principle. Although 25 percent more reward by most standards is reasonably large, the effort required to get it makes it seem much smaller.

Second, the size and timing principles tend to offset each other. In other words, the timing of the reward becomes less important as the size increases, and similarly, the smaller the reward, the shorter the period of time should be. Since it is unlikely that supervisors will have large rewards to give to subordinates, this further emphasizes the importance of using rewards over shorter periods.

Third, size becomes relatively unimportant if the contingency principle is violated. No matter how large a reward offered, if employees don't know what they have to do to get it, it will not significantly affect behavior. Even games of chance (lotteries, for example) have a degree of the contingency principle operating in that if you don't buy a ticket, you can't win the prize.

Finally, size tends to become less important with intangible rewards. This is largely a perceptual problem, which means that it is more difficult to measure the size of an intangible reward (like a feeling of satisfaction or token of recognition) than it is to measure a cash award. In fact, in those situations in which it is impossible to reward in a manner consistent with the effort, token rewards generally are effective. Note, for example, that tokens of recognition are often given to individuals who make outstanding contributions to civic or volunteer organizations.

The Type Principle

The **type principle** pertains to the types of rewards offered and can be looked at from two points of view. The first is the general categories of rewards possible: these are *tangible* and *intangible* and *extrinsic* and *intrinsic*. These four categories interact as illustrated in Figure 8.2 to provide several combinations of rewards. **Tangible rewards** are those that have a physical property to them, such as money, trophies, promotion, time off. **Intangible rewards** are those that are psychological in nature such as job satisfaction, pride, approval from a supervisor. **Extrinsic rewards** are those provided by an outside source. For example, if a supervisor tells an employee he or she is doing a good job, this is an extrinsic reward. **Intrinsic rewards** are those which people give themselves and are not dependent upon an external source. Examples of combinations of these four would be:

1. *Tangible-Extrinsic:* An employee is presented with a plaque recognizing twenty-five years of service.
2. *Tangible-Intrinsic:* As a reward for making a particular sale, a salesman buys himself a new suit.
3. *Intangible-Extrinsic:* A supervisor tells a subordinate he or she is doing a good job.
4. *Intangible-Intrinsic:* An employee accomplishes a difficult task and feels good about it.

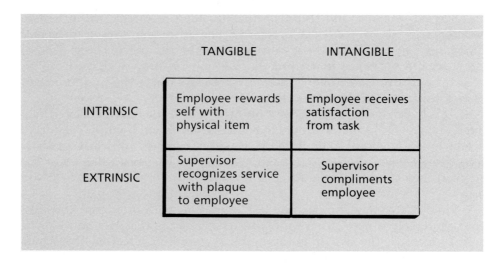

Figure 8.2. Possible Types of Rewards.

As the previous examples suggest, the supervisor can play either an indirect or direct role in rewarding employees. Probably the most control supervisors would have is in the intangible-extrinsic type. In fact, the example of a supervisor telling an employee he or she is doing a good job can be one of the most effective rewards supervisors can use, provided it is used properly. This will be discussed in greater detail later in this chapter.

Within the tangible-extrinsic type, supervisors could manipulate job responsibilities, working hours, type of supervision, or other physical factors. Pay would also fall into this category, provided the supervisor had authority over pay. With the intrinsic categories, supervisors play an indirect role. Since the rewards are internal to the individual, the most the supervisor can do is create an environment in which the employee can realize the rewards.

Creating the proper environment relates to the second meaning of the type principle. Supervisors must realize that not all people find the same things to be rewarding. Something that is very important to one person may mean little or nothing to another. Therefore, before applying any reward system, supervisors first must know what kind or types of rewards are meaningful to subordinates. This statement is consistent with the discussion in the previous chapter regarding the importance of the supervisor's knowing employees well.

There are basically two ways of finding out what types of rewards employees want. The first is simply to ask. Many people, but not all, will be open about it and tell what they find rewarding. The other method is through observing behavior over time and deducing what rewards the individual is working for. This requires experience with people and a degree of sensitivity, but coupled with the first method, it makes it possible to get a good picture of what a person finds rewarding.

Once this is done, then the supervisor has better control over the rewards. Many of the rewards will be intrinsic, so the supervisor is in a position to create an environment in which they can be obtained. For example, if a person finds working by himself or herself to be rewarding, then the supervisor might change the workflow and job design patterns in the department so the person could receive the intrinsic satisfaction of working alone.

The Consistency Principle

The **consistency principle** states that reward systems should be consistent over time and among individuals. In other words, the supervisor should reward all subordinates for the same things (although different rewards might be used), and the same things should always be rewarded. For example, if one subordinate performs well and gets a pat on the back from the supervisor, others who are also performing well will probably resent not getting a similar pat on the back. The consistency over time aspect also means that the same things should be rewarded all the time. For example, if an employee gets the pat on the back for doing something but does not get it the next time he does the same thing, he or she may become resentful. Of course it is not realistic to expect supervisors to reward something each time it occurs, but there should be some element of consistency so that employees know they are on the right track. The importance of the consistency principle will again become apparent in the later discussion of effective discipline.

The Banker's Reward System

The effect of reward systems on employee behavior was made clear to me years ago while I was a part-time employee at a bank. My supervisor unconsciously created a reward system that worked against him. Although he told us what he expected in terms of performance, he unfortunately rewarded something else. After about a year or so it became clear that what he really wanted was to have a well-dressed work group. We learned this through our performance appraisals. We noticed that our evaluation on appearance seemed to influence our evaluation on the other factors such as initiative and dependability. Also, he constantly made reference to everyone's appearance, both on the job and off. Like most employees, we decided our life would be easier if we gave our supervisor what he wanted. So within a year, he developed the best-dressed group of goof-offs you have ever seen! Unfortunately, he was never aware how his reward system affected our productivity.

The Control Principle

This last major principle, the **control principle,** pertains to the degree of control the employee has over the behavior wanted by the supervisor. If the employee has complete control over the desired behavior (such as being punctual in arriving at work), applying reward system principles can affect that behavior. If the employee cannot control what is wanted, then the supervisor should not try to use reward methods. For example, if an employee cannot perform properly because another department prevents him or her from doing what is expected, using a reward system would only create frustration in the employee. Another example would be employees who are just learning their jobs. These people are often not able to produce at levels expected of more experienced workers, so these types of reward systems would be unfair, although the supervisor can use reinforcement to improve learning (this aspect is discussed more fully in Chapter 13).

It is also important to realize that the application of rewards and punishments is something that goes on all the time. A supervisor's behavior is *ALWAYS* affecting subordinates, either positively or negatively. The idea behind learning about reward systems is for supervisors to better understand how their behavior affects others so that changes can be made if necessary.

The application of these principles suggests the following: supervisors should tell subordinates what they want, utilize whatever rewards they have for subordinates when they get what they want, and make sure the rewards are fair and actually rewarding for subordinates. If the rewards are consistently and fairly applied over time, then, all things being equal, the supervisor can create a situation in which performance is high and individuals achieve personal satisfaction as well.

Exercise 8.1

Identifying Reward Systems

Effective reward systems can be important determinants of productivity. However, to be effective they must be managed properly and have a solid theoretical foundation. This exercise allows you to examine any reward system which you have experienced in a job. Briefly describe this system, and then evaluate how well it adhered to the principles discussed in the previous section. Then make a judgment whether the system was effective or not. Is there a relationship between effectiveness and the system's utilization of the principles? Why or why not?

Using Punishment for Effective Discipline

The use of **punishment** — the application of unpleasant consequences following undesirable behavior — in organizations has been a controversial subject. Opinions vary all the way from recommending that it never be used to those who believe the only way of getting people to do something is to punish them for not doing it. Although we do not often think of supervisors as sources of punishment, the principles of applying punishment serve as a basis for establishing and maintaining discipline in the workplace, and it is with this approach in mind that we discuss the principles.

It should be no surprise to note that punishment must be used carefully. Used inappropriately or in the wrong situation it can create more problems than it solves. Also, managers who use only punishment with no positive rewards will create a punitive, negative climate that, at best, will result in only a minimum level of productivity. At worst, there can be high turnover, low morale, and in some cases, even sabotage. In other words, the negative effects of punishment can be drastic.

Regardless of the potential problems with punishment, it is a necessary part of every supervisor's job. The key is to establish a climate of positive discipline rather than one in which behavior is controlled by fear. As this section will show, discipline need not be negative and a supervisor can be tough, fair, and supportive while maintaining good discipline.

When to Use It

Punishment can be used in situations in which employees are aware of the rules or expectations but choose to violate them. Under these conditions, punishment will tend to have fewer negative effects. People resent punishment if they feel they have been had or if the situation is unfair.

Provided the above conditions have been met, punishment can achieve positive change in many instances. For example, if a manager wishes to communicate that a particular rule is important, then punishing the violator will communicate to others that the behavior will not be tolerated. Punishment is also useful if what is desired is the opposite of what is being punished. For example, if an employee is late to work, this can be punished because to avoid the punishment in the future all the employee must do is be at work on time. However, in other cases punishment may not teach the person what is right. For example, if an employee cannot do a task correctly, punishment will not teach the right way.

When Not to Use It

Since punishment is a negative act, we can learn more about it by examining when it should *NOT* be used.

Punishment should never be used for employees who are learning. During the learning process, mistakes are made out of ignorance, not out of purpose. The learning environment should be a positive one in which people are encouraged to take risks, try new ideas, or learn new behaviors. Punishing people who are learning will quickly extinguish all such behavior.

Punishment should also be avoided in emotional situations. The emotional reaction of punishment from a supervisor may be confusing to the employee and create bad feelings toward the supervisor. The supervisor should point out the undesirable behavior as soon as it occurs, but it is generally a better idea to reserve the discipline act for a later time when more rational thinking may prevail. Then the employee will view the punishment as a rational act by the supervisor instead of the result of an emotional outburst.

There is one exception to this principle that has to do with the difference between the supervisor's *attitude* and his or her *behavior*. Punishment, it should be remembered, is an act of discipline. The decision to engage in an act of punishment (such as a suspension or formal reprimand) should not be made in an emotional state. However, there are situations in which the employee's actions warrant disciplinary action, but none is available. In these situations, the supervisor should express his or her feelings to the employee, and this is best done while emotional. An example would be in the situation described at the outset of this chapter regarding employees who take advantage of the company sick leave policy. Since they are operating within the policy, the supervisor cannot use a formal means of punishment. However, he or she is entitled to have feelings and to express them. Not only is it all right, it can also have an effect on the employee's behavior. This is also a safe method of handling these situations since, so far at least, there are no rules or laws against expressing one's feelings.

Punishment generally should not be used in a group setting. If an individual's behavior warrants punishment, then it should be done in private. Punishing someone in front of others can create any number of feelings such as embarrassment, resentment, or a negative group reaction, and the learning value of the punishment is overridden by the bad feelings.

How to Use It

The principles regarding how to use punishment effectively are listed on the next page with brief explanations for each.

1. *Punishment should follow the act as quickly as possible.* With the exception just noted regarding emotional situations, supervisors should discipline as soon after the infraction as is possible. Time lapses only create anxiety in the employee and can create distortions in perception and judgment. Time lapses also reduce the learning effect that punishment is designed to provide.

2. *Punishment should be for the act, not the person.* Punishing the act takes the personal impact of the disciplinary action out of the situation. The supervisor is essentially saying, "You are a good person but have committed a bad act." No one likes to be criticized personally.

3. *Discipline is best accepted in a positive climate.* If punishment is the only method a supervisor uses to influence behavior, then it will be resented. However, if positive methods are the primary ones used, then disciplinary action tends to have fewer negative outcomes. People can accept the negative consequences better if their positive attributes are also recognized.

4. *Discipline should be for behavior, not attitudes.* When disciplinary action is used, it should be for an act, not for how a person feels, or for his or her general attitudes toward something. Few supervisors would actually discipline someone's attitude, but the word itself might creep into the conversation and have the same effect.

5. *Discipline should be for a specific act.* Punishment that is only for general reasons is resented and the person punished does not learn what he or she did that was wrong. Supervisors should always specify for what act the employee is being disciplined.

6. *Punishment should be a learning experience.* Punishment for punishment's sake is not necessarily a learning experience for either party. This is why punisment for revenge purposes seldom improves behavior. The subordinate must learn *why* the behavior is unacceptable, otherwise it may occur again.

7. *Disciplinary action should be intense.* This does not mean that punishment should always be harsh (though it might in some cases), but rather its impact should be felt over a relatively short period of time. Remember when you were a teen-ager and your parents grounded you for three weeks for doing something wrong? Over the three weeks your resentment increased more and more as you suffered — unduly, you thought — for an interminable period of time. Since resentment can decrease learning value, extended periods of punishment are not recommended. Far better to let the axe fall all at once and then get on with improvement.

8. *Punishment should be applied the first time.* The tendency, both at home and at work, is to warn people about their behavior. Warning is recommended when people are learning right from wrong. Once this is accomplished, warning serves no useful purpose for either the supervisor

or the employee. If an act is not disciplined the first time it occurs (once learning is complete) the employee will resent being disciplined at some later date. There can even be a legal problem in some circumstances; there have been cases in which employees have won arbitration cases for a grievance filed on the grounds that they had been doing the same thing all along but were never disciplined.

9. *Be careful of the discipline reward.* Strange as it may sound, discipline is a positive experience for some. It may be that it draws attention to them, or reinforces a feeling that the supervisor is out to get them, or serves some other personal purpose. In any case, discipline will only make these problems worse, so they must be dealt with in a different way. One alternative is counselling, which is discussed in Chapter 18.

Combining Rewards and Punishments

The most effective systems for supervisors are those that use both rewards and punishments to control behavior. On the assumption that most employees do more things right than wrong, a system should be weighted toward the positive side. Not only does this help maintain the good behaviors of employees, but it also makes the discipline process more effective.

Unfortunately, many people are more adept at pointing out peoples' mistakes than recognizing when they are doing things right. Traditionally, managers have *assumed* that employees did their jobs well, and therefore concentrated on those few times when they did not. This practice can create an extremely negative climate in which employees feel

Discipline Me Again! Please!

The story is told about some social workers who visited a prison to study the behavior patterns of the inmates. One aspect of behavior they found most interesting was that the same inmates were being disciplined consistently. The worst punishment in the prison was The Hole, a small hole in the ground covered by a metal lid with a breathing apparatus. The worst disciplinary action at the prison was to send a prisoner to the hole for several days to be fed bread and water. The social workers reasoned that if the hole was so bad, why were the same people going back time after time? Subsequent analysis showed that living in the hole on bread and water was a status symbol for the informal leaders of the prison population. Whenever they felt their leadership waning, they committed an infraction of the rules so they could be sent to the hole. Surviving that ordeal increased their stature considerably. To solve the problem, the prison changed the diet from bread and water to baby food. The behavior problems stopped immediately. It seemed that to live in the hole on baby food was not a very rewarding experience.

that no one appreciates a job well done and everyone is always willing to point out mistakes.

There are some excellent lessons to be learned here from the area of Transactional Analysis (TA). The concepts in TA analyze the types of interactions (i.e., transactions) that occur between people, and the effect those transactions have on individuals. Terms such as *positive strokes* and *warm fuzzies* describe the pleasant or rewarding things we say to people, and *negative strokes* or *cold pricklies* are the negative or punishing comments.[1] The colorful terms themselves describe the effects they have on others. Some examples of each are:

- *Positive stroke.* "Thanks for meeting that deadline yesterday, Don. That really helped me out."
- *Negative stroke.* "Can't you ever do anything right? I don't know what I'm going to do with you!"
- *Mixed stroke.* "I noticed you were on time today. It's about time."

The theory of TA states that typically, most people receive far more negative strokes than positive ones and we therefore retaliate with negative strokes of our own to get even (to create a balanced transaction). Supervisors, therefore, can create a more positive work environment by

The One-Minute Manager

In their popular book, *The One-Minute Manager*,[2] authors Ken Blanchard and Spencer Johnson use reward system concepts in a unique way to describe a particular manager. They describe a manager who uses "one-minute goal-setting" (to clarify expectations), "one-minute praisings" (to reward performance), and "one-minute reprimands" (to discipline those who know better). Their point is that it doesn't take that much of a supervisor's time to manage people when rewards and punishments are used properly. They also make the point that a manager's major responsibility in managing people is to "catch people doing things right." By doing this a positive climate is established, employees enjoy learning and growing, and discipline is much more effective.

Interestingly, this philosophy sheds a different light on the term *close supervision*, which is often associated with a negative supervisory style. However, if the supervisor is closely supervising employees to "catch them doing things right," then few employees would ever object to close supervision. Clearly, the *quality* of time that a supervisor spends with employees is more important than the quantity.

1. Eric Berne, *Transactional Analysis in Psychothrapy* (New York: Grove Press, 1961).

2. Kenneth Blanchard and Spencer Johnson, *The One-Minute Manager*, (New York: William Morrow, 1981).

giving positive strokes when they are deserved, and using negative strokes sparingly.

Applying Rewards in Practice

In this final section several examples of rewards will be discussed with special consideration of how they should be applied in practice. Although no two situations are the same, the types of rewards discussed below are common to most organizations. The emphasis is upon the concerns the supervisor should have when using these rewards.

Using Money As a Motivator

As we have noted on several occasions, many supervisors do not have control over salaries. This is unfortunate since, properly used, money can be an effective incentive. For those supervisors who can control employees' pay, there are certain principles that should be kept in mind.

Regardless of who controls pay, it is frequently not a good motivator because its application violates the principles already discussed in this chapter. The most common error is violation of the contingency principle, that is, pay does not affect behavior because it is not contingent upon performance. A monthly salary, for example, is contingent only upon an employee remaining with the organization for a month. This may not have much to do with performance on the job. In fact, any pay system that is based upon the passage of time will generally not affect behavior, except to encourage people to maintain some minimally acceptable level of performance to avoid being fired.

As the principles discussed earlier indicate, money can be a motivator if (a) it is contingent upon behavior, (b) the amount involved is large enough, (c) the effort required is seen as fair, (d) the employees desire more money, and (e) employees can control the behavior that affects their pay. An example of a situation in which the supervisor might use these principles would be in discretionary or merit increases. The organization might give the supervisor either a pool of discretionary funds or a range of increases that could be given to each employee. The supervisor could then use the above principles to decide on the merit pay.

Recognition As a Reward

One of the most effective methods of rewarding subordinates is through recognition. Informal means of recognition are completely within the control of the supervisor and can therefore be applied without anyone else's approval. They frequently cost nothing except the supervisor's time.

One of the reasons recognition is so powerful is that most everyone needs it. In the previous chapter the discussion of Maslow's hierarchy of needs pointed out how the ego (or status) needs can be a dominant motivational force today. Recognition for good performance is one way of satisfying that need.

Recognition can take many forms. It can be a compliment to a worker about his or her performance, a memo to other department members recognizing an achievement of a fellow employee, an Employee of the Month program, or any other method that recognizes the individual worth and achievements of employees.

The major caveat to using recognition as a reward is that it must be sincere, real, and focused on the behavior being recognized. Telling someone he or she has done a good job when that is not true makes the supervisor appear a fool. Overusing the recognition strategy also reduces its value. Not only does overuse risk reaching the employees' saturation point, but too much recognition probably means that much of it is phoney. For example, Employee of the Month programs often lose their value if it becomes obvious that sooner or later everyone will be employee of the month.

A Warm Fuzzy

My feeling is that in general, people have difficulty giving "warm fuzzies" to others, especially at work. There may be cultural reasons for this (for example, the Latin Americans are much more open with their feelings), but I think a more important reason is simply that we don't practice it enough. Therefore, I always try to give supervisors practice at it whenever possible. At the close of a three-day supervisory training program several years ago, I ended with a practice session in giving warm fuzzies. I asked each participant to reflect for a moment about the person sitting to the right. I then told them we would close the program with each person, one at a time, turning to that person and paying a sincere compliment. As would be expected, the first person had considerable trouble and stumbled through in an embarrassed manner. They got better, however, as we went around the room. As we got close to the end, one of the participants had the opportunity to give the warm fuzzy to a fellow supervisor who worked for the same organization. He spoke for about two minutes, though it seemed much longer to the rest of us. His comment was warm, sincere, and specific. He said he admired how effective the man was at his job and made a specific reference to one of his recent major accomplishments. The other supervisor's reaction was a surprise to us all. He began crying — not openly weeping, but we all could see his eyes get a little misty as he thanked his colleague for what he said was the best warm fuzzy he had ever received. The sad part of this story is that his fellow supervisor was the first person ever to comment on his recent personal achievement.

Job Assignments As Rewards

Another type of reward usually within a supervisor's control is job assignment. Although union contracts can be restrictive regarding job assignments, there often is some room for the supervisor to maneuver. The manner in which job assignments can be used varies considerably. An employee might be assigned complete control over an area of responsibility if previous performance indicates he or she can handle it. There may be some plum tasks available that the supervisor can assign on a contingency basis, or jobs with higher prestige, more freedom, or other perks that might be attractive.

As is the case with any reward, using job assignments as an incentive means the supervisor might be accused of playing favorites. As long as the supervisor plays favorites according to accepted performance criteria, this should be considered a normal cost associated with using reward systems properly. However, supervisors should recognize that not everyone will see this as fair and will perceive favoritism by the supervisor.

Making Performance Appraisals Rewarding

Chapter 18 contains a more complete discussion of **performance appraisal,** the periodic evaluation of performance, but the topic is very relevant to the concept of developing good reward systems. Experience suggests that performance appraisals are frequently unpleasant for both supervisor and employee. This can change, however, if the principles of reward systems are applied to the performance appraisal process.

It seems that the most frequently violated reward principle is the

Exercise 8.2

Identifying Potential Rewards

Several examples of rewards supervisors might use have been presented in this section. In practice, there are many different types of rewards and it only takes a little creative thinking to identify some.

This exercise requires you to do some brainstorming, i.e. think of as many different rewards that supervisors would have available to influence subordinates. If you are in a group setting, you may use the group's creativity to generate the list. Most groups come up with as many as forty or fifty different rewards!

timing principle. Most organizations schedule performance appraisals on an annual basis. This means that the supervisor is appraising behavior that may have occurred a year ago! One can imagine the conflicts and bad feelings that would result from this type of appraisal. A more effective approach is to *appraise performance when it occurs.* This means the supervisor should be communicating with subordinates about their performance on an ongoing basis, in a process separate from the annual, formal performance appraisal program. If communication is open and ongoing during the year, then the annual appraisal process becomes a summary of all that has occurred, and is more a record-keeping summary and not part of the behavioral reward system.

A second problem is that performance appraisals can tend to dwell on the negative at the expense of the subordinate's good points. Even if the positive and negative are 50-50, this still is not an accurate portrayal of most people's behavior patterns. Most of us do far more things right than wrong. This negative climate puts the subordinate on the defensive and the appraisal interview frequently ends up in a heated argument.

Another common problem is that subordinates are often not aware of where they are going wrong. With little or no feedback about their performance, except on an annual basis, they have no choice except to proceed on their own. Finding out they have not performed as expected can be a very negative experience.

One final point is worth noting. Effective performance appraisal requires great skill on the part of supervisors. Like any skill, it requires practice and if you only do it once a year you won't be very good at it.

A Set-Up for Failure

One of my former students called me one day about a year after her graduation and asked to speak to me about a problem she had. It seemed that she had recently received her first performance appraisal and had been rated extremely low by her supervisor. She felt she had been treated unfairly and disagreed with her evaluation. Her side of the story (which I assumed to be mostly true) was that when she was hired and placed in the department she was given no direction at all. She was given a job description that was five years old and told that was what she was to be doing. She was virtually left on her own for a year except for occasional meetings with the supervisor for budgetary approval. The essence of her supervisor's criticisms was that she had failed to set objectives, had not integrated her work with department priorities, and had failed to maintain satisfactory relationships with others. My ex-student was upset because for the entire year she felt she was doing an excellent job. My advice to her was to voice her concerns to her supervisor and her supervisor's supervisor and follow up these conversations with a written letter. She did this and it seemed to take care of that particular situation; the supervisor agreed to change the performance evaluation. However, the personal relationship between the two became so strained that my student quit six months later.

Key to Success

The degree of control that supervisors have over their employees will largely depend upon (a) how many and what kind of rewards are available to the supervisor, and (b) how these rewards are used. Diminished authority in many supervisory roles has made the effective use of those remaining rewards more important than ever. Supervisors cannot help but influence their employees' behavior, either positively or negatively. Understanding reward systems and how they can be used can create a positive behavioral climate which increases productivity as well as the satisfaction of employees.

The first step for supervisors is to identify the rewards available. The list is often longer than most people think. Some rewards will be extrinsic and some intrinsic, but many can be used in some way by supervisors. The key is to identify what specific rewards motivate each individual and then to create a contingency relationship between desired behavior and the reward. It is dangerous to assume that subordinates know what behavior the supervisor wants. They should be told and told in no uncertain terms. When that behavior occurs, it should be rewarded in some fashion.

The best reward systems are those in which everyone wins. If a supervisor rewards subordinates for good performance, the system is not completed until the supervisor is rewarded as well. These rewards could come either from subordinates or from higher management — but ideally from both. Just as parents need strokes from their children once in a while, supervisors need the occasional stroke from their employees. Perhaps we need a bumper sticker that reads something like "Have You Hugged Your Supervisor Today?"

Summary

This chapter has described the theory and application of reward systems and suggested several ways that supervisors can increase their effectiveness through the proper application of rewards and punishments. The basic concepts are (a) rewards must be contingent upon behavior, (b) employees must be aware of what the contingency relationship is, (c) rewards should follow behavior as quickly as is feasible, (d) the size of the reward should reflect the effort it takes to achieve it except in the case of token rewards, (e) rewards should always take into account individual differences, (f) rewards should be consistently administered between employees and through time, and (g) supervisors should concentrate on the rewards over which they have control.

An important part of any reward system is the discouragement of certain behavior, that is, the application of punishments to create effective discipline. This chapter discussed the purpose of discipline, when to use it, how to use it, and when not to use it.

Reward systems are most effective when a proper combination of rewards and punishments are used to influence behavior. Rewards available to the supervisor include recognition, job assignments, and occasionally money. All of these can be important influences on behavior if the basic reward system principles are met.

Performance appraisals, one of the formal reward systems in organizations, can be made more effective by using the principles discussed in this chapter. Appraising performance, both bad and good, when it occurs is one method of improving the process.

Opening Incident Revisited

George Friesen has made what should now be some pretty obvious mistakes in dealing with this performance problem. It is not surprising that Starke is upset. Whether or not this becomes a union matter is now relatively immaterial. The important point is that the learning value of Friesen's comments have been lost because the situation has been handled poorly.

First, Friesen should not have waited until the last day of the probationary period to talk to Starke about his concerns. Presumably, he has had this information for some time now. Why wait this long to tell Starke? Had he told Starke of this when it first occurred, Starke would have had time to improve his performance (if, indeed there really is a problem). As it stands now, Friesen has no choice but to request that the probationary period be extended or to dismiss Starke.

Friesen has also made a mistake in talking about Starke's attitude problem. By doing this, he is criticizing Starke as a person rather than concentrating on his behavior. Starke will resent this and it will reduce the learning value of the conversation considerably. In other words, he will dwell on his negative feelings toward Friesen rather than on improving his performance.

Starke's reaction is predictable given that Friesen has mentioned only his shortcomings. Isn't Starke doing *something* right? He probably is, but Friesen neglects to mention those factors. This annoys Starke even more and increases his dislike for Friesen.

And finally, it has never been established that there is a performance problem. Friesen obviously thinks so, but we have no evidence that Starke knows about it. If Starke doesn't agree that there is a problem, then there will likely not be any change. If Friesen had spoken to Starke when he first thought there might be a problem, then the two of them could have talked about it under much better circumstances. Friesen may have found out that Starke was not aware he was taking longer than normal on some jobs, and that there was more information available on the customer relations issue. As it is now, Starke will feel that the feedback has been very one-sided.

Review Questions

1. Why is the contingency principle important for reward systems to be effective?
2. What is the awareness principle?
3. How does the timing of a reward affect behavior?
4. What is the size principle?
5. What is the type principle?
6. What are tangible and intangible rewards?
7. What are intrinsic and extrinsic rewards?
8. What is the consistency principle?
9. What is the control principle?
10. When should punishment be used by supervisors?
11. When should punishment not be used by supervisors?
12. What are the essential characteristics of using effective discipline?
13. What are positive, negative, and mixed strokes?
14. What conditions must be present for money to be a motivator?
15. What kinds of rewards are available for use by supervisors?
16. Why is recognition usually an important reward?
17. How might the principles of effective reward systems be used to make performance appraisal systems more effective?

Chapter Glossary

Reward systems.	The formal and informal methods used by organizations and managers to influence behavior toward goals. Involves the application of rewards and punishments to shape behavior.
Contingency principle.	Reward system principle that states that rewards received by employees should be tied to specific behaviors, that is, rewards should depend upon performance.
Awareness principle.	Reward system principle that states that employees must know which behaviors will be rewarded by the system or supervisor.
Timing principle.	Reward system principle that states that rewards should follow behavior as quickly as is feasible. Long time periods reduce the effectiveness of the contingency principle.
Size principle.	Reward system principle that states that the size of the reward should match the effort or achievement as closely as possible.

Type principle.	Reward system principle that states that rewards must consider individual differences. Not all people find the same things to be rewarding.
Tangible rewards.	Rewards that have a physical property to them, such as money, trophies, etc.
Intangible rewards.	Rewards that are psychological in nature and do not have a physical property attached to them. Examples are compliments or look of approval.
Extrinsic rewards.	Rewards administered by someone other than the person being rewarded, such as a boss or organization.
Intrinsic rewards.	Self-administered rewards, such as personal satisfaction in doing a job well.
Consistency principle.	Reward system principle that states that the administration of rewards should be consistent over time and between individual employees. The same behaviors should be rewarded for all people.
Control principle.	Reward system principle that states that supervisors should be concerned only with the rewards over which they have control, and these rewards should be emphasized and used effectively.
Punishment.	The application of an unpleasant consequence following an undesirable behavior. Can be an effective determinant of behavior if used properly.
Strokes.	Transactional Analysis term for applying interpersonal rewards such as a compliment. Positive strokes, negative strokes, or mixed strokes can be applied. Probably derived from the phrase "stroking the ego."
Performance appraisal.	Evaluation of the performance of a subordinate. Can be formal (such as the regular performance review) or informal (as when the supervisor communicates his or her evaluation of performance on an ongoing basis).

Case Problem

First Federal Savings & Loan

The First Federal Savings & Loan is a relatively large organization employing almost a thousand people in several locations throughout the city. In recent years, the company has noticed a significant increase in absenteeism, particularly in the clerical and nonmanagerial ranks. Although there is no direct cash expense associated with the problem, the supervisors and managers have expressed annoyance at constantly having to find someone to fill in for an absent employee. Most attribute the cause of the problem to the generous sick leave policy (20 paid sick days per year).

For some time there have been discussions regarding possible ways of reducing the absenteeism. The executive committee of the company has agreed to entertain solutions from all managers and then decide which, if any, should be implemented. It was announced at one of the managers' meetings recently that supervisors and managers should write up their ideas and submit them to the executive committee.

After several weeks the suggestions were collected and distributed to all managers and supervisors. There was some duplication among the ideas, but the following list is representative of the recommendations:

1. Abolish the present sick leave policy and have no paid sick leave except for individuals who produce a medical certificate.

2. Reduce the number of paid sick days from twenty down to some lower number (most recommended ten but a few suggested it be as low as five).

3. Leave the sick leave policy alone but point out to employees the problems associated with high absenteeism.

4. Start a demerit system in which sick days taken would be tabulated and translated into demerits. These demerits would then be used in other decisions such as promotions, transfers, and layoffs.

5. Allow employees to trade sick days not taken for vacation days. After a year, unused sick days could be used as vacation days the following year on a ratio of 2:1 (one vacation day for every two sick days).

6. Create a new policy that would state that any absent employee who was discovered not to be sick would be fired.

7. Have a cash bonus system in which employees who had a perfect attendance record for the year would be awarded $100 cash.

8. Publish the names of those with perfect attendance records in the monthly company newsletter.

9. Establish a lottery in which every employee with perfect attendance for the week would be eligible for a draw for $10.

Questions for Discussion

1.   Which of these proposals do you think would be the most effective? Why?
2.   Can you think of a better method?

Working with Groups

9

Chapter Learning Objectives

After reading and studying this chapter you should be able to:

1. List the reasons why an understanding of work groups is important for the supervisor.

2. List and explain the reasons why employees form work groups.

3. Explain and identify group norms operating in a group.

4. Explain the role of informal group leaders.

5. Explain the differences between formal and informal group leaders.

6. Describe the concept of group cohesiveness and explain how the supervisor can make a group more cohesive.

7. Explain the nature and purpose of the informal organization and how the supervisor might use it.

8. List and explain several ways a supervisor might build a more effective team.

9. Suggest several ways supervisors could use group concepts to have more effective meetings.

10. Describe the concept of group decision making and how a supervisor could use it.

11. Explain how the supervisor can work through informal leaders.

12. Suggest five ways a supervisor can influence group norms.

Key Terms

Work group
Formal work group
Informal work group
Work to rule
Group norms
Informal group leader
Group cohesiveness

Informal organization
Team building
Groupthink
Group decision making
Consensus
Quality circles

201

Changing Norm

Charlie Cox just took over the Accounts Receivable Department of the company, having been transferred from a similar department elsewhere in the company. One of his first instructions from his manager was to "solve that coffee break problem." It seems that under the previous supervisor, things got pretty lax and the fifteen-minute coffee breaks stretched out to twenty to twenty-five minutes on a regular basis. Complaints have been received from other departmental supervisors because their employees wonder why they cannot take long coffee breaks as well.

Charlie has watched the situation for about a week, and it is clear that Norm Davidson is the basic cause. It is Norm who seems to suggest when it is time to go for coffee, and no one leaves the coffee room until he does. Also, it is apparent that this practice has been going on for several years. Charlie's previous experience with work groups left him with the impression that they can be difficult to deal with. On the other hand, he feels that if he could change Norm, the rest of the group will be easier to deal with.

The problem he faces is how to change Norm.

Understanding group behavior is especially important to a first-line supervisor. Although supervisors must manage individuals, these individuals will invariably belong to one or more groups that will have an effect upon the individual's behavior. Lack of understanding of *why* and *how* groups affect individual behavior can cause problems for supervisors, and attempts to solve these problems on an individual basis can be ineffective and frustrating.

This chapter will show why the supervisor should be concerned with groups. Some fundamental group concepts will be explained and related to some typical problems that supervisors might encounter. Finally, we shall explore some ways that the supervisor might use group concepts to improve group satisfaction and productivity.

The Role of Work Groups

Except in rare instances, every supervisor will encounter work groups in the organization. In fact, it is difficult to imagine an organization functioning without work groups. Most of them contain between two and twenty members, although larger ones will exist in some circumstances. Each of these groups will have a supervisor who must understand group behavior.

What Is a Work Group?

To understand groups we must first understand their properties. Groups exist everywhere and all have some properties in common, but work groups are special because of their potential power on the job, which can affect productivity as well as the effectiveness of the supervisor.

As far as this book is concerned, a **work group** *is any set of two or more people who are working toward a common objective and are in physical proximity with each other.* This means that two people working in different areas of the same physical plant would not form a work group, even though they may be working toward the same overall objective. In other words, some degree of social interaction is required for the group processes to operate. Similarly, people can be physically close to one another, such as a crowd in a shopping center, but because they have no common goal they are not a group.

Other factors affect group processes, such as how much time the group spends together, how large the group is, and how stable the membership is. As a general rule, the more time spent together, the smaller the group, and the more stable the membership, the more the group will act as one. Later we shall explore this important aspect of groups—called *cohesiveness*—in greater detail.

Groups also can be categorized as formal or informal. **Formal work groups** are defined by the authority structure and work procedures designed by the organization itself. Therefore, all employees working under a common supervisor belong to the formal work group. **Informal work groups**, however, are defined by the group members, and are not bound by official lines of authority. The informal group may extend beyond the boundaries of the work unit, or more than one group may exist within a formal work group. Figure 9.1 shows how the formal and informal groups may differ. This chapter will emphasize the informal work groups and the formal groups will only be noted when an important difference occurs that would affect supervisors.

Why Do Workers Form Groups?

Employees form informal groups for many different reasons. Among the more common ones are security, friendship, recognition, and support.

SECURITY. "Strength in numbers" describes one of the primary reasons why workers join groups. The group protects the individual from outsiders and gives him or her a feeling of belonging. Few people can function without the security of a group since groups provide a degree of certainty and predictability in interpersonal relationships.

The type of security provided by the group can include economic, social, physical, and psychological security. From an economic stand-

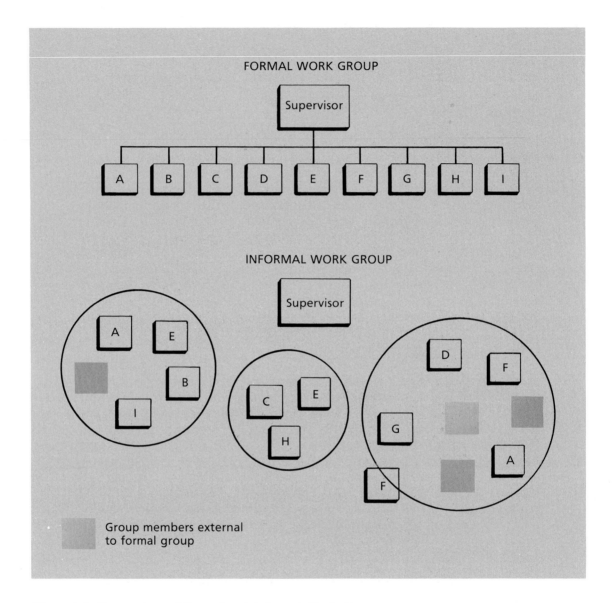

Figure 9.1. Comparison of Formal and Informal Work Groups.

point, groups can protect the individual from loss of earnings or even loss of a job, as in the case of unions protesting layoffs or dismissals. Groups have been known to carry some members by compensating for their weaknesses or covering for them when they are unable to bear their share of the load. Group pressure can force some high producers to reduce their effort in order to protect the group from the negative effects of overproduction. In the classic Hawthorne studies conducted at Western Electric Company during the early part of this century, it was found that groups exerted considerable influence upon the productivity of individual members. If someone produced above the level the group considered acceptable, he was labeled a ratebuster and pressure was exerted on him to reduce production. One of the ways this was accomplished was by a process known as 'binging,' giving the ratebuster a sharp rap on the arm. After several 'bings', the ratebuster got the idea and reduced his output. The interesting point of this study was that the workers really did not know what would happen if they produced considerably above or below their normal level of output. They did know, however, that consistent deviation from standard would attract management's attention and they assuredly wanted to avoid that.

Groups also offer psychological security to members. People tend to need to know that their behavior is acceptable to others and will either seek out groups that will reinforce their behavior, or will adapt their behavior to that required by the group. People become anxious when they have to interact with others whose values, attitudes, and objectives are significantly different, so workers form groups based upon these important characteristics.

For similar reasons, groups offer individuals security in their social relationships on the job. The close ties that often occur in groups provide the social satisfaction that is frequently necessary to individuals. The importance of these relationships is made apparent by the number of people who continue their social contacts off the job. The stability provided by a strong group can be a major factor in determining productivity levels of a group.

FRIENDSHIP.   Many people belong to groups to form friendships with other members. It was noted in Chapters 5 and 6 that social needs can be an important motivator and this motivation is often manifested by the strong social ties found in groups. It is not surprising that strong

How Groups Can Influence Individuals

Recently, one of my students conducted a research project that illustrated the importance of groups quite well. A labor strike occurred at a manufacturing company and the student decided to write a paper on the attitudes of the strikers. The newspaper had reported that ninety-five percent of the employees had voted in favor of the strike by a show of hands at a union meeting. The student interviewed a sample of the employees individually and was surprised to learn that very few of them were in favor of the strike!

social ties are formed in work groups, since employees spend a considerable amount of their waking hours in the company of the same group. In some cases, because jobs have been designed to minimize the skill required, social satisfaction is one of the few motivators left, so these friendships — and the activities associated with them — acquire considerable importance for the employees.

RECOGNITION.   Small groups are also attractive to individuals because of the potential for recognition they offer. In large groups — or alone — there is little opportunity for recognition. A person may feel that he or she is treated like a number in large groups and that unique individual qualities are not recognized. In the small work group, there is considerable opportunity for individual recognition. In sports teams, for example, individual accomplishment is praised by teammates as well as by fans. On the job, individual behavior that is ignored by the larger organization can be the center of attention for the small group. One person may be the best joke-teller, another a skillful bowler, another a new father or mother. In each case, the group will provide the individual attention and recognition that individuals need. It is not uncommon, for example, for some work groups to celebrate members' birthdays or other significant personal events.

SUPPORT.   The supportive function of groups recognizes that formal systems at work are not perfect. For example, formal communication does not always tell what is *really* going on, jobs are never perfectly designed, tools and equipment are never perfectly suitable for the task, and so on. Consequently, employees require considerable support in coping with the realities of everyday organizational life. While it would be expected that employees would turn to their supervisor for such support, that is often not the case. For all the reasons listed previously, the work group becomes the major source of support.

Some common examples of the supportive function of groups are:

- providing important information to group members through the grapevine;
- improving work methods to reduce the effort required to meet standards of performance;
- assisting group members in learning jobs;
- covering for members when they cannot cope with their responsibilities;
- offering emotional support to the individual experiencing difficulties;
- socializing of new employees to make them aware of how the organization operates.

THE POSITIVE ROLE OF GROUPS. As the preceding list indicates, work groups can perform many positive functions. In fact, many organizations should be glad that work groups function as they do. One of the best examples of how groups contribute to productivity can be seen when groups decide to **work to rule**. When a group works to rule, it is really saying that it will no longer perform a supportive role in the organization, and will do precisely as the formal system says it should do — nothing more and nothing less. Given the imperfections that always exist in formal systems, this can create chaos. Consider, for example, the problems created when the air traffic controllers, post office employees, police officers, or other public employees work to rule. While these are large groups, the same effect occurs in companies when work groups decide not to perform their supportive role.

To sum up, people form informal work groups for many different reasons, and no single reason is more important than another. The reasons for forming groups will always be present, although the strength of any particular reason will vary from situation to situation. In any case, the supervisor will not be able to prevent groups from forming unless, of course, employees are prohibited from interacting with each other. The emphasis of this chapter is upon understanding why they form so that supervisors can use the energy and motivation that characterizes these groups and channel their efforts toward increased productivity.

Important Group Concepts

Although all groups are different, they nevertheless have certain common properties. It is these common properties that have significance for supervisors, as they are the key to understanding and managing groups effectively.

Group Norms

The most important characteristic of groups, **group norms** are the standards of behavior that are accepted by the group and are required of group members. Supervisors must constantly deal with group norms because they determine the collective behavior of the members. For closely knit groups, some norms are readily observable (a code of dress, for example), but others may be more subtle. A supervisor might know that a closely knit group has clear norms of behavior, but may not know exactly what those norms are. Also, some norms may be important to a supervisor (such as a productivity norm, for example) but others may have little direct bearing on work activities, such as who eats lunch with whom.

Norms are the means by which groups control the behavior of their members. Norms are communicated and enforced (as with binging) and those who do not conform to the group's norms are excluded from the group itself. Note, however, that the excluded ones may remain *physically* part of the group even though they are *socially* excluded. For example, even though eight employees might work together in an office, only five might be in the group. The other three may, for a variety of reasons, decide not to adhere to the group norms and are therefore psychologically and socially excluded from the group.

Norms can pertain to virtually any type of behavior, such as manner of dress, production levels, social activities, or personal objectives, to name but a few. Although norms tend to remain relatively constant, they can change over time, especially if group members change. Normal turnover in a group can appreciably affect norms, as would the loss of one of the more important members of the group.

It is important to understand that norms, though important influences upon individual behavior, are not consciously decided by the group. That is, the establishment of group norms is not a formal process in most situations. Norms are set through the social processes that occur as the group members interact with one another. While the supervisor can have an impact upon group norms, the norms themselves develop to a large extent from the group, not the managers of the group. Later in this chapter we shall discuss how a supervisor might attempt to change a group norm.

Group Leaders

Group leaders, also referred to as informal leaders or natural leaders, are an important part of working with groups. First, we have to draw the distinction between the **informal group leader** and the formal leader. The formal leader is the supervisor, or whoever has formal authority over the group. The informal leader is the individual to whom the group looks as most exemplifying the group's values and norms. The informal leader, therefore, can exert considerable influence over group members since, by definition, they hold the same values and norms to be important.

In practice, informal leaders often have more influence over group members than the supervisor. This is not surprising because informal leaders are chosen by their members whereas the supervisor is selected by another group (management). This can be a difficult situation for supervisors, who may see the informal leader as a challenge to their own authority. If the group's norms are contrary to the goals of the supervisor, the situation becomes worse. It is important for the supervisor to remember that there are *always* informal leaders and that they do not reflect upon the supervisor personally. It is important, therefore, that

Exercise 9.1

Identifying Your Group Norms

The definition of a group provided earlier clearly applies to your class. The class is a collection of individuals working toward a common objective, and the members are in reasonable physical proximity for an extended period of time. So your class will have developed norms of behavior.

This exercise requires that you do the following:

1. Divide into small groups of four to six members.
2. Discuss and decide what the norms of the class are at this point of your course. List these.*
3. Discuss and decide if different groups have formed around different norms, that is, are there subgroups in your larger group?
4. Have the norms of the class changed over the period you have been together? If so, how?
5. Discuss the norms identified by each of the discussion groups. Are the lists the same? Why or why not?

* One of the most common norms in a class is the seating arrangement. Even though many instructors do not assign seats, individuals tend to occupy the same seats. Is this the case in your class?

---

the supervisor learn to *use* the natural influence of the informal leader to achieve the unit's objectives. How this can be done will be discussed later in this chapter.

A question frequently asked by supervisors is, "Would it not be better if I were the informal leader of my work group?" The answer, strangely enough, is "no." The primary reason is that informal leaders owe their support to the group, whereas formal leaders owe their allegiance to the management (or shareholders). This means that the informal leader will behave in a manner that is in the group's best interests, whereas the supervisor must behave (and make decisions) in the organization's best interests. Also, as we noted in Chapters 2 and 3, supervisors must be held accountable for the performance of their managerial roles and being the informal leader of a group would jeopardize this accountability. It is important for the supervisor to be considered as excluded from the work group (although still a member of other groups), and thus in a position to be objective, as the role requires.

The difference between the informal and formal leaders of groups presents some interesting problems in many organizations. As Chapter 2 noted, it often happens that a group member is promoted to be supervisor of the work group. If this individual has been the informal leader of the group, he or she will (and should!) lose this position. But the transition can be difficult for many new supervisors because of the conflict between their new and old loyalties. The difficulty can be avoided to a large degree if informal leaders are promoted to positions *outside* their previous work groups. In any case, when informal leaders are promoted (or leave the group) new informal leaders will continue to emerge, as long as the group remains in existence.

Group Cohesiveness

Group cohesiveness refers to the team spirit of a group. In a very cohesive group, the members feel a strong attraction to each other and there is a lot of the *we* feeling. Group norms are widely shared in a cohesive group and outsiders are often seen as a threat. Groups develop cohesion over extended periods of time, once the social processes and interaction have had a chance to create acceptable norms of behavior.

At first glance, it may appear that supervisors should always try to create cohesive groups. There are times when group cohesion is a desirable factor, but this is not necessarily always true. For example, a cohesive group whose cohesion is based upon a norm of low productivity can create problems for a supervisor. If the supervisor attempts to increase productivity, the group may become more cohesive (as groups often do when threatened by an outsider) and resist the supervisor's requests more strongly.

Another cost incurred with cohesive groups is reduced flexibility in staffing. Inserting a new employee into these cliques can be difficult if the group finds that the new member does not adhere to the group norms. In cases where the norm relates to an uncontrollable factor (such as age or sex) there is little the new member can do to respect the group norms. In these instances the supervisor faces a difficult problem; to remove the employee because he or she doesn't "fit in" is managerially (and legally) an unsound move.

Cohesive groups can present another potential problem for supervisors. Since the power of the group is greater than the power of the individuals, resistance to change can be greatly magnified in a cohesive group. Even if the change negatively affects only one member, a cohesive group will tend to stand behind their member by presenting a united front against the change. In some cases, the resistance may not be overt but will be manifested in subtle ways. For example, a group may express resentment by allowing mistakes to occur even though the members know the mistakes should be corrected.

In general, the effects of group cohesion are to magnify both the

The Effects of a Move upon Group Productivity

One of Harvard Business School's most famous cases, "The Case of the Changing Cage," illustrates how important it is to understand cohesive groups. The case describes a work group of about ten clerks whose job was to file and retrieve canceled check vouchers in an insurance company. Because of the security associated with the vouchers, the work was performed in an enclosed room with a cage front. Morale was high in the group and productivity was satisfactory. The group engaged in quite a bit of horseplay and over the years clear norms of behavior emerged. For example, they used a side door to sneak out during the day to bring snacks into the cage. All of this came to an abrupt halt when the cage was moved. The new cage had no side door and the supervisor purposely removed the filing cabinets in front of the cage door so he could see in better. He outlawed the snack breaks and criticized the cage workers for keeping a messy work area. The cage workers resisted the change and began to sabotage the move. The supervisor was quite surprised when, at the end of the normal accounting period, a check on productivity showed that the unit was far below their previous performance levels and that the unfiled vouchers had been hidden in the cage workers' desk drawers.

positive and negative outcomes of supervisory decisions. Decisions perceived as good will have a proportionately greater positive effect upon productivity, and decisions perceived as bad will have correspondingly greater negative effects. Thus far we have dealt primarily with the potentially negative influence of cohesive groups; later in this chapter we shall show how supervisors can use cohesive groups to advantage.

The Informal Organization

Thus far we have concentrated on the behavior of small groups, which is the day-to-day contact for most supervisors. Similar processes occur, however, in the larger organization environment and this is referred to as the **informal organization.** In contrast to the formal organization (which consists of official policies, rules, job descriptions, and so forth), the informal organization structure describes how things *actually* happen. A humorous (but perhaps realistic) comparison of the formal and informal organizations is shown in Figure 9.2.

The informal organization is of considerable importance for supervisors. It also plays a supportive role in assisting in getting the work done. It is useful to view the informal organization as the real work-doing part of the organization. Things which supposedly cannot be accomplished officially are often done quite expeditiously in the informal system. For example, one supervisor may need some work done by another supervisor's department, but official policy states that departments must have a minimum of three days' notice for such work. A simple telephone call

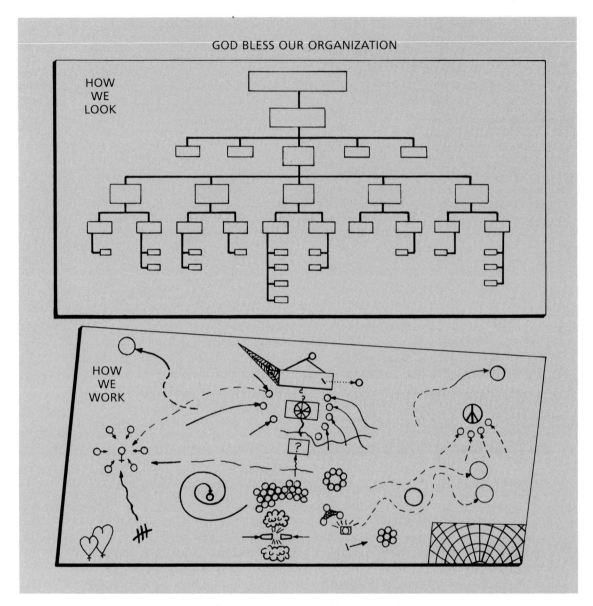

Figure 9.2. Comparison of the Formal and Informal Organization Charts. Reprinted by permission from Jerry L. Gray and Frederick A. Starke, *Organizational Behavior: Concepts and Applications* 2nd ed. (Columbus, OH: Charles Merrill, 1980), p. 205.

from one supervisor to his or her friend in the other department can often get the work done within hours.

The informal organization is characterized by a separate power sys-

The Need for an Organizational Credit Rating

In his popular course "Managing Management Time," William Oncken refers to the credit rating of managers, a concept which refers to the degree of positive relationships created by one manager with another. Oncken maintains that having a good credit rating with those upon whom you depend can save time for a manager. As an example of how to build up a *poor* credit rating, Oncken gives the example of a supervisor who calls the foreman of the shipping department and requests that a special shipment be placed on the dock so that he can pick it up immediately. The shipping department foreman goes to great lengths to comply with his request, including paying overtime to get the shipment on the dock. Two days later the shipment has not been picked up. You can imagine what will happen the next time the supervisor needs something from the shipping department! However, according to Oncken, begging and pleading are not necessary if you have a good credit rating in the organization. He advocates the conscious cultivation of the few people in the organization upon whom you depend. Developing these informal relationships can save you considerable time when you really need something from someone else.

tem (as opposed to authority system), communication system (the grapevine; see Chapter 10), and status system. A few examples follow.

1. Secretaries can acquire considerable power in informal systems because of the knowledge they acquire in their positions.
2. The son or daughter of the president has considerable influence over others even though his or her job may have little authority.
3. A vacant position is posted and candidates are interviewed. Frequently, the co-workers of the new employee know who the successful applicant is before the supervisor does.

Because of the inevitability of the informal organization, supervisors must learn to use it. This requires knowing who the powerful individuals are and being able to tap into the system. Interdepartmental cooperation is perhaps the best example. Most supervisors depend upon the cooperation of others to get their work done, and having good relations with those people can be crucial.

Applying Group Concepts

Knowing how and why groups behave as they do can make supervisors more effective managers of people. In this section, we discuss some specific strategies that supervisors can utilize to tap into the energy that is inherent in groups.

Team Building

Most supervisors would like their work group to act like a team. Implied in this statement is that group members should help one another, personality conflicts should be minimized, and the groups should work towards a common goal. **Team building** is not a haphazard process, and such behaviors do not happpen accidentally. Some of the more important factors that can affect the team spirit of a group are highlighted in the following discussion.

KEEP GROUPS SMALL. Large groups are more difficult to mold into teams since there are fewer opportunities for all members to interact. With small groups, however, individuals have greater opportunity to form close relationships with each other, thereby increasing the cohesion of the group as a whole. In small groups it is also easier for clear group norms to develop, a factor that is necessary for cohesion to occur.

CREATE OPPORTUNITIES FOR INTERACTION. If group members have little opportunity to interact it will be difficult for them to become cohesive. In some organizations, it is difficult for co-workers to interact because of noise on the job, the design of the work itself, or geographical separation. For example, it would be difficult for a sales supervisor to get the sales force to act as a team if each salesperson is located in a different part of the country. In some cases, it may be difficult for a supervisor to stimulate interaction on the job because the factors which determine interaction may be beyond his or her control. In these situations, the supervisor may have to initiate interaction off the job.

SHARE INFORMATION. One of the unique properties of effective teams is that members share information equally. There are no secrets, hidden agendas, or forked tongues operating in the group. Supervisors can assist in team development by sharing — with all members — information the group needs to perform its tasks. This act of openness can create a bond of trust between the supervisor and the group which can have a positive effect on group cohesiveness.

AVOID COMPETITION IN THE GROUP. Competition, while sometimes healthy for an organization, can destroy the team spirit in a group. It would be difficult, for example, to have employees act as a team if they are governed by an individual reward system. Sales supervisors frequently encounter this problem when they design a sales contest to motivate the sales force. If the prize goes to the one who sold the most, each salesperson is in competition with the others, and team spirit can be destroyed. The reward for being a good team member is to be a loser in the contest.

STIMULATE COMPETITION WITH OTHER GROUPS. While competition within the group can be unhealthy, competition between two different groups can increase the team spirit within each. We see this principle on a larger scale when two countries are at war; differences within each country are put aside as they concentrate on the enemy. The supervisor, of course, cannot create an enemy, but if one exists naturally, it can be used to improve cohesiveness. Care should be taken, of course, that the competition does not get out of hand and have a negative effect on the rest of the organization.

KEEP THE GROUP A GROUP. Depending upon the circumstances, supervisors can have some flexibility in creating the group feeling. For example, if the group has its own definable territory, this can contribute to cohesiveness. Also, the smaller the territory, the greater the cohesiveness. This means that the supervisor who wishes to increase the team spirit of the group should try to keep the group together as much as possible. The more they are spread out and the more their territory is open to others, the more difficult it will be to create a cohesive group.

MINIMIZE MEMBERSHIP CHANGES. The reasons for this are perhaps obvious, but it can be difficult because of the cause-and-effect relationship between cohesion and changes in group membership. The principle is that the fewer the changes in membership, the more cohesive the group can be. However, it is the cohesiveness of the group that will minimize membership changes. It is truly a chicken-and-egg problem. The best strategy for a supervisor is to emphasize the effective management of individuals in their jobs, so that turnover will be reduced to a minimum; if other processes in the group are managed effectively, the group spirit will maintain the cycle. Of course, there are some instances in which changes in membership not only cannot be avoided, but are desirable—such as promotions. In these instances the supervisor should encourage the turnover and place extra emphasis upon the replacement as described in the next section.

MATCH INDIVIDUAL ATTRIBUTES. Group cohesion occurs because the members find each other attractive. Therefore, team spirit can be enhanced if group members are chosen according to a common set of personal attributes. Care must be taken, however, since undue weighting on this dimension could result in hiring discrimination problems. This criterion must be used within the limits of proper hiring and placement practices.

Building Effective Work Teams

Team behavior and spirit are well exemplified by sports teams. By examining how sports teams are treated, we can learn some important lessons for supervision. While the specific activities will vary from sport to sport, in general the members of the team dress alike, travel together, sleep together, ride buses together, take showers together, practice together, eat together, and of course, work together. It should be no surprise that when individuals do all these things together, they will begin to act and think like a team. Not all of these can be used by supervisors, but there are some interesting possibilities.

TREAT THE GROUP LIKE A TEAM. This may sound like a simplistic statement, but closer examination shows important meaning. Groups will act like a team only if they are treated like a team. Each of the above factors describes one strategy of treating a group like a team. There are more subtle strategies, some of which are used in sports.

Meetings

One of the most common interactions between the supervisor and the group is the meeting. Running an effective meeting is an important skill for supervisors because unproductive meetings waste everybody's time and get little accomplished. Many people hate attending meetings, not because of any inherent dislike of meetings themselves, but rather because they have found them to be of little value. Understanding group processes can help supervisors turn meetings into positive and productive experiences for all.

One of the biggest barriers to effective meetings is the restraining influence of the group on the individual which makes members unwilling to voice their private opinions and ideas in the group setting. The supervisor may propose an idea, ask for reactions, and receive no feedback. The silence is taken as tacit approval of the idea, whereas in fact the participants at the meeting do not want to express their opinions in front of the group. One way of overcoming this problem is to ask individuals directly for their ideas rather than leaving participation to a volunteer effort. The supervisor can also encourage individual participation by creating a positive work climate on the job, such that employees see that he or she is open to suggestions and ideas. A negative, threatening work climate will usually be carried over to a meeting.

Another problem with meetings is referred to as **groupthink,** the tendency of the group to go along with itself and not question its own wisdom.[1] Instead of exploring new alternatives, groups with the groupthink problem spend most of their time justifying the decision already reached. The supervisor can combat this tendency (especially prevalent in cohesive groups) by appointing a devil's advocate to question the group's thinking. On the understanding that this is just a role to be played, the devil's advocate does not seriously jeopardize the group's team spirit. A healthy dose of skepticism is usually productive for a group. One precaution that the supervisor should take is to rotate the role regularly among group members.

A problem that can be frustrating for supervisors is the opposite of groupthink. Sometimes the conflict and disagreement is so pronounced that supervisors cease to hold meetings. Since this solution is not really a solution at all, it is well to know how destructive conflict can be avoided at meetings. Here an understanding of the informal organization is helpful. Many people have no outlet for their feelings and ideas except at meetings. Consequently, they take every opportunity to dominate the discussion and in some cases, even try to sabotage the meeting itself. Supervisors should realize that this is a sign that these people need to be listened to, and failure to do so creates problems for the rest of the group. Cultivating the informal organization to find out how people feel and what their concerns are, can save valuable time in meetings. The supervisor can meet with these people on an individual basis and iron out many of the difficulties before the meeting takes place. Often just listening to people will solve many of their concerns and make for more productive meetings. More on how to do this is contained in the following chapter on communication and in Chapter 18 on interviewing.

Group Decision Making

The thrust of this chapter has been that effective groups can make a positive contribution to productivity if they are well managed. Nowhere is this possibility more evident than in **group decision making.** It is widely recognized that under certain conditions, groups can exercise their creative talent to make better decisions than individuals. The task of the supervisor is to establish these conditions so that groups can reach their full potential.

The principles of effective group decision making generally arise when the supervisor invites group participation in a problem. By presenting the problem to the group the supervisor is attempting to increase both the *quality* and *acceptance* of the decision. The process of group decision making involves four principles:

1. Irving Janis, *Victims of Groupthink: A Psychological Study of Foreign Policy Decisions and Fiascos* (Boston: Houghton Mifflin, 1973).

1. The problem must be of importance to the group.
2. The supervisor, as the leader of the group, must ensure that each member's ideas are solicited.
3. The group seeks consensus in the decision.
4. Voting on the decision is not allowed.

Group decision making is based upon the theory that, when no expert exists, groups can generate more alternative solutions and therefore the probability is increased that a better decision will be reached. Up to the final decision, any member of the group has the right of veto: **consensus** is reached when the group has agreed that everyone, at minimum, can live with the decision. It should be emphasized that consensus within a group does not mean that everyone has to agree with or be enthusiastic about the decision. It simply means that no one is willing to veto the group's decision. Or, to put it in other words, not using the veto means that no one strongly disagrees with the decision. The reason why voting should not be used is that split votes divide the group into winners and losers. Since losers are likely not to be very committed to a decision in which they were outvoted, the implementation of the decision may be jeopardized. Using the consensus method, therefore, can improve not only the quality of the decision, but the commitment to it as well.

Group decision making is useful for meetings when the supervisor and subordinates must engage in joint problem solving. The method should not be used when (1) the supervisor is a recognized expert in the group, (2) time pressures prohibit group involvement, or (3) the group does not share the goals of the supervisor.

Working Through Informal Leaders

As we noted earlier in this chapter, informal leaders can be a valuable resource for supervisors. These people are often the key to motivating the group because of the influence they have over group members.

The first step, of course, is for the supervisor to identify the group leader. Research has indicated that some groups have two leaders, one known as the task leader and the other as the social leader. The informal task leader is the one who is most influential in matters pertaining to the work to be done, whereas the social leader performs more of a human relations function in the group. The task leader and social leader can be the same person, but that is unusual because the leadership skills required are different and are seldom found in one person. Assuming that two leaders do exist in the work group, the supervisor would deal with the task leader for work-related matters, and the social leader for other types of activities. Once the informal leader(s) is identified, the supervisor can make use of this leader's influence with the group. The informal leader can be a valuable source of information for the supervisor by communicating how the group feels about certain issues, what things they would like as a group, and so forth. The informal leader can also serve to stimulate upward communication from the group.

Another way the informal leader can be useful is for downward communication, although the supervisor would not want only this means of communicating with the group. For some situations, however, it may be wise to test the waters by discussing a problem or proposed change with the informal leader, suggesting that he or she talk the matter over with the rest of the group, and then receiving feedback from the group or informal leader.

Exercise 9.2

Do Groups Make Better Decisions Than Individuals?

As we noted in the text, groups can make better decisions than individuals, provided that certain conditions are met. This is an exercise that will allow you to understand how the process works and see if groups make better decisions than individuals. Fifteen occupations are listed in random order. Your task first is to rank them in order of occupational prestige, from the highest status occupation down to the lowest. Then form into groups of four to seven individuals and do the ranking again using the group decision method described in the text. When you have completed both steps, your instructor will give you the correct answers so that you may compare the individual and group methods.

Occupations

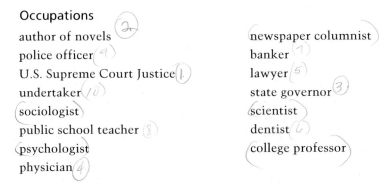

author of novels _2_
police officer _9_
U.S. Supreme Court Justice _1_
undertaker _10_
sociologist
public school teacher _8_
psychologist
physician _4_

newspaper columnist
banker _7_
lawyer _5_
state governor _3_
scientist
dentist _6_
college professor

Source: J. William Pfeiffer and John E. Jones, *Structured Experiences for Human Relations Training*, Vol. 2, (University Associates Press, 1970). Data based upon 1963 survey in the United States.

Saved by the Informal Leader

How to work successfully through informal leaders is a lesson some of us must learn the hard way. Several years ago I was in charge of a project that involved the coordination of two different groups. Since we all had the same objective, I saw little need to involve others in the decision process. Figuring that I would save everyone considerable time, I forged ahead making all the decisions. About two weeks prior to the close of the project, I heard a rumor that some of the people in one group were unhappy with what had been planned. Since I had done my job so well, I couldn't believe that someone could be unhappy, so I checked with the informal leader of the group to make sure. For about thirty minutes he filled my ear with the concerns and feelings of his group. After I listened to their concerns and we worked out a few compromises to satisfy their wants, he left saying, "I'll deliver their cooperation."

Involving the informal leader in decision making can make subsequent acceptance of the decision more likely. Of course there is no guarantee that the informal leader will agree with the supervisor's decision, so compromise is usually required to gain some acceptance. But the alternative, that of trying to sell the decision to the group, is generally less attractive because of potential resistance.

If all this sounds terribly manipulative, it probably is to some degree —but in a positive sense. It should be remembered that informal leaders like to have influence over their groups. It gives them satisfaction and reinforces their feelings of importance. Therefore, when you put the informal leader in a position where he or she can use the natural influence processes available, you are satisfying a very important need of the group. Manipulation in the negative sense would occur if you attempted to get the informal leader and the group to do something they naturally would not do anyway. Using secrecy or false information to influence the group would also be negative manipulation.

Importance of Social Interaction

We have come a long way in organizations over the last decades. There was a time when any form of social interaction on the job was forbidden. Employees were expected to work a complete day (often twelve hours) and it was believed that if they were talking on the job, they were not working. Unfortunatey, some traditional supervisors today still hold to these beliefs and think that if they can eliminate the social aspects of work, productivity will improve.

Our contemporary view of social interaction is that, within limits, it actually contributes to productivity. We recognize that employees have many needs that must be satisfied on the job, among those the need for social contact and stimulation. Understanding the importance of groups shows how social interaction can contribute to productivity.

Although most organizations allow coffee and rest breaks, the primary purpose of these is not to drink coffee and rest. If that were true, then employees would welcome having coffee at their work stations and private rooms in which to rest. Closer examination reveals that the major purpose of these breaks is for employees to satisfy their social needs. It is now understood that employees occupying relatively boring and unchallenging jobs need a greater amount of social interaction than others (notice that company presidents do not normally take coffee breaks). A supervisor who attempts to suppress social interaction on the job may actually be hindering productivity in situations where employees need a break from their routine.

Notice the qualification *within limits.* No one would advocate that social interaction occur constantly on the job. Nevertheless, a certain level of social interaction should not only be tolerated, it should be encouraged. The task of supervisors is to decide the level of interaction that does not detract from productive behavior.

Changing Group Norms

Changing group norms is decidedly not an easy process. It should be remembered that it is the group who decides what the norms are, not the supervisor. In other words, by definition group norms are the norms of the group, not the supervisor. The supervisor may attempt to establish a new norm, but it will be the group who will decide whether or not it becomes a norm. The best the supervisor can do, therefore, is to create the conditions under which changes in norms generally occur. The most common norm that supervisors wish to change is a productivity norm, as when the group norm is not to produce above a certain level. Changing this norm will be the focus of this discussion, but the general process will be the same for any norm. Five strategies can be effective in changing a group norm.

1. *Change the reward system.* Norms develop because certain behaviors are rewarding to the group. If external rewards change—either in type or in magnitude—different behaviors will be reinforced.

2. *Change interaction patterns.* Since norms are the result of patterns of employee interaction, changing these patterns can affect norms. This would normally mean redesign of jobs, workflows, and/or reporting relationships.

3. *Change group members.* Breaking a group up through transfers or attrition can affect norms. If new members are brought in, they can be socialized to a new set of norms.

4. *Adding new members.* For organizations in a state of growth, a

less painful method of changing norms is simply to add new members to the existing group. If enough new members are added, they can change the norm.

5. *Remove the informal leader.* Easier said than done, but to transfer, promote, or otherwise get rid of the informal leader will change the norms. If the person who sets and supports the norms is removed, there is greater opportunity for a new norm to develop.

Changing a group norm, particularly if it is a strong one, is a slow and sometimes painful process. Groups do not easily give up their valued ways of doing things. Supervisors must exhibit considerable patience and understanding when consciously attempting to change a group norm. The group will need an unusual amount of support in adapting to the new requirements and the supervisor will be responsible for providing that support. Punitive methods of changing norms can also work, but often at a very high cost.

Quality Circles

One of the most recent applications of group processes, this is a technique popularized by the Japanese. Its proven success has caused many North American companies to adopt the technique as well. There is nothing about quality circles that could not be applied on an individual basis as well, but the group method is more effective because of the inherent properties of groups.

Based largely upon the principles of group decision making, **quality circles** involve employees meeting in groups to discuss quality defects and methods to eliminate them. The groups usually consist of employees who work together so the orientation toward quality is an extension of the everyday work group. The group concept appears to work well because (1) well-managed groups can make better decisions and recommendations than the average individual, (2) quality problems are often caused by improper job and workflow design and the group is better equipped to see the total picture, (3) the group meetings also satisfy social needs, and (4) participation by the group in any methods changes will increase the likelihood of acceptance.

Not all quality circle programs are successful. It appears that when they are unsuccessful, one of the major reasons is the first-line supervisor. Managing a quality circle group requires strong interpersonal and behavioral skills which many supervisors lack. Some feel threatened by the group and are not able to give the group the autonomy it needs. Companies often fail to understand these problems and do not give their supervisors the proper training to make the groups effective. In sum, for these quality circles to achieve their potential, the climate of the organization must be positive and management must be trained in understanding how groups operate.

Key to Success

In one sense, groups are the central focus of energy in an organization. Organizations hire individuals, but human nature causes them to join informal groups, which can make measurable changes in their behavior. To be effective managers of people, supervisors must understand group processes and how they can be used.

Groups can be changed or they can adapt to the demands of the supervisor, but over the short run, the supervisor must learn to use the natural forces within the group. The power of groups to resist can overcome most pressures forthcoming from a single supervisor, and many times has been the cause of the supervisor's failure. Knowing how to utilize the energy and motivation inherent in a group not only makes the supervisor more efficient (cohesive groups manage themselves, you know) but also more effective at achieving the unit's objectives.

Group concepts have many useful applications for supervisors. The supervisor who can get the group on his or her side will have a tremendous advantage. Group participation, be it through meetings, decision processes, or quality circles, can enhance team spirit and contribute substantially to productivity.

Summary

This chapter has discussed the importance of work groups to the supervisor and the ways in which they can either help or hinder productivity. Work groups are sets of two or more individuals who are working toward a common objective and are in physical proximity with each other. How closely knit a group becomes is a function of the number of people in the group, the degree of interaction they have, and the degree to which they share a common set of values.

People join groups for many reasons, including security, friendship, recognition, and support in performing their jobs. Once they join groups, their behavior is influenced by the group norms, which are the accepted standards of behavior for group members. The informal leader of the group tends to set the norms and have influence over other group members. The cooperation of the informal leader is a valuable asset for the supervisor if his or her influence can be channeled toward the supervisor's objectives. Closely-knit groups in which the norms are widely shared are called cohesive, and can be either helpful or harmful. The supervisor can reduce the cohesiveness of a group (or change its norms) by changing the reward systems, the interaction patterns, or the group membership, or by removing the informal leader. Another problem with cohesive groups is groupthink, in which the group rejects any ideas that violate the group's way of thinking.

Knowledge of group concepts can help supervisors in several ways. It can help in team building, group decision making, running more effective meetings, and working through informal leaders. Knowledge about group behavior can also help in understanding individual behavior because groups affect individuals.

Opening Incident Revisited

Charlie Cox's problem is not an easy one to solve. At first glance, it might appear that it would be easy: simply tell the group to reduce their coffee break time. Although this might solve the problem over the short run (and, in fact, may be the best approach) Charlie must realize that norms are formed over long periods of time and are therefore changed in the same way. In other words, even though Norm and the group may begin taking regular coffee breaks, it may be in response to Charlie's instruction, not because the norm has changed. This means that Charlie will have to stay on top of things to allow for the new behavior to become part of the group norm.

Another way that Charlie might approach it is to deal with Norm on a one-on-one basis. This has two advantages; first, Norm may react differently as a group member than he might if talked to individually. In other words, even though he may understand the reasons why the breaks have to be shortened, he may perceive Charlie's move as a threat to the group. Despite his true feelings, he may react to protect the group. The second advantage is that if Charlie can convince Norm of the need to shorten the break, there is a greater probability that the group will go along with the request.

The text mentioned several strategies that can be used to change a norm. Several of those strategies would not be workable in this case, largely because this problem is not a major one. For example, Charlie would not want to have Norm transferred because of a minor problem like this. The strategy discussed thus far falls into the first category — changing the reward system. That is, by speaking with either Norm or the group, Charlie is letting it be known that taking long coffee breaks will not be rewarded. Charlie also has the alternative of punishing the group for violating the coffee break regulations, but as Chapter 8 pointed out, there are potentially serious problems associated with this strategy. However, if Charlie makes it clear to the group that the behavior is unacceptable, punishment may be in order if it continues.

Review Questions

1. What is the definition of a work group?
2. How do informal groups differ from formal groups?
3. What are the reasons employees form informal groups?

4. What are the functions of group norms?
5. What are informal group leaders?
6. What is group cohesiveness and how can this affect the supervisor?
7. What is the informal organization?
8. How might a supervisor build an effective work team?
9. How might a supervisor use group concepts to have better meetings?
10. What is groupthink and how might the supervisor guard against it?
11. What is group decision making and when should it be used?
12. How might social interaction on the job contribute to productivity?
13. What things could a supervisor do to assist in changing group norms?
14. What are quality circles and how do they use group concepts?

Chapter Glossary

Work group.	Two or more people who are working toward a common objective and are in physical proximity with each other.
Formal work group.	Two or more individuals who report to a common manager.
Informal work group.	A group whose makeup and goals are defined by the members.
Work to rule.	Following job descriptions to the letter and refusing to let the informal organization correct the deficiencies in the formal organization.
Group norms.	Acceptable standards of behavior for group members. They serve as a control on the behavior of group members.
Informal group leader.	An unofficial position in the group. The informal group leader is the most influential individual in the group and can change from group to group. Also called the natural leader.
Group cohesiveness.	A measure of the closeness of group members. Cohesive groups have shared norms and values and tend to resist external pressures.
Informal organization.	The organization that is created by the interaction of the people in it. Often called the social organization, it is characterized by the way people behave, not what the formal system says they should do.
Grapevine.	The informal communication channel that exists between individuals in the informal organization, and carries rumors and misinformation, as well as information, about issues that concern the group.
Team building.	The process of creating cohesive work groups.
Groupthink.	A characteristic of highly cohesive work groups in

which everyone in the group begins to think alike, to the point where the group rejects any ideas that disagree with its own. Belonging to the group takes precedence over making correct decisions.

Group decision making.	Exercise of the creative talents of a group to decide on solutions and reach consensus on the decision. This method seeks minimum agreement. Should be used only under certain conditions.
Consensus.	Group agreement on a decision reached by the group.
Quality circles.	The application of group principles and processes to production or performance problems in an organization. Groups seek out problems and work out solutions, and make recommendations to management.

Case Problem

The Centerville Bank

Sally Foreman supervises four clerks and seven secretaries at the Centerville Bank. Several years ago, the bank decided to consolidate its clerical and secretarial services in a pool, in which many managers share secretaries. Sally was appointed supervisor at that time and the move has since improved the efficiency of the secretarial function.

Sally's group has been together for some time. There has been little turnover and of the eleven people, nine have been with the bank for at least seven years and in the pool since it was created. There was some initial resistance by the secretaries when the pool was created, but things seem to have settled down and are working well.

One of Sally's problems is with the group's equipment. Much of it is outdated and repairs are frequent. For some time she has been requesting some new typewriters, but since the bank is in the process of upgrading its computer installation, no funds have been available for new typewriters.

A few days ago, Sally received a call from the operations manager who is her immediate superior. She informed Sally that some funds have finally been freed up and they can now begin replacing the old typewriters in the secretarial pool. However, at this time there is only enough money for one typewriter and, although things look promising for more, they cannot be guaranteed at this time. Consequently, all Sally can count on now is one new typewriter.

Her problem now is to decide which one of her employees should have the new typewriter. As she was thinking over the possibilities, the following facts went through her mind.

- Brenda Smith does most of the typing for the senior executives.
- Noreen Martin's typewriter is the oldest in the group.
- Marla Klassen's typewriter generally requires the most repairs.
- Jane Brentwood has already received training on the new typewriter in one of her evening secretarial courses.

- Lisa Jones, one of the newer employees, has talked about quitting because of the "antiquated equipment we have to work with."
- Charles Wilson, one of the up-and-coming middle managers (and son of the bank president, Henry Wilson) has requested that the person who usually does his typing, Betty Stern, get the new typewriter.

As Sally ran all these thoughts through her mind, it occurred to her that probably everyone could make a good case for getting the new typewriter. One of her major concerns is that if the situation is handled poorly, it could create major problems in a group that works well together.

Question for Analysis and Discussion

How should Sally handle this situation?

Communication

Chapter Learning Objectives

After reading and studying this chapter you should be able to:

1. List and describe the four roles that supervisors play in organizational communication.

2. Diagram the basic communication model and the stages in the communication process.

3. Describe the specific function of the supervisor in each of the communication stages.

4. Describe the nature and value of feedback in communication.

5. Describe how perception, the receiver's role, and emotional bias can affect communication and what the supervisor can do to overcome these problems.

6. List and describe the major barriers to communication in organizations.

7. List four ways supervisors might stimulate upward communication.

8. Describe how the grapevine operates and how it affects the supervisor's job.

Key Terms

Communication models
Encoding
Communication channel
Decoding
Noise
Feedback
Nonverbal communication
Perception
Emotional bias
Stereotyping
Organizational climate
Upward communication
Grapevine

229

Opening Incident

Communicating with Chico

The Best-Way Department Store is a large chain of stores located primarily in suburban shopping centers on the west coast. Each store employs from fifty to two hundred people, depending upon its size. Ralph Anderson is a supervisor in the Receiving Department and it is his department's job to accept and catalogue all incoming shipments of merchandise before they are sent to the warehouse.

Ralph has fifteen receiving clerks reporting to him, one of whom is Chico Sandez. Chico has been with Best-Way for over twenty years and is considered by the other employees to be the most knowledgeable about the receiving function. Even though he has had little formal education and has difficulty reading English, Chico has memorized the stock numbers of every piece of merchandise in his area and also has an uncanny knowledge of when shipments are coming in. If anyone wants to know anything concerning receiving, they go to Chico if Ralph is absent.

Because of various inefficiencies that have developed over the years in the purchasing function, Best-Way recently initiated a new system which includes changes in the receiving function. All supervisors attended regional meetings to be briefed on the new procedures, which were scheduled to be implemented in two months on a specific date.

When Ralph returned from the meeting he put the matter aside because the implementation date was still two months away. During that time, however, he wrote a six-page document summarizing the new procedures so the employees could begin using them on the specified date. The week before the implementation date he announced at a department meeting that there would be a change in the receiving systems beginning the following Monday. On Friday he inserted his written instructions in the pay envelopes of all employees, noting that the new procedures would be in effect first thing Monday morning.

About mid-morning on the Monday Ralph was sitting in his office when June Rider, one of the other employees, walked in. She said, "I think you had better talk with Chico. He's still doing things the old way and its causing problems for the rest of us." So Ralph stormed out of his office and encountered Chico on his way for a coffee break.

RALPH: Chico! Dammit you're doing it all wrong! I told you last week we were going to change the system and here you are still doing it the old way. What's the matter?

CHICO: Look, Mr. Anderson, things have been going fine around here before this new system and I don't see why we should change now. You do your job and just let me do mine.

Effective communication is the lifeblood of any organization. Without good communication, people can feel left out, instructions can be misunderstood, important information may not be transmitted, and rumors can abound. Communication is the process that helps the organization to hang together as a united whole.

Although everyone acknowledges the importance of communication, it is probably the most common source of problems in organizations. We tend to take communication for granted and often do not give it the attention it deserves. It has been said that "the greatest enemy of effective communication is the illusion of it," and this probably describes how most of us get ourselves into trouble. We assume we are communicating with people and therefore do not bother to check to see if this is true. Or, alternatively, we assume people know what is going on so we don't bother to keep them informed.

In the following dialogue we have a supervisor (Bill) talking with a subordinate (John).

BILL: John, I've looked over that project you just completed and I think you've make a few mistakes. Some of these figures are wrong and I think the customer will be upset when he finds them.
JOHN: Un-huh.
BILL: Go back and review your figures again and correct those errors.
JOHN: OK.
BILL: Get some help from purchasing if you have to.
JOHN: OK.
BILL: Any questions?
JOHN: No.
BILL: OK, then, get right on it.

At first glance it might appear that this communication has been effective. In other words, the supervisor has given an instruction and the subordinate has indicated he will obey it. However, there may be other things not so obvious. For example, John's agreeable responses may indicate a withdrawal because of the criticism from his supervisor. John may not understand the task and might be afraid to ask for more help from his supervisor. Or, John may be angry because he didn't want the job in the first place. Regardless of which of these is true, they do illustrate that the communication process is more complicated than simply giving clear instructions.

Being an effective communicator is more than just understanding its importance. The process of communication—from sending a message to its final understanding—is a complicated one that demands the attention of all supervisors and managers. It is relatively easy to explain and illustrate how effective communication can be accomplished; however, in the final analysis, it must be practiced if skill is to be attained. The exercises in this chapter provide an opportunity to engage in practical applications of the theory.

The Supervisor's Role in Communication

Most studies of supervisory behavior indicate that supervisors spend anywhere from fifty to seventy-five percent of their time in some form of communication. This could be through memos, meetings, personal interactions, telephone calls, or simply talking shop over lunch. One reason for this high level of communication is the unique position of the supervisor in the organization. As Figure 10.1 illustrates, the supervisor is the hub of the communication process. All of the official communications from higher levels must be channeled through the supervisor, and the supervisor is responsible for channeling information upwards as well. Also, the distance from the sources of many communications (the top) to the receivers (the bottom) places additional responsibility on the supervi-

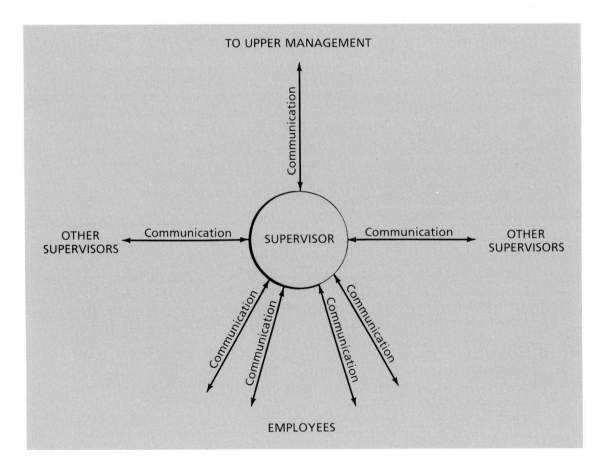

Figure 10.1. The Supervisor as the Hub of the Communication Process.

sor. Because of the supervisor's unique position he or she must occupy several roles in the communication process.

Translator

Information is seldom in the proper form and this often prevents understanding of the message. There may be technical terms not understood, details omitted, or a connotation that is not obvious. The supervisor's job is to translate communications—going up as well as down—so that the receiving party can understand the message. For example, subordinates may address a complaint to upper management and the supervisor might translate this complaint by stating the context of it, as well as providing additional explanatory information.

Buffer

The supervisor's buffer role serves several purposes. First, there is some communication downward that is of little or no interest to employees. If the supervisor is the sole channel for this communication, then it can be stopped so that employees' time is not wasted on something that is of little or no interest to them. A buffer role is also needed for potentially emotional communications. For example, if a client or customer is extremely unhappy with a product or service and complains vigorously to the subordinate, emotions may run high and a customer may be lost. However, if the supervisor occupies the buffer role between the two, communication may be more rational. The supervisor may play a similar role in communication from first level employees to upper management.

Listener

In this role the supervisor serves as a sounding board for ideas, suggestions, or problems. Employees prefer to have a supervisor who is willing to listen to the ideas of others and also put some of these ideas into action. Other dimensions of this role pertain to the behavioral aspects of communication. Chapter 18 on counselling and performance appraisal describes how supervisors must be willing to listen to subordinates who have emotional problems such as fear, anxiety, or depression. It is also important for supervisors to be sensitive to the communications of others so that they can understand what people *really* mean when they say something. All of these require that supervisors see themselves as listeners and occupy that role when required.

Informer

Subordinates depend heavily (but not totally) upon the supervisor for information. If they cannot get what they want from the supervisor, they

The Big Picture

Several years ago I was doing an interviewing program designed to learn more about employees' attitudes toward their jobs. One interview was with a young man about 20 years of age. His story reinforced the importance of communication and keeping people informed. He claimed that he had worked for the company for six weeks operating a punch press machine but never knew what he was actually making. He was never told by his supervisor what the final product was and how his particular job fitted into the rest of the production process. Finally, on one of his days off he joined the company tour conducted for the public. Only then did he see how his job related to the rest of the company and what the final product looked like.

will usually get it somewhere else if the information is important enough. They also resent it when they do not know what is going on, partly because this means to them that the supervisor does not consider them to be important. Supervisors often underestimate the importance of keeping others informed of the big picture. Simply telling people enough so they can do their own jobs is not sufficient. All workers should be kept informed about events or activities that are important to them.

(*★ OVER-INFORM than UnDER-Inform*)

The Basic Communication Model

To better understand how the communication process operates and the supervisor's role in it, we shall first examine a communication model. Figure 10.2 is the basic model, showing that communication consists of a sender, a message, and a receiver who interprets the message. The sender might be a supervisor, the message might be an instruction to perform a certain job, and the receiver might be a worker. But communication is far more complicated than simply sending messages to people. Many things can happen between the time a message is sent and the time it is received. The eight stages that communication must go through are illustrated in Figure 10.3, which is a more realistic description of the communication process. These stages may be described briefly as:

※   1. *Source.* The source could be the supervisor, upper management, the union, or any other person or group. The origin of the message.
※   2. *Encoding.* Putting the message into an understandable form is **encoding**. The form may be the spoken word, a written memo, mathematical symbols, or a picture.

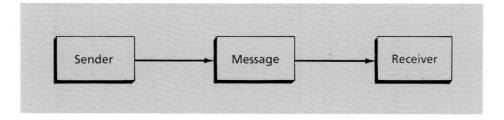

Figure 10.2. The Basic Communication Model.

3. *Message.* This is the actual information the sender wishes to be transmitted. It may be a question, an instruction, or a statement of fact.

4. *Channel.* The **channel** is the actual means by which the message is communicated, such as letter or memo, loudspeaker, bulletin board, company newsletter, or word-of-mouth. Note that the method of encoding determines the channel used.

5. *Decoding.* When the message is received, it goes through the process of **decoding**; it is translated—that is, given a meaning—by the receiver. If the message cannot be decoded properly then it will not be understood.

6. *Receiver.* The receiver is the person or persons to whom the message is addressed. Like the sender, the receiver is subject to many influences that can affect the understanding of the message.

7. *Noise.* The term **noise** designates any type of interference that can affect the understanding of the sender's message. In the case of verbal communications it could be actual noise which would prevent one person from hearing another. In a more general sense, it refers to influences such as attitudes, perceptions, biases, and emotional barriers between sender and receiver.

8. *Feedback.* The process which communicates to the sender that the message has been received is termed **feedback.** It may be a direct reply (in which case the process begins all over again), or it may be an act of behavior that communicates how well the message has been received.

The Supervisor and the Communication Model

How might the supervisor make use of this model? In this section we shall examine the implications of the model for supervisors and suggest ways that communication can be improved.

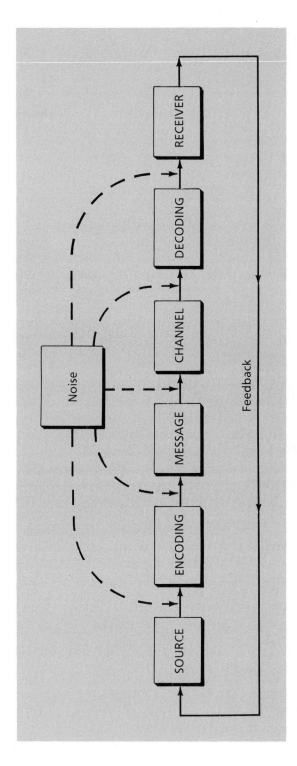

Figure 10.3. The Stages in the Communication Process.

Supervisor As the Source

It is pretty obvious that the supervisor will be the source of many communications. But one of the major factors which determines whether the message has the correct impact is the supervisor's *credibility*. When we hear a message from a credible source, the message tends to have a greater impact upon us than it does if the source is someone we do not trust. Therefore, it is important for supervisors to concentrate on improving their credibility with their subordinates.

How might this be done? First, actions must always be consistent with communications. If a supervisor says one thing and is seen to be doing another, his or her credibility will be jeopardized. This credibility gap may be intentional (generally called lying) or unintentional. The unintentional happens when something beyond the control of the supervisor occurs that is not consistent with what employees have been told.

Another way of improving credibility is to use a credible or prestigious channel to carry the message. In the example below, if the supervisor had asked the president himself to tell the employees their jobs were secure, the message would have probably had a greater impact. General respect can also improve one's credibility. If a supervisor has proved to be a good supervisor in the past, credibility often follows. And finally, being open with communication can improve credibility. Supervisors who communicate only part of the message or withhold information to gain more power over employees will lose credibility. Employees will eventually learn that their supervisor seldom tells them the whole story.

Encoding Messages

Although this may seem to be the most obvious part of the communication process, it is frequently the most difficult. The supervisor must decide *how* he or she will communicate a certain message. Should it be written, oral, or both? This decision will be largely determined by (a) how important the message is, and (b) how likely it is that the message will be misunderstood. If a message is both important and complicated, oral communication followed by a written message may be best. This way, if the spoken message is not fully understood, the receiver has the

The Credibility Gap

In one company a supervisor was having difficulty convincing his employees that they would not be laid off. He had been assured by top management that no one in his department would be laid off. But it seemed the more he told workers this fact, the greater their disbelief, which was understandable because in the previous six weeks the company had laid off one-third of its work force.

opportunity to review it in more detail. For a message that is important but easy to understand, the written follow-up might still be advisable as a reminder. But for messages that are not of critical importance and easy to understand, written follow-up is usually not necessary.

Encoding messages must always take into account the skills and experience of the receiver. What is clear to the supervisor may not always be as obvious to the employee. A supervisor may use terms that are unfamiliar to others, or couch the message in such a way that no one understands its real meaning. Proper encoding also means that all necessary information should be included. It should not be assumed that most people already know what is going on.

Deciding upon the Channel { *needs to be consistent* }

This is critical because selecting the wrong channel means the message may not be fully received. As an example, let us assume that a supervisor has designed a new work schedule and wishes to communicate this to the department. What channel should be used to communicate this? Some alternatives would be: (1) an announcement on the department bulletin board showing the new schedule, (2) a meeting of all employees to announce and explain the new schedule, (3) a notice included in each employee's pay envelope that week, or (4) individual conversations with employees showing them their new schedule.

To decide which channel is best, it is helpful to consider the following criteria.

- How complicated is the message? Is there a chance it will be misunderstood?
- Is feedback on the message important? Is there likely to be resistance?
- What has been done in the past? Is this channel the normal way this sort of message is communicated?
- How important is the speed (or timing) of the message?

We can see that if this is the first schedule change ever done and some resistance (or questioning) is anticipated, and if the change is a complicated one that will be implemented in one month's time, a meeting with all employees to announce, explain, and get feedback on the schedule would be the best channel. On the other hand, if schedule changes are made regularly and are expected by employees, a simple written announcement on the bulletin board may suffice.

The Value of Feedback

Without some form of feedback, the supervisor really doesn't know if the message has been received. Even if there is feedback, it must be interpreted properly to be of any value—as the earlier example of John and Bill shows. Feedback is normally obtained through two-way communication, that is, reversing the process so that subordinates can communicate their understanding back to the supervisor. Two-way communication must be stimulated by the supervisor. A supervisor who communicates mostly by written memo, for example, would receive less feedback on messages than a supervisor who communicates orally.

Although two-way communication can occur in written form, feedback is usually best in face-to-face communication. This is why supervisors are encouraged to hold meetings with subordinates (although this in itself is no guarantee that two-way communication will occur) and to interact with them frequently. In a face-to-face situation, supervisors are able to observe physical reactions to messages as well as hear the verbal feedback. These nonverbal clues are often important to understanding how a subordinate has reacted to a message. Here are some common examples of **nonverbal communication.**

- Listening with arms folded may indicate a psychological defense against the communication.
- Facial expressions, generally self-explanatory, may communicate such reactions as surprise, disbelief, disagreement, or questioning.
- Silence may communicate a variety of reactions, such as apathy, listening, boredom, or embarrassment, depending upon the circumstances.
- Leaning forward while conversing indicates interest; leaning back generally indicates lack of interest.

Exercise 10.1

One-way Versus Two-way Communication

This exercise will be conducted by your instructor to demonstrate one-way versus two-way communication. One person from the class will be chosen to communicate something to the rest of the class using the one-way method. The same person will then communicate a second item using the two-way method. When the exercise is completed, the following questions can be used for discussion:

1. What were the major differences between the two methods?
2. Even though the rules stated that no feedback was allowed in the first situation, was there any feedback? How was it expressed?
3. How did the communicator feel in each of the situations?
4. is there any time in which the one-way method would be superior to the two-way method?

Although some forms of feedback are obvious, others, as with the examples above, are more subtle. The supervisor must be a sensitive listener to feedback for its real meaning.

Feedback should be encouraged because of its self-correcting value: plans and decisions can be changed as a direct result of the feedback obtained. More about the role of feedback will be covered later in this chapter when we discuss creating a climate for effective communication.

Understanding the Receiver

One of the complicating aspects of good communication is that only part of the process is within the control of the supervisor. The supervisor can control message, encoding, and channel, but has less influence over the decoding and the properties of the receiver. However if the supervisor understands what factors affect comprehension, he or she can avoid some of the more obvious errors.

Perception

Perception is the term used to describe how individuals see their environment, and is part of the decoding process. Employees' perceptions are determined by their needs, attitudes, emotions, and previous experiences. All of these affect or color how an individual will react to a communication. For simplicity's sake, all of these can be lumped under the general heading of experience (since, as we noted in Chapter 5, experiences are the source of attitudes). This suggests that people will interpret information according to their previous experiences. For example, an employee who has consistently had conflict with a supervisor will perceive

Beauty in the Eyes of the Beholder

Many exercises and experiments have been done with perception to illustrate how if affects communication. One of the more frequent experiments is to show a quotation to a group of subjects; half of them are told that it came from a union publication and half are told it came from a management newsletter. As you might guess, how the quote is perceived is largely determined by the background of the receiver. Union people generally see the statement as accurate if told it came from a union publication, and management people see it as a distortion of the truth. A similar effect occurs when the source is reversed; management people perceive it as accurate and union members see it as management propaganda. These effects occur regardless of the actual content of the message.

communication from that supervisor differently than an employee who has had a positive relationship.

Perception also relates to the source credibility noted earlier. A supervisor who has low credibility with employees because of previous experiences will find their perceptions of messages to be vastly different from what was intended. A common example is the communication (or lack of it) that occurs between unions and management. Information contained in a union bulletin is perceived differently by management—and vice versa—because of the credibility gap that often exists between the two.

The Receiver's Role

This example also illustrates the importance of the receiver's role in the communication process. Because a role includes experiences as well as the expectations of others in defining that role, information received is filtered by the individual in the role. For example, consider two roles that often interact at work: the shop steward and the supervisor. Each of these roles has very different expectations associated with it which can interfere with the communication process. If the shop steward sees his or her role as champion of employee rights, any communication directed to the shop steward must be consistent with that role. Similarly, if the supervisor sees himself or herself as protector of management's policies and regulations, communication must take that perception into account. Since everyone occupies several different roles, there are many opportunities for communication to conflict with role expectations. A common example is the self-image that a person has. Most people see themselves as competent, so if the supervisor communicates in a way that implies the opposite, communication will be ineffective.

The primary lesson for supervisors is that communication must be consistent with the roles people see themselves as occupying, both within the organization and outside. Supervisors can sometimes avoid conflicting with role expectations by placing themselves in the other person's shoes and imagining how they would react.

Emotional Bias

The combination of the receiver's attitudes, values, experiences, and feelings constitutes his or her **emotional bias** in communication. Emotional biases serve as filters that change factual, logical information into something consistent with emotional state. This process is diagrammed in Figure 10.4. In order to communicate effectively, supervisors should understand that any piece of information that affects an individual personally will have an emotional bias to it. To counteract the bias there are several things that supervisors can do. First, it is necessary to understand

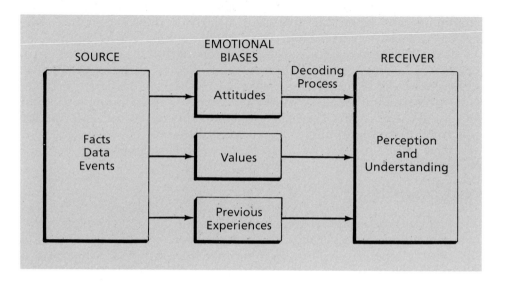

Figure 10.4. How Emotions Affect Understanding.

that facts will seldom solve emotional resistance. Facts, figures, data, and logic are meaningless if they conflict with an individual's emotional biases. Moreover, using factual communications to try to convince someone with emotional biases can make the situation even worse. Overcoming emotional resistance will be discussed in more detail in Chapter 19, Managing Change.

Second, communication can be couched in such a way that it avoids the receiver's obvious emotional biases. For example, a supervisor who wished to reprimand an employee would avoid personal criticism, which would probably be rejected. However, the supervisor could point out the unsatisfactory behavior. The technique of doing this was discussed more fully in Chapter 8.

Finally, one way of reducing emotional biases in communication is to be a good listener. Supervisors who show empathy with people's feelings through good listening will lessen emotional bias and have a better chance of following up with a communication that is accepted. A useful format for dealing with emotion and tension is contained in Table 10.1. As Planty explains, "Many of our problems and failures in communicating with other people are failures in responding to their emotions. Employees' problems, where fear or a conflict of interests or values exist, are often surrounded with tension, fear, confusion, anxiety, suspicion, bias, distortion, or other neurotic behavior. Behavior in such cases often is not reasonable, logical, rational. There may be hostile, aggressive, negative and even destructive attack, verbal or more physical in nature. Or there may be silent, sullen, fearful, depressive, withdrawal symptoms. To handle these situations one should do or refrain from doing the follow-ing:"

Table 10.1. Communicating When Emotions Are High and Conflicts Exist.

Things To Do	*Things to Refrain From Doing*
1) Set a supportive, quiet situation for discussion; give your *full* attention.	1) Don't let phone, assistant or secretary interrupt.
2) Expect, prepare yourself, to hear negative, critical, sometimes unpleasant, confused, distorted talk or silence and reluctance to speak.	2) Don't interrupt or be shocked or surprised.
3) Draw off; release these emotions, feelings, sentiments.	3) Don't disagree or argue, don't agree either.
4) Do the above by listening, listening, listening.	4) Don't correct or deny.
5) Listen, especially to feelings, attitudes, sentiments, values, perceptions, beliefs as well as to more objective data.	5) Don't blame or criticize.
6) Restrain your own emotions in face of the above. Remain neutral (neither agree nor disagree).	6) Don't judge; be neutral.
7) All during the above steps try to *understand* — (a) get in the shoes of; (b) *feel* with the subject; (c) empathize, see and feel from his frame of reference as he or she talks.	7) Don't reason, or lead the person back to reason. Don't expect a logical, honest or calm presentation.
8) Echo back — reflect back — the person's emotions, fears, feelings, beliefs. Summarize the feelings expressed. Say, for example, "You feel pretty rejected?" or, "You think you have been taken advantage of, have been used?"	8) Don't play FBI. Don't question suspiciously.
9) When the above steps have been taken, the employee oftentimes releases even more negative comments, followed eventually by the desirable result given in #10 below.	9) Don't talk too much or the employee won't.

Table 10.1. Communicating When Emotions Are High and Conflicts Exist.

Things To Do	*Things to Refrain From Doing*
10) *Positive, constructive, logical, offerings usually come from the emotional person, leading, with your help, to conflict reduction and often to problem solutions.* He or she moves from seeing the situation emotionally towards seeing things reasonably, rationally. Once the person becomes rational like this you may help by getting him or her to see and take appropriate actions. You may ask for alternative courses of action, if the employee does not suggest them. At this time you may guide a little, but give the employee a chance first. When you do guide, do it by questions.	10) Don't fear silence.
	11) Don't become emotional yourself.
	12) Don't direct until step #10 at the left is reached. Don't do it even then unless it's needed.

Source: Professor Earl Planty, personal communication. Used with permission.

Barriers to Effective Communication

Among the barriers to good communication that especially deserve the supervisor's attention are our tendency to evaluate the comunications of others, our own defensiveness, our emotional state, the distance between communicators, stereotyping, and fear and insecurity.

Tendency to Evaluate

The influential psychologist, Carl Rogers, maintained that the greatest barrier to effective communication is our tendency to evaluate what someone has said to us, since this causes the other person to become defensive. For example, if an employee says, "This job is too much for one person," and the reply from the supervisor is, "No, you're wrong. We've done it that way for years," a disagreement will probably arise over the supervisor's evaluative statement rather than the issue. An alternative way of handling the same situation would be for the supervisor to reply, "Why is it you feel that way?" Note that in this case the supervisor has not evaluated the subordinate's comment, but only responded to it, and now they can proceed to discuss why the subordinate feels that way. The discussion is likely to be less emotional.

Defensiveness

One reason why the tendency to evaluate has such a negative impact upon communication is because it evokes a defensive reaction from the receiver. Two people attempting to defend their own ideas will not communicate very well, because neither will be listening to the other.

Difficulties can also arise when someone else initiates a conversation with us. Suppose, for example, that an employee enters your office and says, "That last change you made was all screwed up. Now I have to do the job all over again!" The defensive reaction might be, "We had to do it that way because of the new design change. If you weren't sure how to do it, you should have come and asked." A better response might have been, "I'm sorry you had difficulty. Let's go over it together and see what we can do with it."

The trouble with defensiveness is that it is a natural response for most of us. To defend ourselves is a natural instinct and we often do not consider how this affects communication. Overcoming our own defensiveness must be a conscious process and not be left to chance.

Emotional State

"Now let's keep calm and talk about this rationally" is easier said than done. As we noted in the previous section, emotions play an important role in our ability to communicate. While we noted that the emotional state of the receiver was important, it should be pointed out that the sender's emotions can also play a part. The techniques in Table 10.1 confirm how important it is for the supervisor to keep a cool head whenever possible. Otherwise, emotions will prevail and the interaction will degenerate into a full-blown argument.

Distance

It is easier to communicate with those close by than with those who are in some distant location. In fact, there are many physical barriers in organizations that prevent good communication. For example, although there are good reasons why supervisors should have their own offices, it is well to recognize that this does inhibit the communication process to some degree.

It is not uncommon for some supervisors to manage people who are in different locations. This means that the supervisor should make a special effort to keep communication flowing. Otherwise, the employees could easily feel left out and morale could drop.

Without physical barriers, a lot of communication would occur in the normal course of events. However, when physical barriers (including distance) are present, the supervisor must give added attention to the communication process.

Stereotyping

Stereotyping means that we tend to classify people into categories such as good and bad, or union and nonunion, and so forth, and then evaluate their communications in terms of how we have classified them rather than according to the substance of their messages. Supervisors must try constantly to keep an open mind and attempt to receive communications in terms of their content, not their source.

Fear and Insecurity

It is common for supervisors and subordinates to talk frequently to each other. But are they necessarily communicating? Often not, because of the fears and insecurities of both individuals. In other words, because of the fear of what might happen to them, people do not always express their true feelings about matters openly. This lack of openness is partly built into the relationship, in that supervisors do have authority over subordinates and can control rewards and punishments for them. This in itself can cause subordinates to choose their words carefully. We also tend to

Turning the Tables on the Communicator

I once had a supervisor who had apparently studied communication from a how-to manual and tried to practice every principle strictly according to the book. One of these principles must have dealt with how a supervisor should behave when communicating something unpleasant. He apparently had learned that in these situations the supervisor should come out from behind his or her desk, and sit beside the employee, making sure to be on the same level. Unfortunately, this was the only time this supervisor ever communicated to us from any position except behind his desk. So the net effect was that every time he left his desk and sat beside us, we knew we were in for trouble. Instead of reducing our defenses—as his method was supposed to do—he actually increased them. Our resentment increased even more because we suspected he really didn't believe in communicating on an equal basis, but was using this as a gimmick to try to get his point across. As the situation worsened, we tried various methods to screw up his little gimmick. The most effective seemed to be to refuse to sit down. Since he was shorter than most of us, this really destroyed his strategy and seemed to really confuse him.

be closemouthed with people of very different status because we are unsure of how our behavior will affect them—and vice versa. For example, a vice-president visiting with first-level employees may not get a true picture of what their feelings are because of the large status differences between their jobs.

This particular barrier can cause difficulties for supervisors. Many supervisors, for example, have an open door policy supposedly designed to encourage subordinates to come in and talk about whatever bothers them. When no one ever comes in, the supervisor might erroneously conclude that everything is going well, whereas in fact, subordinates just don't feel comfortable voicing their concerns to the supervisor. Supervisors who are poor listeners and use these occasions to argue with subordinates rather than trying to understand their feelings will find that their so-called open door policy breeds resentment instead of solving problems.

There are other barriers to communication, such as personal biases, our self-image, and language difficulties, but these can be at least partially overcome by a planned strategy of communication that addresses them directly. One such strategy involves creating an organizational climate that is conducive to effective communication.

Creating an Organizational Climate for Effective Communication

The **organizational climate** of a department can be described as the general atmosphere of that unit. A climate can be classified as positive or negative, depending upon the attitudes, feelings, beliefs, and experiences of those in the unit. In negative climates, communication is often one-way instead of two-way, there is little expression of true feelings, and fear and anxiety permeate the entire unit. The real danger of a negative climate is that on the surface it usually appears that everything is all right. There are few complaints, employees appear to be agreeable, and an acceptable level of output may exist. But the undercurrents of feeling in such climates can be destructive. Employees cannot make their maximum contribution under such conditions and they usually resent the climate in which they must work.

Creating a positive climate for communication goes far beyond the communication principles themselves. It involves leadership styles, reward systems, job descriptions, performance appraisal systems, and group relationships, to name but a few. We shall outline some things that supervisors can do to improve the climate for better communication, but these will be ineffective if the other factors that influence organizational climate are not attended to.

Stimulating Upward Communication

Upward communication, the flow of information from employees to management, is one of the most useful feedback tools available to supervisors. However, it cannot be left to chance or to happen on its own. The supervisor must consciously do things to stimulate it. If employees perceive that knowledge of their ideas, feelings, and attitudes is sincerely wanted by their supervisor, a more positive climate will result. Several methods for stimulating upward communication are explained in the following sections.

ASKING FOR IDEAS. The obvious first step in stimulating upward communication is to ask employees for their ideas or feelings. The "no news is good news" philosophy can be catastrophic for supervisors. Some information will filter up to the supervisor in the natural course of events, but it will probably be very selective and will not communicate the whole picture.

When asking for information, it is usually advisable to be as specific as possible. People have difficulty responding to general questions such as "How do you feel about things around here?" or "Is anything bothering you?" More direct (but nonthreatening) approaches usually have a better chance of providing useful information. A question such as "How do you like the new procedure on reporting travel expenses?" is likely to give the supervisor a much better picture of how the person feels.

Sometimes there may be considerable upward communication but it is not representative of the whole group. There may be one or two relatively vocal members who appear to speak for the group but actually do not, and a supervisor who listens only to those who are vocal may be misled. Upward communication should be solicited from everyone so as to get a reasonable picture of the whole group.

USING MEETINGS. A more formal method of stimulating upward communication is through the careful use of meetings. Meetings can have many different purposes and if these purposes are confused, the supervisor may not get the quality of communication expected. For example, in some meetings the supervisor may wish to announce a particular decision or explain a policy. To solicit feedback *after* a decision is announced will seem pointless to employees. A different meeting should have been held for feedback purposes before the decision was made.

Another problem with meetings is group behavior. We know that because of group role expectations, people can behave one way as individuals and another way as members of their group. Some may not be willing to voice their true feelings in a group meeting and the supervisor may not get accurate feedback.

Meetings on the Farm

One of the best examples of how meetings can improve communication was given to me by a farmer who owned and managed a large vegetable farm employing three hundred workers in peak season. Each morning before any work began, he held a fifteen-minute meeting with all of his supervisors. They gathered in the main yard, with the farmer sitting in the back of a pickup truck, and talking about the work plan for the day. The farmer began by giving his plan for the day, which was then modified by ideas and suggestions from the supervisors.

When the meeting was over, each supervisor knew what everyone else was doing that day and what the manager's expectations were for the entire crew. The supervisors then had brief meetings with their individual groups to explain what had transpired at the supervisors' meeting, and again received feedback on the plans. The farmer believed that these brief meetings ended up saving much more time than they used because of the extensive communication that took place.

Notwithstanding these potential problems, meetings can be used to stimulate upward communication. If a supervisor shows himself or herself to be receptive to the ideas of others, there can be a considerable amount of two-way communication. One of the major reasons why meetings are useful is that they can be planned and scheduled, thereby reducing the probability that upward communication will be left to chance.

FOLLOW UP WITH ACTION. "Actions speak louder than words." This is certainly true of upward communication. Employees like to know that their ideas are listened to, but they also expect some action to be taken as a result. If supervisors continually encourage upward communication but employees perceive that no action is ever taken on it, they will quickly lose interest. In situations where employees' ideas cannot be used, they should be told why. This at least communicates back to employees that their ideas have been given serious consideration.

Effective Listening

One of the major characteristics of a good climate for communication is good listening skills on the part of supervisors and other managers. As with the rest of the communication process, most of us consider ourselves to be good listeners, but we often really are not. Listening is more than just hearing people speak. It involves being sensitive to the real meaning behind the spoken word, allowing people to express their true feelings, and communicating understanding back. It is listening to the

An Exercise in Listening and Understanding

As we have noted in the text, there are many barriers to effective communication. This exercise gives you the opportunity to practice your listening skills and avoid some of the barriers. The exercise can be done either with many groups of two operating simultaneously, or with two individuals in front of the rest of the class.

Your instructor will give you a topic to debate, specify a time period, and designate who will speak first. Before the second person can reply, he or she must summarize what the first person has said, and the first person must agree that he or she has been properly understood. When this is done, the second person can speak, followed by a summary by the first person, and so on. In other words, after the opening remarks, each can give his or her point of view only after summarizing the words and feelings of the other party.

When the exercise is over, the following questions can be discussed.

1.   How did you feel about this communication situation?
2.   How did it differ from other debates you have had?
3.   How might a supervisor use the principles learned in this exercise to be a better communicator?

positive and negative feelings, as well as the factual and emotional content.

Specific applications of good listening skills are covered in Chapter 18, on counselling and performance appraisal. But the need for good listening goes far beyond these two situations to participative management, interviewing, and good interpersonal relations with employees. Everyone likes a good listener.

Climate and the Quantity of Communication

While few would argue with the value of good communication, there is frequently a question of how much a supervisor should communicate to employees. Should they be told everything? Is it possible to communicate too much? These are difficult issues which will have to be analyzed in each specific situation, but there are some useful principles that can be given.

As a general rule, the climate for communication can be improved by providing employees with as much information as possible. Not only does this have important implications for the grapevine (which is discussed in greater detail in the following section), but it also serves to set the stage for the psychological climate of the supervisor's unit. Openness of information establishes feelings of trust and security that are important for both morale and productivity.

There are three types of information that should not be communicated. The first is, of course, confidential personal information about other employees, items communicated to a supervisor in confidence, or anything that has legally been declared confidential. The second is trivial information. It is possible to communicate so much that overload occurs and employees are not able to separate the important information from the trivial. Finally, supervisors should be careful of communicating to employees information that they are not likely to understand. If it must be communicated, then it should be translated so it will be meaningful to employees. The decision as to whether information will be understood or not should not be made lightly. Withholding information on these grounds could be taken as an insult by employees and cause resentment.

Communication and Informal Leaders

We have already noted that informal leaders are the natural channel of communication between supervisors and employees. The climate of a work group can be enhanced if the role of the informal leader is respected by the supervisor. Bypassing this person is tantamount to attempting to undermine his or her influence in the group and is likely to be resented by all. This does not mean that supervisors should communicate only with the informal leader and ignore the group. This would also create serious problems. However, some situations can be better managed if the informal leader is consulted first before beginning the communication process with the group.

The informal leader can provide valuable feedback for a supervisor. Good communication between this leader and the supervisor can help avoid other communication errors that the supervisor might make. Ideas can be tested before they are communicated to the group, or the informal leader can inform the supervisor of the group's reaction to previous communications. This does not mean that supervisors should check with the informal leader all the time, but there are instances in which he or she can serve a useful role in establishing a positive climate for communication.

The Grapevine

The grapevine, or rumor mill as it is often called, is present in every organization. Like many other aspects of human behavior, it should be looked upon as a natural phenomenon of organizational life. It cannot be eliminated, nor should it be. It can be destructive or helpful, depending upon how it is used and managed. In this section, we examine what it is, how it starts, and how supervisors can manage it effectively.

What Is It?

The **grapevine** is the informal channel of communication that exists in work groups and other informal groupings of people. It carries the information that is passed on from person to person — usually by word of mouth — during the informal interactions that inevitably occur in organizations. As noted in the previous chapter, the grapevine satisfies some important needs of employees such as security, social contact, and ego satisfaction.

Although the grapevine is more active at some times than others, it is constantly transmitting information. We can see it when a group of people are talking while having lunch together or two employees stop to talk during work, or, in more clandestine moments, when a group of employees whisper together in a storage closet.

The grapevine is noted for its speed in transmitting information. Information that would take days to travel through formal channels may be communicated almost instantly through the informal system. But what it gains in speed it loses in accuracy. Because information must travel through many different encoders and decoders, the chances for distortion of the facts increase dramatically. Each person's perceptions, biases, and experiences will distort the original message a little, until in some cases, the end message hardly resembles what was originally communicated.

How Rumors Start

To understand how rumors start we must first recognize that the grapevine carries only information that is important to those using the grapevine. Information that is of no interest to people is, by definition, not carried by the grapevine. Rumors generally start because there is a need for information and none is forthcoming from the formal sources, that is, upper management. Therefore, to satisfy this need, information may be created, placed into the channel, and then transmitted as long as the receivers find it important.

There are many individual motives for starting rumors, but they all boil down to the same general source — the desire for power. Information is power and those who are seen as having important information — regardless of whether it is right or wrong — are treated as powerful people. Employees who have strong feelings of insecurity, for example, may try to start rumors to overcome their personal feelings of inadequacy. Others may do it to gain acceptance by other individuals or a group. In some cases, rumors are started as a means of getting revenge against another person or group.

Managing the Grapevine

Although supervisors cannot manage the grapevine in the traditional sense of the word, if they understand how it operates they can minimize its negative effects and occasionally use it to their advantage.

The most effective method of stopping rumors would be to provide the actual information that employees want. When the facts are known, there is no need for the grapevine. However, life is never as simple as this. Depending upon what the rumor is, providing the facts will have different effects. Basically, the principle is that if the facts confirm the rumor, the rumor will stop; however, if the facts are contrary to the rumor, they will have much less effect. For example, if there is a rumor that a supervisor is quitting and then it is formally announced that the supervisor has quit, the rumor will cease — as well as any negative effects associated with it. However, if it is announced that the supervisor is not quitting, the rumors will likely persist, especially if experience tells employees that the organization has lied in the past. This phenomenon is frequently observed when professional sports figures announce their retirement. As a public, we are so used to seeing them come out of retirement that we pay little attention to their original announcements.

The grapevine can be useful to the supervisor provided that he or she can tap into it. In most cases, the supervisor will not be a member of the employees' grapevine, so other methods must be used to get the information. Asking employees what information the grapevine is carrying is one method, or talking with someone who has access to some of the information but is not a regular member of the group is also useful. Finding out what is in the grapevine can be useful feedback for the supervisor, in determining what information should be communicated. For example, if the grapevine is carrying rumors that layoffs are about to occur, the supervisor might respond to this in a formal communication (unless the facts are confidential).

It is sometimes recommended that supervisors plant information in the grapevine and use it as a tool for communication. While there may be instances in which this works, it can be dangerous. We already know how information can become distorted in the grapevine, so it is unlikely that whatever information the supervisor plants will be communicated accurately. If the supervisor wants to make sure that communications are accurate and properly understood, he or she should not use the grapevine.

Key to Success

"The greatest enemy of communication is the illusion of it." This chapter has pointed out many ways in which our illusions regarding good communication interfere with getting our message across. Our biases, emotions, defensiveness, personal experiences, and attitudes all color our perception of what is being communicated. We know now that Jack Webb's famous line on *Dragnet* — "Just the facts, Ma'am" — is in reality an impossible request given all the things that can get in the way of a receiver and sender.

It sounds strange that something we spend fifty to seventy-five percent of our working lives doing may be our greatest weakness, yet evidence from employees suggests that this is true. We often speak of the importance of getting employees to feel that they belong, yet we shut them off from information that is important to them. We want our employees to act like team members, yet we do not share information that is so important to the spirit that makes good teams. We consider ourselves to be good listeners, yet many of our conversations with others end up in arguments.

All of this suggests that there is a lot that most of us could do to improve our communication with others. Perhaps the best place to begin is to draw a parallel between communication and McGregor's Theory X and Theory Y (which will be described in Chapter 12). In the past, maybe we have believed that because employees weren't part of the team, did not feel as if they belonged to the organization, and did not share their feelings with supervisors, there was little point in trying to communicate with them. Perhaps if we turned it around and believed that practicing good communications would bring about teamwork, the feeling of belonging, and openness of communication from below, the self-fulfilling prophecy would cause it to happen.

Summary

This chapter has described the communication process in organizations and how this process affects the role of the supervisor. Communication is the lifeblood of any organization and the supervisor plays an important role as a translator of information, as a buffer from unnecessary or unwanted information, as a listener to the communications of others, and as an informant or provider of information to employees.

Models of the communication process depict the important stages in the process. A simple model includes only the sender, the message, and the receiver. A more realistic (and complicated) model shows how communication is complicated by the nature of the source, the encoding process, the message itself, the channel used, the decoding process, the nature of the receiver, the noise in the system, and the feedback that occurs after the message is received.

One of the most important factors affecting communication between supervisor and subordinates is the credibility of the supervisor. A poor organizational climate and a lack of trust between supervisor and subordinates will have a negative influence. Other factors are the perception process, the role of the receiver, and emotional biases on the part of both the sender and the receiver.

Barriers to good communication exist in all organizations. Some of the more common ones are our tendency to evaluate, defensiveness, emotional state, physical and psychological distance, stereotyping, and fear and insecurity.

Supervisors can establish a climate conducive to communication by stimulating upward communication, developing better listening skills, creating trust within the work group, working through informal leaders, and understandng the nature and role of the grapevine.

The grapevine is the informal communication system that operates in every work group. Some of the information transmitted is inaccurate (rumors) and supervisors must take appropriate action to curtail rumors before they do serious damage. Understanding and managing the grapevine can help the supervisor to be a more effective communicator.

Opening Incident Revisited

Ralph's outburst at the end is clearly a problem in this situation, but the important learning value is in the understanding of what has led up to it. Ralph has made several errors in this case, some having to do with the communication processes and some having to do with Chico himself.

Ralph has failed to realize how this communication and change will affect Chico. Chico has difficulty with the English language and feels threatened by anything he can't understand. To guard against this he apparently has developed his memory as a compensatory mechanism. His expertise in the department is widely recognized because of this and he probably feels pretty good about himself.

This change — and the way it was communicated — will have a devastating effect upon him. In view of the short notice for the change, he may be unable to understand the new system and will attempt to keep using the old one. Ralph's method of communicating the change has allowed for no feedback, and therefore Ralph's first indication that Chico doesn't understand is when June Rider tells him. Ralph has made a classic error in communication: he has assumed that because he understands the system, everyone else also understands.

The other error Ralph made was in waiting so long to communicate the change. He had two months to let his people know about it, so the short notice (and the way he communicated it) was bound to create some problems.

The incident also illustrates how emotions can affect understanding. It may be, for example, that Chico does understand the new system but resists it because of the psychological harm that it does to him. His personal system of memorizing all the stock numbers will now be useless and he will lose his important position in the informal organization. Of course this is not a reason to scrap the new system, but Ralph could have handled the change better.

Review Questions

1. What are the primary roles that supervisors occupy in the communication process?
2. What is the basic communication model?
3. What are the stages in the communication process?
4. How might the encoding process affect communication?
5. Why is channel selection important for the supervisor?
6. Why is the decoding process important for good communication?
7. How can noise affect communication?
8. Why is feedback important for effective communication?
9. What role does perception play in communication?
10. Hoe does the role of the receiver affect communication?
11. How does emotional bias affect communication?
12. What are the major barriers to effective communication?
13. How can a supervisor create a better organizational climate for effective communication?
14. What is the grapevine?

Chapter Glossary

Communication model.	Representation of the stages of the communication process, in which a message is transmitted from a sender through a channel to a receiver.
Encoding.	Putting the message into a form that the receiver can understand, for example, spoken word, writing, or mathematical symbols.
Communication channel.	The medium through which a message is sent to the receiver, for example, communication, letters, and the grapevine.
Decoding.	Translation of the message by the receiver is called **decoding.** For example, if the message is written, the decoding process will involve reading.
Noise.	Any type of interference in the communication system which affects understanding, such as distractions, competing communications, or actual acoustic disturbances.
Feedback.	The part of the communication process that allows the communicator to judge whether the message sent has been received and understood. Feedback can be verbal or nonverbal.

Nonverbal communication.	A communication that relies on physical symbols (e.g., body language). A communicator can receive feedback by understanding nonverbal methods of communication.
Perception.	The way a person sees a communicaton and interprets it. Information is filtered through personal experiences, biases, values, and attitudes.
Emotional bias.	The effect of the personal feelings of individuals on communication. Previous experiences, values, attitudes, and feelings color an individual's perception of the meaning of information.
Stereotyping.	Generalizing the meaning of a communication on the basis of a preconceived image of the source.
Organizational climate.	The behavioral atmosphere or the psychological environment of a work unit or organization.
Upward communication.	The upward flow of information from employees to managers.
Grapevine.	The informal communication channel that exists in all organizations. It transmits information and rumors speedily but not always accurately.

Case Problem

Central Industries, Inc.

Central Industries is an old, established firm in the northeastern United States that was started by the Stewart family two generations ago. The current president, Emily Stewart, is the granddaughter of the founder, Josh Stewart, who started the business seventy-five years ago. The company is involved in the boat business, its primary product line being aluminum and fiberglass fishing boats.

In the past ten years Central has developed a full line of luxury "bass boats" that have become the best-selling boat of its type in the industry. Demand has been so great that plant capacity was expanded three times in the last ten years. The problem Central now faces is another plant expansion to accommodate the increased demand for their product. Unfortunately, there is no more room at their present site and Emily Stewart has been contemplating how the expansion can be accomplished. One alternative is to purchase another piece of property close by and build a new facility capable of handling their production needs for the foreseeable future. However, Emily has become increasingly concerned about the firm's distance from its primary markets. In previous years there was no problem because their aluminum boats were used almost everywhere. However, for their bass boat product line, their markets are further away, as most of these boats are sold in the southern and western parts of the U.S. This means that shipping costs are higher than for firms located in the south and that Central is in danger of losing its competitive edge. Therefore, Emily has been considering moving the firm to another city, in either the south or the west.

So far she has told no one of the possible move except for the three vice-presidents of the company (two of whom are family members). She is reluctant to say anything to the employees until something more certain has been decided.

Questions for Discussion

1. Should Emily tell the employees about the possible plant relocation? Why or why not?
2. Should she have said something when the idea first came to her?
3. What will likely be the reaction of the employees when they find out?
4. What should Emily do then?
5. In general, how should this type of situation be handled?

Leadership
and Supervision

After reading and studying this chapter you should be able to:

1. Describe the problems associated with leadership traits.

2. List and describe four traits that are generally associated with effective leadership.

3. Describe the relationship that leaders should have with their group.

4. Differentiate between leadership and supervision.

5. Describe the role that personality plays in leadership effectiveness.

6. List and describe the major roles that supervisors occupy as leaders.

7. Differentiate between power and authority.

8. Define power.

9. List and define the major sources of power available to supervisors.

10. Describe the ways that supervisors can increase their power.

Key Terms

Leadership traits
Trait theory of
    leadership
Power
Authority
Leadership roles
Influence
Information power

Position power
Skill power
Identification power
Acceptance power
Reward and punishment
    power
Zone of acceptance

261

The Joker Is Wild

Sam Robbins is angry. This is the third time this week someone in his department has pulled a practical joke on him. On the two previous occasions he let the group know he didn't appreciate these pranks, but apparently the message has not gotten through. Just now, when he sat down in his chair, it collapsed because someone removed the bolts that held the seat to the wheels.

Sam has been the supervisor of this group for only about a month. His predecessor was known to run a pretty loose operation and there was considerable talk about how the employees did pretty well as they pleased. Sam is determined to tighten ship because he doesn't want to have the same reputation.

While putting his chair back together, he has been reviewing his options. He could go to the group and ask who had played the prank and deal with that particular individual. He has also thought about examining his job description to see what authority he has to deal with this type of problem. Or, he could just ignore the situation, hoping that the group has had its fun and things will get better.

Probably the most sought-after skill in management is leadership ability. On the national scale, we speak of wanting the President to be a strong leader, and in organizations there is no less need for developing good leaders in the managerial ranks. Many millions of dollars are spent annually on leadership training, not only in business organizations but also in hospitals, churches, volunteer organizations, and government.

This chapter begins our analysis of the complicated phenomenon known as leadership. Our primary goal is an understanding of the process itself, that is, what leadership is as well as what it is not. First we look at some important issues in leadership such as leadership traits, the relationship between leadership and the group, the role of the supervisor, and personality and leadership. Next we examine the roles that supervisors are expected to occupy as leaders of groups. Finally, we explore the relationship between power and leadership and how supervisors can use power to become more effective leaders.

Important Issues in Leadership

For every supervisor, there are probably several important questions about leadership that are particularly troublesome (for what its worth, they are troublesome to every level of management!). These seem to be:

Are good leaders born or are they made? Are there certain traits that good leaders should have? Can I be a leader as well as one of the boys? Are leadership and supervision synonymous? What is the relationship between leadership and personality? And, what is the best style of leadership? With the exception of the last question, which will be covered in the next chapter, this section will provide an understanding of these issues.

Leaders: Born or Made?

Historically, it was believed that good leaders were born and not made. Depending upon one's definition of born, that still may be true. It is a fact that some people become very effective leaders for reasons we do not fully understand. To that extent, then, some leaders are born. However, deeper analysis often reveals why they became effective leaders. Two factors, situation and personality, are plausible explanations for born leaders.

The situational context suggests that these born leaders are very effective in some situations but not others. For example, Sir Winston Churchill is often cited as a born leader because of his leadership ability during World War II. However, when the war ended, he was not re-elected to the British Parliament. His supposedly innate leadership skills, therefore, may not have been innate at all, but rather a function of the situation he faced and his ability to make good decisions in that environment.

Personality (to be discussed in detail later in this section) is an abstract phenomenon that is not fully understood, especially in terms of its causes. No doubt some leaders are successful because of their personalities and, since we cannot fully explain personalities, we attribute their effectiveness to being natural. A complicating factor is that the cause-and-effect relationship between personality and leadership effectiveness is not clear at all, so even though some good leaders may have outstanding personalities (whatever that means), we aren't really sure that one causes another.

In the absence of adequate evidence to the contrary, we must still admit to the possibility that some effective leaders are born. It appears, however, that the good-leaders-are-born theory is more a dumping ground for things not clearly understood, and that, if the recent trends in leadership research are any indication, this theory will continue to lose credibility. Perhaps the most important consideration is that, assuming the born leader theory is correct, we have not yet learned to breed good leaders. This, of course, has important implications for leadership training.

The modern view of leadership is that many leadership skills can be learned. Note the careful wording of the statement. It does not say that we can make everyone an effective leader (primarily because we do not fully understand the leadership process), but that we can teach leadership skills. Whether or not these skills will make an individual an effective leader in any given situation is not something that can be guaranteed.

Leadership Traits

Closely related to the born-leader theory is the issue of **leadership traits.** It is believed that certain traits tend to be associated with leadership effectiveness and if we could identify these traits we could do a better job of selecting people for supervisory and managerial positions. Or alternatively, we could train the traits into people to make them more effective leaders.

The search for a good list of traits has been long and thorough. Researchers have examined physical characteristics (such as height or the shape of the head) as well as more psychological characteristics such as intellectual and emotional factors. Recent research has even gone so far as to examine such things as the sign under which a person was born, handwriting style, and order of birth.

It appears, therefore, that the trait theory of leadership has not proved to be a reliable method of analysis. However, there are a few traits that appear to have some relevance to leadership effectiveness, though by themselves they would not ensure that a person would be a good leader.

1. *Desire*—not surprising, since it suggests that motivation to lead is a key ingredient in leadership performance.

Pick a Trait—Any Trait!

The trait approach to leadership is basically a manifestation of our desire to simplify something that is really quite complicated. Our nature compels us to seek to make order out of chaos, thus the desire to discover a finite list of traits that can be used to identify good leaders (one can only wonder at the impact this would have upon personnel departments if we ever did come up with a good list). Perhaps the best description of where we stand on this problem is contained in a study reported by Ralph Stogdill in his *Handbook of Leadership* (New York: Free Press, 1974). One researcher reviewed over one hundred trait theory studies that examined traits such as intelligence, perseverance, cooperativeness, willingness to change, emotional stability —over one hundred and fifty traits in all. The study found that only five percent of the traits appeared in four or more of the studies!

2. *Intelligence*—means that the intelligence of the leader should be slightly above the average of the group. Does not mean that the more intelligent a person, the better leader he or she will make.
3. *Communication Skills*—again, not surprising given that leaders must communicate with followers.
4. *Confidence*—although to be avoided in the extremes, confidence in oneself apparently tends to rub off on subordinates.

The relative inadequacy of the results of the search for leadership traits is further illustrated by the fact that of the above four traits, only communication skills can be learned through training.

The primary lesson to be learned from the trait approach is probably that there is hope for almost everyone. There is no such thing as one best supervisor, nor is there a specific set of psychological or physical attributes that good leaders and supervisors must have. Later we shall see that supervisors should do certain things, but these will be specific behaviors that can be learned, not inherent psychological or physical traits. The above four traits would be a useful starting point for supervisors, but they would not necessarily mean the supervisor would be a good leader.

Leadership Versus the Group

Another nagging issue is whether the leader can (or should) be part of the group, or one of the boys (or girls), as it were. Here we need not be as cautious as we were with the traits. Although there are exceptions, as a general rule the supervisor should *not* be part of the group, at least not in the social sense.

To understand this principle, we must distinguish between supervision and leadership. Effective supervisors must possess leadership qualities because they are leading other people. Leaders, however, do not have to be supervisors since, strictly speaking, leaders do not *need* positions of authority—they need only to have influence over others. In Chapter 9 these individuals were referred to as natural or informal leaders, and they are part of the work group. Their role in the group is very different from that of the supervisor. The major difference is that informal leaders owe their allegiance to the group, whereas the supervisor holds his or her position at the discretion of the authority structure. Consequently, supervisors must often make difficult decisions (such as, who is to be laid off or transferred) and must remain as objective as possible. A supervisor who is too close to the group risks losing objectivity when making these decisions.

As evidence of this principle, a study was once done comparing the effectiveness of two types of supervisors—the psychologically close manager and the psychologically distant manager. The study confirmed that the psychologically distant manager was the more effective.[1]

As in the case with most behavioral patterns, some degree of normalcy is necessary. For example, a manager who is psychologically distant to the point of being aloof and uncaring would be as ineffective as the psychologically close manager, though for different reasons. The key is to find that middle ground that allows for objectivity without the appearance of being too distant.

Leadership and Supervision

As we have already suggested, leadership and supervision are not necessarily synonymous. In addition to the reasons already given, other factors separate the two. The process of supervision requires other behaviors, activities, skills, and responsibilities that are not inherent in the leadership role. For example, the supervisor must possess some degree of technical skill in order to supervise effectively, although the degree of the skill required will vary from position to position: the technical skill required of a nursing supervisor is probably higher than that required of a supervisor in an assembly line operation. Furthermore, none of the managerial activities discussed in Chapter 4 are necessarily found in leadership roles. Some good leaders, for example, may be very poor planners.

The major difference between leadership and supervision is that the process of leadership is largely behavioral in nature, whereas supervision goes far beyond the psychological and sociological determinants of behavior. As we noted at the outset of this book, good supervisors must be more than just good managers of people. In fact, one of the major difficulties in selecting good supervisors is finding individuals who have *both* good leadership and supervisory skills.

Leadership and Personality

There is little doubt that effective leaders must be well liked, but this is not a very scientific statement. What does *well liked* mean? What if a supervisor is only somewhat well liked? Is he or she then half as effective as a supervisor? There are many things supervisors could do to be liked which would be detrimental to performance. For example, giving every

---

1. Fred E. Fiedler, "The Leader's Psychological Distance and Group Effectiveness," in D. Cartwright and A. Zander, eds., *Group Dynamics*, 2nd ed. (New York: Harper & Row, 1960).

Exercise 11.1

Identifying Leadership Traits

The following experiment will give you some realistic insights into leadership traits. First, think of someone you have known in the past who you believed was a good leader. Next, jot down the *traits* this person had which you believed caused him or her to be a good leader. Third, share your list of traits with others who have done the same thing for someone they believed to be a good leader.

How many of the traits are common to all leaders? What does this tell you about leadership?

---

employee two hours for lunch might make the supervisor more popular, but would hardly be conducive to better productivity.

Personality plays an important role in the selection of informal leaders by a work group, although even here other factors can also come into play. Personality is an important factor for supervisors, but only insofar as interpersonal concerns can affect productivity. For example, the discussion in Chapter 6 regarding the role of morale would suggest that certain aspects of the supervisor's personality may increase morale, but may have no effect upon productivity.

In general, personality is not considered a major determinant of supervisory success, although there are two major exceptions. First, some individuals place considerable importance upon how well they get along with their supervisor. Studies have shown that in specific cases, interpersonal relations with supervisors can be a motivaing (or demotivating) factor. However, should a case arise in which an employee did not like the supervisor, improvement would be difficult because basic personalities cannot be changed. The second instance is broader in nature and therefore more useful. Research by Fred Fiedler into situational leadership has indicated that interpersonal relations are a more important determinant of leadership effectiveness than the task design or the inherent position power of the leader. In other words, Fiedler is saying that leaders who have good leader-member relations have more flexibility with the group than leaders with poor leader-member relations. This increased flexibility means that the group would probably be more tolerant of a leader's other limitations than would otherwise be the case.[2]

2. Fred E. Fiedler, *A Theory of Leadership Effectiveness* (New York: McGraw-Hill, 1967).

Supervisory and Leadership Roles

Since we now have made the distinction between leadership and supervision, for the remainder of this chapter we can treat the two as a single role. We know that effective supervisors must have leadership skills and we can now develop the two concepts simultaneously.

Chapter 2 noted the importance of the concept of role, and specifically how the expectations of others influence the roles we occupy. This is also true of the supervisor-leadership role. One way of learning how this role should be played is to understand the expectations of others—subordinates in this case. Understanding what they generally expect of supervisors gives important clues as to how the leadership part of the role (as opposed to the supervisory part) can be performed. The various roles that supervisors are expected to occupy are depicted in Figure 11.1. A description of the nature of these roles and how supervisors can use them to increase their effectiveness follows.

The Leader As Supporter

One of the most important roles of a supervisor is that of supporter—or helper—to the subordinates. This means that subordinates expect their supervisor to engage in whatever activities are necessary to help them perform their tasks more efficiently, more quickly, or more easily. For instance, the supervisor might fill in in someone's absence, pitch in to meet an important deadline, or remove blocks to productivity. In its basic sense, this role means that employees expect their supervisor to help them do their jobs, not hinder them. Its implementation is also simple: the supervisor might ask, "What can I do to help you?"

The Leader As Technical Advisor

On several occasions we have made reference to the need for technical skills in supervisors. We have always pointed out that (a) some degree of technical competence is important for supervisors, (b) the degree of technical skill necessary will vary from situation to situation, and (c) the higher the supervisory level, the less important technical skills become.

Technical skills are closely related to the supervisor's supportive role. If employees need help in technical matters, a supervisor unable to provide such help would lose influence. For example, if a typist needed help in setting up a complicated system of financial tables and the supervisor knew nothing about typing or the problems usually encountered in this situation, the leadership role of the supervisor would suffer.

Again, however, the danger of being too much of a technical advisor should be noted. There is a risk that supervisors may spend too much time on technical matters at the expense of their managerial duties. Perhaps the best reason for having a degree of technical competence is the respect it creates, a respect which can carry over to other areas of leadership.

The Leader As Power Figure

The concept of power is an important one for supervisors. No one likes to see weak people in positions of leadership. Companies do not like weak union officers (they can't control their members) and unions do not like weak company presidents (they can't control their managers). Unfortunately, power has an ugly connotation, such that many people become deathly afraid of being labeled power hungry. Admittedly, power can get out of hand, but to be an effective supervisor requires the ability to exercise power judiciously. We deal with power from another perspective later in this chapter, so our focus here will be upon how subordinates expect supervisors to use power.

Years ago a study was done comparing effective and ineffective su-

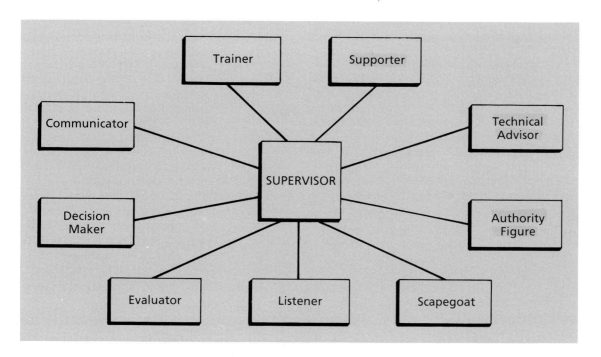

Figure 11.1. The Roles of the Supervisor as Leader.

pervisors. It was found that supervisors who were rated highly by their subordinates engaged in three activities.[3]

1. They were seen as going to bat for the subordinates, using their influence at higher levels for the betterment of the unit or department.
2. They were able to use their influence successfully, that is, on occasion, they delivered what was needed.
3. They were seen as using their influence primarily for the good of the subordinates rather than their own.

Items (1) and (2) establish that a supervisor is powerful; that he or she can successfully go to bat for the subordinates to obtain whatever they need to perform their jobs. This might be better equipment, more staff, or better working conditions. The third item is important because it establishes the trust relationship that has to exist between supervisors and subordinates. Without the trust, powerful and influential supervisors may be perceived as using their influence for their own good at the expense of the subordinates. Therefore, powerful supervisors are effective only if the power is utilized on some type of a shared basis. If the

The Incompetent Nursing Supervisor

Several years ago I encountered a situation that emphasized the importance of technical skills in the leadership role, especially with regard to the nursing profession. A hospital had hired a new nursing supervisor who came with excellent recommendations from a larger hospital. She had many years of experience as a supervisor and all indications were that she could handle this job with no difficulty. The hospital administration was concerned because of a noticeable drop in the morale of the nursing staff since the arrival of the new supervisor. I interviewed all the nurses to find out what was bothering them. My interviews revealed the usual list of complaints, but nothing that seemed to relate to the new supervisor directly. I was getting desperate for an answer (as was the hospital). One day I was having lunch with an individual who happened to work for the hospital where the new supervisor had previously been employed. In the conversation her name was mentioned and I was surprised to learn that she had last worked there ten years ago! Upon checking her application form, we discovered that she had lied about when she had worked there and, in fact, she had not worked as a nurse (or supervisor) for ten years. My interview data now made sense. The nurses had picked up that she was out of touch with current nursing practices (although they didn't say so directly) and they therefore resented her attempts at supervising them, especially in her in-service training function. When confronted with her fraudulent application form, she resigned. A respected and competent nurse from within the ranks was appointed supervisor and the morale problem disappeared.

3. D. C. Pelz, "Influence: Key to Effective Leadership in the First-Line Supervisor," *Personnel* 29 (1952), pp. 209–17.

An Untrustworthy President

During the early 1970s, many universities began to feel the impact of reduced funding from governments. The same problem arose at private universities, and at one such institution the president asked the faculty and staff to engage in a major cost-cutting campaign to reduce expenditures, and proposed faculty layoffs, reduced support staff, increased class sizes, higher teaching loads, and reduced travel budgets. The campaign seemed to be reasonably well accepted until one day in the local newspaper it was revealed that the president's Mercedes-Benz was paid for by the university, and that recently he had negotiated a lifetime pension of $70,000 per year with the Board of Trustees to be effective upon his retirement in three years. When this information became pubic, enthusiasm for the cost-cutting program dwindled, and within one year the faculty had unionized.

trust factor is violated, the supervisor can be in for some serious problems.

The Leader As Scapegoat

This may seem like an unfortunate role for supervisors and perhaps in one sense it is. Nevertheless, it is necessary. The scapegoat role means that the supervisor must be prepared to accept responsibility for the actions of subordinates. This does not mean that undesirable behavior or poor decisions should be condoned—for they should not; but it does mean that the supervisor cannot always shift blame away from himself or herself.

Subordinates resent a supervisor who consistently tries to blame others for unacceptable behavior. Suppose, for example, a worker makes a mistake that costs the company a small amount of money. If the supervisor sends him or her upstairs to explain the mistake, then the supervisor is not accepting the role of scapegoat. To play the role properly, the supervisor should go upstairs, explain the mistake, accept responsibility for it as a supervisor, and then deal with the subordinate separately. Again, it should be emphasized that playing the role of scapegoat does not mean that supervisors should condone or ignore mistakes of subordinates; it only suggests that as the manager, the supervisor should share in the accountability and deal with the mistake itself as the situation requires.

The Leader As Listener

In Chapter 18, "Interviewing, Counselling, and Performance Appraisal," this topic will be examined in depth but it warrants mentioning here as well. Every employee, the supervisor included, sooner or later experiences some degree of anxiety on the job. The anxiety may not be directly related to the job, but it can affect job performance if it is not dealt with. One of the more positive roles a supervisor can play is that of a listener, an individual who is willing to listen when people are upset, mad, afraid, or insecure. Subordinates like to have a supervisor who is seen as understanding and willing to listen to a person's expressions of feelings.

The role of listener, however, goes beyond dealing with upset employees. Participation, which is discussed in the next chapter, requires that the supervisor listen to their ideas and suggestions also. Goal setting, which was discussed earlier, requires active and positive listening by the supervisor. Developing good communication between supervisor and employees requires effective listening. Good listening serves a managerial purpose as well as a therapeutic one.

The Leader As Evaluator

No doubt one of the more unpleasant roles required of supervisors is the evaluative one. Earlier we discussed the managerial requirements of supervisors and pointed out that supervisors *should be* required to evaluate subordinates' performance and be held accountable for that evaluation. That doesn't change, of course, but this discussion is more concerned about that role as seen from the subordinate's perspective.

Evaluation is the primary means for subordinates to receive feedback on their behavior. They need to know where they are going right and where they are going wrong. No one enjoys hearing about his or her mistakes, but having no feedback can create more serious problems in the long run.

Another dimension of evaluation pertains to how subordinates expect their supervisors to deal with other employees. If a supervisor should be evaluating the performance of others but is not doing so, resentment may arise. Discipline is a common case of supervisory neglect. If one employee is consistently causing problems for others, the supervisor will be expected to deal with the problem, otherwise resentment can affect the morale of the entire group.

Some supervisors have difficulty handling problems such as these, partly because of the interpersonal conflicts involved and partly because they haven't been properly trained. The discussion in Chapter 8 on how to discipline, as well as the material in Chapter 18 on performance appraisal should provide some guidance.

The Leader As Decision Maker

''The only thing worse than a bad decision is no decision at all.'' This statement, though it may not be entirely accurate, does reflect a major expectation of the suprvisory role. However, it does not mean that supervisors should make decisions merely for the sake of making decisions. Although decision making is discussed in greater detail in Chapter 15, here we will concentrate on the expectations of the supervisor in the decision-making role.

First, supervisors are not expected to make decisions without having the necessary information. What is annoying to subordinates is to see that a supervisor does have all the information necessary, but then will not make a decison.

Second, this role expectation does not mean that supervisors have to make decisions themselves. Perhaps a better wording would be, "supervisors are expected to get decisions made." It may be, for example, that the supervisor wishes to involve the group in the decision-making process. This would be consistent with the role expectation, provided that a decision is reached.

The decision-making function is important to subordinates because it lets them know what to expect. A supervisor who sits on a decision unnecessarily causes uncertainty and anxiety. Furthermore, decision making is the one area in which employees see the supervisor as having complete control. Therefore, when a decision is not forthcoming, they may see the supervisor as weak, incompetent, afraid, or any combination of these.

The Leader As Communicator

As we noted in Chapter 10, the supervisor is the pivotal point for all formal communication in the unit. Informal communication will flow through the unit via the grapevine, but employees will depend upon the supervisor for most of their job-related information. This means that supervisors need to see themselves as communicators and transmitters of information, rather than just collectors of information.

As we shall note later in this chapter, there are times when supervisors should withhold information; but generally speaking, as much information as possible should be passed on to employees. If the information is important enough, the workers will probably find out anyway, so they may as well find out the correct information from their supervisor.

Another aspect of the supervisor's communication role is task related. Employees need information in order to perform their jobs efficiently. Nothing is more exasperating than to find out that something was done needlessly simply because of poor communications. Rarely are these types of errors made on purpose, but they are nonetheless annoying. In fact, forgetting to tell someone something is probably an indirect admission that you did not consider the person important—which is why people resent it so much.

Nobody's Perfect!

One of my most embarassing moments occurred several years ago while I was in charge of a renovation project in our campus building. Planning started in late June in order to have the renovations completed by the time school started in September. Many people were involved: faculty, students, staff, and various administrators. Since it was a small project, it was to be handled internally by the campus architect's office, so a junior designer was assigned to the job. After some initial consultation, a working plan was drawn up for the group's approval. There was considerable disagreement between group members and a lot of time passed before consensus could be reached. It then appeared that there was not enough time left to complete the work before school started, so it was decided to postpone the renovations until spring. On the following Monday morning, the architect showed up with a work crew to begin the renovations. I had forgotten to tell him the project had been postponed.

The Leader As Trainer

A part of the helper or supporter role mentioned earlier is the role of trainer. This includes not only training new employees in job skills and work methods, but also socializing them into the work group. As the new employee learns the ropes and increases his or her job skills, the trainer role of the supervisor diminishes, though it never is eliminated.

The role of trainer requires somewhat different attitudes and behaviors, because people who are learning need greater understanding, support, empathy, patience, and tolerance from the supervisor. The learning environment should be positive, not threatening, so that employees are encouraged to develop their skills and abilities. More will be said about this important role in Chapter 13, "Selecting, Inducting, and Training Employees."

⋆ Barriers to Performance

There are other roles not mentioned here that supervisors have to play from time to time: coordinator, policeman, representative, and organizer, to name but a few. These could be considered minor, however, in the sense that they either occupy a relatively small portion of the supervisory role or, for various reasons, are not part of every supervisory role. Those we have discussed seem to be common expectations of most supervisors and are therefore covered in greater detail elsewhere in this book.

There are two barriers often encountered by supervisors in attempting to engage in these role behaviors. The first is lack of training. In Chapters 2 and 3 we alluded to the fact that many supervisors lack preparation for their roles, and the previous role analysis illustrates the problem areas that can arise. The role of listener, for example, requires specific communication skills that must be learned, understood, and practiced. Performance evaluation is another skill area that requires training and practice. Better training can assist in improving role performance so that supervisors can exhibit leadership in a manner consistent with the expectations of their employees.

The second barrier is the potential for conflict among the different roles. Success in one may sometimes interfere with success in another. For example, the most frequent conflict tends to be between the supporter and evaluator roles. The supporter role requires creating a positive climate, while the evaluator role often requires criticism and discussion of negative factors. It takes a very skillful supervisor, indeed, to engage in both roles effectively.

The initial step to successful supervisory leadership is awareness of what followers generally expect from their leader. That has been the primary purpose of this section. After awareness come experimentation and practice with the role behaviors on the job (or in a simulated work environment) to develop the skill levels required for effective leadership.

Power, Influence, and Supervision

The importance of power and influence for supervisors should be obvious by now. A supervisor with little power or influence would not be able to control employees and, regardless of his or her other qualities, would probably be ineffective. The purpose of this section is to explain more fully what power and influence are, how they can be used, and how the supervisor can acquire them.

What Is Power?

The first step in understanding power is to differentiate it from authority. **Power** is the *ability* of an individual or group to influence another person or group, and is exercised only at the discretion of those being influenced. In contrast, **authority** is the *right* to influence another person or group and is delegated to the individual by the organization. It is therefore possible to have power without authority, and authority without power (although the two will often go hand in hand). Another way of examining the two concepts is to note that power is a concept attached to an individual (or group), whereas authority is a property associated with a formal organizational position. For example, supervisors have authority by virtue of their job descriptions, but any power a supervisor might have would be a function of personal qualities and behaviors beyond the authority in the job description.

As an example of these two concepts, consider the informal leader of a group as described in Chapter 9. These leaders have no formal authority, but they can possess considerable power, or ability to influence others. Another example would be a famous sports or television personality who tries to sell us a new car in a radio or television commercial. Again, he or she has no authority but is attempting to influence our behavior through personal qualities (power).

As we have explained, authority would be present in a supervisor's job description. However, if a supervisor never used that authority, we would say he or she had little power over subordinates. A different supervisor could occupy the position, use the authority, and then be seen to have considerable power.

The ideal situation for supervisors is to have sufficient authority available from the job description, and also to use that authority in addition to any personal power attributes. Relying on only one of the two makes the supervisor's job more difficult.

What Is Influence?

Influence is the result of the exercise of power and authority. To have **influence** means that one person can effect a change in the behavior of another person or group. Theoretically, at least, influence can result from either power or authority, but practically speaking, influence results from power since power relates to a person's ability to affect behavior. In other words, it is possible to have authority but no influence, but not to have power without influence.

If all the above seems somewhat confusing, you are on the right track. Power and authority *are* confusing, both in theory and in practice. However, the importance of the distinction becomes apparent in the next section concerning sources of power.

Sources of Power

We have already noted that the source of authority is the job description. In contrast, power has several sources which can be classified into several categories, all pertaining to personal qualities, abilities, or situations.[4]

4. This discussion is heavily based upon French and Raven's theory of sources of power. See J. P. French and B. Raven, "The Bases of Social Power," in Dorwin Cartwright, ed., *Studies in Social Power* (Ann Arbor: University of Michigan Institute for Social Research, 1959), pp. 150–67.

INFORMATION. **Information power** allows one person to influence another because the second person needs the information that the first person possesses. if no one needs the information, no power or influence relationship is present.

Examples of this can frequently be seen in organizations. Some managers and supervisors withhold information from employees to make the latter dependent upon them. Employees are unable to operate on their own and make their own decisions because they do not have all the information they need. Thus, the supervisor becomes more powerful.

Another example is the rumor mill described in Chapter 10. One reason why people like to start rumors is because the information they possess gives them power over others, regardless of the accuracy of the information. This means that one way of stopping rumors is to make the correct information available to all.

SKILL. In one sense, **skill power** is a variation of information power. In this case, one person possesses a specific skill or ability that someone else needs. As long as the need persists, an influence relationship will be present. For example, a person in a department may have an important and specialized skill that everyone else needs (such as mathematics or budgeting), which will place him or her in a more powerful position relative to others. In the larger context, computer people acquire considerable power over other departments because of the skill and knowledge they possess about computers.

Power and Word Processing

An area in which many organizations are experiencing difficulty is the placement of word processing machines into their office systems. The problem arises because of the power and authority conflicts that develop out of knowledge and skill power held by word processor operators. In one case I observed that *fewer* people used the word processing machine because they resented the power that the operator had over them. For example, a senior person (with lots of authority) would want a rush job done right away. For reasons not fully understood by the senior person, this was not always possible ("I can't do it now because the thermo-memory has cross-filed with the megabyte disk"). Eventually, every job was labeled rush, which created even more tension. The resentment became so strong that many began avoiding taking their work to the word processor and instead gave it to a typist—someone whose work they could understand—even though it usually meant a longer delay. The problem was eventually solved by creating a job priority list, and posting the list by the word processor itself so that everyone could see how much work was in the queue ahead of them. Thus, information was shared and some of the power (though not all of it) of the word processor operator was removed.

POSITION. Power accruing to individuals or groups who have positions perceived by others as rewarding is **position power.** Supervisors will, of course, acquire a certain amount of position power by virtue of the authority vested in their position. Presidents of companies, obviously, exert considerable position power.

On an informal level, position power results from the perceived influence a person has in his or her role. For example, the secretary to a senior executive may have considerable position power because of the perceived influence that he or she has with the executive. Or, a particular position may acquire power because of the rewards that are perceived to accrue to that individual, such as the stage manager for a famous rock group.

Position power is usually made up of information and skill power, since these generally accrue only to those people in specific positions. In other words, in order for a position to possess power and influence, it would have to have some information, skill, and/or rewards associated with it.

IDENTIFICATION. This type of power is potentially the most influential. **Identification power,** potentially the most influential because of its deep psychological roots, is based on the desire to imitate (or model) the behavior of someone else. The most obvious example of this is with young children; they identify with all sorts of heroes such as sports figures, cartoon characters, and television stars, and consequently they imitate their behavior in ways such as dressing like them, buying models and games, and generally acting out the roles of their heroes.

Adults do the same thing, although not quite as obviously, and the choice of hero is usually made for better reasons than the number of criminals he has put in jail. Because people do not make these choices lightly, these models exert considerable power and, generally speaking, for long periods.

From the standpoint of supervision, this type of power is not easily acquired, largely because it is difficult to predict what type of behavior employees will model. However, since modeling is based upon seeing our hero receive rewards we would like to receive, supervisors can attempt to set a good example, hope that the example is rewarded (for example, by a promotion), and that the employees also will see promotion as desirable.

ACCEPTANCE. This is perhaps the most common source of power possessed by managers and supervisors because it is closely tied to the formal organizational position. **Acceptance power** means that people will accept your influence because it is considered normal to do so in the situation. In organizations, we expect subordinates to be influenced by

Exercise 11.2

Informal Leaders and Formal Leaders

Now you know that informal leaders have power within their groups, although they have no formal authority. Formal leaders, on the other hand, are given authority but must acquire power. Putting the two concepts together can create some interesting problems. Imagine that you must decide who will fill a vacant supervisory position. One of the applicants is the informal leader of that group who has the technical qualifications necessary for the job. Make a list of the factors that would be in favor of this person's appointment, as well as a list of the factors that would be against it. On balance, should the informal leader be made the formal leader?

---

their supervisors to some degree because of the nature of the relationship. Because of this, subordinates allow it to happen; they accept it as being normal.

Acceptance power is limited by the definition of *normal.* This means that if a supervisor attempts to exert influence in a manner that goes beyond what is considered to be normal, he or she will be unsuccessful. For example, acceptance power would be rejected if a supervisor ordered a subordinate to do something illegal, although there are cases on record in which subordinates did commit the illegal act because the power of the manager was so great.

REWARD AND PUNISHMENT. This category is a catch-all that includes all of the above as well as some others. Any time an individual or group has the ability to impose rewards or punishments on another person or group, an influence relationship will be present, that is, **reward and punishment power.** Notice, for example, that each of the above categories has a degree of reward and/or punishment power attached to it. A supervisor could acquire this type of power by praising and disciplining subordinates as described in Chapter 8. Reward and punishment power can also be used independent of the formal authority. Recognition for good work or expressing disappointment at lack of performance would both be examples of using this type of power.

Acquiring Power

As the previous discussion illustrates, there are some types of power that are beyond the control of the supervisor. However, there are certain things that supervisors can do to increase their power base and therefore become more effective leaders.

IMPROVE TECHNICAL KNOWLEDGE AND SKILL. It is in these two areas that supervisors can effect the greatest change in their power base. Subordinates will be more likely to respect and follow a leader who is seen as being knowledgeable and skillful in the task at hand. The common term for this is respect, and it is known that respect can increase influence. Knowledge and skill improvement apply to technical as well as managerial areas. In fact, both would be necessary for the supervisor to function well as a leader.

OBTAIN AND USE AUTHORITY. In the early chapters the importance of having sufficient authority in the supervisory role was noted. In addition, it is important for the supervisor to use (and to be seen to use) whatever authority is available. Using the authority establishes that the supervisor has the *ability* to use whatever authority is available.

ENLARGE THE ZONE OF ACCEPTANCE. The **zone of acceptance** defines how much latitude the supervisor has in using acceptance power. Supervisors with a narrow zone would find that subordinates frequently question their decisions or bypass the supervisor and take their concerns and problems to higher managers. While increased knowledge will help enlarge the zone of acceptance, the best way is by generally being an effective supervisor. In other words, as employees learn that the supervisor knows what he is doing, they will tolerate a wider variety of decisions and instructions from the supervisor.

SERVE AS A ROLE MODEL. It has always been known that supervisors (as well as other managers) should always set a good example. In terms of using identification power, this is about the best a supervisor can do. The decision to imitate another's behavior is always made by the chooser, not the model.

USE REWARDS AND PUNISHMENTS. Supervisors who are seen as using rewards and punishments frequently will acquire more power than those who do not, all other things being equal. This means using not only the rewards and punishments that are required (that is, recommendations for promotion or disciplinary action for violating rules), but also the informal ones. In fact, there is probably greater opportunity for using the informal rewards and punishments than the formal ones. As Chapter 8 pointed out, supervisors should learn to be free with their compliments as well as their criticisms, and to deal out each according to the principles developed in that chapter.

Key to Success

Leadership skills are a necessary (but not sufficient) part of every supervisor's job. Being an effective leader involves more than just giving orders to subordinates. The people-managing part of supervision requires that supervisors understand the fundamental nature of the leadership process, how it relates to supervision, and the role behaviors that leaders are usually expected to perform.

The acting out of the leadership role requires the use of power to influence others. Supervisors who rely only on the authority contained in their job descriptions will encounter resistance from their employees and will probably end up very frustrated. There probably was a time when the primary supervisory quality required was the ability to communicate directions clearly. But in today's complex supervisory world, supervisors have to be effective leaders.

Understanding the role of leadership and supervision is the first step toward becoming an effective leader. We have yet, however, to relate the concept of supervisory *style* to the leadership process. The next chapter will explore the alternative styles available to supervisors and provide assistance in deciding which ones are appropriate for which situations.

Summary

This chapter has examined the relationship between leadership and supervision, and discussed the roles that supervisors must occupy when exercising leadership. First, several issues regarding leadership were presented. The conclusions were: leadership skills can be taught, the trait approach to leadership has not yielded much assistance in selecting or training leaders, supervisors must adopt a role that is detached from the group so that more objective decisions can be made, leadership and supervision are not synonymous, and the personality of the individual can affect leadership ability in certain situations, although this is generally not considered to be a major determinant.

The chapter examined the various roles that supervisors must occupy. These are the role of supporter, technical advisor, power figure, scapegoat, listener, evaluator, decision maker, communicator, and trainer. Each of these roles requires slightly different behaviors and occasionally the roles are incompatible.

Power is a necessary attribute for good leaders. Power is the ability to influence people and can have several sources. Although supervisors have authority, they cannot rely on authority alone to get things done. One of the best ways for a supervisor to increase his or her power is to establish a reputation for using authority and to be competent at the job.

Other sources of power exist: information, skill, position, identification, acceptance, and reward and punishment. Each of these will be used from time to time, depending upon the circumstances.

Opening Incident Revisited

Sam's problem is that he has no power over his group—yet. Since he has followed a supervisor who apparently exerted little control over the employees, it is not surprising that they expect him to behave in the same way. Since power is the *ability* of one person to influence someone else, Sam will have to demonstrate that he has the ability.

In view of that, let's examine the alternatives that he's considering. First, if he asks the group who pulled the prank, they may not own up to it. From what we know of group theory, the group may protect its members by disavowing any connection with the prank. Sam certainly could not prove otherwise. However, this does not mean that his strategy is without merit. Confronting the group with his feelings may be the first show of power that the group needs. In other words, they may learn that Sam will not let these pranks go unnoticed.

His second strategy—to look at his job description to see how much authority he has—would probably have only limited value. The problem is not his authority, but his influence. However, he may find something in his job description that will help him to acquire some power, such as rewards and punishments.

His third strategy is likely to be the least valuable of the three. Doing nothing will reinforce the group's perception that he has little power. The effect of this would probably be to decrease his zone of acceptance even further.

In sum, Sam must do something to show the group that he has authority and is willing to use it to establish his role as leader of that group. It should also be noted that whatever action Sam decides to take should be taken as quickly as possible. The longer he waits to exert some influence the more difficult it will be.

Review Questions

1. Are good leaders born or are they made?
2. What is the trait theory approach to leadership?
3. What traits are often associated with leadership effectiveness?
4. What problems are associated with the trait approach?
5. How does the group affect the supervisory leadership role?
6. How are leadership and supervision different?
7. What is the relationship between leadership and personality?
8. What are the various roles that supervisors must perform as leaders?
9. Why is power important for leaders?
10. What is the relationship between power and trust with regard to the supervisor as leader?

11.   What is the scapegoat role?
12.   What is the evaluator role?
13.   What is the supporter role?
14.   What are the supervisor's primary sources of power?
15.   How are power and authority different?
16.   What things can supervisors do to acquire more power?

Chapter Glossary

Leadership traits.	Behavioral and attitudinal characteristics that are assumed to be associated with effective leaders.
Trait theory of leadership.	The approach to leadership that attempts to find which leadership traits are associated with effective leadership.
Power.	The ability of a person or group to influence another person or group. It is a social process and functions at the discretion of the person or group being influenced. Cannot be delegated.
Authority.	The right of a person or group to influence another person or group. The right originates with the organization and can be delegated.
Leadership roles.	The various roles that supervisors must occupy in order to perform the leadership function. The roles are defined by the expectations of the organization and subordinates.
Influence.	A change in behavior of one person or group as a result of an interaction with another person or group. Can be the result of power or authority.
Information power.	Power that allows one person who has information to influence another who needs it. Influence relationship lasts as long as the second person needs the information.
Skill power.	Power accruing to an individual or group who possesses skills needed by others. Influence relationship lasts only as long as those being influenced need the skill.
Position power.	Power accruing to individuals or groups who have positions which are perceived by others as rewarding. Can also be a source of authority.
Identification power.	Power based upon one person's desire to be like another person. Usually called modeling. Influence relationship lasts only as long as the modeling principle operates.
Acceptance power.	Power based upon the norms of a specific situation which allow influence to occur. One person accepts the influence of another because that is the norm in that

	situation. Lasts only so long as the norm exists, or the persons involved remain in that situation.
Reward and punishment power.	Power that accrues if one person or group is in a position to reward or punish another person or group. Influence relationship lasts only as long as the rewards and punishments can be controlled.
Zone of acceptance.	The limits within which the influence of a leader is accepted by others. The wider the zone the leader is able to establish the more influence he or she has.

Case Problem

Tom Jones

Tom Jones is the maintenance supervisor at Valley Community College and supervises a staff of twenty-five employees, all of whom perform various maintenance duties around the college. He has been in his job for ten years and the majority of his staff have been with the college for a number of years as well.

Over the past several years the college has been experiencing difficult times. Although enrollment is at an all-time high, the funds available to operate the college have diminished over the last few years. Every year at budget time, Tom has submitted his request to the president, and every year his budget has been further reduced. His present staff of twenty-five is down from a high of forty just three years ago. Every year he has had to lay off more employees and ask the remaining to take up the slack, and each year it becomes more difficult to get all the work done with fewer people. In addition, the morale of his staff is at its lowest. Several of his best employees have quit, and although that reduces the need for layoffs, he is left with less capable employees to do the same amount of work.

Last week the annual budget meeting for all the department managers and supervisors took place. Each department's request was reviewed and the president announced what the budgets would be for the coming year. At that meeting, Tom learned that his budget is being cut another ten percent, which means laying off at least two more employees. Today his manager, the vice-president of operations, informed him that he had just received a letter signed by most of the maintenance staff asking that they be given a new supervisor.

Questions for Discussion

1.   Why do you think the staff sent this letter?
2.   Is Tom at fault here? Why or why not?
3.   What could Tom have done to avoid this situation?

Supervision and Leadership Styles

12

Chapter Learning Objectives

After reading and studying this chapter you should be able to:

1. Define Theory X and Theory Y.

2. Describe the cause-and-effect relationship between Theory X and Theory Y and employee behavior.

3. List several examples of Theory X and Theory Y behavior or characteristics in organizations.

4. Describe the importance of distinguishing between leadership attitudes and leadership behaviors.

5. Compare Theory X and Theory Y with personality traits.

6. List the limitations of the Theory X–Theory Y analysis.

7. List and define the three basic leadership styles and give the advantages and disadvantages of each.

8. List several behaviors that supervisors would use to be autocratic and democratic.

9. List and describe each of the contingency models of leadership.

10. Describe the contingency approach to leadership and list its advantages and disadvantages.

Key Terms

Leadership style
Theory X
Theory Y
Stretching
Autocratic leadership
Democratic leadership

Abdicratic leadership
Contingency theories of leadership
Leadership continuum model
Managerial grid

Situational leadership
Leadership decision-making model
Path-goal theory

McBurgers Hamburgers

Susan Weston was amazed. As a new management trainee for McBurgers Hamburgers, a national chain of fast-food restaurants, she never saw such organization before. She sat through the lunch-hour rush and couldn't believe that they served so much food in such a short period of time.

But as she watched, something else struck her, the restaurant manager's autocratic style of leadership. He was barking orders right and left (though he always said "please"), never seemed to ask anyone else's ideas on how jobs should be done, and generally ran things like a dictator. The reason Susan was amazed at this is that she just completed a course in supervision at a local college and the instructor literally preached about the value of participative management. Yet here was an obviously successful organization that had no participation whatsoever.

Later, when she spoke with some of the employees, most of whom are part-time high school students working for spending money, they confirmed her suspicion that the manager is very autocratic and that he will not tolerate the least deviation from the specified method of performing a job.

This evening, Susan has been reflecting on her career with this organization. She is worried because according to a leadership style questionnaire she recently completed in class, her preferred style is predominantly participative.

One of the most researched topics in the area of managing people is leadership style. As usual, the research has focused on finding the best leadership styles and, although it has not yielded the answer sought, it has provided some useful insights for appropriate supervisory styles.

Whereas Chapter 11 described the general nature of leadership and the roles that leaders must play, **leadership style** pertains to how the supervisor actually treats subordinates. Style also relates to specific behaviors of the leader, and recent research has concentrated on behaviors that can be taught in supervisor training programs. After all, the concept of effective leadership styles would be relatively meaningless if the styles could not be learned by others.

As this chapter will illustrate, one of the trends in leadership research has been away from the simple, two-dimensional models to situational models. This is a direct result of the fruitless search for the "one best way" and indicates that leadership is a complicated process. However, the advantages of the situational models are that (a) they tend to deal more with behavior than with attitudes, and (b) they offer concrete solutions to leadership problems.

In this chapter we begin by analyzing the simplest of models, the basic assumptions that supervisors make about employees, and show

how these attitudes relate to leadership behaviors. We then discuss the alternative leadership styles available and show how each might be appropriate in certain situations. Finally, the chapter concludes with an examination of the most accepted models of leadership behavior and shows the situational nature of the leadership process.

Theory X and Theory Y

In the 1950s, management theorist Douglas McGregor studied various leadership styles in an attempt to understand which styles led to better productivity levels. He was fascinated by the difference in productive behavior that occurred on the job and this formed the basis for his theory.[1]

McGregor saw basically two types of employees at work: those who were responsible, mature, productive, and who could be trusted with responsibility, and those who were the opposite, that is, needed close supervision, could not be trusted, and generally produced at some minimum level. The question McGregor addressed was, "How do workers get the way they are?"

The answer to this question resulted in his now famous "Theory X and Theory Y" formulation. McGregor believed that people responded to the environment in which they worked, with a large part of that environment being the leadership styles to which they were exposed. He believed that workers reacted to the *assumptions* of their managers and that these assumptions, described as either Theory X or Theory Y, influenced the behavior of the workers.

The Theory X assumptions are negative:

1. Employees basically dislike work and must be coerced into working.
2. Employees are lazy, irresponsible, and indolent.
3. Employees cannot accept responsibility.
4. Employees need to be controlled.

The Theory Y assumptions are positive:

1. Employees like to work and seek out responsibility.
2. Employees can be trusted to work on their own.
3. Imagination, creativity, and ingenuity are normally distributed throughout the population, not narrowly distributed.
4. Employees will work toward organizational goals as a means of self-satisfaction.

1. Douglas McGregor, *The Human Side of Enterprise* (New York: McGraw-Hill, 1960).

McGregor believed that a manager with Theory X assumptions would cause that type of behavior, and a manager with Theory Y assumptions would cause positive types of employee behavior. This cause-and-effect formulation is depicted in Figure 12.1.

In other words, McGregor proposed that if a manager assumed (**Theory X**), employees were lazy, irresponsible, stupid, and needed to be controlled, this would cause them to act that way. Similarly if managers held positive assumptions about employees (**Theory Y**), these assumptions would cause positive behaviors. As Figure 12.1 suggests, managers had traditionally believed the opposite cause-and-effect model to be true. That is, they believed that *because* employees were lazy, indolent, and so on, they must be treated accordingly. So McGregor's analysis placed the responsibility for change on the shoulders of managers because it was their assumptions about people that created the behavior — both bad and good — that occurred on the job.

X and Y In Practice

Although McGregor's initial formulation of the X-Y attitude theory was primarily concerned with individual leadership styles, other aspects of work environments are illustrative of the same basic assumptions about people. Some of the more obvious examples of Theory X factors are:

- close supervision,
- jobs with narrow scope,
- time clocks,
- external motivators, such as money,
- rules,
- controlled coffee breaks, and
- rigid work schedules.

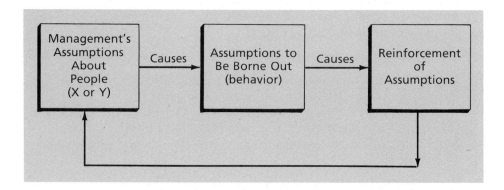

Figure 12.1. The X-Y Cause-and-Effect Model.

Theory Y factors include:

- participative management,
- jobs with broad range of responsibility,
- few controls over individual behavior,
- emphasis upon goal achievement,
- two-way communication,
- shared influence between manager and subordinate, and
- satisfaction of internal as well as external needs.

There are several things here that are of interest to supervisors. First, many of the characteristics that define a Theory X or Theory Y work environment are beyond the control of the supervisor. For example, many control systems — such as time clocks and work schedules — are designed, implemented, and managed by senior management. Given all the Theory X factors that would exist in many large organizations, the Theory Y attitude of a supervisor might have little impact on employees.

Second, these examples suggest that Theory X need not be viewed as entirely negative. Everyone would agree on the need for some control in organizations. Without it, chaos would be rampant. Therefore, it is important to distinguish between the control system itself, and the motivations (or assumptions) behind it. For example, time clocks can have two purposes: to provide cost data for product pricing (a positive motivation), and to check on when employees arrive at work (a negative motivation). According to the X-Y formulation, the effects upon behavior would be different.

And finally, these examples suggest that the perception of what is X and what is Y may vary with the employee. This is particularly true of leadership styles. A style that is perceived as Theory Y by a relatively low-level employee may be perceived as too controlling by a higher-level person. If we view X and Y as various degrees of freedom allowed employees, then it is not surprising to find that one person's freedom is another's prison.

Applying X and Y

As Chapter 5 pointed out, human behavior is a complex phenomenon. Any theory that simplifies behavior into two categories must therefore be used with caution. If we keep this in mind, the X-Y formulation does have possibilities for improving the supervisor's understanding of his or her impact upon employee behavior.

Putting Theory X attitudes into practice would mean:

1. close supervision;
2. directions on what to do, when to do it, and how to do it;
3. solving problems for employees;

4. mostly downward communication;
5. close control over all behavior;
6. use of rules and punishments to control behavior; and
7. centralization of authority in the supervisor's job.

Putting Theory Y attitudes into practice would mean:

1. relatively loose supervision;
2. delegation of authority to subordinates;
3. mutual agreement upon subordinates' objectives;
4. two-way communication between supervisor and subordinates;
5. participation of subordinates in decision making;
6. consultation with subordinates by supervisor; and
7. emphasis upon results, not how results are achieved.

ASSUMPTIONS VERSUS BEHAVIOR. An important point to remember is that X and Y describe attitudes or assumptions about people. Attitudes about people may or may not have anything to do with how they are managed. Although it may sound strange, it is perfectly possible to feel one way about people, yet treat them in another way. This point is very important for the application of X and Y since we know that attitudes are difficult to change. If we had to rely on attitude change before supervisory styles could change, we would be waiting for a long time indeed. However, once we realize that our assumptions about people can differ from how we treat them, then there is real possibility for a supervisor to change from being an X leader to a Y leader. This notion will become an important concept when we examine the situational ap-

A Theory X Parent

During a supervisory training course, one of the participants approached me about a family problem. It seemed that he was having difficulty with his thirteen-year-old son — a problem he had diagnosed as the generation gap, but could also be called the X-Y gap. The immediate problem was the degree of control he wanted over his son, and his son was resisting. The father had just completed an X-Y questionnaire that showed him to have strong X attitudes. Recently he and his son had been arguing over what time the son should be home on weekends. The father demanded the son be home by 11:00 P.M. and the son was resisting what he thought was an unreasonable rule. After some discussion, the father agreed that he should be more Y in his relationships with his son and decided that the following weekend he would tell the son he could come home at a time he thought was reasonable. As it turned out, the son came home at 4:00 A.M. that weekend, the father went through the roof, and the boy was grounded for six weeks. The father's comment: "I knew he couldn't be trusted to handle responsibility!"

What went wrong?

proaches to leadership. For the remainder of this analysis, however, we shall assume that attitudes and behavior are synonymous.

MAJOR SHIFTS IN STYLE.   Throughout the years of applying the X-Y theory several lessons have been learned. One is that leaders should avoid making major shifts in their supervisory styles over short periods. An employee's reaction to the environment is something that has been built up over a long period. Regardless of what the organization thinks of that behavior, it is functional for the employee. A major shift in either leadership style or environment can produce considerable anxiety and, in fact, lead to lower performance. If a supervisor wishes to change either the style or the environment (or both), the changes should occur in small steps and over extended periods to give workers a chance to adapt.

MATCHING STYLE WITH PEOPLE.   It follows from the previous principle that leaders must match their style to fit the needs of the employee. We learned in Chapter 5 that, with some exceptions, behavior does not change significantly over short periods. Therefore, the supervisor will initially have to adapt the style to fit the person. For example, if a supervisor inherits an employee from another company who has been conditioned by a very structured, control-oriented atmosphere, providing Theory Y leadership will probably result in a situation like that described by the Theory X parent. Shifts in leadership style should be made gradually.

STRETCHING EMPLOYEES.   The application of Theory Y principles involves stretching employees. Assume that you have subordinates who behave according to Theory X assumptions and you want to develop them into more of a Theory Y type. **Stretching** means that you would slowly delegate more and more responsibility, always giving the employee a little more than he or she is capable of. Increasing expectations a little at a time gives employees a challenge or target that is only slightly beyond their present capabilities, but is within their grasp. The stretching principle is one of the most useful for developing the potential talent in people.

X and Y and Control

It may appear that Theory X is a very control-oriented philosophy and Theory Y is not. This is only partly true. The major difference is that Theory X relies on *external* control, whereas Theory Y is oriented toward *internal* control. Under external control systems, employee behavior is controlled by such things as the supervisor's behavior, organizational control systems, rules and punishments, and so forth. Theory Y is designed to develop responsibility in employees so that they exhibit control over their own behavior. In other words, Theory Y attempts to develop employees who will do the right things because they want to, not because they have to.

X and Y Versus Personality

Much confusion has existed over the years regarding the relationship between theories X and Y and the personality of managers. It has erroneously been thought that Theory X managers were rude, obnoxious, or otherwise were unlikeable people. Similarly, Theory Y managers have typically been pictured as nice guys, friendly, pleasant to work for, and so forth. Neither description is correct because both confuse personality with leadership style. As we noted in the previous chapter, being well-liked by employees will no doubt make a supervisor's job easier, but it does not describe leadership style. Leadership style has to do with communication, direction, structure, control, and other sets of behaviors, not with the interpersonal qualities and skills of the supervisor. Although style and personality would not be completely divorced, it is possible to be a nice Theory X manager or an obnoxious Theory Y manager.

Which Is Better: X or Y?

This question has had some confusing answers over the years. For a long time it was believed that the Theory Y style of leadership was better than the Theory X, and in one sense that is true. Theory Y is better in that it allows for more growth and development of employees. Also, because it relies on self-control rather than external control, the supervisor is freed up to perform managerial duties other than just supervising employees. After all, close supervision is a very time-consuming activity.

However, it would be incorrect to say that all supervisors should

Understanding X and Y

The confusion in many people's minds about X and Y was brought home to me several years ago in a supervisory training course while I was attempting to develop the concepts of X and Y. The group was divided in half and one person from each group was asked to lead the group in a task. One leader was instructed to lead in an X manner and one in a Y manner. After giving the teams time to get organized, I visited each to see how they were doing.

Upon entering the X leader's room, I found him standing on top of a table, shouting and cursing his group members. He thought that was the way that X supervisors behaved. I then went to the Y leader's room, only to find him gone. After a short search, I found him sitting in the lounge drinking a cup of coffee. When asked what he was doing there, he replied, "Being Theory Y — letting the group do what it wants to do."

adopt a Theory Y style of leadership. As we have already noted, some employees need a more structured environment and would have difficulty working in a situation where they were required to make decisions. Some people need to be controlled, told what to do, and "goosed" now and then. Extreme Theory Y leadership would be quite inappropriate for these situations.

Therefore, there is a place for both X and Y *behaviors* and *attitudes* in supervision. The key to effectiveness is to have the skill to apply the right style to the right employee, and to avoid extremes. The situational nature of good leadership is now widely recognized. Later in this chapter we shall discuss in detail the situational analysis supervisors should be prepared to make.

Basic Leadership Styles

Over the many years of leadership research, different labels have been given to the various leadership styles. Terms such as participative, permissive, people oriented, supportive, relationship oriented, and considerate, have all been used to describe the style that is directed primarily towards concern for people. The opposite style has been labeled directive, task oriented, production oriented, or structured. Regardless of the label used, one thing that is agreed upon in leadership theory is that leader behaviors can be divided into two categories: those that deal with people, and those that deal with the job or task at hand. The common labels for these are *democratic* for the former, and *autocratic* for the latter. The *abdicratic* style — which may not be a style at all — is also worth noting. Below is a discussion of each style: note that the autocratic style corresponds to the Theory X assumptions, and the democratic style corresponds to the Theory Y assumptions.

Autocratic Style

The **autocratic style** is basically one in which the supervisor makes most or all of the decisions, at least those of any importance. Autocrats practice centralized decision making and generally allow employees little opportunity for participation and involvement. Communication upward is generally limited and the leader makes sure everyone knows where he or she stands. Autocratic leaders generally have strong confidence in their own ability and believe their way of doing things is best. Instructions tend to be clear and detailed to make sure employees do the job the right way.

Autocratic leaders have, unfortunately, been given some bad press in recent years. One possible reason for this is the confusion between per-

Exercise 12.1

Diagnosing Your X and Y Attitudes

Directions: The following are various types of behavior which a supervisor may engage in in relation to employees. Read each item carefully and then place the number from the key beside each statement.

Key: 1 = Make a Great Effort to Do This
2 = Tend to Do This
3 = Tend to Avoid Doing This
4 = Make a Great Effort to Avoid This

If I were a supervisor, I would:

1. Closely supervise my employees in order to get better work from them.
2. Set the goals and objectives for my employees and sell them on the merits of my plans.
3. Set up controls to assure that my employees are getting the job done.
4. Encourage my people to set their own goals and objectives.
5. Make sure that my employees' work is planned out for them.
6. Check with my people daily to see if they need any help.
7. Step in as soon as reports indicate that the job is slipping.
8. Push my people to meet schedules if necessary.
9. Have frequent meetings to keep in touch with what is going on.
10. Allow employees to make important decisions.*

After you complete the exercise your instructor will provide you with scoring instructions.

* Exercise adapted from *The 1972 Annual Handbook for Group Facilitators* (Iowa City, IA: *University Associates Press,* 1972).

---

sonality and leadership styles mentioned previously. This has caused us to overlook the positive aspects of autocratic leadership and the fact that it is at times more effective than participative leadership. Experience with leadership styles suggests that autocratic leadership, properly exercised, would be effective in the following situations:

1. in crises;
2. when employees are new and have little ability;
3. if employees lack initiative and a sense of responsibility;
4. when communication and coordination is of utmost importance (e.g., military).

5. if the leader is a clearly recognized expert on the problem;
6. when the quality of a decision is of critical importance and acceptance of the decision by subordinates is of little importance;
7. if initial organization and coordination are required.

It is worth noting that with the exception of item (3) above, none of these situations contradicts Theory Y assumptions. In other words, the supervisor could exhibit autocratic behavior, yet still hold Theory Y assumptions about subordinates in these situations. Also, autocratic leadership in itself becomes more palatable once it is realized that a supervisor can be nice, yet autocratic.

The other side of the coin, of course, is that autocratic supervisors can create serious problems. If the conditions mentioned earlier do not exist, autocratic methods might be resented and cause low morale and low productivity. Many employees expect to have a voice in their jobs and working conditions. If they are competent, they resent having a supervisor looking over their shoulders and telling them how to do their jobs.

As a society, we seem to be moving away from autocratic methods to a more participative style of management. For example, part of the success of the "Japanese Method" of management involves democratic management styles where workers are consulted regularly about how objectives should be accomplished. Although the idea of participative management originated in North America, recent experience suggests

My Autocratic Friend

I am very fortunate to have a friend who happens to be one of the best autocrats in the world. By "best," I mean he exhibits all of the good qualities of autocrats, and none of the personality problems that are usually (wrongly) associated with autocratic leadership. For several years he was kind enough to assist me in leadership experiments in which autocratic and democratic leaders were compared. These experiments usually involved some type of competition between two groups working on a timed project that required very basic skills. In over ten years of experiments, he has never lost a contest. Whatever the goal was, his group did it better, faster, and more efficiently than the democratic group. In hindsight, he always had an advantage.

First, he never had the same group twice, so any low morale associated with his style never had an opportunity to affect future performance. Second, he always won, and the winning feeling he generated in his group probably compensated for any misgivings about his leadership style. But more importantly, he knew his style and he knew it well. Therefore, in these experiments (as well as his normal business life) he always created situations in which autocrats had an advantage, that is, he created crises, set himself up as the expert ("I've done all this before"), and so forth. That's why he is a good autocrat. As you might guess, he's also smart enough to avoid situations in which autocratic leaders would not function well.

that the Japanese have made better use of it. We can also see that many other aspects of our daily lives such as schools and educational systems, churches, civic organizations, and families have moved toward more democratic systems.

Autocratic supervision is often called traditional management because of its origins years ago when participative methods were unheard of in organizations. Even today it is not difficult to find traditional supervisors who keep a tight rein on their employees, make all decisions themselves, and expect obedience and compliance in a manner reminiscent of slavery. Provided that these supervisors are managing traditional employees, there may not be a problem. However, when faced with a new generation of workers who have been raised in a more democratic environment, these supervisors will create serious problems.

Democratic Style

The **democratic** (or participative) **style** is the opposite of the autocratic style. On the basis of Theory Y assumptions about people, democratic managers delegate authority to subordinates, involve them in decision making, trust them to handle responsibility, and exert little direct control over their behavior. Democratic managers believe that employees have something to contribute to the organization beyond just their physical capabilities, and they therefore create an environment in which these contributions can be stimulated and utilized.

Research has indicated that groups with democratic supervisors tend to have higher morale, although this does not always mean higher productivity (as we noted in Chapter 5). However, since morale is a long-run requirement for consistent productivity, the democratic style would seem to be more desirable in many situations. It is safe to say that, all other things being equal, democratic methods of supervision will tend to generate better attitudes (such as loyalty, commitment, and morale) than autocratic supervision.

There are, however, several disadvantages to democratic supervision. First, it takes more of the supervisor's time. Participation, involvement, and communication all require face-to-face contact with subordinates. There is no doubt that it would be faster for the supervisor to make the decision and announce it. This, of course, is why autocratic methods are recommended for crisis situations.

Another potential problem with democratic supervision is the possibility of disagreement between supervisor and subordinates. Sometimes supervisors mistakenly assume that with participation and better communication, subordinates will end up agreeing with what the supervisor wants to do, and some supervisors attempt to use democratic methods as a trick to gain subordinates' agreement. In reality, if true participation is used, the supervisor must be prepared to compromise his or her own ideas to include the input or subordinates.

MISCONCEPTIONS ABOUT DEMOCRATIC SUPERVISION. There are generally two common misconceptions about how democratic supervision operates. The first is that the supervisor should take every decision to subordinates for participation. This is false. The supervisor must be very selective about participation, which should be implemented only under these general conditions:

1. The decision must be of some importance or consequence to subordinates;
2. Adequate time must be allowed for meaningful participation to occur;
3. Subordinates must be qualified to participate; and
4. Subordinates must have adequate information about the problem.

If these conditions cannot be met, the attempt at participation will be a frustrating process for all. The subordinates will probably feel they are being manipulated, and the supervisor will view the whole process as a waste of time.

The second common misconception about democratic supervision relates to the more common meaning of the term *democratic.* In democratic political systems, decisions are voted upon by constituents and therefore some believe that supervisors should allow employees to vote on decisions. In organization and management theory, the term democratic has a different meaning than it does in political circles. If subordinates were allowed to vote on decisions, the supervisor would, in effect, be abdicating the role of supervisor, since accountability for the decision must lie with the supervisor, not the group. In addition, voting would probably not generate good decisions since the voting process could be contaminated with all sorts of nonmanagerial factors. In democratic or participative supervision, the supervisor is still accountable for getting good decisions made and cannot turn the decision-making function over to the group.

WHEN DEMOCRATIC SUPERVISION WORKS. As in the case of autocratic supervison, there are certain types of situations in which the democratic or participative style is more effective.

- The leader is not a recognized expert in the problem.
- Acceptance of the decision and its implementation by the group is a critical factor.
- The group has knowledge that the supervisor needs to solve the problem.

- The supervisor's authority or power base is low.
- Resistance to a decision is anticipated.
- The employees are skilled and motivated.
- The overall objectives of a decision are agreed upon.

These conditions should be understood as guidelines. Each situation must be examined on its own merits. Also, there are degrees of being democratic (as well as autocratic) so the supervisor can vary the amount of participation depending upon the situation.

Abdicratic Style

As we noted at the beginning of this chapter, the **abdicratic style** is really not a style at all, in the sense that an individual is the formal leader but does not perform any leadership functions. What sometimes happens in these situations is that one of the group, perhaps the informal leader, takes over the leadership of the group. This could be bad or good depending upon a number of factors, but the major point is that the person selected for the leadership position has failed to function properly.

There are several reasons why people would abdicate the leadership position. Some may simply find the leadership role uncomfortable, that is, the role (as described in the previous chapter) may place too great a psychological burden on them. Others may operate from a very weak power base, and although they would like to be effective leaders, have only their desire (but little authority) to work with. Some might abdicate because they face a very strong informal group leader, with whom the conflict is so great that the formal leader gives up and acquiesces to the

Measuring Supervisory Styles

One of the more popular training instruments these days is the questionnaire that measures supervisory style. Participants answer a series of questions (much like Exercise 12.1) which, when scored, reveal their primary supervisory style. A few years ago I began experimenting with these instruments in the following way. I would first give the questionnaire to the supervisors and have them score it. Generally speaking, in about seventy-five percent of the cases, the supervisors described themselves as being participative. I would then give the same questionnaire to their employees and ask them to answer the questions as they thought their supervisor would. When these questionnaires are scored, they generally show the supervisors to be more autocratic than they believed themselves to be. This suggests that there may be a degree of self-deception operating when we examine our own leadership styles. A more realistic view probably can be obtained from our employees.

A Day in the Life of an Abdicrat

The following is taken from a conversation with a middle-level supervisor in a large government organization. However, the situation could—and does—arise everywhere, and is one of the major enemies of effective leadership.

"When I first came into this job ten years ago I was a real ball of fire. I really wanted to make things happen and impress the brass with my ability. It didn't take long to figure out where to start. There was so much deadwood and slacking around here I was amazed that anything ever got done. After about a year of laying the proper groundwork,

I went after one of the worst slackers. I proposed to my boss this guy be fired and provided him with all my documentation. You know what he said? 'Don't rock the boat. That guy has been around here for fifteen years and will likely be around for another fifteen. If you try to fire him, he'll just file a grievance and we'll probably lose it. Then you'll really have a problem. I don't need those headaches. Just do your job and don't cause any trouble with the union.' I tried several other things and got the same answer. After a while, I just said to hell with it! Life is too short for that kind of grief."

informal leader. Finally, some supervisors abdicate their leadership role because they lack the necessary support from the rest of the organization. For example, a supervisor may try to tighten ship but finds that when the conflict goes upstairs, higher mangagement provides no backing and reverses his or her decision.

Supervisory and Leadership Behaviors

Thus far we have described leadership assumptions, attitudes, and styles, and made general reference to how supervisors implement these styles. With this background, it is now possible to be more specific regarding what supervisors should do to implement either a democratic or autocratic style.

During the 1950s and 1960s, several research projects on effective leadership were conducted at Ohio State University. These studies attempted to discover which leadership styles were most effective under what conditions, and still stand as a landmark today in our knowledge about leadership and supervision.

In measuring leadership styles, the Ohio State studies used a series of questions that were answered by employees about their supervisors. These questions are particularly useful here since they describe what leaders actually do, as opposed to their attitudes, assumptions, or feelings. The questions have been adapted for our purposes to provide statements which show what a supervisor would do to be either democratic or autocratic.[2] Some sample participative (democratic) behaviors are:

1. waits patiently for the results of a decision;
2. allows group members complete freedom in their work;
3. publicizes the activities of the group;
4. makes pep talks to stimulate the group;
5. permits members to use their own judgment in solving problems;
6. does little things to make it pleasant to be a member of the group;
7. keeps the group working together as a team;
8. encourages initiative in the group members;
9. puts suggestions made by the group into operation;
10. lets the members do their work the way they think best;
11. lets some members take advantage of him/her;
12. treats all group members as his equals;
13. settles conflicts when they occur in the group;
14. assigns a task, then lets members handle it;
15. gives advance notice of changes;
16. looks out for the personal welfare of group members;
17. allows the group a high degree of initiative;
18. trusts the members to exercise good judgment;
19. permits the group to set its own pace;
20. maintains a closely knit group.

Sample directive (autocratic) behaviors include:

1. acts as spokesman for the group;
2. lets group members know what is expected of them;
3. makes accurate decisions;
4. becomes anxious when he/she cannot find out what is coming next;
5. encourages the use of uniform procedures;
6. argues persuasively for his/her point of view;
7. speaks for the group when visitors are present;
8. decides what should be done and how it should be done;
9. pushes for increased production;
10. makes sure his/her part in the group is understood by the group members;
11. sees to it that the group's work is coordinated;
12. takes full charge when emergencies arise;
13. reduces a madhouse to system and order;
14. maintains definite standards of performance;

2. Adapted from Leader Behavior Description Questionnaire—Form XII (Columbus, OH: The Ohio State University, College of Commerce and Administration, Bureau of Business Research, 1962).

15. refuses to explain his/her actions;
16. asks that group members follow standard rules and regulations;
17. acts without consulting the group;
18. anticipates problems and plans for them;
19. schedules the work to be done;
20. doesn't allow the members any freedom of action.

The behavioral descriptions given in these lists serve two major purposes for us. First, they can be used to show what supervisors should do when they want to exhibit a particular style. Second, they indicate that the autocratic and democratic styles are much more complex than their names imply. It is for this reason that terms such as *directive* and *participative* or *production oriented* and *people oriented* are better descriptions of the styles than *autocratic* and *democratic.* Indeed, most people would rather be called directive than autocratic.

Contingency Models of Leadership

The contemporary view of leadership, as proposed in the **contingency theories**, is that it is situational and that it is complex. Both of these conclusions are in stark contrast to the historical view that tried to find the one best way. Even McGregor, just prior to his untimely death, was beginning to reformulate the X-Y theory into more of a situational framework. The complexity dimension recognizes that leadership behaviors cannot be accurately described using two-dimensional scales, al-

Exercise 12.2

Effective and Ineffective Leaders

The situational nature of effective leadership should now be apparent. A style that is good in one situation could be totally inappropriate in another. This exercise gives you the opportunity to think about effective and ineffective leaders (or supervisors), their styles, and their situations. Think of one leader for each of the four possibilities: an autocratic leader who was effective and one who was ineffective, and a democratic leader who was effective and one who was ineffective. Then describe in detail the type of situation that each leader faced, and that made him or her effective or ineffective.

though that is still a common trend. This section presents and analyzes the popular contingency (i.e., situational) theories of leadership today. You should be able to see the influence of earlier theories in the contingency models, and have a better understanding of the conclusions reached earlier regarding appropriate situations for autocratic and democratic styles. The leadership models most relevant for supervisors are the Leadership Continuum Model, the Managerial Grid, Situational Leadership, the Vroom-Yetton Model, and the Path-Goal Model.

The Leadership Continuum Model

One of the earliest attempts at formulating a contingency approach to leadership is the Tannenbaum and Schmidt **Leadership Continuum Model** pictured in Figure 12.2.[3] Though not based on empirical research, the model was an intuitive attempt to recognize that leadership styles must vary to fit the situation. At the far left side, the boss-centered style, the leader has all the authority and uses it. This would be the equivalent of the autocratic approach. However, as one moves from left to right, the style changes in degrees to subordinate-centered leadership. One of the major insights of this model is to show that leadership styles can range over many variations and are not just either-or.

Tannenbaum and Schmidt state that in order to choose the right syle, the manager must be aware of the forces operating in the situation. These are (a) forces in the manager, (b) forces in the subordinates, and (c) forces in the situation. After analyzing these three factors, the supervisor can then decide which point along the continuum is the best style.

Although Tannenbaum and Schmidt offer some ideas regarding how the forces should be analyzed, the problem remains as to exactly how one decides which point on the continuum best describes the situation. However, the other models to be discussed overcome this problem to some degree. In any case, the Leadership Continuum Model is a useful starting point for understanding the contingency approach to leadership.

The Managerial Grid

One of the first leadership models to discard the traditional labels of autocratic and democratic was that of Robert Blake and Jane Mouton.[4] They created the terms *production-centered* and *people-centered*, which generally correspond to autocratic and democratic, respectively. The

3. Robert Tannenbaum and Warren H. Schmidt, "How to Choose a Leadership Pattern," *Harvard Business Review* (November–December, 1964).
4. R. R. Blake and J. S. Mouton, *The Managerial Grid* (Houston: Gulf Publishing Company, 1964).

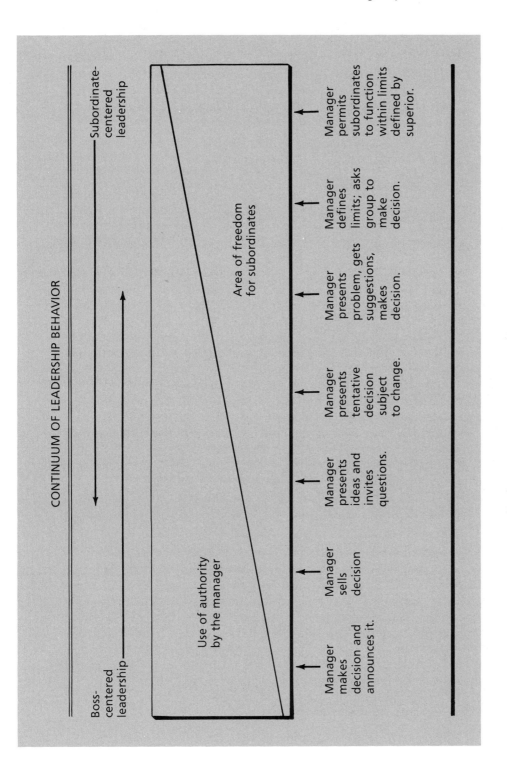

Figure 12.2. The Leadership Continuum Model.
Adapted from Tannenbaum and Schmidt, 1964. Copyright © 1964 by the President and Fellows of Harvard College; all rights reserved.

Managerial Grid was also one of the earliest attempts to describe the independent relationship between concern for production and concern for people. Prior to the grid formulation, leadership behaviors were placed on a continuum such as the Tannenbaum and Schmidt scale just discussed. By placing the two sets of behaviors on a graph format the grid recognized that the two sets of leader behaviors could be present in varying degrees.

The Managerial Grid leadership model is illustrated in Figure 12.3. Although there are theoretically an infinite combination of leadership styles available, the grid concentrates on five. These are:

1. 1,1 *Impoverished Management*. This style describes the manager who really doesn't lead at all, and most closely resembles the abdicratic style discussed earlier. This manager has little concern for people and production.

2. 9,1 *Task Management*. This style is heavily concerned with the production side of leadership, and has little concern for people. The major emphasis is to get the stuff out the door, regardless of the human cost involved.

3. 1,9 *Country Club Management*. This is the opposite of the production-oriented leader. This leader's main concern is that people be happy in their jobs; if you can just make people happy, everything else will work itself out.

4. 5,5 *Middle-Road Management*. This is the leader who is trying to find a reasonable compromise between what appear to be opposing alternatives. Rather than take a strong stand on either one, this leader does a satisfactory amount in each. A classic fence-sitter.

5. 9,9 *Team Management*. This style is considered by Blake and Mouton to be the ideal style, although it is acknowledged that other styles will have to be used from time to time. The 9,9 manager has high concern for people *and* production, and is therefore able to maximize results in both dimensions.

The Managerial Grid has been an extemely popular approach to leadership training and development. As part of the grid training program participants complete a series of questionnaires that feed back to them what their personal profile is on the grid. Once this is done, training can commence to develop those areas in which the person is weak. The grid approach is also used as a method of long-term development in an organization or work group. The goal of achieving team management (9,9) requires that people be able to deal with intergroup and interpersonal problems so that destructive conflict can be managed more effectively. The grid teaches techniques of conflict management so that the barriers to effective work teams can be removed.

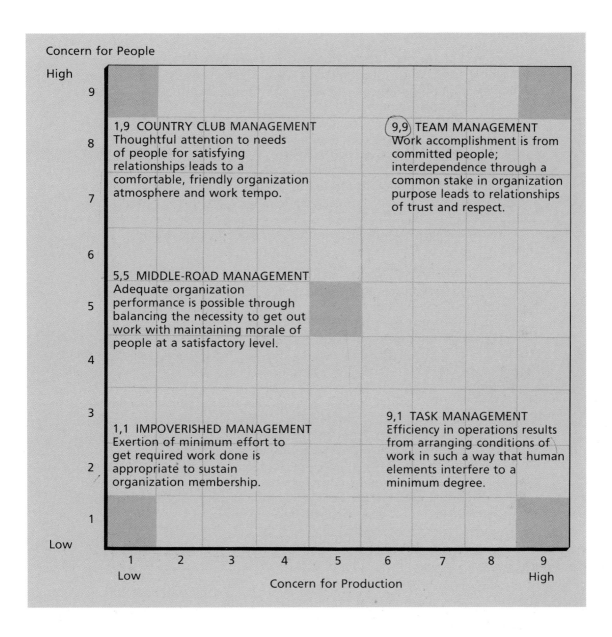

Figure 12.3. The Managerial Grid.
Adapted from Robert Blake, Jane Mouton, Louis Barnes, and Larry Greiner, "Breakthrough in Organization Development," *Harvard Business Review* (March-April, 1958). Copyright © 1958 by the President and Fellows of Harvard College; all rights reserved.

Situational Leadership

A more recent formulation of leadership behaviors in a grid format is Situational Leadership, developed by Paul Hersey and Ken Blanchard.[5] Although the foundation of the model is similar to the grid, there are some important differences.

Situational Leadership recognizes the two basic dimensions of leadership behavior (called directive behaviors and supportive behaviors), but takes the analysis one step further into a true situational framework. Whereas the Managerial Grid proposes that the 9,9 style is the *ideal* style, Situational Leadership maintains that any style can be effective in specific situations. The Situational Leadership Model is presented in Figure 12.4.

Situational Leadership describes four distinct styles available to the manager.

1. S(1)—*Telling Style.* Primarily directive in nature, this style consists of behaviors such as defining roles, giving instructions, setting goals, and telling people how, when, and what to do in their jobs.

2. S(2)—*Consulting Style.* The "high task, high relationship" style, this style provides considerable direction but also considerable support. The leader consults with subordinates (the supportive approach) but retains the final decision (directive approach).

3. S(3)—*Participating Style.* In this style the leader reduces the directive content of his or her role, but maintains the supportive behaviors. By allowing subordinates to participate in decision making, the leader is relinquishing his or her power base from which directions were given. Primary function of the leader is communicating and facilitating.

4. S(4)—*Delegating Style.* This style recognizes that some people need little active leadership. Because of their skill and motivation, leaders often just get in their way. This style is very low in profile and provides little direction and support to these employees.

Situational Leadership maintains that any of these styles can be effective, depending upon the nature of the person or group being supervised. The model then goes further to define four development levels (D levels) of employees, based upon the premise that performance on the job is a function of an individual's ability and motivation.

1. D(1)—low ability, low motivation
2. D(2)—low ability, high motivation
3. D(3)—high ability, low motivation
4. D(4)—high ability, high motivation

5. Paul Hersey and Ken Blanchard, *Management of Organizational Behavior* (Englewood Cliffs, NJ: Prentice-Hall, 1982).

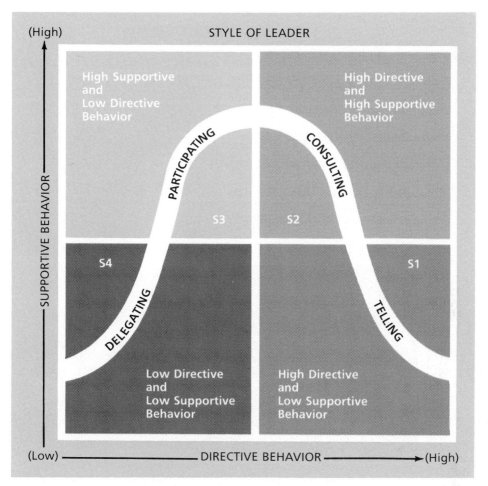

Figure 12.4. The Situational Leadership Model.
From Paul Hersey and Kenneth H. Blanchard, *Management of Organizational Behavior: Utilizing Human Resources*, © 1982, p. 200. Reprinted by permission of Prentice-Hall, Inc., Englewood Cliffs, N.J.

The model then relates leadership style to the development level of the person or group as illustrated in Figure 12.5. To find the correct leadership style to use for a certain employee, the supervisor has only to decide at what stage the employee is in the development process.

It is not difficult to think of situations in which the Situational Leadership model would be useful. New employees, for example, would be the most likely candidates for D(1), and the model prescribes the S(1) style, that is, a lot of direction. This seems reasonable because new employees would be unable to function properly if not initially told what to

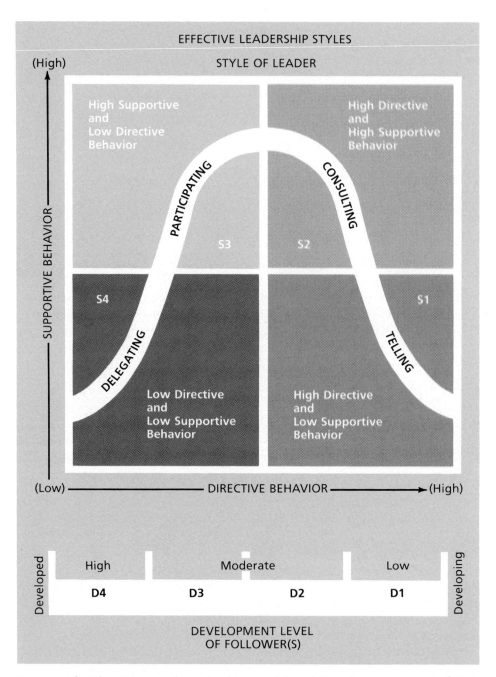

Figure 12.5. The Situational Leadership Model and Development Level of Followers.
Adapted from Paul Hersey and Kenneth H. Blanchard, *Management of Organizational Behavior: Utilizing Human Resources,* © 1982, p. 248. Reprinted by permission of Prentice-Hall, Inc., Englewood Cliffs, N.J.

do. As they increase their motivation, the supervisor can increase the supportive behaviors while maintaining the directive ones. This builds confidence in the employee and strengthens the interpersonal relationship. The S(3) style would be useful for an employee who has the ability, but lacks motivation. Task direction here would be futile since the employee already knows how to do the job. However, by emphasizing the supportive behaviors (communicating, listening, participating) the supervisor can increase motivation. And finally, the S(4) style is appropriate for employees who are both skilled and motivated. These would most likely be the more senior, long-term employees who need little direction. Although the supervisor should not ignore the D(4) employees, they do not need as much attention as the others.

Leadership Decision-Making Model

The **Leadership Decision-Making model** developed by Vroom and Yetton is yet another attempt to define how situations affect leadership behavior.[6] This model starts with the framework established by the Tannenbaum and Schmidt continuum, but then develops the continuum further to specify what factors in the situation affect the leader's decisions about how to lead.

Table 12.1 shows the ranges of styles in this model and gives a brief description of each. Again, notice the similarity between these styles and the descriptions given by the Tannenbaum and Schmidt continuum. The model itself is pictured in Figure 12.6 and shows the decision process that a manager must go through to determine which style is most effective. One of the differences between the Leadership Decision-Making model and the previous contingency approaches is that this model recognizes that *more than one style may be effective in a given situation* (called the "feasible set"). Note that in the last column of Figure 12.6, some alternatives indicate more than one feasible style. This means that the supervisor can have more flexibility in dealing with people than was previously thought to be the case.

One of the major advantages of the Leadership Decision-Making model is that it minimizes the guesswork that the leader has to do in order to decide which style is best. The specific questions in the model provide a very structured approach to the problem. The model is, however, more complicated than the others discussed because it attempts to include more variables in its analysis. Since we know that human behavior is a complex phenomenon, any model that includes a large number of variables is likely to be more useful than one that oversimplifies the problem.

6. V. Vroom and P. Yetton, *Leadership and Decision-Making* (Pittsburgh: University of Pittsburgh, 1973).

Table 12.1. Ranges of Leadership Styles in Leadership Decision-Making Model.

1. You solve the problem or make the decision yourself, using information available to you at the time.

2. You obtain the necessary information from your subordinates, then decide the solution to the problem yourself. You may or may not tell your subordinates what the problem is in getting the information from them. The role played by your subordinates in making the decision is clearly one of providing the necessary information to you, rather than generating or evaluating alternative solutions.

3. You share the problem with the relevant subordinates individually, getting their ideas and suggestions without bringing them together as a group. Then you make the decision, which may or may not reflect your subordinates' influence

4. You share the problem with your subordinates as a group, obtaining their collective ideas and suggestions. Then you make the decision, which may or may not reflect your subordinates' influence.

5. You share the problem with your subordinates as a group. Together you generate and evaluate alternatives and attempt to reach agreement (consensus) on a solution. Your role is much like that of chairman. You do not try to influence the group to adopt "your" solution, and you are willing to accept and implement any solution which has the support of the entire group.

Source: Reprinted from *Leadership and Decision-Making*, p. 13, by Victor H. Vroom and Philip W. Yetton, by permission of the University of Pittsburgh Press. © 1973 by the University of Pittsburgh Press.

The Path-Goal Model

The Path-Goal model is the least developed of the leadership theories, but nevertheless offers promise for supervisors. It is related to the expectancy theory of motivation discussed in Chapter 7, and describes the role that the leader can play in the motivation process.[7]

Expectancy theory, it will be remembered, proposes that motivation occurs when an employee perceives that effort will lead to an outcome which the employee sees as important. The **Path-Goal theory** of leadership proposes that the effective leader is one who can clarify the path

7. Robert House, "A Path-Goal Model of Leader Effectiveness," *Administrative Science Quarterly* 16 (September, 1971), pp. 321–38.

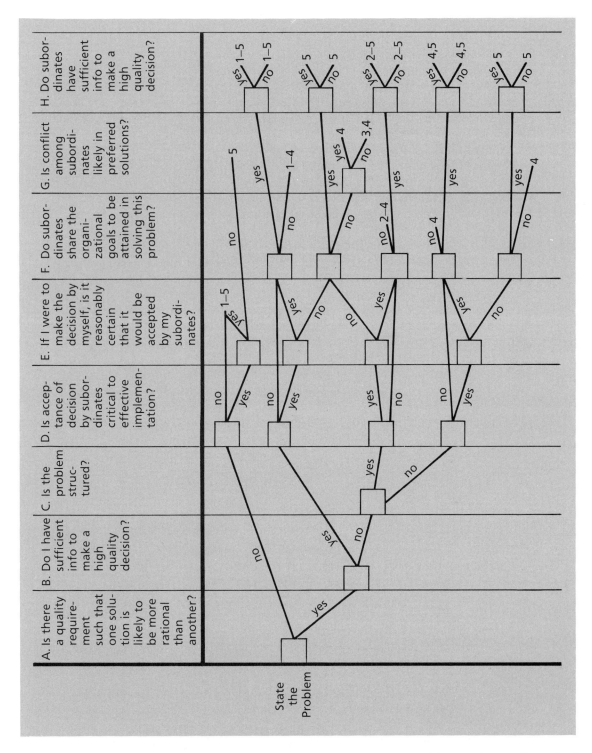

Figure 12.6. Decision-flow Process for Leadership Decision-making Model. Numbers at the end of the diagram correspond to style numbers in Table 12.1.

Adapted from *Leadership and Decision-Making* by Victor H. Vroom and Philip W. Yetton, by permission of the University of Pittsburgh Press. © 1973 by University of Pittsburgh Press.

from effort (or performance) to the employee's goals. The supervisor does this by specifying what behaviors will lead to what rewards, by removing blocks that may prevent employees from reaching the goals, or by behaving in a way that will increase employee satisfaction on the way to achieving these goals.

One of the promising aspects of the path-goal approach is that it reconciles all of the previous models. For example, directive behavior by the supervisor would be useful for an employee who didn't understand the task at hand because direction would clarify the path between effort and reward (assuming, of course, that the supervisor rewarded good performance). Conversely, a senior, experienced employee would resent direction since it might be interpreted as a lack of trust or sensitivity. In other words, direction in this instance would be a block to satisfaction rather than assistance.

In practice, the application of the Path-Goal model is relatively simple. The supervisor has to know (a) what the employee wants from the job, and (b) if motivation or performance will be useful in attaining what the employee wants. Once this is known, the supervisor can then proceed to make the relationship between performance and reward as clear as possible, and provide the necessary support for the employee to work at a level commensurate with his or her abilities. In situations where effort and performance cannot be related to the employee's goals, the best the supervisor can do is avoid annoying behaviors—such as too much direction and close supervision.

Key to Success

Choosing a leadership style will seldom be a simple proposition, if for no other reason than that all people are different. However, the years of research on the leadership style question have yielded some useful conclusions that will help supervisors perform their leadership responsibilities.

First, it is generally agreed that leadership is situational in nature, that is, that different behaviors (styles) are required for different situations. A single style may work, but only if the situation remains constant.

Second, the situational context of leadership requires flexibility on the part of the supervisor. One of the unanswered questions regarding leadership is the extent to which most people can be flexible in their styles. There is some evidence to suggest that people are relatively inflexible, but recent developments in leadership training indicate that it is possible to teach people to adopt a wider range of behaviors.

Third, our awareness of the differences between leadership *attitudes* and leadership *behaviors* has helped us to understand the leadership process much better. It is difficult, for example, to train a Theory X supervisor to become Theory Y because these are attitudes toward people and attitude is very difficult to change. However, it is possible to teach different leadership behaviors—which can be independent of attitudes. Thus, for example, a supervisor can have strong Theory Y attitudes toward people in general, but still use directive behavior with a new employee.

Finally, effective leadership is a combination of knowing one's basic attitudes toward people, proper diagnosis of the situational determinants facing the leader, and the ability to apply the proper behavior in the situation. The proper mix of people orientation and production (or directive) orientation to be adopted is, in the final analysis, a judgment call by the leader. This suggests that rather than choosing *one* of the contingency models, the supervisor would be wise to utilize *all* of them, as each gives a slightly different perspective on leadership.

Summary

This chapter has reviewed the major theories and styles of leadership that are popular today. The most general formulation is Theory X and Theory Y developed by Douglas McGregor. He maintained that the attitudes of the supervisor caused the behavior of subordinates, and that behavior would not change until the supervisor's attitude changed. The X-Y theory is useful for diagnosing problems on a broad scale, but difficult to apply in practice because of its general nature.

There are three main styles of leadership: autocratic, democratic, and abdicratic. The autocratic leader dominates the work group by making most decisions, practices one-way communication, and generally does not solicit employees' ideas and suggestions. The democratic leader is more people oriented and uses the group to make decisions and set objectives. Democratic leaders believe that employees have much to contribute to the organization and they practice a management style that develops workers' abilities. The abdicratic leader does not engage in the leadership role, preferring not to take an active part in the work group and often turning the leadership function over to the informal leader. With the possible exception of the abdicratic style, all leadership styles can be effective in certain situations. The key is knowing which situation requires which style.

Contingency theories describe various leadership styles as well as the situations in which each is most effective. The chapter reviewed five of the current theories: the Leadership Continuum Theory, the Managerial Grid, Situational Leadership, the Leadership Decision-Making Model, and Path-Goal Theory. Each of the contingency theories examines leadership in a situational context and suggests that specific factors determine the appropriate leadership style to use.

Opening Incident Revisited

Are Susan's concerns justified? Is this organization really as autocratic as it seems? Is it possible for an organization to have strong autocratic leadership, yet still be profitable? The answers to these questions, which will be developed below, are "no," "yes," and "yes," respectively.

The fast-food business is only one example of the positive aspects of autocratic leadership. In this business, profit is determined largely by volume, and volume depends upon getting as many customers served as possible. During peak periods, therefore, there just isn't time for anything but pure task behavior from the leader. Systems must be properly organized in order to serve literally hundreds of people in a short period.

Another aspect of the fast-food business affects leadership style. When people visit chain restaurants, they do so primarily because they know the quality of the product they are buying. Regardless of the restaurant's location, as long as the name is the same, the product will be the same as well. To maintain these standards, the organization needs standardized work procedures and equipment at each location. Some person or group has studied the production process at length and has decided the best way to cook the hamburger to maximize efficiency. Having a cook try a different method will affect the entire production system. In other words, the possible benefits of any participative process by employees are far outweighed by the potential costs involved.

Why, then, do these restaurants not have a mutiny on their hands? Don't people resist autocratic leadership? As the chapter has poined out, not necessarily. First, being autocratic does not mean the leader has to be obnoxious about it. A show-and-tell style can be made quite palatable in the right circumstances. There is no evidence in the incident of the manager being anything other than directive. Second, the type of employee being managed will have an effect upon the style used. Young, part-time employees are not likely to be capable of making too many decisions on their own and, in fact, probably find the directive style quite satisfying since it helps them perform their jobs better and gives them fewer worries on the job.

So how about Susan's chances of adapting to this system? She probably has little to worry about, since leadership methods used in this organization can be learned relatively easily. For one thing, all of the employees probably expect an autocratic manager and would be lost under a participative mode. Also, she will receive a great deal of training in the proper leadership behavior because this organization knows the cost of having poor leaders. Finally, Susan has only to realize that she is perfectly free to keep her participative *attitudes,* so long as her leadership *behavior* is primarily directive. Later, however, once she succeeds at this job, her next position may require a shift in leadership behavior to a more participative style.

Review Questions

1. What are Theory X and Theory Y.
2. How did McGregor propose that attitudes of managers affected the behavior of employees?
3. How is it possible for a leader's attitudes to be different from his or her behavior?
4. How should changes in X and Y occur? Why?
5. How do X and Y differ in their philosophy of control?
6. Which is better: Theory X or Theory Y?
7. What is autocratic leadership?
8. What is democratic leadership?
9. What is abdicratic leadership?
10. What are the advantages and disadvantages of autocratic and democratic leadership?
11. Under what conditions could the manager allow employees to participate?
12. What are some of the behaviors that indicate that democratic or autocratic styles are being practiced?
13. What are contingency theories of leadership?
14. What is the Leadership Continuum Model?
15. What are the five styles of leadership covered by the Managerial Grid?
16. What is Situational Leadership and how does it work?
17. Of what importance is the development level of the employees in choosing a leadership style?
18. What is the Leadership Decision-Making Model?
19. What does the Path-Goal Model suggest a leader should do?

Chapter Glossary

Leadership style. A set of consistent behaviors by an individual designed to influence the behaviors of others.

Theory X. A set of attitudes which sees employees as lazy, indolent, irresponsible, stupid, and in need of external control.

Theory Y. A set of attitudes which sees employees as motivated, having a sense of responsibility, wanting challenge, and capable of self-control.

Stretching.	A developmental concept which suggests that individuals can be developed by giving them greater levels of responsibility. Consistent with Theory Y.
Autocratic leadership.	A style of leadership in which the leader makes decisions without employee participation or consultation, practices one-way communication, tells employees what to do, how to do it, when to do it, and where to do it. Style consists mostly of directive or production oriented behaviors.
Democratic leadership.	A style of leadership in which the leader involves subordinates in the decision-making process, practices two-way communication, and gives employees freedom to make their own decisions within specified guidelines. Style consists mostly of supportive or people-oriented behaviors.
Abdicratic leadership.	A style which avoids taking an active role in the leadership process. Generally adopted by a person with a weak power base or no desire to lead.
Contingency theories of leadership.	Theories or models which propose that effective leadership styles depend upon the situation. Most models attempt to diagnose the situation and prescribe the appropriate style. Opposite of the one-best-way approach.
Leadership Continuum Model.	One of the early contingency approaches by Tannenbaum and Schmidt which notes that autocratic and democratic management can occur in degrees. Proposes that the correct style is a function of the forces operating in the situation.
Managerial Grid.	A situational approach to leadership which uses two attitudes—concern for people and concern for production—as the basis for a leadership model. Five styles are used to describe various combinations of the two sets of attitudes.
Situational Leadership.	Leadership theory devised by Hersey and Blanchard which uses four styles of leadership to be matched with the four development levels of the followers. Effective leadership is achieved by matching the correct style to the correct development level.
Leadership Decision-making Model.	Model proposed by Vroom and Yetton which sets out questions the leader should ask to determine the correct leadership style. Answers to these questions constitute the decisions the leader must make to find the correct style. Proposes that more than one style may be used in a given situation.

Path-Goal Theory.   Theory which proposes that the leader's job is to clarify the path between the behaviors desired by the organization (productivity) and the goals of the individual employee.

Case Problem

Continental Bridge Company

Fred Smith is the supervisor of the mechanical drafting department for Continental Bridge Company. He supervises fourteen employees, all of whom do drafting work from rough specifications or layout drawings. Most of the employees have been in the department for several years, with the exception of two persons who are drafting trainees from a local community college.

Fred has been supervisor of this department for two years, and is becoming increasingly disturbed over the problems he has been having with his employees. Relationships have become so strained that Fred has been considering looking for another job.

It all began about a year ago when Fred noticed that many of the employees were slacking off. A few began arriving late several days each week, despite his repeated warnings that they should be on time. After reminding them of their tardiness several times, he instituted a policy that anyone arriving late to work had to make up that time by staying later in the afternoon. To make sure the policy was consistently enforced, he began arriving at work early to make sure he was there to catch those coming in late.

Reaction to his policy was negative. Although punctuality seemed to improve slightly, he was sure that some employees were signing in their friends, claiming that the friend had to go somewhere else in the plant to see someone about a particular job. He therefore changed his policy and now has everyone sign in on a piece of paper in his office so he can be sure they're actually there.

Fred also noticed that some of the employees were stretching their coffee and lunch breaks beyond the allotted time, so he required those who were late coming back from coffee or lunch to make up the time in the afternoon. Again, the group's reaction was negative and they accused him of being a nitpicker. Fred replied that they were paid to do a full day's work and he intended to see that they did it.

His most recent problem pertains to the overall quality of the group's work. Several times in the past several weeks he has received drawings back from the engineers pointing out errors made by his people. This angers him since he knows they are capable of doing better work. To prevent this from happening again, he has informed all employees that in the future, all drawings are to be approved by him before they are sent out.

Today he received a call from the Engineering Department complaining that a set of drawings that was to be submitted two days ago has not been received. Apparently, Fred's department has been holding up a major project. When Fred approached the employee assigned to do the drawings to find out what the problem was, the employee replied, "I'm just checking them over again to make sure they're right. You wouldn't want me to send over something that was wrong, would you?"

Questions for Discussion

1. How would you describe Fred's leadership style?
2. What has he done to get himself into this situation?
3. How should it have been handled?
4. How can Fred get himself out of this situation?

Effective Supervisory Management

Selecting, Inducting, and Training Employees

13

Chapter Learning Objectives

After reading and studying this chapter you should be able to:

1. Describe the processes of selection, induction, and training, and the role of the supervisor in each.

2. Explain the function of nondirective interviewing in employee selection.

3. Give examples of nondirective interviewing questions.

4. Explain the psychological contract and what the supervisor can do to create a strong one.

5. Explain how supervisors can improve the match between the qualifications of the applicant and the requirements of the job.

6. List the errors often made in the selection process.

7. Describe the relationship between selection and induction.

8. List some things a supervisor could do to create an effective induction process.

9. List the errors often made in the induction process.

10. Describe a positive climate for training.

11. List the learning principles that supervisors should practice in the training process.

12. Describe the part aptitude plays in the training process.

13. Describe the learning curve and show how the supervisor might use it to improve training.

14. List the errors that are often encountered in the training process.

Key Terms

Selection
Induction
Training
Directive interviewing
Nondirective

interviewing
Psychological contract
Development rate
Halo effect
Organizational

socialization
Training climate
Learning principles
Aptitude
Learning curve

Ace Hardware Company

Frank Williams is the manager of the local Ace Hardware Store, which is part of a national chain. Four weeks ago Frank hired an assistant store manager after the previous one left to become the manager of a store belonging to a rival chain.

After interviewing several applicants, Frank decided to hire Dorothy Walker, who began work three weeks ago. Frank hired Dorothy because of her previous experience in the hardware business. Her father owned his own hardware store for many years and Dorothy worked for him off and on during her schooling. Her most recent position was as assistant manager of a store belonging to a rival chain in another city, but she left that job when her husband was transferred back to this city. Frank felt he had really lucked out with Dorothy, given her previous experience as an assistant manager, and looked forward to having her take some of the burden of managing the store off his shoulders.

The first sign of difficulty was during Dorothy's first week when Frank overheard her talking to one of the customers, who had asked for advice on some paint. Dorothy exlained the technical aspects quite clearly, but then told the customer that if the paint didn't work out, the store would refund his money. The policy of Ace Hardware has always been to provide advice and assistance whenever possible, but to make it clear that once the customer has purchased the item, it is his responsibility. Several similar events occurred after that, and Frank had to tell Dorothy that Ace Hardware operated differently from other stores.

Today came the final blow. Dorothy walked in and told Frank she will be leaving in two weeks. She has accepted a position as manager of a hardware store owned by another chain.

Many problems in managing people can be traced directly back to deficiencies in the selection, induction, or training phases of supervision. In the **selection** process the supervisor attempts to match the needs of the job to the skills, aptitudes, and motivations of the employee, i.e., tries to find the right person for the right job. The **induction** phase pertains to how the employee is brought into the work situation itself. Since the employee will be joining a complex social system, it is important that he or she become a part of that system and that appropriate behaviors be encouraged. The induction process involves not only the psychological and sociological aspects of getting the employee into the system, but also the actual work part of the job in which he or she learns how the job is to be performed.

Good selection and induction are complemented by effective training programs. As we learned in Chapter 7, performance is determined by both motivation and ability; the major purpose of **training** is to improve employees' ability, although there can be motivational side effects as well. The effectiveness of training is partly determined by how well the selection and induction processes were performed. For example, workers who are not suited for the requirements of their jobs will be more difficult to train.

This chapter will provide some principles designed to improve the fit between employees and the organization; this will in turn reduce the number of problems occurring later, as well as improve employee commitment and productivity. A thorough study of selection, induction, and training would require more than a single chapter. However, supervisors often have a limited role in these processes, particularly with regard to selection, and knowledge of a few basic principles can help them to avoid some of the more common errors. Because our focus is upon the behavioral side of managing people, the technical aspects of each topic, such as legal requirements, application forms, and specific types of training programs will be minimized.

The Selection Process

As the first step in the employment process, selecting the right people is obviously important. To emphasize its importance, it is useful to think in these terms: there is no such thing as bad employees, only good people who have been selected for the wrong roles. Although this may be an extreme viewpoint, it does highlight the need for good selection. There are many good employees around who have been poorly selected for the jobs they have, and the companies they work for would have been better off never hiring them in the first place. The unfortunate part is that the employees themselves, instead of the selection process, are often blamed

The Improved Secretary

The importance of matching people with roles was brought home to me several years ago in a situation involving a former secretary. In the selection process she appeared to have outstanding qualifications and experience, so I decided to hire her. Over the next year I was only marginally satisfied with her performance. One day she informed me that she had successfully applied for another job and would be leaving in two weeks. I tried hard to show my disappointment but I suspect she knew I was not too upset. About six months later I met her supervisor in her new job, who was elated at her performance. In fact, he said, "Boy, I sure was lucky to get her away from you." I couldn't believe we were talking about the same person! Obviously, she had found a role that suited her and was performing well.

for their poor performance. This means that the same mistakes in selection may be made over and over again. Therefore, the primary thrust of this section will emphasize the matching of people with roles and role expectations of the supervisor.

The Role of The Supervisor in Selection

In Chapter 3 we discussed how the supervisor related to other roles in the organization, including staff functions. It was noted there that the personnel function, being a staff function, should act as an advisor to the supervisor in selection matters. This means that supervisors can — and should — take advantage of this service if it exists. If it does not, then they will have to follow whatever procedures the company has for initiating the selection process.

The primary role of the supervisor in the selection process (assuming there is a personnel department) is to specify the qualifications required for the job, describe the responsibilities of the job, and make the final selection from applicants. The personnel department should conduct the search, perform initial screening of applicants, and then recommend a short list of applicants, from which the supervisor will select the best one.

The important factor at this stage, as we noted in Chapter 2, is for the supervisor to have, at minimum, the right of refusal of any candidate. There are two reasons for this. First, a supervisor will be more committed to properly inducting and training a subordinate chosen by himself or herself, if for no other reason than personal interest in seeing the employee succeed. Second, it will be more difficult for higher management to hold supervisors accountable for the performance of employees who have been foisted upon them. One of the basic rights of a supervisor should be the right to select subordinates.

A common practice is to allow the supervisor to have the right of refusal. In other words, instead of actually selecting a particular applicant, the supervisor is given the right to refuse the one who has been selected. Although this allows the supervisor some part in the selection process, it is a second-best system because it does not allow him or her to select the best applicant, only to reject one not wanted. Of course, refusal to accept the recommendation is valid only if it is done on the basis of reasonable criteria.

Selection Interviewing

In Chapter 18 the topic of interviewing is discussed in considerable depth, but in this section we concentrate on the basics of interviewing and how selection interviews might be conducted.

There are two basic approaches to interviewing: the directive and nondirective approaches. In **directive interviewing,** the supervisor determines the content of the interview, the questions asked, how long it lasts, etc. The interviewee plays a relatively passive role and responds strictly to the supervisor's questions. Sample directive questions are:

- Where have you worked?
- Did you get along with your last supervisor?
- Do you like challenging work?
- Why did you leave your last job?
- Do you think you will like working here?

Nondirective interviewing reverses the process. Questions are very general and allow the interviewee considerable latitude in answering. Rather than looking for specific answers, the supervisor is more concerned with the pattern of responses, the subjects the interviewees choose to talk about, and how they express themselves. Sample nondirective questions are:

- Tell me about your work history.
- Tell me about your previous supervisors.
- What sort of work do you like?
- Tell me about your previous job.
- What do you know about this organization?

One approach is not necessarily better than another. Each can be used in certain situations and both will probably be used to some extent in every interview. The directive approach is best suited for gathering facts. It is therefore important for the supervisor to know what information is needed before entering the interview. Once this is done, good interviewing is largely a matter of asking the direct questions.

As noted above, direct questions tend to get only the specific information requested. Therefore, there will probably be times when the supervisor wants more general information, and here is where the nondirective approach is more appropriate. Questions are phrased in very general terms so that the interviewee cannot bias his or her answers purposely. Because the interviewee does not know what the interviewer is after, he or she will tend to provide much more information. It is then the supervisor's job to understand the meaning behind all the information.

The key to good interviewing is to know when to be nondirective and when to be directive. The choice will depend partly upon how much factual information is known prior to the interview. Since application forms contain most of the hard data, the interview may be more concerned with information that can be generated by nondirective questions. But if the supervisor needs to know where the applicant lives, it would be stupid to try to find out by the nondirective method.

Interviewing is not something that can be completely learned by reading a book. It takes practice to develop effective skills and one of the exercises in this chapter will give you the opportunity go gain some practice. Additional reading on the subject is in Chapter 18.

Establishing a Psychological Contract

When two parties enter into an agreement, they often write up a contract that spells out the expectations and obligations of each of the parties. A similar process should occur in the selection process. The term **psychological contract** is used to describe the expectations of each party in the employment process. While it usually is not written down (although it certainly could be and in many cases this would be a good idea), it is just as important as any other agreement that might be established between two people. The psychological contract is a meeting of the minds regarding the expectations and obligations of the supervisor and the applicant.

This contract is important because it establishes the initial expectations of both parties. These expectations can be either positive or negative, depending upon what transpires in the interview. If the supervisor is not clear on what he or she expects, a weak contract will be established. If, for some reason, the supervisor creates a negative impression in the mind of the applicant, probably no contract will be established; the applicant will not take the job.

The advantages of a strong psychological contract should be obvious. The subordinate will accept the job with full knowledge of what is expected. Therefore, the possibility of "I didn't know this was what you expected!" is greatly decreased. It also means that the initial step toward a positive relationship between supervisor and subordinate has been established. Over the long term, this can mean increased loyalty and commitment to the supervisor and to the organization.

Establishing a strong contract requires open communication, honesty of expectations, a climate of trust between the two parties, and, as will be seen in the following section, a mutual acceptance of the parties' expectations.

SETTING INITIAL EXPECTATIONS.   Part of the psychological contract is letting the applicant know what he or she can expect from the job. The primary danger here is that the supervisor may create false expectations, either positive or negative. We are most likely to create false positive expectations when we really want someone badly. To entice the applicant to take the job, we paint the brightest picture possible. If the picture is unrealistically bright, we may not be able to live up to those expectations. Consequently, even though the organization may be a pretty good place to work, it may fall short of the employee's expectations.

Painting a negative picture can have a two-pronged effect. If people aren't told the negative things they are likely to encounter, they may be disappointed when they find out what things are really like. However, if initial expectations are set too low, the applicant may not take the job at all.

The solution to this dilemma is to avoid exaggerating in either direction. It is best to be as honest as possible about what the job has to offer, both positively and negatively. A few desirable applicants may be lost, but the supervisor will also avoid hiring people who may develop into discontented employees later on. There is no advantage in misrepresenting what people are likely to experience.

LEARNING THE EMPLOYEE'S EXPECTATIONS. Since there are two parties to the contract, it is the responsibility of the supervisor to learn the employee's expectations. Not only will the information gathered by the supervisor be helpful in future relations with the employee, but the *process* of getting the information is helpful as well. More will be said on how this might be done later in this chapter.

In sum, the psychological contract is an important determinant of behavior, particularly in the early stages of employment. The contract may be strengthened or weakened later, depending upon the experiences of each party. The selection process is the first step in establishing the contract, which can be consolidated by the supervisor's wise action during the induction period, as we shall see.

The Impact of Expectations

The point made in the section above about how expectations can affect our attitudes and behavior are well known to most everyone. It is surprising how often we ignore these principles and create false expectations. For example, advertising brochures from resort areas always show the best weather and describe the ideal vacation, but many people leave disappointed because it rained two days out of five, a figure that is consistent with the average. Politicians make outlandish promises to get elected, but often cannot live up to them through no fault of their own, and the disappointment of the voters shows at the next election.

The really surprising thing is that the tendency to exaggerate flies in the face of all the research evidence regarding effective communications and influence. Study after study has indicated that giving *both* the pros and cons of an argument is more persuasive than giving only one side. This is an important point to remember in the selection interview, as well as any other situation involving communication and influence.

Completing the Contract

Good contracts are two-way streets. Each party has rights as well as obligations. Although it is important for the supervisor to tell the applicant what is expected, it is equally important to learn what the applicant expects from the employment situation. Not only does this assist in establishing the psychological contract, but the supervisor may learn of an expectation that cannot be met. Finding out at this early stage allows the supervisor to deal with the issue immediately instead of waiting for it to become a problem later on.

Understanding what applicants are seeking in their work will also help the supervisor to be more effective in the day-to-day management of that person. Given knowledge about expectations, the supervisor can then tailor his or her management style to the needs of the employee. For example, an applicant may state that he or she resents a supervisor who is constantly checking on how things are going. So the supervisor can avoid that behavior whenever possible if the employee's performance warrants.

It should be noted that finding out what someone expects on the job may not be as easy as it sounds. Of course one can ask directly, but in a selection interview, if the applicant wants the job, he or she may not be very open about likes and dislikes for fear of saying something that will jeopardize chances of getting the job. It is here that the nondirective technique can be useful. By asking relatively general questions, the supervisor may gather enough information to get a good idea of the applicant's true expectations.

Perhaps the major value of learning about applicants' expectations is not so much the actual information gained, but more the psychological impact the process can have upon the applicants. Showing sincere interest in their expectations of the job creates a positive impression for them and can pay off in the form of better attitudes and productivity. In one sense, discussing the applicants' expectations is an initial form of participation.

Matching Qualifications to the Job

One of the more difficult aspects of selecting employees is matching them to the requirements of the job. On the one hand, it may seem like a fairly simple process; you just hire the person who is most qualified. On the other hand, even the most qualified applicant can cause problems later.

For the moment, let us look at the relationship between an employee and the job as being composed of only two factors: the qualifications of the applicant and the responsibility contained in the job. If it is possible for both of these to progress together at the same rate, the person will

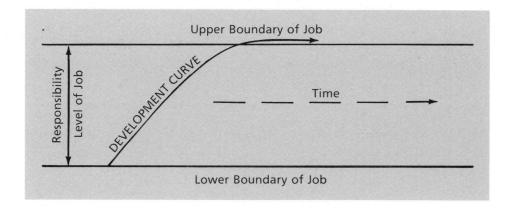

Figure 13.1. Development Curve of Employee Developing at Fast Rate.

always be matched to the job. However, if the responsibility level of the job remains constant while the ability of the person increases, job dissatisfaction will result. The person will become bored with the job and this frustration can manifest itself in all sorts of ways. If people would leave when their jobs became boring, there would be fewer problems. However, many people get permanently locked into their jobs for a variety of reasons. Good selection can prevent these problems to some degree.

One method of improving selection is to analyze the general **development rate** of employees and compare these rates with the demands of jobs. Figure 13.1 illustrates an individual who is developing at a relatively fast rate as shown by the steep slope of the development curve. If the horizontal lines represent the minimum and maximum levels of responsibility in the job, then it is obvious that the employee will outgrow the job in a relatively short period of time. In some cases, this may take only several months.

Figure 13.2 illustrates the opposite case; the employee never develops to the point where the job is beneath his or her abilities. Although the employee would probably never be bored in the job, a different type of problem arises because the supervisor would not be able to delegate the full responsibility required in the job.

The ideal situation is illustrated in Figure 13.3. The employee is hired at the minimum level of ability required to do the job, and then progresses at a rate that slowly brings him or her up to the ceiling of the role, but never above it. In this situation, the employee's capabilities are being fully utilized. Of course, it is impossible to attain this ideal situation for every employee, but the diagrams do illustrate the problems that can be created when the match between the job and the employee is considerably off the mark.

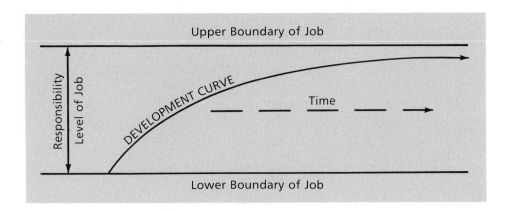

Figure 13.2. Development Curve of Employee Whose Growth Never Surpasses Job Level.

The previous analysis leads to what may seem a strange conclusion: *The person who is the most qualified should not always be the one selected.*[1] Although a new, highly qualified employee may be more productive at the outset, he or she may lose interest in the job and become bored very quickly. It may be better to select someone who will grow *into* the job instead of out of it. Although more training may be required at the outset, the long-term benefits outweigh the cost.

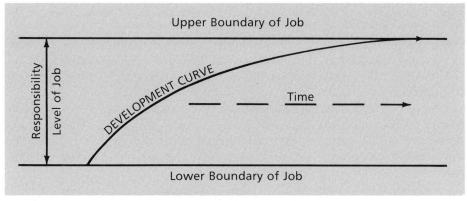

Figure 13.3. Ideal Match Between Employee Growth and Job Requirements.

1. This statement should be viewed with caution since it represents one of the many divergences between the application of sound behavioral science and the requirements of the real world. For example, many union-management agreements would require that, all other things being equal, the most qualified person must be selected.

Hiring Qualified Employees

Several years ago I was visiting a company and happened to sit in on a committee meeting which was reviewing applications for a supervisory position that had been advertised. There were quite a few applications and they were being passed around the group for each person to examine. One committee member consistently made the same comment for many of the applications: "This person isn't qualified for this job." No one responded since all were deeply engrossed in the other applications. After about the tenth time he made the comment, one of the committee members responded in a rather testy manner:

"Of course he isn't qualified for this job. Why would he apply for it if he was qualified? The job he's qualified for is the one he's got now! I have no interest in hiring someone who is qualified. I want someone who isn't qualified!"

The statement took everyone by surpise. But after they discussed the point he was making, there was a big difference in how they reviewed the applications.

Of course this principle does not hold if the job can be changed to match the employee's development level, or if other positions of higher responsibility are available. However, in many situations this is not the case, especially in low-level jobs in companies whose growth rate has leveled off or is declining. Promotions are few and far between, so employees are likely to be stuck in their present jobs for some time.

Making the Final Selection

Making a final selection is usually difficult, especially if the applicants are similar in background and qualifications. One method of making the decision easier is to get the input of others. We learned in Chapter 9 that groups can frequently make better decisions than individuals under certain conditions, and the selection decision is one that fits those requirements. It usually is a good idea to have each candidate interviewed by more than one person if time permits. In senior managerial jobs, candidates may be interviewed by as many as ten or twelve different people before a final choice is made. This would be unnecessary for rank-and-file employees, but at least one other supervisor's opinion would be valuable.

Since no two people conduct an interview in the same way, the second interviewer will probably get different information than the first. Or, even if the information is the same, the two might see it differently. In any case, the more opinions that can be brought to bear on a selection decision, the better that decision is likely to be. It would be expected, of course, that one would return the favor for other supervisors when they are hiring.

Finally, it should go without saying that supervisors should never make a selection decision that cannot be defended on objective, observable criteria, whether it be to their own manager or to an arbitration hearing. It is worth remembering that the *only* defensible evidence is behavior or past performance, not the employee's attitudes, feelings, values, or beliefs.

Common Errors in the Selection Process

In addition to the problems and pitfalls noted already, other errors are frequently made in selecting employees. On the assumption that awareness of their existence will be a major step toward their elimination, we shall describe them briefly.

1. *The halo effect.* The **halo effect** means that we find one attribute or characteristic that we like or don't like in a person, and judge his or her other characteristics accordingly. For example, if you have a strong preference for a high aptitude test score, you might perceive other positive traits in someone who has a high score.

2. *Too much emphasis upon attitudes.* In an interview, attitudes are deduced through what the applicant says. Words are cheap, particularly when someone is hoping for a job. A better measure of potential is past behavior, not attitudes. Thus, checking with previous employers or examining an applicant's accomplishments will give a more accurate picture of a person's abilities.

3. *Inadvertently communicating your decision.* In your enthusiasm over finding a good candidate for the job, you may inadvertently (or on purpose) give the impression that he or she has been chosen, or at least has the inside track on the job. Later, you discover someone who is better and hire that person. You have now created some bad feelings in the first candidate because of the expectation you created. In situations involving internal applications, this may result in a grievance.

4. *Assuming confidentiality.* Although it is understood that all selection interviews are confidential, this is more binding on you than on the applicant. Never say anything in a selection interview that you wouldn't say to anyone else at any other time.

5. *Comparing applicants with others.* People resent being compared to others, or being asked to compare themselves with others. Such questions are often seen as a personal challenge and can cause bad feelings. Moreover, whatever information you get would probably be so biased it would be worthless anyway.

Inducting New Employees

The primary purpose of the induction process is to complete the establishment of the psychological contract. The verbal agreement of the se-

Exercise 13.1

A Selection Interview

As we have noted in the text, interviewing is a skill that must be built up and practiced. This exercise gives you the opportunity to conduct a selection interview. It involves a role play between two members of your class, with a third person observing. Your instructor will provide you with all the information you need to play your roles.

---

lection process is given more meaning as the employee is being inducted into the work group and the organization. As in the first section, we minimize the technical factors of induction (such as employee orientation manuals, etc.) and concentrate on the behavioral processes that occur during induction.

Relationship Between Selection and Induction

One of the principles that ties these two processes together pertains to the relative difficulty of gaining admisssion to the organization. Generally speaking, the more difficult it is to be selected, and the more diffi-

The Effects of Poor Selection and Induction

Several years ago I had the opportunity to do some research on employee turnover in several companies. One of the companies was experiencing an annual turnover rate of over 100 percent in its first-level workers. There were many reasons for this, but one of the major causes could be traced back to the selection and induction process. The selection process took no more than ten minutes, long enough for the personnel department to decide if the applicant had any serious physical defects and to get any personal information necessary (address, phone number, etc.). The supervisor had no part in the selection and often didn't even know anyone was being hired. Usually the applicant was hired on the spot and sent immediately to work. Since the selection process was conducted poorly, the induction process failed as well. The supervisor had not been involved in the selection and therefore had no induction plan ready. Consequently, for the first several days new employees were usually assigned busy work. Turnover was affected in this way: when another job became available to an employee, his or her feelings were, "They didn't really care when I came, so they probably won't care when I leave." The company, of course, had the cause and effect reversed, and thought that since no one ever stayed around very long, it was stupid to spend any time on employees at the outset.

cult the induction process, the greater the commitment of the individuals after completing these two steps. Many organizations use this principle to attract and retain new members. The Marine Corps, for example, uses the phrase, "If you're good enough . . ." and follows it up with the rigorous induction process of basic training. Professional groups such as doctors and lawyers have stringent selection procedures as well as examinations to pass before being admitted to the profession.

While supervisors cannot normally use these specific techniques, they can still take advantage of the principles. The selection process should be rigorous instead of just covering the bare minimum. Similarly, the induction stage will add meaning to the experiences the applicant received in the selection process. It is here that the new employee will gain his or her first real experience as a member of the work unit. If the induction process proves to be a positive experience, it can pay off in better performance further down the road.

How to Induct Employees

There are many things a supervisor can do to induct new employees effectively, but they all fall into the general category of *time*. In other words, one of the most important things supervisors can do in the early days of employment is to spend time with new employees. This offers two benefits. First, it shows employees that the supervisor does care about them, enough at least to spend time helping them get adjusted, and therefore strengthens the psychological contract that was initiated in the selection interview. Second, it gives the supervisor the opportunity to communicate expectations to the employee in addition to what was discussed in the selection process.

Except for rare instances, all employees eventually acquire the knowledge necessary to cope with their organizational lives. They acquire values, attitudes, and beliefs based upon their organizational experiences. If they do not acquire these basic attitudes from the supervisor, they will most likely get them from their co-workers. This process — the acquisition of the norms and values of the work group, the management, and the organization — is called **organizational socialization.** The supervisor should have a major role in managing the socialization process because he or she represents the goals, values, and attitudes of the organization's management. If the supervisor does not perform the socialization role effectively, the employee may end up adopting the values, attitudes, and goals of the work group. There is nothing inherently wrong with this, except that the group may instill expectations that are not consistent with those of the organization. The principle here is this: employees always learn the name of the game early on in the job; the question is, will they learn it from the supervisor or from someone else who may see things differently?

Spending time with new employees is a good strategy, but equally important is what the supervisor does with this time. Here are some possibilities.

1. *Introduce them to co-workers.* If nothing else, this is just common courtesy. It also makes what can be an awkward process much easier for the new employee.

2. *Introduce them to your manager.* This can often be a nice touch that makes the new employee feel part of the team, getting to know all the players in the game.

3. *Introduce them to other departments.* Sometimes an employee's job will require interaction with members of other departments on a regular basis. This is a good time to make those introductions so the relationship does not have to start off cold.

4. *Introduce them to the company.* If the time and physical layout permit, it is always a good idea to give the new employee a tour of the entire facility, with the idea of showing how his or her job fits in with the rest of the organization. Personal introductions are not necessary.

5. *Conduct an informal orientation session.* Some organizations have orientation sessions for all new employees, but the informal one is often more important. This is where the supervisor meets one-to-one with the new employee to finalize expectations. This is not a training session, but is the last step before the employee starts to work.

6. *Get them into the group.* Introductions are necessary, but they do not get the employee into the group itself. This is often accomplished by assigning a co-worker to look after the newcomer. This may be yet another instance in which the supervisor can work through the informal group leader.

Follow-Up in Induction

It is impossible to specify how long the induction period should last. Many organizations have a formal probation period but this does not necessarily coincide with the end of the induction period. Theoretically speaking, the induction period is not over until the employee has adopted the norms, values, and expectations of the work unit.

Regardless of how long this takes, induction is not something that ceases on a certain day. It is an ongoing process and the supervisor should follow up on a regular basis. At the outset, the follow-up sessions may occur daily, and then with decreasing frequency and intensity. These debriefing sessions give the supervisor the opportunity to find out how the employee is adapting to the work environment, and the employee a chance to ask questions that may be important for personal development. Both are necessary to strengthen the psychological contract.

Common Errors in the Induction Process

Proper induction is frequently the most neglected area of the employment process. Some common errors in induction are described below:

1. *Assuming that experienced people need no induction.* Most agree that newly-hired young employees could use some induction, but it is often assumed that older, more experienced employees do not need it and might even resent being inducted. Although the two groups would need different *types* of induction, the process is still necessary. The induction process has a wider purpose than just showing someone where the washroom is. It is an important part of the psychological contract.

2. *Forgetting the other half of the contract.* Most of us are good at detailing our expectations of the employee but often forget the other half of the contract. One of the best ways of preventing a mismatch of person and job is to learn as much as possible about what the new employee expects from the job, the company, and the supervisor.

3. *Leaving induction to the wrong person.* Induction is not something that should be delegated, at least at the outset. Again, the psychological value of the induction time spent by the supervisor with the new employee should not be underestimated. Some aspects of the process can be delegated later, but at the outset, the experience of receiving the supervisor's personal attention can be a meaningful one for the employee.

4. *Induction after the fact.* By definition, induction takes place beginning on day one. There is no such thing as having an induction period two weeks after a person has begun the job. If you as a supervisor find that you will not have the time to induct someone properly the first day, it would be better to postpone the starting date until you do have time.

Exercise 13.2

Improving the Induction Process

This section has given you some general ideas about how to induct new employees. However, the list of possibilities is almost endless. This exercise gives you and your group the opportunity to brainstorm various things that could be done to improve the induction process.

The class will be divided into groups of three to five persons. Each group will brainstorm a list of things that supervisors can do to induct new employees properly. This list can then be shared with the larger group. In most classes of thirty to forty people, this process can generate as many as fifty specific things that supervisors can do to improve the induction process.

Selection and induction go hand in hand. If either is done poorly, the effectiveness of the other will be jeopardized. Induction is an important behavioral process that is designed to make the new employee aware of the norms, values, attitudes, and expectations of the organization. It has been proved that rigorous and challenging induction programs have a positive effect upon loyalty, morale, and commitment to organizational goals. Much of the responsibility for the behavioral aspects of the induction process rests with supervisors. *Induction takes place only once;* if the supervisor does not induct properly, the negative effects can be felt for the duration of the employee's tenure with the organization.

The Training Process

Effective training of employees is what makes the selection and induction processes pay off. No matter how well the first two have been handled, if the employee cannot do the job properly there has been little gained. Training is more than just showing someone how to do a job. It is a process that is fraught with pitfalls and risks, all of which must be understood by the supervisor.

The Climate for Training

In many cases, supervisors will not do training themselves but will delegate it to someone else. However, even in these cases, supervisors will have an impact on the training process because they are the ones who establish the **training climate**. A positive climate is necessary for learning to occur and to contribute to productivity. It is possible to learn in a negative climate, but the effects of the learning may not be transferred to improved productivity.

Certain qualities characterize a positive climate for training.

1. *Employees are accepted for what they are.* Training does not mean that employees are changed into something they are not. Effective training is utilizing people's natural skills, abilities, and aptitudes, and developing them to fit the needs of the organization.

2. *The Trainer is seen as a helper, not an evaluator.* The best trainers are those who can help people learn in a supportive manner. Evaluation or judgment about competence can inhibit the learning process. Many supervisors have difficulty being good trainers because their roles require them to evaluate performance as well.

3. *Mistakes are accepted as natural.* A major part of the learning process is making mistakes. If mistakes are punished or ridiculed, people will not enjoy learning.

4. *Employees are encouraged to learn and develop.* Without this, employees will feel that their organization cares little about their per-

sonal advancement and growth. They will remain in dead-end jobs and probably blame the organization for it.

5. *Training is a group process.* While it is normal to have a single individual designated as the trainer, in a positive climate training can be done by anyone. People should feel free to rely on anyone in their group to teach them new and useful skills.

6. *Training is a collaborative effort.* Competition between employees can destroy training efforts. People do not like losing and will therefore avoid taking on new responsibilities if they will be compared competitively to others. They will prefer to stick with the things they can do best.

7. *Training is an ongoing effort.* There may be specific training programs from time to time, but the development of people should be an ongoing concern of all supervisors.

It should be remembered that a positive or negative climate for training is the *result* of how training is conducted, not the cause of it. Some suggestions as to how a positive climate can be established follow.

Motivation Versus Ability

As we pointed out in Chapters 6 and 7, the distinction between ability and motivation is important. Training is used to improve employees' ability, not their motivation. (The exception to this is that if the decision to train is perceived as a form of recognition it could have a motivating effect.) Therefore, training should be used only in conjunction with motivation, not in place of it.

Similarly, motivation methods should not be used to solve ability problems. People who are *unable* to do something need to be trained in how to do it, not motivated. In real life, of course, these two are not totally separate but it is useful to view them that way at the outset when dealing with performance improvement.

Principles of Learning

Training, of course, is based upon the learning process and the principles associated with learning, which have been scientifically developed to maximize the efforts of the learner. It is useful to review these **learning principles** here and show how they can make the training process more effective. Note that they are closely related to the discussion in Chapter 8 on reward systems.

1. *Learning is most effective with experience.* Classroom training, reading books, and watching others are all useful, but the significant, long-lasting learning comes through experience. This means that supervisors should provide ample opportunity for employees to gain experience and practice in their skills.

2. *Learning should occur in small units.* Most jobs or tasks consist of a wide variety of activities. Expecting someone to handle the entire job at once is unrealistic. People learn best if the material is presented in small units. This not only allows employees to master one part adequately, but also gives them the feeling of accomplishment necessary to motivate the further desire to learn.

3. *Learning should have targets.* Most people enjoy reaching goals that are reasonable yet challenging. When the job is broken down into small units, the mastery of the unit can be defined by a specific performance target. This helps trainees to know that they have learned what was expected and provides valuable feedback.

4. *Learning should have positive reinforcement.* Since there will always be some type of reinforcement, it is imperative that the supervisor ensure that it is as positive as possible. The units and targets provide the best opportunity for reinforcement to occur. Positive reinforcement makes the learning a positive experience.

5. *Speed is developed through practice.* It is one thing to learn *how* to do something, but another to learn to do it quickly. Speed is a function of both motivation and ability, but the ability part is primarily determined by doing the job again and again,

6. *Learning is affected by expectations.* We observed in Chapter 5 that the expectations of others can affect our behavior. This is also true with learning. The supervisor who says to the trainee, "This is a difficult job. No one else can do it right and I doubt if you can either," is conditioning the employee to expect failure. This conditioning may cause him or her to fail. Supervisors should always communicate positive (but realistic) expectations.

These general principles of learning can be applied to any type of training. Their implication is that supervisors need to have patience and understanding and must be supportive of the employee's efforts to learn. If these principles are followed and the employee cannot seem to develop the necessary abilities, the problem is with either motivation or aptitude. **Aptitude** can be defined as the propensity or potential to develop a specific skill or ability, and is generally thought to have genetic origins. Therefore, aptitude problems usually cannot be solved. If the employee does not show aptitude for the job, he or she was improperly selected in the first place. (Motivation problems can be dealt with using the concepts developed in Chapters 6 and 7.)

Training and the Learning Curve

One important issue facing most supervisors is how long it should take an employee to learn a job or specific skill. The relationship between skill level and learning time is known as the **learning curve.** Depending upon the amount of time it takes to learn a job, the learning curve shows

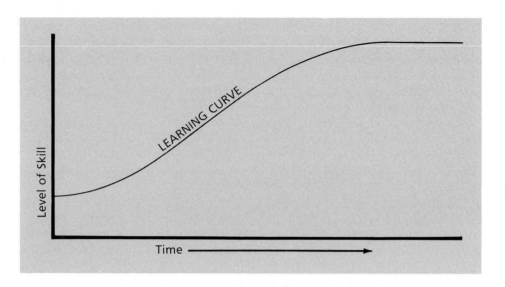

Figure 13.4. Sample Learning Curve Showing Relationship Between Level of Skill and Time.

the supervisor what levels of skill can be expected at what intervals of time. An example of this curve is contained in Figure 13.4.

Among other things, the learning curve is useful for establishing standards for training time. If many people have been trained previously, an averaging of their learning times can establish a standard for others. Not only can this serve as a target for the trainee, but also it can indicate to the supervisor the possibility of an aptitude problem if learning is

The Role of Aptitude

Aptitude is a complex concept and we really don't know all about how it develops. It is defined as the potential for skill, but how that potential develops is still a mystery. It is for this reason that considerable effort has been spent on developing aptitude tests. These tests are designed to discover whether or not an individual has the *potential* for developing certain skills, but are no guarantee that he or she will develop them. They are most commonly used for measuring mechanical aptitude. Firms hiring people to repair equipment want to know if the applicant has mechanical aptitude before spending large sums of money for training.

Aptitude tests are less useful for jobs requiring mental skills rather than physical ones. This is because mental skills cannot be defined as precisely as physical skills. So far, no one has been able to design a test to measure a person's aptitude for supervision. If someone ever does, it would be a useful selection tool, indeed!

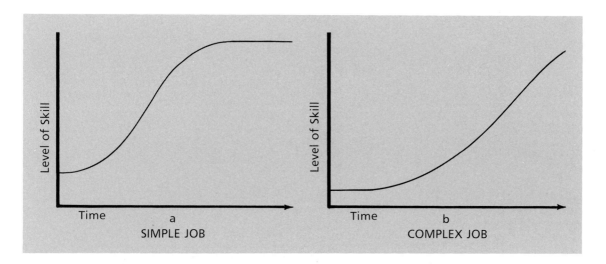

Figure 13.5. Comparison of Learning Curves for Simple and Complex Jobs.

abnormally slow, or a person-job mismatch if the learning time is unusually short.

All other things being equal, the more difficult jobs will have a longer learning curve than easier jobs. Figure 13.5 compares the learning curve for a relatively simple job with the curve for a more complex job.

The learning curve is also useful for determining the strength and frequency of the reinforcement (discussed in Chapter 8) that is so important for learning. Positive reinforcement is needed more at the outset when the trainee may be insecure and need reassurance. Since we have already noted that the learning should occur in small units, the reinforcement could be patterned after these units.

Figure 13.6 shows the various stages along the curve that would determine the frequency for reinforcement. At the early stages where the curve is horizontal, positive reinforcement is needed most (section a). When the curve begins to rise, reinforcement can be reduced, but not significantly (stage b). As the curve begins to taper off, reinforcement can be reduced even more (stage c). The final stage (stage d) shows that the employee has mastered the skill and is now performing satisfactorily. Even here the supervisor needs to provide the occasional positive reinforcer to maintain existing performance. If positive reinforcement ceases, the employee may slide back down the curve.

On some occasions a situation such as that illustrated in Figure 13.7 may be encountered. In this learning curve there is a *decrease* in performance after the training begins. This can happen if an employee needs to be untrained before being trained, a common occurrence when hiring

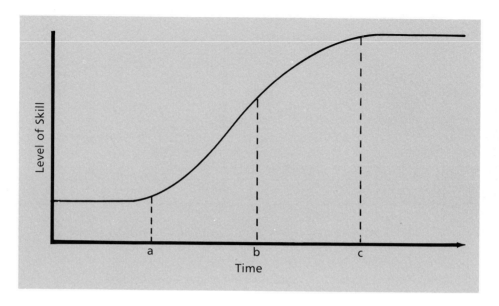

Figure 13.6. Learning Curve Showing Stages of Reinforcement Application.

someone from a similar organization that uses different work methods. The drop in performance occurs because of the conflict generated by having learned the job one way and having to change to a new way. Should this happen, the supervisor should give a lot of direction and reinforcement. The direction shows the employee how the job is done in the present organization, and the support is the motivating force that encourages him or her to do it properly. It is also useful to emphasize why the job is done this way so the employee will see a reason for the difference.

Common Errors in Training

As with the two previous sections, this section closes with a summary of some of the more common errors made in the training process.

1. *Punishing employees who are learning.* Not only does punishment not teach employees how the job should be done, but it causes resentment that can affect performance when the job is learned and discourages employees from wanting to learn.

2. *Expecting too much too quickly.* People who have already mastered a skill can become impatient with those who are learning. It is useful for the trainer to remember how difficult it was to learn and the conditions under which he or she learned.

3. *Providing a poor environment for training.* Learning occurs best

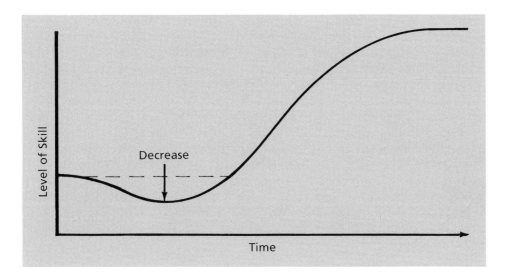

Figure 13.7. Learning Curve Showing a Decrease in Performance Early in Training Period.

in a physical and mental environment that is designed for training. For example, it is best not to place employees in a situation in which their mistakes can be observed by others who have already mastered the tasks, unless it is certain that the experienced employees will offer positive reinforcement and support to the learners.

4. *Failure to recognize individual differences.* People learn at different speeds and in different ways. While training is designed to teach people how things should be done, supervisors should always be willing to accept another way of doing the task that produces the same results.

5. *Failure to provide follow-up training.* People can develop bad habits as well as good ones during training. Training does not stop at the end of a formal program or training session. There must be follow-up to see how effective the training has been. Performance deficiencies can then be corrected, provided they are the result of inadequate training.

Key to Success

Proper selection, induction, and training are the prerequisites to good and lasting performance on the job. There are several reasons why these three areas are of critical importance to the supervisor.

First, selection and induction are, by definition, one-time events. In other words, the supervisor has only one opportunity to select and induct. If either of these is not done properly, it is difficult (if not impossible) to reverse the effects. Training is more of an ongoing process, but potential behavioral problems may arise if it is not done properly. Of course this also means that if selection, induction, and training are done well that they can have a long-lasting positive effect on the employee. In essence, therefore, the down-side and up-side potential is very great for the supervisor.

Second, depending upon the specific organization, each of the three processes can be within the control of the supervisor. In virtually all cases, the supervisor would have a large impact on the induction process, and in some he or she may have input into the selection decision as well as the training component. In terms of establishing a strong, positive relationship between supervisor and subordinate, the induction process is perhaps the most important. Also, the supervisor can use the induction process to establish the psychological contract if that was not done in the selection process.

Summary

This chapter has described the three processes that have a major impact upon the initial attitudes and behavior of employees: selection, induction, and training. Each of these affects the other two and must be analyzed carefully by the supervisor.

Selection involves finding the right person for the right job. Placing an individual in a job that is not suitable will cause serious problems that cannot be solved by induction and training. Supervisors should have a voice in the selection of their subordinates so they will be more committed to helping the employee succeed. Selection decisions can be made through interviewing; nondirective interviewing is useful for obtaining general information from applicants, and directive methods are best for obtaining factual information. It is often advisable to have other supervisors interview applicants as well.

An important aspect of the early employment process is the psychological contract that is established between supervisor and employee. This contract is an understanding between each party about the expectations of the other. To complete the contract it is important for the supervisor to learn about the employee's expectations.

Although it is useful to hire individuals who are qualified for the job, care must be taken to avoid hiring individuals who are overqualified, or soon will be. A better choice may be someone who is minimally qualified, but will grow into the job through time. The final selection decision should be made on measurable criteria, not the applicant's attitudes, beliefs, or values.

The induction process pertains to getting the new employee into the social and technical systems of the organization. Good induction creates a strong psychological contract and minimizes the psychological anxiety that new employees often experience.

The training process is designed to develop new employees into skilled individuals who can contribute to the organization's goals. Effective training is conducted in a climate that is supportive of learning and follows the principles of learning. Poor training environments cause employees to resist change and hide their mistakes. Training should not usually be used as the solution to motivational problems. Supervisors can monitor the training process through the use of learning curves, which relate learning level to time, and give an indication of how successful the training has been.

Opening Incident Revisited

Frank's feelings about the situation are understandable, but the events were also reasonably predictable. His initial feelings about hiring someone with so much experience in the business have now turned to frustration because she is leaving for another job. In one sense, Dorothy was ideally suited for the position; in another, she was not. There was little doubt she could handle the job (given a proper induction and training program, of course), but this also meant that she would be looking for something beyond what she is capable of doing now. Although the period of three weeks may be unusually short, she was almost bound to leave eventually for a better job.

She was unsuited for the position in the sense that there was no room for her to grow in the job, short of taking Frank's position. If she had no other alternatives, she might have stayed for quite some time. But she would eventually feel confined by the job and resent not being able to do more. Frank would probably pay the price for her resentment.

Does this mean that Frank should have hired someone who was less qualified? Perhaps, but it all depends upon his objectives as well as his alternatives. If all other applicants had no experience in the business or were unqualified for other reasons, then Dorothy was possibly the best choice. If Frank's goal was to get as much assistance as possible in the shortest time, then Dorothy was probably his best choice. However, he should have understood the risk involved in hiring someone so well qualified.

Although there may have been nothing Frank could do to change the outcome, he might have been able to postpone the inevitable by improving his induction and training programs. He assumed that because Dorothy was experienced in the business she needed no training. His only attempt at training, therefore, was to watch her performance and point out all the things she did wrong. Dorothy probably resented this because she would not have done things that way if she had been told differently at the beginning.

If Frank finds her resignation a total surprise he must not have conducted a proper induction. He may have expected her to remain for a minimum period of time, but he obviously failed to communicate that to Dorothy. If that matter had been discussed at the outset, things might now be different.

Review Questions

1. What is the relationship among selection, induction, and training?
2. What role should the supervisor play in the selection process?
3. What role would directive and nondirective interviewing methods play in the selection interview?
4. What is the psychological contract?
5. How can a supervisor create an effective psychological contract with employees?
6. How should a supervisor view an applicant's qualifications in making a selection decision?
7. What are the errors often made in the selection process?
8. How could the halo effect influence a supervisor's selection decision?
9. Why is the induction process important?
10. Why is a rigorous induction process recommended?
11. What are some of the things supervisors might do to improve the induction process?
12. Why is follow-up in induction important?
13. What is a positive climate for training?
14. What things can supervisors do to establish a positive training climate?
15. How is the motivation-versus-ability distinction important to the training process?
16. What are the major principles of learning that affect training?
17. What is the learning curve and how might supervisors use it to increase the effectiveness of training?
18. What are the errors often made in training?

Chapter Glossary

Selection.	The process of matching the skills and qualifications of job applicants to the requirements of the job.
Induction.	The process of fitting the employee into the organization and work group. Involves orientation, communicating expectations, and socialization of the organization's norms and values so that the employee adopts the behavior patterns desired by the organization.
Training.	A planned process of improving skills and abilities.
Directive interviewing.	A method of interviewing in which the interviewer (supervisor) directs the flow, content, and timing of the

	interview. Interviewee responds with factual information to the interviewer's direct questions.
Nondirective interviewing.	A method of interviewing in which the interviewer (supervisor) plays a passive role by posing only general questions that allow the interviewee to respond as he or she sees fit. Objective is to get the interviewee to talk as much as possible.
Psychological contract.	An understanding between the supervisor and employee about what is expected of each. The process of creating this contract develops a feeling of trust between the two parties.
Development rate.	The relative speed at which an individual grows in his or her job, that is, changes in ability to handle responsibility.
Halo effect.	A perceptual process in which one person forms generalizations about another based upon a single trait or characteristic. Halo effect can be negative or positive.
Organizational socialization.	The process through which individuals adopt or reject the norms and values of the organization and work group. One part of the induction process.
Training climate.	The psychological atmosphere created by the supervisor that either encourages or discourages learning new skills and behaviors. Negative climates discourage training, positive climates are supportive of it.
Learning principles.	The set of principles that have been scientifically developed to maximize the individual's learning efforts. Proper use of the principles develops a good training climate.
Aptitude.	An individual's potential to learn a skill or acquire certain knowledge. Complex in origin, thought to be partly hereditary in nature. More easily measured for mechanical skills.
Learning curve.	A graph showing the relationship between time and performance. Generally speaking, complex tasks have a long learning curve, simple tasks a short one. Can be used to estimate learning time, set learning standards, and monitor learning progress.

Case Problem

Beaver Trucking Company

John Stinson was in the office of Clyde Lowell, the terminal manager of Beaver Trucking Company, being interviewed for a position as dockhand in the warehouse. His responsibilities would primarily be loading and unloading of trucks, and he would report to a supervisor in charge of a specific area of the terminal. He completed the application the previous week, and was called in by Lowell for an interview. After the usual pleasantries were exchanged, Lowell's conversation went like this:

> I think you'll like it here. Most of the guys are a pretty good bunch, although like any barrel you'll find a few rotten apples. We've tried to take care of most of the bad ones, but there are still a few left. We expect a fair day's work for a fair day's pay around here. I don't mind telling you that we don't tolerate goofing off and a few guys have had to hit the road because of it. I would also advise you to keep away from Bruno Watkins and his crowd. They're basically a no-good bunch — drinking, playing cards during lunch, and God knows what else. We're trying to get something on them now but it's going to take a little while. If you do find something we can use, let me know because everybody's life would be a hell of a lot easier around here if Bruno and his clan were gone. You'll find your supervisor, Kip Brown, not a bad guy either. He's got his bad points but he sure tries like hell. But if he gives you any trouble, just come to me. You look like you've got something on the ball and I'd like to see you be around here for a while. We have lots of supervisory jobs open up around here and if you keep your nose clean you may have a shot at one. Of course, there's the union to deal with on the seniority problem but we can handle that somehow. Usually if you write long enough sentences the union jerks can't make heads or tails of it anyway. So if that's all, go home and be back first thing in the morning and I'll get you started.

Questions for Discussion:

1. What problems do you see with this interview?
2. What good things do you see in the interview?
3. How would you think the interview will affect Stinson?
4. How should Lowell have conducted the interview?

The Delegation Process

14

C. Give the Necessary Authority to Carry Out the Task
D. Let Others Know of the Delegation
E. Show Confidence in Subordinates
F. Don't Delegate Just Trivial Tasks
G. Don't Expect Others to Do the Job as Well as You Can
H. Don't Delegate Haphazardly
I. Don't Be an Autocratic Delegator
J. Don't Check Constantly to See How Things Are Going
K. Don't Take Credit for Results Achieved by Subordinates
L. Don't Overload Subordinates
VI. Key to Success
VII. Summary

Chapter Learning Objectives

After reading and studying this chapter you should be able to:

1. Describe the delegation process and what it is designed to achieve.

2. Define the exception principle.

3. List and explain the advantages of good delegation.

4. List and explain the disadvantages of the delegation process.

5. List and explain the reasons why subordinates often resist delegation.

6. List and explain the dos and don'ts of delegation.

Key Terms

Delegation
Final responsibility

Exception principle
Overload

353

John Brown's Delegation

John Brown supervises ten clerks in the Cumberland Community College Bookstore. The store provides all the textbooks and supplies for the various departments of the college. Each spring John asks each department to submit its textbook orders for the coming term, and other requests are sent prior to the other three terms of the year.

John believes in delegating as much responsibility as possible and has been constantly on the lookout for tasks that can be assigned to his subordinates. He believes this frees up his own time and provides good experience for his staff.

After thinking about it for some time, John decided about a month ago to delegate the task of soliciting textbook orders to the staff. There was no reason, he thought, that they couldn't do the ordering themselves, thus saving him considerable time in dealing with the different departments. So at a staff meeting, he informed the employees that they would each be responsible for soliciting textbook orders from specific departments, and for making sure that the proper number of books were on hand at the start of each term. He noted that any unusual problems should be referred to him. The staff seemed excited by the new tasks and most felt that this would give them more control over the academic areas they had to deal with on a day-to-day basis.

In the past few days John has received telephone calls from several department heads. It seems that they are upset at the changes in the textbook ordering procedures. One complaint is that now departments are being asked to submit textbook orders once during the year instead of before each term. It seems that they are also upset that they are not supposed to deal directly with John on their textbook problems.

Effective delegation is the core of the supervisory process. Without it, the supervisor becomes little more than a high-level employee who measures effectiveness by how many more hours he or she works compared to subordinates. Good delegators often seem to have time on their hands (they really don't but it appears that way) and poor delegators seem overburdened to the point of exhaustion. It has often been said that to become a good manager you have to work *smarter*, not harder. Delegating effectively is one way of working smarter.

The phrase "delegate effectively" has a very specific meaning. Merely delegating responsibility is itself not a magic answer to being a better supervisor. Effective delegation involves knowing when to delegate, what to delegate, and to whom it should be delegated. Many supervisors create substantial problems with their employees because they do not know how to delegate properly. Learning the principles in this chapter will help you avoid those problems.

There are aspects of delegation that can be learned from a book, but ultimately one must practice the concepts to see how they work in particular situations. Each supervisor has an individual style and the effectiveness of the delegation process will be partially determined by that style.

What Is Delegation?

In its most general sense, **delegation** is defined as the assigning of decision-making authority to the lowest possible level. In practical terms, this simply means giving decisions to the subordinates who are capable of making them. Since no supervisor would want to delegate to someone who wasn't capable of making the decision, this means that the supervisor must have a good idea of subordinates' skills and ability to handle responsibility. The theory underlying delegation is that managers are inefficient if they are making decisions that those below them could be making. It also means that employees are not being utilized to their full potential, thus making the entire chain of command inefficient.

Although in theory delegation has to with delegating decisions, it can also be viewed as delegating *tasks*. In other words, the supervisor assigns to subordinates certain tasks that were previously part of the supervisor's job. These tasks can be either ongoing types of tasks, or special in that they occur infrequently or only in unique situations. In either case, the supervisor considers that the subordinate is capable of handling the task and delegates the responsibility to him or her.

Delegation and Responsibility

Even though a supervisor may have delegated a task to a subordinate, the **final responsibility** cannot be delegated. The supervisor is still accountable to his or her own manager for the effective performance of that task. If the task is not performed properly, it is the supervisor's head that is on the line, not the subordinate's. However, the supervisor can (and should) hold the subordinate accountable providing, of course, that proper principles of delegation were followed. So the key to understanding the relationship between delegation and responsibility is the difference between responsibility and *final* responsibility. As noted in Chapters 2 and 3, it would be inappropriate for the supervisor's manager to hold the supervisor's subordinate accountable for substandard performance on a delegated task.

Decision and Delegation

At our university we have a set formula for admitting graduate students. The formula consists of a weighted score that includes grade point average and aptitude test scores. Admissions clerks are instructed to admit any student who scores above a certain level using the formula. Most of the students are admitted by the clerk. A few cases, however, do not fit the formula. For example, an applicant may have low grades and aptitude scores, but the grades may have been obtained many years ago and the individual may now be in a responsible managerial position. This applicant would be referred up to an admissions committee for the final decision.

Delegation and the Exception Principle

The limiting factor in delegation is the **exception principle.** This classical principle of management states that routine decisions should be made by subordinates, leaving only the exception (i.e., unique) decisions for the manager. The supervisor can inform subordinates either implicitly or explicitly that "As long as decisions fit our standard pattern, you go ahead and make the decision. Anything that is different, let me look at it first." To make this process effective, the supervisor must correctly communicate what the standard pattern is so that subordinates can recognize an exception when they encounter one. This is not a particularly difficult task and will be explained in greater detail in the following chapter on problem solving and decision making.

What Delegation Is Not

One way of learning about delegation is to understand what it is not. First of all, delegation should not be viewed as a system for passing the buck. As we have just explained, supervisors cannot avoid final responsibility for the actions of subordinates. Supervisors who use delegation as a means of avoiding responsibility will quickly find that subordinates develop an extreme dislike for delegation (and their supervisor!). Second, delegation is not just a way of getting rid of unpleasant or undesirable tasks — although this does not mean that these tasks cannot be delegated. Subordinates resent being given all the garbage tasks, particularly if they know the supervisor is delegating them for this reason. As we shall see later, the garbage tasks tend to cause less resentment if the interesting jobs are delegated as well.

Also, delegation is not necessarily a way of making your life easier, although we have to be careful about the meaning of the term *easier.* The point is that delegation should not be used to free you to do nothing.

Admittedly, the prospect of sitting back in a comfortable chair day-dreaming while an army of subordinates does your job for you is appealing, but this would be a short-run benefit at best. Subordinates would undoubtedly feel used and taken advantage of in a situation like this and the resentment caused would be costly in the long run. While delegation can be used to free up some of your time, this time should be used (and be seen to be used) constructively. All managers need time to engage in the mental managerial processes — planning, organizing, directing, controlling, and staffing. If too much time is spent on the routine aspects of supervision, the managerial aspects are left wanting. It is here that delegation can make you a more effective manager because you have more time to manage.

Finally, delegation is not, by itself, a way of overcoming staff shortages. Delegation can be a useful tool for utilizing staff more effectively, but the process is more concerned with *quality* of tasks delegated rather than the *quantity*. If delegation is used to overcome shortages in man-power, the result is more likely to be overload of subordinates rather than increased productivity.

There are many pitfalls along the path to learning effective delegation. As is the case with any managerial tool, applied properly it can increase employee productivity as well as job satisfaction. Improperly applied, it can breed resentment and poor job satisfaction. Later in this chapter we shall discuss in greater detail the potential problems with delegation and the errors supervisors commonly make.

Delegating Everything

Several years ago I was doing a research study at a large bank. My contact at the bank was a vice president of the personnel area. During the course of the study, I was amazed at the time the man had to devote to me and my work. He seemed never to be in the office and even drove me around to visit the various branches of the bank used in the study. On the days I wasn't there, he was either on the golf course or doing "site visits" (whatever they were). We became quite good friends during the study, close enough, in fact, that I felt I could go right to the heart of the matter and ask him how he managed to have so much free time. He replied, "I have the best bunch of people working for me you could ever hope for. They are perfectly capable of handling anything that comes into the office. I would even delegate my monthly meetings with the president if I thought he would stand for it. I hired each one of them personally and trained them for their jobs. They now know more about their areas than I do."

Three months later he left the bank to take a similar position with a much larger organization.

```
┌─────────────────┐
│  Exercise 14.1  │
└─────────────────┘
```

Deciding What to Delegate

It is generally agreed that delegation is a useful process for both supervisor and subordinate, providing that subordinates are delegated the proper tasks. Assume that you are a supervisor and are contemplating delegating more to one of your subordinates. What factors will you consider in deciding which tasks to delegate?

If you are now working as a supervisor, which tasks and decisions do you delegate? Are there any you could delegate but do not? Why?

Advantages of Delegation

When used properly, delegation has advantages for the supervisor, the employee, and the organization. Some of the more important ones are listed below.

Training and Development

Delegation can be an excellent training and development tool. In the history of organizations we have never devised a better way of teaching people how to handle responsibility than to give them some. Nothing beats hands-on experience (as was noted in Chapter 5) and delegation provides these experiences. The major reason why delegation is useful for development is that responsibility can be delegated in pieces, thus letting the person learn to handle responsibility in small steps and grow in the job rather than the sink-or-swim approach sometimes used. This philosophy of delegation is consistent with the effective training approaches described in the previous chapter. The supervisor should monitor the performance of the subordinate and increase the delegation as improvement warrants.

More Managerial Time

As we mentioned earlier, supervisors need time to manage their operations. Poor delegators spend too much time doing operational tasks instead of managerial ones, so their work groups are poorly managed. The process then becomes a vicious circle in that because the operation is not well managed, the supervisor finds that more and more time must be spent on operational work (often referred to as firefighting). Unfortunately, many supervisors pride themselves on their crisis style of management whereas in reality, firefighting is usually a symptom of poor management.

A Better Job Done

Although some supervisors are reluctant to admit it, delegating a task often means that it will be done better. This happens because subordinates are closer to the decision and its ramifications and therefore may have more specific knowledge than the supervisor. Also, a subordinate can get more excited about a job because it may be more challenging to him or her than to the supervisor, who may consider it routine. To the extent that satisfaction can affect results, subordinates can often achieve better outcomes than the supervisor.

Downward Communication Improved

Effective delegation requires that the supervisor spend considerable time with the subordinate giving instructions, specifying results, and requesting feedback. All of these increase the amount of communication between them considerably. Learning more about the task and how it relates to unit objectives, and receiving information necessary to complete the task provide an element of communication that can improve supervisor-subordinate relationships.

Job Satisfaction Increased

There are many qualifications to this statement, but in general, effective delegation can have a positive impact upon employee morale. Learning on the job, having a feeling of increased responsibility and involvement, and increased communication between supervisor and subordinate can help to improve morale. As we noted earlier, improper delegation can have a negative effect, but good delegators have an excellent chance of achieving high morale.

Disadvantages of Delegation

There are costs and rewards associated with every managerial strategy. Each supervisor must decide whether or not he or she is willing to pay the price to be a good delegator. Some of the disadvantages are unavoidable, others are a matter of supervisory style and individual preferences. But being aware of the disadvantages can prepare one for the inevitable, thus helping to cope with any problem, real or imagined, that might arise.

Training Time Required

Delegation is not something the supervisor just does on the spur of the moment and then forgets about. The subordinate must be properly prepared and trained to handle whatever task or decision has been delegated. Otherwise, the decisions will be substandard, the supervisor disillusioned, and the subordinate reluctant to take on additional responsibilities in the future. Therefore, effective delegation requires that the supervisor spend adequate time training the subordinate to handle the delegated responsibility. Often supervisors choose not to spend this time on the grounds that "it's faster if I do it myself." This is a very short-sighted view. It may well be that the first, second, third, or even fourth time the supervisor attempts to train the subordinate may be time spent that could have been spent by the supervisor in actually doing the job. But think of the time saved once the subordinate does learn and the task can be delegated every time thereafter! Training time is then repaid many times over.

Another reason why many supervisors do not train for delegation is that they are poor trainers themselves. Some lack patience, others are poor communicators and subordinates never really know what is expected of them, and others do not know the basic principles of how people learn. Each of these topics has been covered in other parts of this book.

Losing Touch with the Situation

Some supervisors like to know everything that goes on in their work area. If something happens that they don't know about, it makes them very uncomfortable. These supervisors generally make poor delegators because when they delegate, they insist on still being involved, thus nullifying many of the advantages inherent in the delegation process. One of the things that a supervisor must be prepared to accept is that effective supervision (and delegation) means that it will not be possible to be involved with everything that goes on. Supervisors must be prepared to trust subordinates sufficiently to let them get on with the responsibilities of their jobs.

Occasionally, one can expect to be confronted with the unexpected, such as a query about a task in the supervisor's unit that has been delegated. In many instances, the supervisor will not be able to answer the query. Provided that this does not cause serious problems elsewhere and does not happen too often, it should be considered as a normal price of the delegation process. It should not be considered a weakness in a supervisor that he or she cannot answer every question on the spot; on the contrary, it should be seen as a strength if it means that subordinates are carrying responsibility on their own.

Unfortunately, many times it is upper management that forces supervisors to get totally involved in their subordinates' work. A manager who expects the staff of supervisors to be able to answer any question from above immediately is implicitly hindering the delegation process. The statement, "I don't know right now but I'll check on it and get back to you as soon as I can" is often seen as a weakness in a supervisor and is reinforced accordingly.

Task Done Differently

This disadvantage is so subtle in its meaning that it is often overlooked. It is very closely linked to leadership style and therefore varies considerably between supervisors. Basically, this concept recognizes that when you delegate a task, *it will be done differently than if you had done it yourself.* The final objective may be achieved, but the process of performing the task (i.e., how, when, and with what) will be different. And even if the objective is achieved, the result may appear different because of the different methods used.

It takes a particular type of supervisor to tolerate these differences. Some equate being different with being wrong or incompetent. Generally speaking, autocratic supervisors have more difficulty with this than other supervisors. They have their way of doing things and expect others to do them the same way. Since it is virtually impossible for one person to do a task exactly the same as another, these supervisors are consistently disappointed with the performance of their subordinates. If the quality and quantity of performance are there, the employee should be allowed some variation in work methods.

Another situation in which this problem manifests itself is when a supervisor manages a job he or she used to perform as a first-line employee. The more skilled the supervisor was in the job, the greater the

Close Supervision in Painting

A colleague of mine recently asked me to help him with some major yard work for his newly constructed house. He had also hired a college student and after several hours the work pace slowed (because of our age limitations) and changed to conversation. It turned out the student had recently quit a painting job that paid considerably more than my colleague was paying him for the yard work. When asked why, he said, "The supervisor treated me like a kid — and he was younger than I was. He showed me how to sand, how to scrape, how to stir the paint, and how to use the brush properly. I've painted houses for two summers and here is this kid telling me how to do the job. He wouldn't get off my back. Every time I turned around he was watching to see if I was doing the job right. After two days I had enough and quit."

temptation to expect subordinates to perform the job in the same way. These situations require extreme tolerance from the supervisor, lest the subordinate feel that the supervisor is supervising too closely and setting expectations that cannot be met. In fact, when employees complain of oversupervision, often what they mean is that their supervisor will not tolerate different ways of performing the job.

Why Do Subordinates Resist Delegation?

Just mention the word delegation to many people and the result is often a lot of groans. Typically, the word has a positive meaning to managers, but is seen as negative by subordinates (and remember, every supervisor is also a subordinate!). Everyone has probably had feelings of apprehension, fear, suspicion, and anger when the manager announces, "I have this job I want to delegate to you." So let us analyze some of the reasons why this happens, and what the supervisor can do to alleviate these negative feelings.

It's Easier to Ask You

We often make it easy for subordinates not to accept more responsibility by readily doing things for them. If a difficult problem arises, they know that their supervisor will solve it for them, so why go to the trouble of trying to do it alone? This becomes a mutually reinforcing situation because some supervisors like subordinates who depend on them and seek their help (it makes them feel important), and subordinates like managers who make their jobs easier. So what appears to be a very satisfactory arrangement is, in reality, doing both parties a great disservice.

Making It Easy For Subordinates

The true capabilities of subordinates can often be seen while the supervisor is away, say on vacation, illness, or out of the office on business. A moment's reflection will show the following facts to be true in many cases. When the supervisor is around, there is a constant parade of subordinates into his or her office. They come in with supposedly important problems to be solved and, sure enough, the supervisor solves them. So what do these same subordinates do with these problems when the supervisor is away for three weeks' vacation? They usually solve them themselves. This suggests that the supervisor is making it very easy for the subordinates to become overly dependent upon him or her. If effective delegation was used, the subordinates would be handling these problems all of the time, not just when the supervisor is unavailable.

The subordinate is not developing properly and the manager is spending too much time doing things the subordinates should be doing.

This, of course does not mean that the supervisor should refuse to help a subordinate with a problem. That would really be a formula for disaster. What it does mean, however, is that the supervisor should be on the lookout for patterns such as that described in our example because these patterns suggest that the supervisor may be providing too much help to subordinates. Or, to put it another way, there is a great difference between being helpful to subordinates and being their permanent crutch. Avoid the role of crutch.

Fear of Criticism for Mistakes

All of us have seen a dog that hangs its head low and cowers close to the ground whenever someone comes near. Even though the person may be softly encouraging the dog and trying to pet it gently, the dog behaves as though it was deathly afraid. No doubt some time in the past the dog ran to someone, jumped happily up and licked his or her face, and was promptly kicked in the backside. After a few instances of this, the dog quickly learns not to trust people and plays it safe.

People behave much in the same way when punished for making a mistake. We generally don't like being punished, so the safest way to avoid punishment is never to take any risks. This is deadly for the delegation process since risk taking by the supervisor and subordinate is an important part of learning. Supervisors should never condone mistakes, but errors in judgment must be separated from errors in intent. Only rarely does a person make a mistake on purpose (this is called sabotage), yet some supervisors treat mistakes as though they were intentional. Subordinates who make mistakes in judgment should be treated with understanding and the entire incident should be used as a learning experience. Recall that in Chapter 5 it was noted that experiences are major determinants of our behavior, such that if a subordinate has a bad experience with delegation, he or she will be less enthusiastic about delegation the next time around. But if the supervisor can create positive experiences while delegating, subordinates will enjoy it rather than resent it.

The negative impact of poor judgment by a subordinate can be reduced if the supervisor also points out the things that were done correctly. Emphasis on the positive will help the subordinate not only to feel that the situation has been dealt with more fairly, but also to learn from the reinforcement of the correct behaviors what the supervisor is expecting.

Mistakes of intent, of course, should be dealt with immediately. The methods for dealing with these instances were covered in Chapter 8 in the discussion of effective discipline.

Lack of Necessary Resources to Do the Job

The term *resources* is used broadly here. It could be information, training, physical resources, financial resources, or job objectives. The two most common resources that are required in any delegation process are information and training. It would be virtually impossible for a subordinate to carry out a delegated task effectively without these. It is unfair for a supervisor to hold a subordinate fully accountable for the delegated task in the absence of adequate information and training.

As it happens, one of the instances in which this type of problem often occurs is in the case of new supervisors. Newly appointed supervisors are often not given any training in supervision, yet are expected to supervise effectively. When they fail, management often attributes it to poor selection.

Subordinates Already Overloaded

Someone who already feels overloaded isn't likely to be enthusiastic about being delegated more to do. Before this problem can be overcome, the supervisor has to find out if the subordinate is actually overloaded, does he or she have more responsibility than can be handled in the normal working day? Perhaps the individual is a poor manager of time or is doing someone else's work and shouldn't be. But once it is established that there is **overload,** then this problem should be solved before more responsibility is delegated. It was noted earlier that delegation cannot be used when a unit is already understaffed, and similarly, a manager should not use delegation to solve staff shortage problems. But one positive by-product of the planned delegation process is that it forces supervisor and subordinate to examine the total workload, something that should be done regularly.

Let Alone — ZAP!

In a video tape series on Situational Leadership (see Chapter 12), author Ken Blanchard describes a popular delegating style known as the "Let Alone — ZAP!" strategy. This style is often practiced by supervisors and managers who have little appreciation for the value of training and development on an incremental basis. They dump the entire load of responsibility on subordinates and then let them alone. Sooner or later a mistake is made, and the subordinates get zapped. They have therefore learned one thing they should not do again. However, the supervisor never tells them what they should be doing or what good performance looks like; they only zap them when they make a mistake. The "Let Alone — ZAP!" strategy is probably one of the most effective ways of turning good employees into deadwood.

Lack of Self-Confidence

Another reason why subordinates may resist the delegation process is that they have little confidence in their own abilities. Often these are either new (or young) employees, or people who have not worked for a period of time and are reentering the workforce, although it is not limited to these two groups. For example, people who have been constantly criticized all their lives or have always been told what to do may develop strong feelings of inadequacy in almost everything they attempt.

These types of employees need a lot of attention and positive reinforcement from the supervisor. They need to be reinforced more often than others and receive more support when they do make errors. In extreme cases, it may not be possible to change the person (see Chapter 5) but in more moderate circumstances the support and reinforcement can slowly build self-confidence so he or she can assume more responsibility.

The key to developing these employees is not to delegate too much initially. Individuals with low self-esteem need to accomplish goals to prove to themselves that they have the capability. Therefore, small, achievable objectives are important for these people. After each success, confidence builds a little, and over time the person may develop more normal patterns of behavior. One of the worst things a supervisor can do to these employees is to delegate too much and let them alone until they make a major mistake. This reinforces feelings of inadequacy and makes the situation even worse.

Efficiency Can Backfire!

I was once told the story of a company president who constantly complained of being overworked. He left the house at seven in the morning and seldom returned until after eight in the evening. To find out why he was so overworked, his wife (in disguise) applied for and got the job of cleaning lady during the day. During her rounds she would watch employees performing various tasks and ask them, "Why are you doing that?" In most cases, the reply was "Because we've always done it." In one instance she watched a secretary duplicate and collate eighteen copies of a thirty-five-page report for a sales meeting. Her investigations revealed that none of the eighteen people read the entire report and it was subsequently decided that they could easily get by with a one-page summary. This single change saved the secretary ten hours per week.

The happy ending to the story is that the wife's careful examination of the workload revealed many more instances of inefficiencies in the company, all of which were eliminated. The company president then had more free time and ended up running off with his secretary!

Exercise 14.2

To Delegate or Not to Delegate

Although delegation is proposed as being a useful tool for improving a supervisor's effectiveness, it is also generally agreed that there are some responsibilities that should not be delegated. Think for a moment about the job of a supervisor, and then make a list of the tasks (or types of tasks) you feel should not be delegated. Be prepared to defend your position.

The Dos and Don'ts of Delegation

Cookbook lists of dos and don'ts can be dangerous because they tend to oversimplify what are often very complex topics. However, the principles of delegation are reasonably valid and a general list of dos and don'ts can be generated. Brief discussions of the principle follow the list.

- Specify the results expected.
- Explain why you are delegating.
- Give the necessary authority to carry out the task.
- Let others know of the delegation.
- Have confidence in subordinates.

- Don't delegate just trivial tasks.
- Don't expect others to do the job as well as you can.
- Don't delegate haphazardly.
- Don't be an autocratic delegator.
- Don't check constantly to see how things are going.
- Don't take credit for results achieved by subordinates.
- Don't just overload subordinates.

Specify the Results Expected

Knowing what is expected is important if the subordinate is to carry out a task properly. The supervisor should spend considerable time explaining what is expected (but not how to do the job). This process essentially sets the goals for the subordinate and gives him or her a measure of task completion. It is difficult to be too precise in explaining what you expect. In the most basic sense, subordinates should know what good performance looks like.

There used to be a belief that leaving the task vague was a motivator, because the uncertainty of what was expected created anxiety in subordinates, which in turn increased motivation and caused them to try harder. This may cause them to try harder, but the increased motivation could easily end up in frustration if they can never give the supervisor what is expected. A better approach is to specify *results* clearly, but leave the *means* of achieving the results up to the subordinate. Thus, whatever uncertainty is created is at least channeled toward the correct objective.

Explain Why You Are Delegating

This may seem obvious, which is probably why it is so often overlooked. The supervisor may feel that the boss is the boss and therefore explanations aren't necessary. The reasons for delegating can be many: to develop subordinates, to free up time for the supervisor, or because the subordinate is better qualified than the supervisor. In any case, there is less chance of creating resentment in the subordinate if the supervisor first explains why the task is being delegated.

Give the Necessary Authority to Carry Out the Task

When you stop to think about it, if a supervisor delegates a task but doesn't delegate the complete authority to carry it out, there has been no real delegation. The subordinate will be forced to come back time and time again to the supervisor for more information, resources, or approval of what has been accomplished so far. All of these negate the advantages of delegation.

Let Others Know of the Delegation

This is often a communication that is overlooked. Whether in written or oral form, it lets everyone else know that a particular area of responsibility has been delegated. This can be a time-saving device because any communication regarding the task can now go directly to the subordinate without first having to go through the supervisor. It also assists the subordinate, who does not have to spend time telling everyone what has transpired. Imagine the plight of a subordinate who has to go throughout the organization to gather certain information, and must explain their arrangement to every person he or she deals with!

Show Confidence in Subordinates

This is a classic chicken-and-egg problem. Supervisors often say, "When he shows that he can do the job, then I'll have confidence in him." Meanwhile, the subordinate is feeling, "If he would just show a little confidence in me, I know I could do the job." The thrust of the message here is that delegation may not be effective if the supervisor is not willing to let the subordinate carry on alone. Trust, it must be remembered, is communicated to others by the manner in which they are treated. If a supervisor delegates a task and then hovers constantly to see how things are going, this communicates to the subordinates that the supervisor really doesn't trust them. Simply to say, "I have confidence in you" isn't good enough; the supervisor must *show* that he or she trusts the subordinates by giving them the freedom to act on their own.

Don't Delegate Just Trivial Tasks

This well may be the most serious threat to the delegation process. It happens like this: a supervisor is not sure a subordinate can handle tasks A, B, and C because they are pretty difficult and challenging. So as a test, the supervisor delegates task E, which is trivial compared to the others. The subordinate may resent being given a trivial task like E and this affects his motivation to do task E properly. Since task E has been performed in a substandard manner, the supervisor concludes that, since the subordinate cannot handle task E properly, he certainly can't handle A, B, and C.

If the supervisor had doubts about a subordinate's capabilities, a better strategy would have been to take A, B, or C and break that one task down into smaller components and work with the subordinate until the task is completed. This accomplishes the same thing but avoids creating the resentment at the trivial task.

This does not mean the supervisor cannot delegate trivial tasks. First, what is trivial for the supervisor may be reasonably challenging for the subordinate, so in essence the supervisor is not really delegating a trivial task. Second, trivial tasks tend to be resented more if that is the only type of task that is delegated. Greater acceptance can be gained if other types of tasks are delegated as well.

Don't Expect Others to Do the Job as Well as You Can

This has already been discussed but it warrants mentioning again. Supervisors must be tolerant of individual differences and methods of performing tasks. Successful task performance should be judged by results achieved, not on the specifics of how they were achieved.

Don't Delegate Haphazardly

Effective delegation is a systematic, planned process that is integrated with the overall objectives of the work unit. It should be part of an overall development plan for subordinates to train them to handle more and more responsibility. Haphazard delegation is often the result of crisis management where the supervisor delegates only because he or she has to and with little thought for the needs of the subordinates. Haphazard delegation creates problems with subordinates, too. They find it difficult to plan and organize their own workload if their manager spontaneously thrusts additional responsibility upon them. The disruptive nature of haphazard delegation creates inefficiencies for everyone.

Don't Be an Autocratic Delegator

With one exception to be noted, this is a useful principle. Participation in the delegation process can enhance the subordinate's chances of success and improve the relationship between supervisor and subordinate. If no participation is allowed, the supervisor may never know when overload is occurring, or if the subordinate perceives any difficulties in performing the task. Good communication between supervisor and subordinate is essential.

One exception to this principle is a corollary of a basic principle of change discussed in Chapter 19. It is recognized that some people resist change because they anticipate having unpleasant experiences with the change. One way of dealing with this type of problem is the try-it-you'll-like-it strategy; the supervisor orders the change to take place and then provides support to subordinates after the change to increase the chances that the experience will be positive. One can easily imagine a similar strategy with a situation mentioned earlier — the employee with no self-confidence. With the participative approach, the subordinate may express considerable resistance to the delegated task. An alternative is for the supervisor to be autocratic (but not obnoxious!) in the delegation, and increase the support and assistance given to the subordinate. This, plus continued reinforcement for successful task performance, will give the subordinate a positive experience with delegation and further enhance development. This would probably not have occurred with the participative method.

Don't Check Constantly to See
How Things Are Going

This can really drive subordinates mad. Few things are more annoying than to be delegated a task and then be asked frequently, "How are things going?" Assuming that a completion time was stated in the instructions (as it should be), unless other information has surfaced that affects the task, the subordinate should be left alone. Assistance can be offered at the employee's request and then only if it is consistent with conditions noted earlier.

Curiously, experience has indicated that few managers and supervisors are capable of *totally* delegating a task. Giving up control, trusting subordinates completely, and staying out of their way seems to be a difficult thing for supervisors to do. They probably feel that the subordinate appreciates their presence so their inability to delegate is well intended. Nevertheless, effective suprvisors realize their presence only inhibits delegation and may breed resentment.

Don't Take Credit for Results Achieved by Subordinates

Even though a task may belong to a supervisor, when it is delegated the subordinate should receive full credit for successful completion of the task. As an example, suppose a supervisor is requested to prepare an inventory report for upper management; the task is delegated to an inventory clerk who completes the task, gives the report to the supervisor, who in turn passes it up to upper management. Since the task was originally delegated to the supervisor, that person will receive credit for doing a good job and the subordinate may be neglected unless the supervisor makes a specific effort to give credit where credit is due. In this situation, it would be satisfactory for the subordinate to sign the report (as the individual who prepared it), and the supervisor sign it as the manager who approved it. In this way, everyone gets credit but it is clear who prepared the report.

Don't Overload Subordinates

Again, this was noted earlier but it is important to put it explicitly in the "don't" category. Overload is an absolute concept in that everyone only has so many hours in a day. There is also a perceptual aspect, however, in that delegation will probably more likely be seen as overload if the delegated tasks are trivial. Overload can be prevented by communicating with subordinates prior to delegation.

Key to Success

Effective delegation is a crucial part of any supervisor's job. A supervisor who is a poor delegator (i.e., either doesn't delegate, delegates the wrong things, or doesn't communicate with subordinates) will be less effective as a supervisor and will not be performing a proper managerial role. Unfortunately, there are no magic answers to the many questions that arise when contemplating delegation. There are general principles — which have been presented here — but these principles must be tested by each individual supervisor in specific situations.

The greatest cost associated with poor delegation is the damaging effect on employee development. If the supervisor has little confidence in employees' abilities, they will tend to respond negatively. Since subordinates are not developed to their full capacity, the organization suffers accordingly. Employees who have not been given increasing levels of responsibility through a systematic program of delegation are not promotable, and this can cause serious morale problems. It is an organizational variation on the Catch-22 problem: because employees aren't developed, they aren't promoted; because they aren't promoted, they can't be developed.

The process of delegation requires that the supervisor learn to toe the fine line inherent in all of the principles of management. Knowing how much to delegate so that the subordinate feels challenged but not overwhelmed, knowing how to help subordinates achieve goals without spoon-feeding them, and being supportive in their learning process without condoning poor performance — all these require understanding and sensitivity which, as far as we know, must be learned through experience.

Summary

Delegation is the assigning of decision-making authority to the lowest possible level in the organization. By delegating decisions to subordinates, the supervisor can become more efficient at performing supervisory duties. Delegation is also a good training technique since it allows employees to handle higher levels of responsibility. Even though decisions can be delegated, the supervisor still has final responsibility and accountability for the decisions made. The exception principle is an important part of delegation since it gives the supervisor control over decisions that are required in unusual circumstances and cannot be made by subordinates. Delegation should not be used as a method of getting rid of unpleasant tasks, or merely to give the supervisor idle time.

There are many advantages to delegation: it provides valuable training for employees, it gives supervisors more time to plan their work, it often results in a better job, it improves communication between supervisor and subordinate, and can increase job satisfaction. The disadvantages to delegation are that it takes time to train employees properly so they can handle the additional responsibilities, supervisors often lose touch with the situation once decisions have been delegated, and the job may be done in a way different from the supervisor's.

Subordinates often resist delegation. They may be afraid of making a mistake, they may lack confidence in their ability to do the job, they may lack the resources necessary to do the task properly, or they may be already overloaded. In some cases, the supervisors make it too easy for the subordinates to rely on them to make the decisions.

The delegation process has been scientifically studied and experiences with managers and supervisors have resulted in a useful list of do's and don'ts in delegation. Although there will be exceptions to the list, it is a useful starting point for improving delegation skills.

Opening Incident Revisited

Although John Brown is having some problems with delegating the textbook ordering task, he is on the right track and the situation can probably be salvaged.

First, let's look at what he did well. The task he chose to delegate is not a trivial one. In fact, it obviously has a lot of meat to it (otherwise the department heads would not care if it was not done right). It also appears that his employees have really become involved in the task and paid serious attention to it. This is evident by the changes they have made in previous procedures.

John also delegated the task and gave the employees a free rein in how it was to be done. Although this caused him problems later, he followed the spirit of proper delegation. This also shows the employees he has confidence in their abilities.

Finally, John followed the exception principle, although he was a little vague about what constituted an exception. Additional information on this might have alleviated some of the problems that arose later.

One of the obvious errors John made was in not informing the department heads of his new system. By discussing the matter with them, he might have been able to deal with their concerns at the outset, rather than waiting until the problems developed. John's delegation policy could have been construed by the heads to mean that he doesn't consider their textbook orders to be as important as they used to be. In other words, they may be reacting more to a perceived drop in status than anything else.

Another thing John could have done better was in the follow-up process. The textbook order task is a major one and the possibility for errors in judgment is therefore greater. Although John would not want to supervise too closely, he should have designed some feedback system so he could monitor how things were progressing. For example, he might have requested monthly reports on the ordering process.

Although there is no evidence in the incident regarding the abilities of his employees, it is unlikely that all are at the same level of development. Yet, it appears that his delegation policy is uniform for all employees. This could be why only some of the department heads have complained. Perhaps John should have been more selective by delegating more to the most experienced and capable employees and less to the others.

The fact that some employees have apparently made a major change in the ordering policy suggests that John may have delegated too much. Oftentimes employees are not able to see the big picture by themselves, and more control over the task might have prevented the unhappiness of the department heads. While a single order once each year would probably make life for the staff much easier, it may be unrealistic from the standpoint of the academic units.

Review Questions

1. What is delegation?
2. Can a supervisor delegate final responsibility? Why or why not?
3. What is the exception principle and how does it relate to delegation?
4. Can trivial tasks be delegated?
5. What are the advantages of delegation?
6. How can delegation make the supervisor a better manager?
7. What are the disadvantages of delegation?
8. What are the reasons why subordinates often resist delegation?
9. What are the dos and don'ts of delegation?

Chapter Glossary

Delegation	The process of systematically assigning authority to the lowest level at which the tasks can be carried out properly.
Final responsibility	The ultimate accountability for performance that rests with the manager or supervisor. Although subordinates can be held accountable for certain responsibilities, final responsibility cannot be delegated.
Exception principle	A classical principle of management that separates decisions that can be delegated from those that cannot. Subordinates are delegated a set of decisions or tasks, but are instructed that exceptions to the normal responsibilities should be referred upward for action.
Overload	A situation in which an employee is given more responsibility than can be handled in a normal working day.

Case Problem

Southside Drug Store

Marlene Simpson is the owner of the Southside Drug Store, a neighborhood store which sells pharmaceuticals and related items. The store employs fifteen people on a full- and part-time basis, including two other pharmacists and an assistant manager, Ron Diebold. Diebold is in charge of the sales and clerical staff, while Marlene supervises the other pharmacists and manages the overall store operations. Diebold has been with the store for three years and has proved to be a motivated employee. Eager to learn about the business, he has always been willing to take on more responsibility and Marlene has delegated most of the day-to-day operations to him.

Marlene has noticed that Diebold spends a lot of hours at the store, far more than she expected. He is usually at work by 7:00 A.M. and seldom leaves before 7:00 P.M. In addition, he is usually at the store for several hours on both Saturday and Sunday. He seems to have an excellent rapport with his staff and Marlene can find no fault with his performance.

On Saturday morning, when Marlene was in her office reviewing the sales figures for the week, Diebold walked in and asked if he could talk with her. The following conversation took place:

DIEBOLD: Marlene, do you have a minute?

MARLENE: Sure, Ron, what's on your mind?

DIEBOLD: Well, I've been meaning to talk with you about . . . well, about the possibility of a raise.

MARLENE: OK, let's talk.

DIEBOLD: Well, I know we agreed on an annual salary with no overtime pay, but at the time I wasn't aware of how many hours this job would take. I find it takes at least sixty hours a week to get all my work done, and . . . well, I feel putting in that much time warrants more money than I'm getting now. Mind you, I really like my job and it's good experience for me, but some of my cashiers are making almost as much as I am when you consider what my hourly rate would be. I think I should be making more.

MARLENE: I see. Have you thought about cutting back on your hours?

DIEBOLD: Sure, I've thought about it, but there's just no way it can be done. Believe me, there's nothing I'd like better than to spend fewer hours here, but it's just not possible. Why, taking the weekly inventory alone takes almost fifteen hours. And with all the additional stock we're now carrying, it's going to start taking more than that.

MARLENE: Can't you get some of the other staff to do the inventory?

DIEBOLD: Not really. You know how important it is that the job be done right. Besides, in the time it would take me to teach someone, I could do it myself. Also, with the high turnover we have, I would teach someone and they'd probably leave two weeks later. All that time would be lost. No, it's faster if I do it myself. At least that way I know it's done right.

MARLENE: So you don't see any way you can reduce your hours?

DIEBOLD: No . . . there's no possibility. But I wouldn't mind so much if I were paid more. Can we agree on some type of raise?

Questions For Discussion:

1. What seems to be Diebold's problem?
2. If you were Marlene, would you give him the raise? Why or why not?
3. Is Marlene to blame in any way for this situation?
4. What suggestions would you have for Marlene to deal with this problem?

Decision Making and Problem Analysis

15

After reading and studying this chapter you should be able to:

1. Describe the difference between problem analysis and decision making.

2. Define decision making and problem analysis.

3. Describe the role of judgment in decision making.

4. Define programmed and unprogrammed decisions.

5. Describe the role that emotions play in decison making.

6. Define the concept of satisficing.

7. Describe the characteristics of an effective decision.

8. List and describe the steps in the problem-analysis phase.

9. Describe the difference between symptoms and sources in problem analysis.

10. Define the systems effect and describe how it affects problem analysis.

11. List and describe the steps in the decision-making phase.

12. List and describe the steps in the decision implementation phase.

13. List and describe the common errors made in problem analysis and decision making.

Key Terms

Problem analysis
Decision making
Computational decisions
Judgment
Programmed decisions

Emotional decision making
Rational decision making
Unprogrammed decisions
Satisficing

Decision effectiveness
Symptom
Source
Systems effect
Decision making steps
Decision implementation

Deciding to Decide

"You've got a problem there and I want you to make a decision about it," said George LeBeau, manager of distribution for *The Daily Herald.* The remark was directed at Tom Sifton, supervisor of the truck drivers who deliver the newspapers to the surrounding towns and local drop-off stations. There are thirty drivers who drive the delivery trucks, sometimes hundreds of miles in one day.

LeBeau continued, "I've been watching the maintenance costs on the trucks and right now our costs are up twenty percent over last year. I've already talked with the maintenance foreman and he assures me that the same maintenance programs are being followed this year as last. That means your drivers are responsible for the increased costs. What do you propose to do about it?"

"I'm not sure," replied Sifton.

"What do you mean you're not sure?" said LeBeau. "The facts speak for themselves. You certainly can't argue with the facts now, can you?"

"Well, I still have some checking to do before I can decide," said Sifton.

"I can't see what checking there is to do. You've got to come to a decision quickly before the V.P. has us both in on the carpet. I just know in my bones he's seen the same figures," said LeBeau. "He will want to know what we're doing about the increased costs, so you give me a decision by this time tomorrow."

"I'll do my best," replied Sifton, as he walked out of LeBeau's office.

"We want someone in this job who can make decisions!" In most organizations, this is a frequent statement and is often the major thrust behind trying to find good managers and supervisors. If life were only as simple as finding someone who will make decisions, many of our problems in management would disappear overnight.

As this chapter will show, problem analysis and decision making are very complex subjects. So complex, in fact, that it is very difficult to teach someone how to make "better decisions." Decisions themselves are easy to make; the tough part is learning to make better ones.

One way of improving skills in these areas is having a clear understanding of what problem analysis and decision making are all about, and how one should proceed in making a decision. Equally important, however is the implementation of decisions. A good decision is worthless if it is not implemented properly. This chapter discusses some of the concerns supervisors should have regarding decision implementation, and Chapter 19, "Managing Change," is also relevant to this topic.

Difference Between Problem Analysis and Decision Making

The two terms in the chapter title were not chosen by accident. Though similar in nature, they have quite different meanings and this chapter treats them as separate processes. For example, problems may be solved and no decision made, and decisions can be made even though no problems have been solved. A supervisor may reach a decision regarding a particular problem, but if the problem has not been analyzed correctly, the decision will not solve the problem.

Sound strange? It probably does because most of us do not make the distinction between problem analysis and decision making. Here are a couple of examples to help understand the difference. Suppose a supervisor decides to implement a new form for employees to sign when they arrive in the morning to minimize tardiness. In this instance, the supervisor has made a decision, but it may not solve the problem. If, for example, employees are consistently tardy because of poor morale and attitudes, the form will not solve that problem. What the supervisor should do is engage in problem analysis first, then decide if a decision is warranted. The supervisor may note that many employees are tardy in the morning, and then begin to analyze that specific problem, its causes and severity. Once the problem of tardiness has been properly analyzed, a decison may or may not be warranted. For example, the supervisor may decide that the problem is beyond the bounds of his or her department, and do little except report the problem analysis to higher management.

For our purposes, we shall treat **problem analysis** as the process by which a problem is identified and defined. Decision making is concerned primarily with reaching a solution to the problem that has been analyzed. The two are obviously closely related but they should be separated, both in theory and in practice.

Before examining problem analysis and the decision-making process in detail, we will discuss the concept of decision making as a function of every manager's job. Important concepts such as what a decision is, the role of judgment in decisions, the programming of decisions, rationality in decision making, the importance of finding the best decision, and the concept of decision effectiveness, are all important to understanding how problems can be analyzed and better decisions made.

Important Decision-Making Concepts

The term *decision* is used so frequently we often don't stop to think what it means. As will be illustrated shortly, sometimes we think we are making decisions when we really aren't. Other times, we choose not to make a decison, forgetting that not making a decision is in itself a decision! And of course there are those times when we intend to make a decision and we do. If all this sounds complicated, you are beginning to appreciate how complex decision making is.

What Is Decision Making?

Simply defined, **decision making** is the selection of a choice between two or more alternatives under conditions of uncertainty. This definition has three critical aspects to it: first, a choice must be made. No decision is completed until a course of action has been selected. Second, one must be faced with two or more alternatives. If only one alternative is feasible, then the decision is essentially made. Finally, and this is often overlooked, there must be uncertainty as to which is the correct course of action. If the decision maker has *complete* knowledge about the alternatives, the correct course of action would be obvious.

To illustrate these characteristics, let us examine **computational decisions,** which are based on perfect information. As the definition of decision making implies, these are not really decisions at all. Assume you have to paint a room and want to decide how much to spend. If you know the area of the room, how much area a gallon of paint will cover, and how much the paint costs, then you can *compute* how much you must spend. If there are decisions to be made, they would be made in other areas such as what color to paint the room, what quality of paint to use, and so forth. But if the room must be painted in the same color, and the color requires that a specific quality of paint be used, it would be

Deciding Who Receives Credit

In one of my classes I was trying to get across the concept of computational decisions. I asked the class members to give me an example of a decision they generally made at work. One member volunteered that in her job as an employee in the credit department, she decided who got credit and who didn't. In describing this decision, she stated that she gathered information on an application form, examined all the information, and then decided if the store should give the customer credit. I then gave her several sample cases to decide. In extreme cases, such as where an applicant earned $100,000 per year and had no debts, she had no difficulty in deciding they would be given credit. In borderline cases, however, she had difficulty. It turned out that she had a formula the company had given her to decide if credit should be given. For each piece of information on the application form, the applicant was given so many points. These points were then added to get the applicant's credit rating. If the applicant had enough points to reach the minimum required, he or she was given credit. So what appeared to be a decision was actually just a computation. The decision as to who got credit was actually made at a higher level by the person who set the minimum number of points required.

incorrect to say that you were going to decide how much to spend in painting the room. In other words, there was only one alternative and perfect information about that alternative was available.

Decision Making and Judgment

The essence of making decisions is the use of judgment. This is the part of the definition that refers to uncertainty. As we have pointed out, the reason why computational decision making is not really decision making is that it doesn't involve any judgment. When you choose between different alternatives without having complete information, you are using **judgment.**

Judgment is often referred to by other names: intuition, gut feel, or seat-of-the-pants decision making. All of these terms describe how we select alternatives under conditions of uncertainty. The interesting thing about judgment is that *it cannot be taught.* This may seem to be a devastating comment in a chapter on decision making, but it is a fact that no one can teach someone how to use better judgment. The most that can be done is to teach methods of reducing uncertainty to a manageable form so that the role of judgment can be controlled. We can teach how to analyze problems, how to gather information on a problem, how to generate more alternatives, and the steps that should be followed in making a decision, but assuming that you will not have all the information you need, your actual decision will be a function of your experience, values, objectives, and a host of other unknown and uncontrollable factors.

The major implication of this concept for you as a supervisor is that the very nature of the supervisor's job is such that you will seldom, if ever, have all the information to make decisions. Sooner or later, you will have to stick your neck out and make a decision based upon judgment. Because you have used judgment in reaching the decision, do not expect everyone to agree with you — as they probably will not — because they have different attitudes, values, and experiences.

As a final point, it is worth noting that people are paid wages and salaries by organizations because of the judgment they must exercise. Company presidents earn more than supervisors because they must exercise more judgment. It would be foolish to pay someone a large salary to compute answers to problems. When computation is possible, computers are used so that people can be assigned to situations that involve uncertainty. Although computers can handle large amounts of information and perform calculations more quickly than people, they cannot use judgment since they are limited to the alternatives programmed into them.

The fundamental role of judgment in decision making is illustrated in Figure 15.1, which indicates that the higher the organizational level,

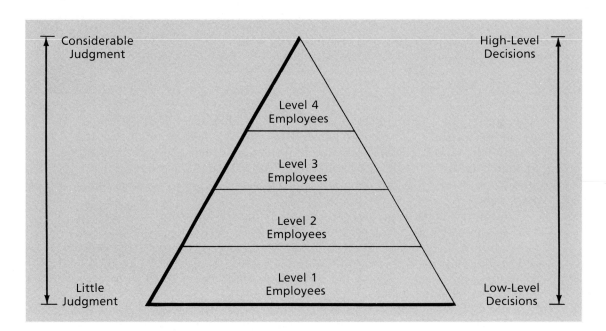

Figure 15.1. The Role of Judgment in Decision Making at Various Levels.

the greater the amount of judgment required. This is the same as saying that managers at the upper levels of the organization have less information upon which to make decisions than do lower-level managers. Again, this is why they get paid more than lower-level employees. And the reason supervisors (we hope) get paid more than their subordinates is because the supervisors must exercise comparatively more judgment in making decisions.

Programmed and Unprogrammed Decisions

Because employees can use both good and bad judgment, organizations must have ways of controlling the amount of judgment required in any job. This is accomplished by programming decisions. The term programming is used here much as it is with computer programming. When we program a computer, we confine it to a fixed set of alternatives. The computer decides which alternative to choose, but it cannot go beyond the alternatives programmed into it. **Programmed decisions** are made within a fixed set of alternatives.

Organizations operate in much the same way. Suppose you supervise a group of salesclerks and, while you want them to use judgment in dealing with customers, you cannot afford the risk of letting them have

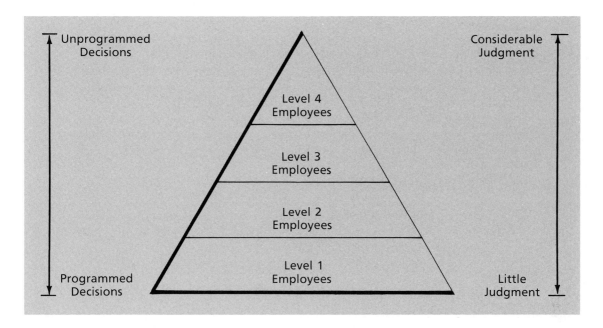

Figure 15.2. Relationship Between Judgment and Programming of Decisions at Various Organizational Levels.

complete judgment in their jobs. You will therefore give them a fixed set of alternatives, with freedom to choose among the set. For example, for customers who are returning some merchandise, you might give them the following alternatives:

1. Allow the customers to exchange the merchandise for the same item or one of equal value;
2. Give a credit slip for the amount of the returned item;
3. Give credit for the return for the purchase of an item of greater value.

You have implicitly allowed them to make a decision within these three alternatives. Notice, however, that according to the program you have set, they could not refund the customer's money. Therefore, you have set limits, that is, programmed their decision.

The relationship between judgment and programming decisions should now be apparent. As illustrated in Figure 15.2, lower levels of the organization have a greater degree of programming than the higher levels. Because of these programs, lower levels require less judgment in decisions than higher levels.

As a supervisor, all of your decisions will be programmed to some degree. Some of the constraints may be determined by external factors such as the legal environment, and some will be given by the organization itself. Recall from Chapter 4 the structure of plans in an organization: objectives, policies, procedures, and rules. These are the primary ways in which the company programs your decisions. Your own manager will also program your decisions to some degree. In fact, it is a good idea, if you are not aware of what some of the programs are, to find out. Otherwise, you may make a decision that is outside the bounds of your set of alternatives. That, of course, makes for a very nervous boss.

Rational Versus Emotional Decisions

Given the reasoning developed so far, it follows that all decisions (if they are consistent with the definition given previously) involve some emotion. In this context, emotion is synonymous with judgment, intuition, or gut feel, and **emotional decision making** allows for feelings and value judgments.

To use the same logic, **rational decision making** requires no value judgment, because all the information needed is available. Perfect information is a virtual impossibility in most situations, so it follows that all decisions will have an element of emotional content to them.

In practice, of course, no decision is completely devoid of either rationality or emotion. There will be a blend of both, with programmed decisions having more rationality than unprogrammed ones. **Unprogrammed decisions,** for which the number of available alternatives is not fixed, are similar to those described in the discussion of the exception principle in the previous chapter.

Another way of viewing the role of emotions in decision making is to examine how the emotional state of an individual can affect his or her decisions. It is generally unwise to make a decision when in a strong emotional state. Supervisors who have strong feelings about a situation (they may be angry or upset about something) have difficulty understanding the significance of the information available and often make decisions they regret later. Our goal is always to make decisions as rationally as possible, recognizing both the positive and negative roles that emotions can play.

Another variation of the emotional decision is the hunch. Hunches are decisions we want to make but cannot explain why. Hunches have a role to play in decision making, but not as substitutes for rational thinking. Hunches sometimes pay off, but because they are hunches, we never know why. Therefore, there is little learning value in hunches and each time we use them we are taking a chance. As in any activity that involves probabilities, it is wise to minimize the risk in our favor.

Finding the "Best" Decision

Supervisors, like anyone else, would like to make the best decision possible. However, there is a danger associated with trying to make the best decision. Since decision making is done under conditions of uncertainty, decision makers understandably will gather information in an attempt to reduce this uncertainty. If the decision maker attempts to gather *all* the information needed to make the decision, the search could be endless. In the language of decision making, this is called *optimizing*, or trying to find the optimal or best possible solution to a problem. At some point in time, however, the search for additional information has only marginal benefit and the person would be better off exercising judgment and arriving at a decision. In other words, it is recommended that managers search only for as *satisfactory* a solution as possible, rather than the optimal one. This process is called **"satisficing."**[1]

The distinction between optimizing and satisficing can also be used to describe decision-making styles. Supervisors whose style is to try to find the best solution possible may end up spending too much time on one decision at the expense of others. Their inability to deal with uncertainty, risk, and judgment can make them ineffective decision makers because they are continually searching for more information to minimize the risk. The satisficing style is not only much more practical, but also usually more effective, providing the supervisor is able to exercise sound judgment.

The main thing to remember in aiming for the best decision is to understand that the "best" decision is a theoretical ideal which, if it can be attained, is often not worth the cost. The effective supervisor is the one who needs only a satisfactory amount of information before making a decision.

Decision Making and Objectives

A decision is defined as good or bad in relation to the objectives it attempts to achieve. Before any decision is made, it should be tested against whatever objectives the supervisor has. It therefore follows that decision making is easier if objectives have been clearly defined. If objectives are unclear or not stated at all, then supervisors and managers have no criterion against which the decision can be judged.

As an example, assume that a supervisor wishes to hire a new employee and has four candidates to choose from. If the supervisor has no clear objectives for the unit, then the choice will be relatively difficult. It

1. Herbert A. Simon, *Administrative Behavior* (New York: Macmillan, 1957).

will be hard to evaluate the qualifications of the candidates in relationship to how they will help or hinder the performance of the unit. However, if the supervisor's primary objective is to increase the range of skills within the department, each of the candidates could be judged against this criterion.

Because it is common to have more than one objective, the decision-making process becomes much more complicated than just described. Having multiple objectives means that you must test your decision against each of them (with some form of priority). This suggests that it is even more important to have your objectives thought out clearly.

Decision Effectiveness

As noted earlier in this chapter, there are actually two components to the decision-making process. One is making the decision, and the other is implementing it. Theoretically at least, it is possible to have a good decision which, when implemented, turns out to be ineffective. One way of looking at this possibility is described in the following equation:

$$ED = Q \times A$$

where ED stands for Effective Decision, Q stands for Quality, and A stands for Acceptance. The meaning of the equation is that **decision effectiveness** is a function of the quality of the decision (i.e., how good it is) times how well the decision is accepted by those who must implement it.

Although this is a simplified way of looking at the decision process, it is still useful for understanding how good decisions can turn into ineffective ones. If we assign values of zero to ten for the Q and A we can see how the effectiveness can vary. If a supervisor has a high quality decision, but the group will not accept it, then our equation might read:

$$Q (8) \times A (2) = ED (16)$$

In other words, this will not be a very effective decision. Notice, however, that participative decision making (as we know from Chapter 12), can increase acceptance because involvement in decision making increases employees' commitment to the decision. This might change our figures to read something like:

$$Q (8) \times A (5) = ED (40)$$

The decision is clearly now more effective than before because we have increased the acceptance. However, a much more likely possibility is that when acceptance increases, quality will *decrease.* Quality often decreases because in the participation process, the goals of the supervisor are contaminated by the individual goals of the participants. In other

Compromising and Decision Making

It is unfortunate that we tend to view compromising as the same as losing. As our last equation below indicates, a compromised solution is often more effective than one that is right but is not accepted. A good illustration of this is a decision made by a company several years ago when faced with the possibility of a wildcat strike by their 3,000 employees. The national union had called for a one-day walkout by all members to protest a recent change in government legislation. Even though the strike was illegal, the union wanted to support it. The company debated the right decision, which was to take the union to court and attempt to recover something in the way of a fine. After all, the walk-out was illegal. However, they decided to meet with local union officials and work out a compromise. After considerable discussion, it was agreed that if the company would allow a hundred workers to march in the demonstration and be paid their regular wage, the union would call the other 2,900 into work that day. So even though the company lost the productivity of a hundred workers that day (thus a lower quality decision as compared to having them all come to work), they gained the productivity of the other 2,900 employees. This makes the actual decision more effective than the original alternative, which was to have all 3,000 employees walk out.

words, the supervisor will have to compromise his or her objectives to gain acceptance. Therefore, our equation might read:

$$Q\ (6) \times A\ (5) = ED\ (30)$$

So even though the quality of the decision has decreased, its overall effectiveness has almost doubled compared to the original situation.

Problem Analysis

At the outset of this chapter it was noted that problem analysis and decision making are different. The reason is that problem analysis is primarily a diagnostic process that defines the problem so that the decision process can begin. At the risk of making the situation overly complicated, we shall treat the two separately at this stage, and then integrate them later in the chapter.

Problem Prevention

Although you will learn some methods and techniques of analyzing problems in this section, it should always be remembered that it is easier to prevent problems from occurring than to solve them after they have occurred. With prevention, you have more freedom to take action because there is nothing to overcome.

| Exercise 15.1 |

The Ideal Decision Maker

Everyone has met someone in the past whom they considered a good decision maker. This exercise asks you to describe that individual in terms of what made you think of him or her as good. Each person in the class will think of a good decision maker and describe the traits, characteristics, and behaviors that made the individual good. Then in small group discussions, members will compare their lists and answer the following questions:

1.   What traits, characteristics, or behaviors are listed by all?
2.   Which ones are mentioned only once?
3.   What does this tell you about good decision makers?

Problem prevention is analagous to planning a trip properly. If you do some initial planning and take action before the trip, you will probably have fewer problems once the trip is under way. However, if you travel the wrong road for fifty miles, you must first overcome those fifty miles before you can begin to make positive progress towards your goal. The same situation exists with supervision. The problems you could have prevented will cost you more — in time, money, or other resources — when you deal with them after they have arisen.

The Distinction Between Symptoms and Sources

When a problem arises, the most critical step is to understand the differences between a symptom of a problem and the source(s) of the problem. If these two are confused, there is a risk of dealing with only the symptom, which is a superficial and often short-run method of solving problems.

Symptoms are indications, such as events, data, statements from employees, or other observable information that tell you a problem exists. This is usually referred to as a deviation from standard or what was expected to happen. The deviation itself is the symptom that tells you something is wrong. Finding out what caused the deviation is the next step in the process.

A comparison between the supervisor's role in problem solving and that of a doctor will illustrate the difference between symptoms and sources. Let's assume your elbow hurts — the deviation from standard. When you go to a doctor, he or she will ask you for your symptoms, such as where, when, how often, and how much it hurts. This information helps the doctor to learn how much deviation from standard has occurred. The list of symptoms then aids the doctor in doing the *diagnosis* of the problem, or trying to determine its **source,** the basic cause. The more symptoms you have, the more accurate the diagnosis can be.

We now come to the reason why the distinction between symptoms and sources is important. If the doctor treats only the symptoms, the problem will return. For example, the doctor could give you pain killer, but if the source of the pain is not discovered the pain will return when the effects of the pain killer have worn off.

Solving supervisory problems follows a similar process. If supervisors deal only with the symptoms of problems and not the sources, the problems will eventually reappear. For example, if employee turnover in a department is high, the supervisor could treat the symptom by hiring and training new employees to fill the positions. However, if the underlying causes of the turnover are not solved, the new employees may leave as well.

As the medical example illustrates, detecting and understanding symptoms are important to the problem-analysis process. In fact, the more time spent examining and discovering symptoms, and the more symptoms identified, the more accurate the diagnosis can be. The key, of

Supervisors As Sherlock Holmes

Analyzing problems requires a combination of behavioral science and Sherlock Holmes skills. The Sherlock Holmes part is the fact finding (creating the list of symptoms) and the behavioral science part is the interpretation of what those symptoms really mean. In one case a supervisor was facing a problem with his work group. They were constantly complaining about working conditions, their supervision, and pay. Since the group worked primarily outside, it was not uncommon for them to complain about the weather and use this as an excuse for not doing the work. The supervisor listened carefully to their complaints (the symptoms) and considered doing something about them. When he analyzed all the information he had, it was obvious that neither working conditions, supervision, or pay had changed significantly in recent years. Moreover, the workers had all hired on with the understanding that they would be working in all types of weather. The supervisor then concluded that improving the working conditions, reducing supervision, and increasing their pay would not take care of the source of the problem. It might reduce their complaints for a short time, but something else would probably crop up. In analyzing what had changed, the supervisor realized that recent mechanization of their jobs had substantially reduced the skill level required, and this was the real source of their exasperation. They had lost their former pride in their workmanship and were showing their dissatisfaction by complaining about other things. With the exception of practicing some good listening skills with the employees, there wasn't much the supervisor could do. But at least he saved himself some pretty expensive solutions that probably would have had no lasting effect on the problem.

course, is to understand the difference between treating symptoms and dealing with the sources. In practice, most problems involve a little of each. The doctor, for example, will give you both pain killer and something to attack the source of the pain. The reason, of course, is that it usually takes longer to deal with sources than it does with symptoms. The same is true in organizations. Some symptom relief is usually necessary to minimize the problems until the source of the problem can be removed.

Problems and the Systems Effect

Not only do problems tend to occur in multiples, they also tend to have more than a single source. A concept known as the **systems effect** states that all variables in a social system are interrelated. Therefore, a change in one part of the system affects all other parts. In terms of problem analysis, this means that one problem has likely been caused by several factors in the system.

The systems effect is also important in solving problems. It means that when you solve a problem, you must be on guard to make sure you do not create another one. In other words, the systems effect of your first solution may have a negative impact on another part of the system. If it were not for the systems effect, most problems would be much easier to solve.

Steps in Problem Analysis and Decision Making

The process of problem analysis and decision making is illustrated in Figure 15.3. This shows three stages, the problem analysis, the decision making, and the decision implementation, each stage consisting of a number of steps.

Problem Analysis Phase

In this stage, the goal is to arrive at a clear understanding of what the problem is. As is often said, "A problem well defined is a problem already half-solved," so a large portion of your time should be spent in defining the problem. In addition to the concerns discussed previously, the **problem analysis** phase consists of the following steps: developing standards, observing deviations from standards, describing the deviations in useful terms, and determining the causes of deviations.

DEVELOP STANDARDS. Standards are the benchmarks used to tell if a problem exists. If no standards existed, we would never know

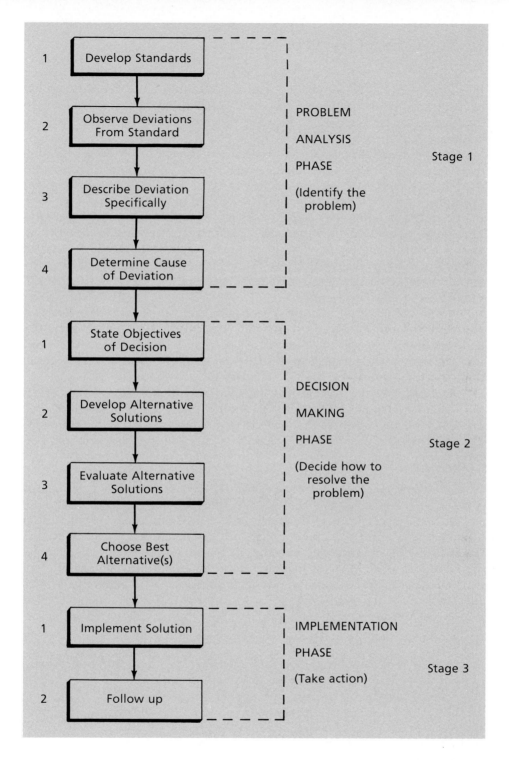

Figure 15.3. Steps in the Problem-analysis and Decision-making Processes. Adapted from Jerry L. Gray and Frederick A. Starke, *Organizational Behavior: Concepts and Applications* 3rd ed. (Columbus, Ohio: Charles Merrill, 1984). Used with permission.

that a problem has arisen, or we would know only after the problem has reached serious proportions. It is the responsibility of the supervisor to establish standards, although in some areas they will be determined by higher management.

Standards may be expressed qualitatively or quantitatively, although the latter is preferable. It is always easier to judge deviation from standard if the standard is expressed in concrete, measurable terms. So, for example, a supervisor in a manufacturing firm may have a standard of so many units per hour, or a certain cost per unit. Or a hospital supervisor may have a standard that measures patients per nursing hour worked, and a government agency might compare numbers of clients served versus man-hours worked. In any case, standards must be constantly reviewed to make sure they are up to date and reflect what could normally be expected of employees.

Whenever possible, employees should have input into standards. If standards are imposed upon them, they are less likely to see them as fair and will often find ways of beating the system. In other words, they may make it appear as though the standard is being met and cover up problems that the supervisor should be aware of.

There is also an informal side to standards. In addition to the formal performance standards, supervisors should know their employees well enough to know when their behavior is not normal. So if an employee who is normally outgoing and friendly behaves in a withdrawn and sullen manner, the supervisor should know that a problem may exist.

OBSERVE DEVIATIONS FROM STANDARD. Once standards have been established, the next step in the problem-analysis phase is to watch for any deviations from standard. The deviations may be either technical (such as a tolerance deviation on a machined part), or human (such as a drop in employee morale). Deviations may be above or below standard, but in either case they are cause for further investigation.

When a deviation from standard is observed, it is generally a good idea to review the deviation with others, either fellow supervisors or employees, to see if agreement exists about the deviation. If no agreement exists, then it is likely that standards are either nonexistent or unclear.

If there is agreement about the deviation, then it should be explored further to see if any pattern exists. For example, if production is down by 10 percent and investigation shows that the deviation usually occurs around 10:30 A.M. and 3:00 P.M., one might investigate the possibility that employees are taking extended coffee breaks. Of course, there could be many explanations for the same deviation.

A word of caution is in order about deviations generally. What may appear as an obvious deviation to you as the supervisor, may not appear that way to someone else — especially the person or persons responsible for the deviation. In Chapter 10 the discussion of perception illustrated how individual biases can affect the individual's perception of the facts. So do not be surprised if your seemingly logical conclusion about a deviation is not accepted by someone else.

DESCRIBE THE DEVIATION SPECIFICALLY.   If a problem is to be solved, its symptoms must be described accurately. It is of little use to say that production is down. How much is it down? In what areas? Is that all that is down? Answers to these and other questions are needed to get an accurate picture of the deviation.

To explain this step it is useful to return to our medical analogy. If the only deviation you give your doctor is, "Doctor, my elbow hurts," this would not be very helpful in diagnosing the source of your deviation. A hurt elbow could be caused by any number of causes. If the doctor immediately jumped to a conclusion based upon hearing that your elbow hurts, you would probably be very suspicious of the doctor's problem-analysis skills. Yet, perhaps because of our emphasis upon being decisive in management, many supervisors will do just that; they will learn of a problem and will prescribe a cure without investigating the deviation in any depth.

DETERMINE THE CAUSE OF THE DEVIATION.   This step requires the use of the information gathered in the first three steps. Since

A Lesson to Remember

As is the case with most important lessons in life, we tend to learn them the hard way. That is certainly true of how I first learned the lessons of problem analysis. As a student in my final year of college, I was taking a course in business policy. The purpose of the course was to teach students to take a broad, integrative perspective about managing organizations, and cases were used as class material. For our first written assignment we were instructed to analyze a problem in a case and recommend a solution. At the next class, everyone brought a written analysis, each one thinking he or she had analyzed the problem properly. Before we handed them in, the instructor asked us to write the name of our major area of study in business at the top of the page. When the cases were graded and handed back to us, the instructor noted that virtually every one of us had seen the problem according to our major area of study. Finance majors saw the major problem facing the company as a financial one, the marketing majors as a marketing problem, and so on. We all received an F on the case for our lack of objectivity in problem analysis. Only at the end of the term did the instructor give in and drop the case from our grades after we assured him we had learned our lesson about personal biases in problem analysis.

we have already discussed how the information should be used to discover the sources of the problem, we concentrate here on the errors usually made in this step.

The most common error is to draw a conclusion first and then try to find the data to support the conclusion. An individual who deep down has already concluded what the problem is, will be very selective and biased in the information he or she gathers to solve the problem. This is why supervisors and managers are always encouraged to have an open mind about problems. For example if a supervisor notices an employee not working as hard as he or she could, and the supervisor perceives the employee as lazy, it is unlikely that any amount of rational problem analysis will occur.

Another common error is to define problems in terms of one's own personal expertise. For example, if an individual is good at solving technical problems, then he or she may have a tendency to see every problem as a technical one. The supervisor can overcome this tendency only by recognizing his or her personal biases and consciously allowing for them.

The Decision-Making Phase

On the assumption that the problem has been analyzed correctly, the supervisor can go on to the next phase, deciding how to solve it. The ideal way to do this is to follow the steps outlined below, which are relevant for any decision that must be made.

STATE THE OBJECTIVES OF THE DECISION.   Define what the situation should be when the problem is solved. To say that you want to solve the problem is far too general. At some point in time you will want to decide whether or not the problem has been solved, so a clear specification at this stage will provide you with a standard to measure your progress.

The objectives of the decision should describe clearly what conditions will exist when the problem has been solved. An example would be, "When the problem is solved, production costs will decrease by 5 percent and rejects will be reduced by 10 percent." If the problem is more people-oriented, an example might be, "When the problem is solved, Tom and Mary will have no more interpersonal conflicts and there will be no other employee complaints about their bickering." Notice that the objectives of the decision will bear a close resemblance to the standards described under problem analysis.

There can be some complicating factors to this step. Just because others may agree that there is a problem does not mean that they will agree on what the situation should look like when the problem is solved. Therefore, the strategies and techniques for gaining acceptance of the problem definition will also apply to gaining agreement on the objectives of the decision. Participation, involvement, and good communication can all assist in this stage. If others are not committed to your attempts to solve the problem, the implementation phase will encounter resistance.

DEVELOP ALTERNATIVE SOLUTIONS. The objective of this step is to develop as many alternatives as possible. Creativity is important here since unique and innovative solutions often work, when traditional solutions cannot.

There are two practical obstacles that often arise in this step, both of which are the enemy of creativity. The first is the tendency to use solutions that have worked in the past simply because they have worked before. The main reason this is dangerous is because it is unlikely that the problems are the same. If you use a solution that has worked in the past for a problem that appears the same but in fact is different, the solution will fail. Also, the tendency to repeat past solutions reduces the effort that would have been spent in thinking of more alternatives.

The second practical problem encountered is the resistance against doing anything different. This is the we've-never-done-it-that-way syndrome. This is most likely to happen in an environment that is threatening and punitive. People may be afraid to take risks and try something different if they feel they will be punished or ridiculed for their ideas. Obviously, a supervisor can encourage new ideas by creating a positive climate that allows people to explore different ways of doing things without fear of repercussion.

EVALUATE ALTERNATIVE SOLUTIONS. This step requires that each alternative be measured against the objectives set for the deci-

The "Yes but . . ." Problem

I once sat in on a problem-solving session conducted by an executive in the restaurant industry. This was a new activity he had initiated in which he visited the various restaurants across the country and sat down with the employees to get their ideas on what problems they had and how they could be solved. The employees were understandably hesitant about being too open with someone from head office but after a while they began to offer some alternative solutions for their problems. After each suggestion was made, the executive prefaced his reply with, "Yes, but . . ." and proceeded to explain why their idea wouldn't work. After about ten or twelve "Yes buts . . .," the group stopped generating more ideas. The executive expressed disappointment that they did not come up with any more alternatives.

sion. Information will have to be gathered regarding each alternative, with the understanding that you will never have all the information you need to arrive at a decision. In the final analysis, all the information gathered will have to be tempered with judgment.

Provided that the people and the situation meet the criteria developed in Chapter 12 for participative management, group decision making can be a useful tool here. The more people involved, the more ideas can be generated to judge the alternatives. This does not mean that you have to conduct a vote on the decision, but you can profit by the feelings and opinions of others.

It is again worth pointing out that under normal circumstances, you are aiming for a satisfactory solution, not necessarily the best one. Satisfactory, of course, is defined relative to the time and resources you have available to evaluate the various alternatives. For example, one might question the value of spending 30 percent more time to improve a decision by only 5 percent.

CHOOSE THE BEST ALTERNATIVE.   Once all the previous steps have been completed, you can make your decision. If all the steps have been carefully executed, the selection of an alternative can be relatively easy.

If reaching a decision is not easy, the reason can usually be traced back to a failure in one of the previous steps. For example, if you have not stated objectives clearly, you will be unable to tell which alternative is the best one. If you have not done a proper problem analysis, there will probably be a dispute about which is the best alternative. Or, if you have not adequately described the deviation from standard, you cannot be sure that the solution you have chosen will actually solve the problem.

The Implementation Phase

In this phase the goal is to convert thought into action. This really requires the consideration of how to implement change effectively because any decision involves a change of some sort. Introducing change is the topic of Chapter 19 so only some of the principles will be highlighted here.

IMPLEMENTING THE SOLUTION.   As we mentioned earlier in this chapter, both quality and acceptance are important for effective implementation. It is critical that the decision be of the highest quality possible and be accepted by those who must implement it. In fact, it is useful to view the implementation phase as something carried out by the subordinates, not the supervisor. The supervisor can order the decision implemented, but if subordinates are not committed to it, implementation will be only superficial at best.

Theory into Practice

This exercise will require you to put into practice the theory of problem analysis and decision making. Be warned that this can be a difficult and tedious exercise, but that will be a good experience for you to understand the difficulty of making effective decisions.

Each person in the class will identify a problem to be analyzed and solved. The problem may be of any kind, but one dealing with a work situation is preferable. You will play the role of the supervisor as if you are responsible for analyzing the problem and deciding upon a solution. Follow the steps illustrated in Figure 15.3 in as much detail as possible. Be as objective as possible in providing the information. When everyone has completed this phase (this can be done before class), he or she will present the analysis and solutions to a small group. Each group will decide on one problem that will be presented to the rest of the class. Groups should select the problem from which the class can learn the most.

Acceptance and implementation can be enhanced by participation and involvement of others, the degree of participation being determined by the decision, the nature of the emplyees, and the situation. Not all decisions will require the involvement of employees, but the major ones certainly will.

This is not to say that employees will not appreciate a good decision. On the contrary, all other things being equal, they will have less resistance to a good decision than to a bad one. Proper performance of the steps in the problem analysis and decision-making phases will go a long way towards gaining acceptance for the decision.

FOLLOW-UP AND CONTROL.   Once the decision has been implemented, it must be monitored to determine the extent to which it has solved the problem. Whatever deviations were originally discovered must now be watched, since these will be the criteria that indicate whether or not the decision has been a good one.

In monitoring the decision's effectiveness, it is important that the systems effect mentioned earlier be taken into consideration. It is possible that the decision has solved one problem and created another. Should this happen, the problem-solving process should begin again. It is also important to note that since the follow-up and control step is essentially a decision process in itself, all the previous problems can arise again.

Common Errors in Problem Analysis and Decision Making

This chapter has touched on many errors that can occur during problem analysis and decision making, but there are several common ones that are not related to any specific step. This final section will describe some of the more common errors or misconceptions that seem to occur.

1. *Not admitting a decision was bad.* It is often said that the only thing worse than making a bad decision is not admitting that it is bad. This probably happens because of our ego involvement in our own decisions. We have a little of ourselves in every decision and we feel it is a bad reflection on us to have made a bad decision. However, it takes a much stronger supervisor to admit to a mistake than to continue to push to prove it is right.

2. *Being indecisive.* This is often caused by the insecurity of the decision maker, or the fear of making a bad decision. Indecisiveness is usually the result of a continual search for additional information to make the decision easier. While no one would recommend making hasty decisions, good decision makers know when to cut off the search for more facts and get on with the decision itself. Working for an indecisive supervisor can be very frustrating to subordinates.

3. *"Any decision is better than none at all."* This is actually the opposite of (2) above. Some supervisors, fearful perhaps of being labeled indecisive, make hasty decisions on the grounds that "something must be done." Obviously, this approach generally means totally bypassing the recommended steps.

4. *Assuming that people are rational.* Many supervisors have been snookered by this misconception. It may appear that everything is logical and rational to the supervisor, but those who are affected by the decision will see things differently. This can be very frustrating for the supervisor and will probably only add to the emotional level of the situation. Though difficult, it is always a good idea to place yourself in the shoes of others and try to see the decision from their point of view. If you have difficulty doing this, then ask them how they see it.

5. *Forgetting to get approval from higher levels.* In the decision-making process it is easy to look only downward. Supervisors must always remember they have a boss to answer to, and that person is also affected by the decisions the supervisor makes. If a supervisor makes a decision that is subsequently reversed by higher management, his or her position is weakened in the eyes of employees. This problem could be avoided simply by reviewing the decision with the boss before finalizing it. This is not to say that supervisors should review every decision with upper management, but certainly the ones that may have repercussions elsewhere or are exceptional situations should be discussed.

6. *Not giving credit where credit is due.* While supervisors technically make decisions, they often make them with the help of others (or at least they should). Because the supervisor announces the decisions most of the credit may go to him or her unless the supervisor takes action to spread the credit around. Subordinates will resent helping their supervisors make good decisions if they do not receive any recognition.

Key to Success

This chapter has described problem analysis and decision making as fairly structured processes. That is, there are specific steps to follow which can lead to better decisions. However, it should be understood that there is no known way to improve a person's decision-making skills beyond this structured process. In the final analysis, both good and bad decisions will be made, no matter how closely the procedures are followed. This is because every decision ultimately involves judgment and uncertainty. There is no sequence of steps that can make you smarter, wiser, or luckier.

The purpose of a series of steps in decision making is to add a degree of logic and system to what could otherwise be a mass of confused information. Our minds are information-processing systems that are quite inefficient without some guidance and structure. The steps described in this chapter can assist you in your thinking about problems and decisions and can be used in any situation, whether at work or at home. But, to look at decision making realistically, probably the most these steps can do is to help you not to make bad decisions; they will not necessarily cause you to make good ones.

In decision making probably the most important quality a supervisor can have is the ability to recognize when a decision is a bad one, together with a willingness to admit that it is bad. In terms of managing people, this requires sensitivity to the behavior patterns of employees and awareness that a decision is having a negative effect upon their behavior. This will at least prevent major disasters and will build a trusting and positive relationship between supervisor and employees.

Summary

Problem analysis and decision making are two distinct processes. Problem analysis is the definition and specification of the problem, and decision making is making the choice between alternative solutions under conditions of uncertainty. Poor problem analysis can result in poor decisions. Decision making, by definition, involves the use of judgment and the use of judgment involves the emotions. Decisions in which all the information is known can be computed and are totally rational. Decisions in which alternatives are fixed are programmed decisions. Unprogrammed decisions are those in which alternative courses of action are not fixed. Although the search for information can result in better decisions, supervisors must ultimately make decisions without full information. This process results in a satisfactory decision and is called satisficing. Searching for the optimal decision is usually unrealistic. Effectiveness is a function of the quality of a decision and its acceptance by those who must implement it. Supervisors will occasionally have to trade off between quality and acceptance.

The problem-analysis phase involves distinguishing between symptoms and sources of problems, developing standards, observing deviations from standard, describing deviations, and determining the cause of the deviation. Preventing problems is more effective than solving them after they occur. The decision-making phase involves stating the objectives of the decision, developing alternative solutions, evaluating the alternatives, and selecting the alternative which most satisfactorily achieves the stated objectives. The implementation phase involves implementing the solution and following up to monitor the implementation process. Supervisors have to be aware that they can make bad decisions and be willing to change their decisions when objectives are not being achieved.

Opening Incident Revisited

This incident depicts an unfortunate case in which a supervisor is apparently attempting to follow the correct procedures in problem solving and decision making, but is being bullied by his manager into making a decision without the proper analysis of the situation. Although LeBeau is no doubt feeling some pressure from his manager, he still typifies the "any decision is better than none at all" syndrome that so often plagues managers and supervisors.

Using the system described in the chapter, it is easy to see where LeBeau is going wrong. First, he has observed a deviation from a standard (which we must assume is reasonably accurate) but has failed to analyze why the deviation has occurred. He checks only one other possible source — the maintenance department — and then concludes that a problem exists. Further checking might indicate that (a) the drivers are driving more miles than last year, (b) the trucks are one year older and therefore may be having more breakdowns than before, (c) the trucks are carrying heavier loads than last year which means more wear and tear, and (d) there simply may be more trucks in the fleet than last year. There are probably many more explanations also possible, but those suggested here indicate that there may not even be a problem. You can imagine the difficulties that Sifton will create if he begins making decisions and implementing them if no problem exists in the first place. The alternative explanations for the deviation also suggest that the standard used for comparing costs may be misleading. In other words, if several different sources can explain a deviation, then the standard itself may be inaccurate.

What Sifton apparently hopes to accomplish is to find the source of the deviation. In other words, he wants to define the problem more clearly. This is a sound move, but may be unrealistic if LeBeau wants a decision by the following day. If the drivers are a source of the problem, it will not be readily apparent without a detailed diagnosis of all the symptoms. Discovering the symptoms and diagnosing the problem will take a lot of time, something that Sifton does not have right now. Unfortunately, he may be forced into taking some type of action that will create a whole new set of problems to be solved.

Review Questions

1. Define decision making.
2. Define problem analysis.
3. What is the difference between problem analysis and decision making?
4. What is judgment and what role does it play in decision making?
5. What are programmed and unprogrammed decisions?
6. What role does emotion play in decision making?
7. What is a rational decision?
8. What is satisficing and how does it affect decision making?
9. What factors make for an effective decision?
10. Why is problem prevention important?
11. What is the difference between symptoms and sources of problems?
12. What is the systems effect and how does it influence the decision process?
13. What are the steps in the problem-analysis phase?
14. What are the steps in the decision-making phase?
15. What are the steps in the implementation phase?
16. What are the common errors made in the problem-analysis and decision-making processes?

Chapter Glossary

Problem analysis. The analysis of events (symptoms) to determine the causes (sources) of deviations from standard or what is expected.

Decision-making. Choosing between two or more alternatives under conditions of uncertainty.

Computational decisions. A decision that can be computed or reached by rational means. Requires perfect information about the problem and alternatives. The extreme form of rational decision making.

Judgment.	A mental processing of facts and information to select an alternative. Composed partly of rational and partly of emotional processes.
Programmed decisions.	Decision limited by a fixed number of alternatives, which restrict the exercise of judgment by the decision maker.
Emotional decision making.	An approach to making decisions that allows for intuition, judgment, values, and feelings.
Rational decision making.	An approach to making decisions that involves using only facts or other types of hard data. In the extreme, decisions can be computed.
Unprogrammed decision.	Decision in which the number of alternatives available to the decision maker are not fixed. Requires considerable judgment.
Statisficing.	A decision-making process which searches for the most satisfactory alternative rather than the ideal one. Recognizes that trying to find the best solution to a problem may not be feasible or cost effective.
Decision effectiveness.	A function of the quality of the decision and how well the decision is accepted by others. Can be expressed by the equation: $ED = Q \times A$.
Problem symptom.	Events or behavioral science data that communicate to the supervisor that a problem exists. Can also be described as deviation from standards or expectations.
Problem source.	The basic cause of a problem. For problems to be solved, the source must eventually be dealt with.
Systems effect.	A social science concept which states that all parts of a social system are interrelated, and a change in one part affects all other parts. Useful in analysing the potential effects of a decision.
Problem analysis.	A phase in problem solving which examines the symptoms of a problem to determing its causes (sources). Also involves developing standards, observing deviations from the standards (symptoms), describing the deviations, and determining the cause(s) of the deviation.
Decision implementation	The final phase of the process of problem solving and decision making. Involves getting decision accepted and following up to determine its effectiveness.

Case Problem

The Blue Form

Roger Martin is the office manager for a branch office of the Western Mutual Insurance Company. Reporting to him are ten clerical employees and five secretaries who serve the thirty-five agents in the office. One of the major problems is the allocation of secretarial help to the agents. Their work requests for the secretaries are very sporadic and are a constant source of irritation to the secretaries. At times they have nothing to do, and other times they are swamped. It is the overload that bothers Roger and the secretaries the most. When the secretaries are overloaded, tempers flare as various agents attempt to get their work done first. Only last week, one of the secretaries quit because she "couldn't take the disorganization around the office." Some of the agents have complained to Roger that they are unhappy with having to wait for a secretary to type a policy application, because the customers may change their minds if it takes too long.

Roger recently decided that the work could be better scheduled if the agents would submit work requests. The request forms could then be analyzed and the work distributed in the most efficient manner to the secretaries. Roger designed a form that requests information about the type of work and the date by which it is needed. The forms were printed on bright blue paper to make them quickly noticeable. He sent a batch to each of the agents with the following memorandum:

Attached you will find a set of blue forms to be used in submitting your work requests. With all the problems we have had recently in getting secretarial work done, this form should help us all. When you have work for the secretaries, please fill out the blue form and attach it to your job. Please submit all work orders to me and I will assign them to the secretaries. In this way we can make the most efficient use of the secretaries and get your work done faster. Thank you for your cooperation.

So far only a few blue forms have been submitted to Roger. Under "date requested," all the agents wrote "immediately." Even though so few blue forms have been sent in, all of the secretaries are as busy as usual. This morning, Roger received a blank envelope containing a blue form. The form had an obscene message typed on it.

Questions for Discussion

1. Why has the blue form failed?
2. What parts of the process of problem analysis and decision making has Roger failed to use?
3. Is his decision a good one? Why or why not?
4. What should he do to salvage the blue form?

Working with Unions

16

Chapter Learning Objectives

After reading and studying this chapter you should be able to:

1. Describe the primary role of unions in today's society.

2. Describe the historical labor-management climate.

3. Define and give examples of the prescribed and discretionary parts of a supervisor's role.

4. Describe how unions have influenced the prescribed and discretionary parts of supervisors' roles.

5. Describe how supervisors can preserve management decisions.

6. List and explain the major advantages and disadvantages of unions.

7. Explain why many supervisors have difficulty in relating to union officials.

8. Explain the accountability of the union representative in relation to the supervisor.

9. Explain why grievances can be a sign of organizational health.

10. Explain the concept of error rates and how it relates to labor relations.

11. Suggest some ways that supervisors might handle grievances.

12. Suggest some ways that supervisors might improve their relations with the union.

Key Terms

Prescribed
Discretionary
Union Contract
Representative
   Accountability

Grievance
Error Rates
Seniority

405

Harassing the Shop Steward

Mike Franklin is the shop steward in the warehouse of the White Manufacturing Company. He represents twenty-five employees in the warehouse and has been the shop steward for only one month. The previous steward left the company and the union appointed Mike until an election can be held.

Mike and his group report to Stan Waters, the foreman of the warehouse. Stan has been with the company for many years and has a reputation as a tough foreman. When Mike was appointed steward, the other union officials warned him to be careful around Stan and not let him run roughshod over the employees' rights.

Recently, Roy Middleton, one of the forklift drivers, spoke to Mike about the way that Waters has been treating him. He said that Waters is constantly riding him and is out to get him. He cited several instances recently in which Waters publicly criticized him for doing something that other employees were also doing, although Waters had made no comment to the other employees. Middleton's latest complaint is that he requested a transfer to a different job because the jostling of the forklift was hurting his back, but Waters refused. A few days later, one of the other employees asked for a change of jobs and it was granted. Middleton asked Mike to speak to Waters about filing a formal grievance.

Mike went to Waters' office and explained the situation. The conversation then went like this:

MIKE: So you can see that Middleton is quite upset about this. I hope we can work something out.

WATERS: Look, Mike, I know you're new at this job but I was hoping you and I could see things eye to eye. You know as well as I do that Middleton is a crybaby and a chronic complainer. If he wasn't complaining about his back it would be something else. You know what he's like. You've worked with him a long time. Do you really expect me to do anything just because he gripes all the time?

MIKE: Well, it would appear as though he's got a legitimate complaint. After all, you did transfer another guy when he asked for it.

WATERS: That was different . . . the guy was a really go-getter. He proved that he was a hard worker and I felt I should do something for him. Middleton hasn't done a good day's work since he's been here. Now look, let's don't let this thing get blown up out of proportion. I don't think your union would like for you to spend your time following up every complaint that Middleton is going to come up with. You've always done a good job in this department and I would hate to see you and me on the outs because of a stupid case like Middleton. Don't blow your chances around here because of a jerk like that.

Unions are playing an increasingly dominant role in management today. Historically, only blue-collar workers were unionized, but now white-collar and professional employees of all types are beginning to look to unions for protection of their employment rights, job security, and other benefits. Although the proportion of union membership fluctuates with the state of the economy (mostly because unionized employees are usually the first to be laid off), there is little doubt that the influence of unions on supervision today is greater than ever. Even in nonunion companies, supervisors and managers are finding that they must be cognizant of contractual relationships in other organizations to maintain their competitive edge.

If you work in a nonunion environment, the behavioral science concepts that relate to effective union-management relations can still be important. With certain exceptions noted in this chapter, *most of what management must do in a unionized organization should also be done in a nonunion one.* In other words, one of the major functions of unions is simply to formalize what should be happening anyway. If you begin your study of union-management relationships by accepting this fact, you will have taken a giant step towards creating a more effective working relationship with unions.

Consistent with the applied behavioral science approach, this chapter supports the belief that understanding how something works is important to managing it. We shall therefore discuss the role of unions — why they exist, what they do, and what they should not do. It was noted in Chapter 2 that the role of the supervisor is a unique one, and that is especially true in managing with unions. The supervisor probably has more contact with the union contract and its ramifications than any other manager. It is therefore important that supervisors know as much as possible about the concept of a union.

Understanding the Union's Role in Society

Unions have been around in one form or another since the late 1700s. They have changed dramatically in both form and purpose, and today are a dominant social institution. This section will review why we have unions and the traditional relationship between unions and management.

Why Do We Have Unions?

To put it simply, we have unions because there is a need for them. Why? To answer this, we need only look at the primary purpose of unions, which is to protect the interests of employees. There was a time when this was considered management's responsibility. When the concept of the formal organization originated, unions were not needed since it was assumed that what was best for the organization was also best for the employees. In view of the situation today in which separate organizations (unions) look out for the interests of employees, we can only conclude that management must not have done a very good job in this area.

This is an oversimplified analysis because unions have deep sociological and cultural roots and we cannot lay the entire blame upon management. There are extremely well-managed companies today that have unions for reasons that have little to do with how workers are treated. Nevertheless, on a broad scale we must conclude that employees have had needs that were not being satisfied by companies, so employees created their own organizations for that purpose.

The fact remains that we have unions and they serve an important purpose in our society. It does little good to wish that they didn't exist; far better to spend time understanding how they operate so that their advantages can be maximized and their disadvantages minimized. For those who would like to do away with unions, it is worth remembering that the best enemy of a union is sound management.

Union-Management Relationships

The relationship between unions and management can best be described by analyzing the overall climate of labor relations that exists today. The climate was originally established in the beginnings of the union movement when employees perceived that they and their employers had different and conflicting interests. This perception created an adversary relationship that still exists. Therefore, the general climate in labor relations has historically been a negative one. The two groups have operated on a competitive basis in which each side views the other as the opponent. If employees do not get what they want, they strike and shut the

Labor-Management Cooperation: A Beginning

One of the more recent examples of how cooperation between unions and management can work is with Chrysler Corporation. During 1980 and 1981 the company was in difficult financial straits. The recession had hit the auto industry and Chrysler was very vulnerable. When negotiations began, it was clear that the company could not afford the level of wages that other companies were paying. Chrysler asked the union to accept a wage freeze until things got better. After a lot of haggling, the union agreed, mostly because the company maintained that a wage increase would bankrupt it. Although several subsequent events also helped Chrysler, it is generally agreed that the cooperation between the union and management played a major role in the company's survival. The cooperation did hit a snag, however. When the company's profits increased, the union requested its fair share. The company defined fair share as being considerably smaller than what the union asked, so a brief strike ensued. However, this strike should not obscure the fact that through cooperation, both groups were better off.

company down. If management does not get what it wants, it imposes a lockout and refuses to let the employees work. In both cases, both groups end up losing: employees lose wages and the company loses profits.

There is some evidence that a few firms are moving toward a more cooperative relationship with unions. We are beginning to realize that the cutthroat competition which has existed is detrimental to both sides and that through collaborative efforts, both groups can win. However it will take a long time to undo all the experiences of the last hundred years. Old habits die slowly.

Understanding the Union's Role in the Company

Within the company, the role of the union is similar to that which it occupies in the broader society; it is there to protect the interests of the employees. However, the limits to the union's role in the company are quite precise, especially as they affect how supervisors are to use their authority. In this section we analyze the union role and study its precise attributes.

The Supervisor's Authority

To understand the role of the union in the company it is necessary to understand what supervisors and managers do in performing their jobs. Every managerial role in an organization can be depicted as in Figure 16.1. This diagram shows the supervisor's role as consisting of two parts: a *prescribed* part and a *discretionary* part.[1] The prescribed portion is that part of the supervisor's role in which there is no choice of action. No decisions are required in the sense described in the previous chapter. In Chapter 2, we described this portion as the limits on supervisors' authority. Some examples of activities that might be prescribed are:

- Forward the weekly payroll to the personnel department.
- Report absences to the personnel department.
- Send weekly production figures to the production department.
- Conduct weekly meetings of the safety committee.
- Receive approval of upper management before hiring new employees.

---

1. Elliott Jaques, *Measurement of Responsibility* (London: Heinemann, 1952).

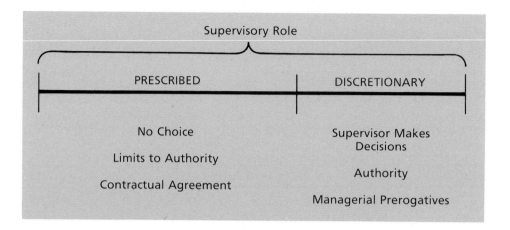

Figure 16.1. Two Parts to the Managerial and Supervisory Role.

These are only examples. In practice, many activities would be prescribed, depending upon how much higher management wishes to control the decisions of supervisors. As the dividing line in Figure 16.1 moves to the left, the supervisor acquires more discretion in managing the work unit. As it moves to the right, the supervisor has less authority to manage. You may have realized the close relationship between prescribed-discretionary activities and the programming of decisions discussed in the previous chapter. Prescribed activities are, of course, those which are programmed, and discretionary activities are less programmed.

The discretionary aspect of the role is the part in which the supervisor makes decisions, that is, uses judgment. These decisions are always made within prescribed limits, but within those limits, the supervisor has total freedom. Accountability of the supervisor is largely oriented toward the discretionary aspects of the role, since it is easier to judge performance in these factors. The organization assumes that the prescribed content will be done as required.

Unions and the Supervisor's Authority

The concepts illustrated in Figure 16.1 can now be used to show the role unions *should* occupy in organizations. *The primary role of unions is to set prescribed limits on the authority in managerial roles.* Bargaining, negotiation, and contract administration are all oriented toward this purpose. Once the limits have been agreed upon, unions have no business getting involved in the decision-making aspect of managers' jobs — nor do they normally want to. They will, of course, attempt to increase the prescribed content in managerial roles, but once the limits have been agreed upon, managers can then make decisions within those limits.

Given the historical development of unions and the labor relations climate, it is not surprising that unions attempt to reduce the discretion available to managers. It is in the discretionary area that unions see managers making decisions that are unfair to employees. Rather than leave these decisions open to judgment (which unions do not trust), they prefer to have them part of the prescribed component.

As only one example, consider a decision to allocate vacation schedules to employees. Under the discretionary method, the manager would examine the needs of the work unit, the preferences of employees, and make a judgment (decision) regarding who takes vacation when. Under the prescribed method, the manager would have to follow the requirements of the labor contract, which may dictate that employees select their vacation times in order of seniority.

Have Unions Reduced Supervisors' Authority?

Of course they have. That is the nature of the collective bargaining process. Over the years, the collective bargaining process has slowly moved the dividing line in Figure 16.1 from left to right, thus reducing the authority of managers and supervisors. However, it is important to remember that all labor contracts are the result of agreement, so if managerial authority has been eroded over the years, it has been done with the consent of managers.

Can this be changed? Perhaps, but not because a few supervisors are unhappy with the arrangement. If our present situation is the result of our labor-management climate, then it will take a different climate to restore managerial authority — assuming that is desirable in the first place (remember, managers got themselves into their present situation by being perceived as misusing the authority they had!).

So, given the present situation, what can supervisors do? Supervisors can do what any manager must do, and that is to make decisions fully within the discretionary areas remaining. No matter how little authority is remaining in the supervisor role, it is important that full authority be exercised within the prescribed limits. Past experience suggests that if the authority is not used (which is another way of saying that it is used improperly), it will be bargained away.

What Is the Union Philosophy?

Do unions believe in this philosophy as well? In concept, yes. Unions do not want to run the company, as some managers think they do. What they want is to set limits on the types of decisions that affect their members. Because they represent sometimes thousands of employees, they are very concerned with equity in treatment. And although things

A Tough Manager!

Several years ago I was having lunch with a colleague and we were discussing the faculty union at our university. My colleague, who managed unionized faculty, voiced some pretty strong opinions against unions. "You can't do anything any more!", he said, "without checking with the damn union first." He then launched into one of his anti-union speeches, guaranteed to bring tears to the eyes of any manager. Of course I had heard all this before, so I decided to test him and see just how anti-union he was. Several weeks previously, we managers had been given a pool of merit funds to distribute among our subordinates. The only prescription was that the criterion for distribution was performance. I asked my colleague how he distributed his merit pool. "Oh, that," he replied, "I gave each person the same." "Are they all performing at the same level?" I asked. "No," he said, "but if you give some more than others, all you get is a lot of grief."

At this point, I must admit that I came unglued. "You," I said, "are the main reason why we have unions today. You were given a managerial decision to make and you chickened out! If I were a union representative I would be in there making a pitch to do away with merit pay because managers like you will not make proper decisions!"

Interestingly, my prediction came true. The following year the union proposed that merit pay be removed from the contract, not because they were against the merit principle, but because of the poor job managers had done in deciding merit pay. Management agreed, and now pay is decided by two prescribed factors, job classification and seniority.

like seniority or position may not be the best definition of equity, at least they are concepts that the employees can understand. In other words, unions do not want to get involved in judgment calls any more than some managers do. This is why they prefer that decisions be largely computational, that is, based upon objective, factual information (such as seniority) rather than judgment.

Sooner or later you will probably encounter a union president, steward, or member who appears to violate this philosophy. That is, he or she wants the union to make managerial decisions. Not only are these people in a minority, but they are behaving this way for reasons other than what you think (we shall cover this later). Also, you will find that the division between prescribed and discretionary activities is not always perfectly clear. After all, a union contract cannot account for all possible decisions. In these situations, take care to check with your labor relations specialist first, but then make the managerial decision if the situation warrants. Your job requires that you undertake certain responsibilities and you have as much right to interpret the contract as anyone else does (again, with the support of your manager or labor relations specialist). If your interpretation is wrong, then the next round of contract negotiations will settle it.

Practicing the Philosophy

Keep in mind that labor contracts, by definition, specify the *minimum* that the supervisor may do. Anything not covered in these minimum prescriptions is therefore open to your discretion. Many contracts do have a general clause that allows an employee to grieve unjust treatment but, like any other contract violation, it must be proven. If you use your discretion wisely, there can still be a lot of latitude in your job for managing people effectively.

Being an effective supervisor with a union does not mean you have to be tough, hardnosed, or any other outdated term. It simply means that you must be aware of the limits to your authority, as well as the areas in which you are free to make decisions. Having sorted these out, you must be prepared to make decisons that, in your judgment, are the best for all concerned.

Interestingly, unions respect this type of manager just as managers respect union officials who behave in the same way. The respect comes from knowing that each party is playing the game according to the rules, rather than trying to shortcut the rules by some devious means. If nothing else, history has shown that trying to undermine policies and prescriptions that have been agreed upon by union and management will, at best, result in short-term victories.

Advantages and Disadvantages of Unions

Unions serve many purposes, though not all would agree on which are positive and which are negative. This section describes some of the general advantages and disadvantages of unions as seen from the point of view of the supervisor.

Advantages

This chapter opened with the statement that unions only required supervisors to do what they should be doing anyway. This means that, with some exceptions, the collective bargaining process compels us to be better managers. If you analyze an organization that has no union, you will probably find that it has many of the same policies, practices, and general treatment of employees that most unionized organizations have. The primary difference is that labor-management relations are handled on a more informal basis than would be the case otherwise.

This sharpening up of management is perhaps the greatest advantage of unions. However, there are others. First, unions add a degree of efficiency to the system. This may sound strange since it is more common to think of unions as causing inefficiency. The context here applies to the relationship between management and the employees. For example, communication becomes much simpler because a primary channel of communication is through the union hierarchy. For matters pertaining to the contract, the supervisor is able to communicate to a single receiver, who in turn will communicate the message to the membership.

Another way unions make supervisors' jobs easier is in decision making. We have already established that through the collective bargaining process unions reduce the discretion available to supervisors. In essence, therefore, this reduces the number of decisions that supervisors must make. For example, without a union the supervisor would have to consider the needs of individual employees when making a decision that affected them. With the discretion removed from this decision, this option would not even be available to the supervisor.

An interesting side effect of this might be that unions could turn poor supervisors into good ones. A supervisor who was ineffective because of poor decisions could improve in a union environment because many of the decisions would be made for him or her!

Unions also establish a degree of stability in the organization that would probably otherwise not be present. The stability results from such things as seniority clauses that reduce turnover among more senior employees, the need for documentation of management policies to ensure consistency in treatment over time, and contractual agreements that can span several years.

Disadvantages

Like any other aspect of organizational life, unions also have disadvantages. These disadvantages are actually the reverse side of the advantages just discussed. For example, one of the major disadvantages of unions is the inflexibility and rigidity they bring to the management of people. Union contracts can affect such things as job assignments, layoff policies, training activities, wages and salaries paid, and promotion decisions, to name but a few. Supervisors will feel an understandable degree of frustration when, for example, they are unable to reassign an employee to another job in the unit when a co-worker is absent because the contract prevents temporary transfers.

Most supervisors would agree that dealing with unions requires more time, despite what was said above regarding efficiency. Implementing agreed procedures, consulting union officials, and documenting practices and decisions will all require additional time. However, it may be that this is time well spent. In other sections of this book we have noted the importance of spending time with subordinates and getting their ideas for change. So if unionization results in greater participation and communication, then this could hardly be a disadvantage.

Some would view the increased prescribed content of supervisory roles as a disadvantage also. Many supervisors feel constrained in attempting to carry out their responsibilities, and would like to have more freedom to manage their people. This may discourage some people from accepting supervisory positions, or cause feelings of helplessness in those who are supervisors.

Finally, one of the major disadvantages of unions is the conflict generated from the adversary relationship that frequently exists between union and management. In a negative climate, this conflict can be destructive and counterproductive. Both groups, union and management, all too frequently react to each other from the perspective of roles and associated expectations, rather than dealing with the real issues. A supervisor, for example, may suddenly become uncooperative as soon as he or she encounters a union official. This form of behavior is a direct outgrowth of the adversary relationship.

Understanding the Role of Union Officials

Most of the day-to-day interaction of supervisors will be with one or more union officials. These could be business agents, shop stewards, or local union presidents. In all cases, it is important to understand the nature of this role so that destructive conflict can be minimized. If the

Perception in Interpersonal Relationships

Several years ago I had the opportunity to work with a group of supervisors in an attempt to improve their relationship with their union. One of the first steps was to get their perceptions out in the open. I gave them an exercise that required them to write down the first thing that came to their mind after I gave them a word. The words came very quickly as I didn't want them to have time to think before writing. First impressions are generally the most useful. I began with several neutral words such as *company, family*, etc., just to get them into the spirit of the exercise. At a random time, I gave

the word *union,* and proceeded with even more words. Afterwards, we went back and examined what each person had written down after the word *union.* Almost three-quarters of the group had written the word *problem.*

After a discussion of what they had done, they agreed that this negative perception of unions was at the root of many of their difficulties.

Interestingly, doing the same exercise with union officials results in the same answer. When they hear the word *management,* they also write down *problem.*

relationship is managed properly, the local union official can be of considerable help to the supervisor.

Sources of Difficulties

For our purposes, we will not distinguish among the duties of the steward, president, or business agent. They do have different responsibilities, although even these vary from union to union. What they have in common is their role within the union organization and our focus will be upon how not dealing with the expectations of that role can lead to difficulties.

The key to understanding the role of union officials is to understand how they see themselves. There are, of course, individual differences, but they generally see themselves as constructive, hardworking, concerned, proud, conscientious persons. In fact, you could include almost any positive term in the list and it would probably fit most union officials — just as it would fit everyone else.

The problems arise when they are not treated in a manner consistent with their self-image. If they encounter a supervisor who treats them as destructive, lazy, stupid, and negative, they will most likely behave that way — again, just as anyone else would. Of course this begins a vicious circle that is difficult to break. Consider communication for the moment. We learned in Chapter 10 that communications that are not consistent with our role or our image of ourselves will be rejected. This is precisely what happens when a union official encounters a supervisor who communicates in a negative manner. If you want to communicate effectively (which means have influence) with a union official, you will have to communicate in a manner that fits his or her self-image. And remember, most people have a positive image of themselves.

Respecting the Role

The other part of the communication process is respecting the role of the union official. Their role requires that they do certain things, *even though they may not believe in them* (just as managers have to!). This is often very difficult for supervisors to understand. Recall from Chapter 5 that role expectations from others can be a major determinant of our behavior. When we accept a certain role, we also accept all the expectations that go with it. If we do not meet those expectations, there is a risk we will be removed from the role. Most of the expectations of the union officials' roles come from the membership. Depending upon what they expect, the behavior of union officials may be different for different unions. For example, some unions are more aggressive and militant than others, so their leaders adopt those behaviors since it is what the members expect.

Putting the role concept together with the positive self-image we know that most people have of themselves, we can see that one of the common problems supervisors have is separating the person from the role. By not distinguishing between the two, the supervisor may inadvertently attack the person (which is wrong) instead of the role (which is all right). For example, you may encounter a union official who is very obstructive and uncooperative. However, this does not mean that he or she is that way personally; it means that the role he or she is in requires that kind of behavior. You can make much more headway by dealing with the role behavior than by dealing with the person.

To understand how to do this, let's go back to the nature of the role. If we understand that the primary role of the union official is to protect the interests of the employees, then it would be useless to attempt to communicate with that official as a helper to the company. That communication will surely be rejected since it is in direct conflict with the official's role expectations. Influence will be gained by appealing to the role of protector of the employees' interests. You can then communicate in a manner that shows you respect the individual as a person (as described earlier) and that you understand the expectations of his or her role. This, of course, is no guarantee that you will get your way, but at least it will minimize the negative conflict and improve communication.

Putting the Shoe on the Other Foot

The principles of behavioral science are not applicable just to management. They can — and do — apply to unions as well. In doing management training for unions (sound strange?), I give them the same principles just discussed. Exaggerating only slightly, I will say something like this:

"Look, if you want to get through to those management people, you have to respect their roles. They see themselves as protectors of the company's interests, the last bastion of intelligence, and the saviors of all that is decent. If you go in there and tell them how stupid they are and how they make dumb decisions all the time, all you will get is an argument and a lot of resistance. You have to understand where they are coming from. They don't see themselves as trying to shaft the employees; in fact, they sincerely believe they are doing what is best for them. If you treat them in any other way, you will get nowhere."

This often comes as much as a surprise to union people as the union role does to management people.

Managing with the Union Representative

In Chapter 3 we developed the various relationships that supervisors have with other roles in the organization. It was pointed out that part of being an effective supervisor was to understand how your role interfaces with others, particularly in the areas of authority, responsibility, and accountability. In this section we will apply the same analysis to the organizational relationship between the supervisor and the relevant union official. We use the term *representative*, but the actual role title could vary from organization to organization.

Managing Accountability

Union representatives occupy a difficult role for many reasons. Ironically, they have many of the same role problems that supervisors have: lack of proper role definition, confused authority relationships, and multiple accountability. It is no surprise, therefore, that many of the principles developed in Chapter 3 also apply to union representatives.

One of the greatest dangers facing supervisors in this relationship is that of improper accountability. Most union agreements allow time for the representatives to conduct union business on company time. Understandably, this can be annoying but since it is prescribed for the supervisor, it cannot be prevented. Of course the supervisor should be watchful for any abuses of this right. Other than that, *it is improper for the supervisor to hold the representatives accountable in their subordinate role for what they do in their representative role.* These are very different roles and must be kept separate. Providing the representative is operating within the confines of the collective agreement, he or she cannot be adversely affected in the accountability for the other role.

A situation in which this might happen is with performance appraisal. You may not like what the representative is doing or may disagree with a position he or she has taken. If you then let this disagreement affect your evaluation of the representative's performance as an employee — in his or her subordinate role — you will be open for a grievance. If there has been improper accountability, the grievance will be upheld.

It is again worth noting the difference between the person and the role. If a representative comes to you with a complaint from the employees, it would be improper to challenge the representative's judgment as to the validity of the complaint. The role requires that the complaint be brought forward, regardless of the representative's personal feelings on the matter. If he or she felt strongly that the complaint was invalid, that issue would be solved before coming to see you. It therefore follows that holding the representative accountable for what you consider to be a stupid complaint is improper.

Accountability of the Representative

One reason, of course, that representatives have difficult roles is because they occupy more than one role at once. What is worse, the two roles are often in conflict for reasons previously noted. Their roles are not unlike that of the part-time supervisor mentioned in Chapter 2. They must switch hats constantly as they go from one role to another.

Nevertheless, union representatives are still accountable for their performance in subordinate roles. Although some aspects of their performance will suffer (especially if the representative role is very time-consuming), this affects only the degree of accountability, not the fact of accountability. If it seems that the representative responsibilities prevent adequate job performance, the company should consider making union representation a full-time job.

In some cases, accountability in the subordinate role is affected in a manner contrary to that described in the previous section. In other words, a supervisor might, for example, be easy on a representative to avoid any conflict simply because the person is the union representative. This is not a wise strategy either, since it would only serve to reinforce the negative aspects of the representative's role.

If the union representative is not performing properly in the representative role, this should be of little concern to the manager. Representatives are held accountable by their members, not by managers. Supervisors should avoid being seen as trying to manipulate the representative role, even though they may feel the job is not being well performed. If the person is not a good representative, this problem will presumably be solved at the next union election.

Handling Grievances

Perhaps the most difficult interaction between supervisors and representatives is the grievance procedure. Most companies, unionized or not, have a formal system for dealing with employee concerns, be they just regular everyday gripes, or legal challenges to an interpretation of the contract. In either case, if the supervisor knows how to handle a problem effectively, many complaints will never have to get to the grievance stage.

Healthy Grievances

Most people view grievances as a sign that something is wrong, and in many instances, this is probably true. However, it is also useful to view grievances as a sign of a healthy organization. There are two reasons for

Understanding "Error Rates"

The idea that mistakes can indicate a sign of health is often a difficult one to understand. However, there are numerous examples in organizations which indicate that error rates are useful tools for judging effectiveness. The key is to put error rates into context; that is, each organization will have a different acceptable rate of errors. A rate too high indicates trouble, but there is some level at which errors are not only healthy, they are expected.

The reason that errors are useful is that they provide benchmarks for measuring effectiveness. For example, banks will consciously manipulate their credit policies to produce a given delinquency rate. If there are too few bad debts, credit policies are loosened; if bad debts are too high, credit policies are tightened. Employee turnover is another example. Some turnover is normally expected in most organizations. So if you encounter a situation in which there is no turnover, it should be investigated. Maybe people are being treated so well that no one leaves, including the deadwood!

A good rule of thumb is this: if you have been a supervisor in a unionized organization for at least five years and have never had a grievance, you are probably not operating at the limit of your union contract. I would therefore question your effectiveness as a supervisor. Anyone who goes five years and doesn't make a mistake is probably operating at too conservative a level. Are you a soft touch? Or are you not exercising some of the managerial prerogatives of the contract? Think about it.

this. First, if employees file grievances, they must feel that the climate of the work unit is such that they can do so without any negative repercussions from their supervisor. In a very negative and punitive climate, for example, employees may be afraid to complain or grieve for fear that the supervisor will get back at them in some way.

The second reason that grievances can be seen as a sign of health is that they show that supervisors are pushing the contract to its limit, rather than letting the contract manage them. If a supervisor is operating at the limits of the contract, mistakes will inevitably be made and a grievance may result. Although grievances should not normally be encouraged, they do not necessarily mean that a supervisor is doing a poor job. There should be concern, however, if the number of grievances is out of line compared to what should normally be expected, or if all grievances result from a single supervisor.

Suggestions for Handling Grievances

Whether grievances are healthy or unhealthy, they still must be handled properly. Most companies, both union and nonunion, will have a prescribed formal grievance procedure. Whatever this procedure is, it must be followed. This section will concern itself with the behavioral and interpersonal aspects of grievances, not the procedural concerns. The vast majority of grievances (or complaints) should be resolved at the supervisory level, and the suggestions that follow should prove helpful to you.

1 *Be open about grievances.* Showing your representative that you are willing to discuss grievances and complaints openly will help establish a good climate for communication. If, when confronted with a grievance, you show displeasure and anger, you are off on the wrong foot.

2. *Don't become defensive.* The first step is to listen with an open mind to the grievance itself. Avoid arguing with the representative or prejudging the case. Your defensiveness will only increase any emotions that may be underlying the grievance.

3. *Don't challenge the role of the representative.* This has been mentioned previously. Understand the role of the representative and do not question his or her motives in presenting the grievance.

4. *Listen, listen, listen.* All you have learned about communcation applies here, as well as the content in Chapter 18 on interviewing. This is a special type of interview and, at the early stages at least, should be nondirective.

5. *Separate fact from feeling.* Grievances will have to be resolved on the basis of fact, not people's motives, attitudes, or feelings. You will get all of these, especially if you use the nondirective method. Drawing off any emotional feelings will help in dealing only with the facts.

6. *Use your advisors.* Always check with other specialists before making a decision. If you have a labor relations department, check with them. Consultation with other supervisors is useful, too. Remember, your decision may set a precedent for other grievances.

7. *Decide as soon as possible.* Delay is the enemy of justice. This does not mean that you must reach a decision on the spot, but unnecessary delays should be avoided, subject to the advice in (6) above.

8. *Explain your decision.* A decision not explained is more likely to be challenged than one that is explained. If you have based your decision on solid criteria, then you should have no fear of explaining your reasons. If you do have this fear, perhaps you should review the decision once more.

9. *Document the decision.* In addition to any formal requirements for documentation, it is still a good idea to make sure that everything is understood. This serves as a feedback mechanism for you. No feedback generally means that your decision has been understood, not necessarily accepted.

Strategies for Supervising
in a Union Environment

This concluding section will detail some specific strategies for more effective supervision in a unionized environment. While all environments are different, these general principles should still be helpful in most situations.

Using Your Authority

The importance of the use of authority in the supervisory role has already been discussed. One example of how this can make you more effective is handling the seniority issue.

Most union contracts have a seniority clause that gives certain rights to employees according to seniority. Common examples are situations involving layoffs, promotions, job assignments, schedules, and pay levels. While the wording will vary from contract to contract, what they have in common is a phrase something like, "All other things being equal, preference is given to the most senior employee." In the case of promotion, for example, the wording might be, "When more than one employee applies for a new position, preference will be given to the most senior employee, providing that qualifications are equal."

In practice, many supervisors and managers perceive this as meaning that they must award the new position to the employee with the most seniority, and therefore feel constrained in selecting the employee they want. If you feel that another employee is better qualified, and you can justify this on concrete grounds, then it is your right to select that person, regardless of seniority. Yes, you may get a grievance, but if your decision is a sound one, you have a good chance that the grievance will be resolved in your favor.

What you should *not* do is award the position to the most senior employee simply because you think you will get a grievance if you don't. This is abdicating the authority vested in your role and tends to lead to a gradual erosion of the authority you have. Remember, if you do not use the authority you have, it will be taken away from you either through the collective bargaining process or through your removal from your role.

The situation also arises in which the supervisor wants to make the right decision, but is prevented from doing so either by higher management or by someone in the personnel department because "we don't want a grievance." Again, you should not stand for this. If you are to be held accountable for the performance of your group, you must have the right to decide who your subordinates will be. Of course if you are advised not to make the decision because you are violating a *prescribed* part of your job, then you should heed the advice of your advisors.

Trying to Manipulate the Contract

Some supervisors try to get what they want by attempting to manipulate the requirements of the contract. As one example, let us assume that a supervisor has posted a job and wants a certain individual to get it. Knowing that there are others in the company with more seniority than the preferred individual, the supervisor may write the job description in a way that only the preferred candidate would be qualified.

This is a very dangerous strategy for several reasons. First, the supervisor is implicitly admitting by this action that his or her decision cannot be defended on the basis of reasonable, accepted criteria. That in itself should be reason to question the act. Second, it will soon become obvious to others what has been done. It may or may not result in a grievance, but if it does this should be considered an unhealthy grievance. Finally, using manipulative methods to circumvent the intent of the contract can only make for a poor labor relations climate. The real effect will not be felt so much in one particular situation as in the spillover it will have on other matters. The trust between the supervisor and the union will be seriously jeopardized.

Keeping the Union Involved

The union will be involved whether you like it or not. The question is, how will its involvement be determined? Will it be through forced means such as wildcat strikes, work slowdowns, etc? Or will it be through the invitation of the supervisor?

Given that you must work with a union, you may as well make its involvement as positive as possible. If you purposely ignore union representatives and pay only the minimum attention required, they will find a way to get your attention more frequently. No one likes to be ignored, especially a union. If you have a decision to make and are unsure whether it falls into the discretionary or prescribed portion of your job, consultation with the union would be advisable. Even in the discretionary portion it is wise to advise the union beforehand of your intentions. A little involvement at this stage can go a long way towards preventing serious trouble later.

Keeping Your Attitudes to Yourself

If you resent unions and how they have affected your job, you are entitled to your feelings. However, if these feelings affect how you behave toward the union they will cause you considerable difficulties in your relationships with union people. Unions are here to stay and nothing you can do as an individual supervisor will affect that. It is a much better strategy to accept the union's role in today's society and attempt to work with it, not against it.

Key to Success

Some of the ideas presented in this chapter may have upset you, some may have surprised you, and some will have reinforced what you may have already experienced with unions. If you were upset or surprised, that is good, for it shows that you are thinking seriously about supervisor-union relations. The first step towards improving your relations with the union is to understand more about it and the role it plays in organizations.

Perhaps some of you were upset because of your negative attitudes toward unions. As we noted previously, that is understandable, especially if you have had some bad experiences with unions. There are some people who believe that unions are the work of the devil and should be banished from existence. This chapter, of course, cannot deal with that issue, but it can help you work more effectively within the union environment, regardless of your feelings about unions.

It is worth returning to our earlier remark that unions compel managers to behave as they should behave anyway. This may be a strong statement and should be taken, not with a grain of salt, but with a degree of caution. There is some truth to it. Many people believe that any company that has a union has done something to deserve it. Again, this may be strong, but it is certainly food for thought. As a supervisor, you can help preserve managerial authority by using the authority given to you decisively and wisely. For that authority you wish you had but do not, respect the role of unions and you may find they can help you become a more effective supervisor.

Summary

Unions are an important factor in supervision in many organizations today. Supervisors, because of their unique position in the organization, often have the most direct contact with union members, union officials, and the union contract. The relationship can be difficult because of the historical conflict between management and unions.

Any manager's job can be divided into prescribed and discretionary components. The role of unions is to bargain for prescribed limits to managerial authority, and the role of supervisors is to make decisions within those limits. Collective bargaining has generally removed discretion from supervisors over the years, and this has often been because of the misuse of authority by supervisors and managers.

Unions have advantages and disadvantages for supervisors. Some of the advantages are: they compel supervisors to be better managers; they make supervisors more efficient in communication and decision making; and they establish a degree of stability in organizations. Some of the disadvantages are: they can bring inflexibility to managerial decisions; they require more of the supervisor's time; and they tend to force employees and managers into an adversary relationship.

Relationships between union officials and supervisors can be improved if supervisors respect the roles and role expectations of union officials, make managerial decisions within prescribed limits, and separate the union official's role from his or her subordinate role.

Handling grievances is an important part of a supervisor's job. Grievances have a positive aspect to them in that they can be a sign of a healthy organization. Handling grievances properly means that the supervisor should have good listening skills and accept grievances as a regular part of being a good manager.

Opening Incident Revisited

Waters is making two critical mistakes in dealing with this situation. First, he is not respecting the role that Mike must occupy as a shop steward. That is, he does not accept the fact that part of the steward's job is to voice the concerns of the employees to their manager. Because Waters does not understand this role, he assumes that Mike believes that Middleton has a legitimate gripe. In fact, Mike may think that Middleton is as much of a jerk as Waters seems to think he is, but his role will not allow him to express these feelings.

Second, Waters is confusing Mike's role as a shop steward with his role as Waters' subordinate. The implication that Mike should sacrifice his performance as a steward for the sake of his long-term career is direct evidence that Waters is holding him accountable in his subordinate role for his behavior in his steward role. This, of course, places Mike in an untenable position because he must violate the expectations of his union members to satisfy the expectations of his manager.

So far we have not mentioned whether or not Middleton's complaints are legitimate. This is because, from the perspective of the relationship between Waters and Mike, *it doesn't make any difference.* In other words, Waters' behavior toward Mike should be the same, regardless of the validity of Middleton's concerns. In either case, Waters has to respect the role of the shop steward and the associated expectations and deal with the problem accordingly. In fact, if he continues to place Mike in a situation of role conflict, Middleton's complaints will likely acquire a much larger importance, even if they are totally unfounded.

Review Questions

1. Why is it important for supervisors to be able to work effectively with unions?
2. What is the major purpose of unions?
3. What has been the historical relationship between management and unions?
4. What are the prescribed and discretionary parts of managers' jobs?
5. What is the relationship between unions and the prescribed part of supervisors' jobs?
6. How have unions reduced the authority of supervisors?
7. What should supervisors do to preserve the authority in their roles?
8. Why do unions prefer computational decision making by supervisors?
9. What are the advantages of unions for supervisors?
10. What are the disadvantages of unions for supervisors?
11. Why is it important for supervisors to respect the role of the union official?
12. To whom is a union representative accountable?
13. Why should accountability in union and subordinate roles be separated?
14. Why can grievances be a sign of organizational health?
15. What are some things supervisors can do to handle grievances more effectively?

Chapter Glossary

Prescribed.
That portion of an individual's job that must be performed. The employee or supervisor has no choice but to carry out the particular task.

Discretionary.
That portion of an individual's job in which judgment can be exercised. Decisions are made within prescribed limits of authority.

Union contract.
An agreement formulated by unions and management which covers the working conditions of union members. The contract prescribes certain procedures, policies, or practices that must be followed.

Representative accountability.
The responsibility of union representatives to their membership, not to their organizational manager, for their performance as representatives.

Grievance.
A formal or informal communication to management regarding a complaint or concern by an employee or group of employees. Many organizations have grievance procedures to resolve the problems.

Error rates.
The measurement of the number of errors expected in any organization. Error rates provide a means for evaluating how well the organization is operating.

Seniority.
The amount of time an individual has been employed by a particular organization.

Case Problem

Portage Manufacturing Corportion

Portage Manufacturing Corporation, located in a small eastern city, employs 700 employees engaged primarily in manufacturing farm implements and related products for the agriculture industry. Portage has been in business for seventy-five years, and for the last twenty-five years its employees have belonged to the United Machinists' Union of America. Although the UMUA has a reputation for being a relatively strong and militant union, relations between the management of Portage and the union have traditionally been reasonably good. There has been only one strike in the twenty-five years and most disputes seldom get beyond the second level of management.

Portage is in the process of filling a vacancy in its tool and die department created by the death of one of the employees. The collective agreement requires that any vacancies be posted throughout the plant, and that present employees be given primary consideration for higher positions according to seniority. Specifically, the wording is: "Provided that two employees are equally qualified for a position, the position will be given to the most senior. Internal applicants will be given preference."

After posting the job and advertising in the local paper, the personnel department has received ten applications for the job, five from present employees and five from outside the company. After interviewing all ten applicants, the personnel manager and supervisor of the tool and die room have narrowed the choice down to three persons, two of the present employees, and one external applicant. Both agree that the external applicant is more qualified than the internal ones, but only marginally so. As they attempt to reach a decision, they are conscious of the contract requirement that union members be given preference.

Questions for Discussion

1. Given the information above, do you think the job should be given to the external applicant or one of the internal ones? Why?
2. Should the union members be given preference in this situation?
3. What do you think the reaction of the union will be if the job is given to the external applicant?
4. How would you deal with the union on this matter?

Safety Management

17

Chapter Learning Objectives

After reading and studying this chapter you should be able to:

1. Describe the five functional areas of safety management.

2. List the important structures and roles associated with safety management.

3. Describe and compute the incidence rate as a means of measuring safety performance.

4. Describe why employees do not want to participate in safety programs.

5. Apply expectancy theory to safety management.

6. List techniques a supervisor may utilize to remove attitude barriers.

7. List techniques to reward employees for participation in the safety program.

8. Describe two main causes of accidents.

9. Describe what supervisors can do to prevent accidents.

Key Terms

Safety management
Functional areas of
    safety management
Occupational Safety and
    Health Act

Canadian Labour Code
Incidence rate
Accident prevention

429

Safety Isn't Important

Harry Black has worked for the Prime Movers Company for the past three years as a supervisor in the shipping department. During this period, he has noticed an increase in the number of accidents in the warehouse. He spoke to the previous manager about this situation and as the manager did not seem too concerned, Harry decided not to push the issue.

A month ago, a new warehouse manager was appointed. Harry thought he might approach the new manager, Mr. Jamieson, about some of his findings, but eventually decided not to, because he thought the new man might be too busy to worry about the accidents that occurred over the last three years. He decided to quit worrying. He thought this manager would be the same as the other — not too concerned about employee health and accidents.

This morning a secretary told Harry that the new boss wanted to see him at three o'clock this afternoon. Harry worried about the meeting all day long, thinking he had done something wrong and was in trouble with the new boss already. At three o'clock Harry walked up to the front office for his meeting. After exchanging greetings, the boss explained why he wanted to see Harry.

"Harry, I have a concern about our safety management program."

Before he could finish Harry blurted out, "I know, Mr. Jamieson, I just happen to have the accident figures in my office. I think we have a major problem here!"

"I know we do, Harry. That's why I called you in here. Not only are the number of accidents on the increase, but when I attended the safety committee meeting the other day, only three people were there. The committee did not seem to be concerned about the accident rate or anything else about safety. What I want you to do is overhaul our safety program, so when the word safety is mentioned, people will be enthusiastic about it. I want your plan for our new program by Monday afternoon."

Harry is not prepared for this. Not only is the boss concerned, but he wants Harry to propose some solutions to the problem. Harry has noticed the problem but he has not thought much about how to solve it. He knows he'd better start immediately. The new boss is expecting results.

One of a supervisor's responsibilities is protection of employees during the performance of their assigned tasks. The execution of any safety program primarily rests with the operations personnel of the organization, with the supervisor being the link between management and the employees. Although the supervisor is the link between these two groups, a great deal of cooperation is needed to make the program effective. Safety requires effort on everyone's part if it is to be successful. Safety management, therefore, is concerned with encouraging positive attitudes toward safety, preventing accidents, identifying hazards, diagnosing causes of accidents, and motivating safe work behavior.

Employees generally understand the importance of safety, but often lack enthusiasm for active participation. Some employees will not even express an interest in safety. This becomes an ever-growing problem for supervisors because many organizations are placing increasing emphasis on the importance of an effective safety program. Senior managers have realized that the costs associated with employee injuries and diseases are rising, and are emphasizing their concerns to their supervisors. Consequently, supervisors must be concerned with the strategies they might use to increase their subordinates' commitment to safety programs.

This chapter begins with an overview of the safety function and how safety programs can contribute to organizational effectiveness. We then use the applied behavioral science approach to analyze the responsibilities of supervisors and employees in safety programs, and to suggest how supervisors might motivate employees to be more safety conscious. Finally, this chapter describes some strategies supervisors may follow to improve safety performance.

Safety Programs

Overview

Accidents and diseases associated with different occupations are, unfortunately, very common in organizations today. Statistics on safety and health in North America indicate an upward trend in accidents and occupational diseases. This trend is caused primarily by increases in the work force and improvements in technology that produce more sophisticated equipment. Even though there has been a decline in the manufacturing work force in recent years, other organizations, such as hospitals and banks, have added employees. Improved technology has caused changes in job procedures requiring retraining of employees. This increases the chances for accidents, especially if the new procedures are complex.

Occupational accidents and diseases can be very tragic to employees and their families. Not only is there the pain at the time of the accident, but there can be lost wages and the possibility of psychological damage as well. Costs are also of serious concern to an accident victim. Seldom can the medical insurance provided by the company cover all the medical bills. Medical compensation insurance plans may not provide the income the person was earning before the accident. If the victim is the sole support of a family, the effects of an occupational injury can be detrimental to the entire household.

Some occupations carry more hazards than others. Firefighters, coal miners, production workers in the chemical industry, textile workers, and welders are exposed to more hazards than most people. There are white-collar occupations that are just as hazardous, such as those of lab technicians, X-ray technicians, and supervisors in manufacturing facilities.[1] But regardless of the occupation, if proper safety procedures are not followed, tragic accidents may take place even in jobs normally considered relatively safe.

As we mentioned earlier, organizations are well aware of the effects of accidents and diseases. Accidents have cost companies billions of dollars per year as well as millions of lost man-hours of work. When an accident occurs, the organization must hire and train a new employee, process accident claims, investigate the cause of the accident, and provide means to educate the rest of the employees on the accident. All this will cost the company extra time and money that could have been directed to other areas. Eventually the organization may pay higher medical and compensation rates based on the number of accidents that occur in the facility. It is no surprise, therefore, that organizations are placing greater emphasis on **safety management** to encourage positive attitudes toward safety on the job. In addition to the human concern, it is sound economics.

Functional Areas of Safety Programs

Organizations develop their safety programs around five **functional areas of safety management:** training and development, hazard prevention, employee accountability and acceptability, safety awareness, and committee administration.

Administration of these five areas is usually accomplished by the personnel department. In large organizations, a full-time safety manager reporting to the personnel manager is employed to administer the program. These individuals are concerned with the development of policies and objectives, review of safety procedures, and public relations for the program.

The functional area usually receiving the greatest attention in the program is _training and development._ Statistics indicate the new employee, generally with the company one year or less, has a higher accident rate than the experienced employee. Therefore, much of the effort is spent training new employees in proper safety practices. Money spent at this stage is likely to be more effective because it is easier to instill good safety habits into employees who have not yet developed poor habits.

Organizations have spent a considerable amount of time and money in the development of new training techniques for safety, with the main

1. John M. Ivancevich and William F. Glueck, _Foundation of Personnel: Human Resource Management._ (Plano, TX: Business Publications), p. 583.

thrust being on accident prevention. Experience indicates that many employees view safety training as a boring subject (no doubt partly because of the it-will-never-happen-to-me syndrome), so trainers have tried to make the material more interesting by utilizing video tapes, skits, expert speakers, and more modern movies. Special emphasis has also been placed on experienced employees, since they are often the most difficult to train. In any case, a continuing educational program in safety is required. Otherwise, employees may develop dangerous shortcuts in work procedures, unsafe work habits, or poor attitudes toward safety in general.

Hazard prevention is another functional area that receives a great deal of attention. Organizations not only try to educate employees on proper safety procedures, but they also try to reduce the number of hazards within their facilities as well. Supervisors and employees have the primary responsibility for reporting, acting upon, or correcting hazardous conditions within the facility. Organizations have stressed special training in hazard identification and correction, development of severity indices (a priority system to correct hazards), and better communication when potential hazards are found.

Two functional areas that have received more attention in recent years are *employee accountability and acceptability* and *safety awareness*. In the past, organizations held employees accountable for their actions if they violated safety procedures. Disciplinary action was taken if the violation was serious. Now, however, managers and supervisors are being held accountable as well. If accidents keep occurring in a particular department, the supervisor may become the target for a lot of questions. In more serious situations, the supervisor may be removed from his or her position.

Management is also trying to make safety programs more acceptable by introducing innovative methods for safety administration. Rather than the traditional model of supervisor instructing employees in safety consciousness, many firms are utilizing other methods for managing safety programs. Some new concepts include the buddy system, in which two employees train and monitor each other's safety habits, and cooperative programs between unions and management.

Safety awareness or publicity has also increased during the recent years. Areas that receive emphasis are better communication about the program, instructional guides on new safety information, higher visibility of safety rules, and improvement of recognition for good safety performance.

The fifth functional area, *committee administration*, is the controlling force for the safety program. Generally, an organization- or plant-wide committee works with the personnel department in administration of policies, procedures, and objectives of the program. Depending upon

Reinforcing Safety

One of the more recent approaches to improving safety on the job is based on the reward principles discussed in Chapter 8. The system is based on the premise that feedback on results can be a motivator, and consists simply of designing a mechanism for feedback on safety performance and rewarding good performance. In a midwestern city transit company, this system reduced accident rates by al-most twenty-five percent. Feedback on accidents was posted on a daily basis and various teams were placed in competition with each other. The winning team each week received either five dollars' worth of gas for each member, or a series of free bus rides. The company concluded that the benefit/cost ratio of the program was over 3:1.[2]

the organization, the membership of the committee could be composed of managers, supervisors, employees, union officials, and external safety consultants. Even with the committee system, it is still the final responsibility of the supervisor to enforce and monitor safety policies and procedures at the employee level.

In large organizations it is impossible to place control of the five functional areas under just one organization-wide committee. Usually subcommittees are organized to operate each of the five areas. An example of the typical organization structure for safety management is illustrated in Figure 17.1.

Policy and procedure changes are generally passed down through lower levels of administration to department safety subcommittees. These committees decide how, when, and where the changes are to be carried out and pass their decisions on to the line managers and supervisors for implementation.

Some of the subcommittee functions may be integrated into the organization-wide committee, or responsibilities of different line managers may be delegated down to supervisors. Even though structures and responsibilities may vary depending on the organization, they will all still work in the five basic functional areas. Examples of activities, responsibilities, and procedures for the five functional areas are given in Table 17.1.

This table identifies examples of only a few of the activities involved in the administration of a safety program. Supervisors participate actively at all levels of the program, serving as representatives on the department committees, and some are members of the organization-wide committee as well.

2. Robert S. Haynes, Randall C. Pine, and H. Gordon Fitch, "Reducing Accident Rates with Organizational Behavior Modification," *Academy of Management Journal* 25:2 (1982), pp. 407-16.

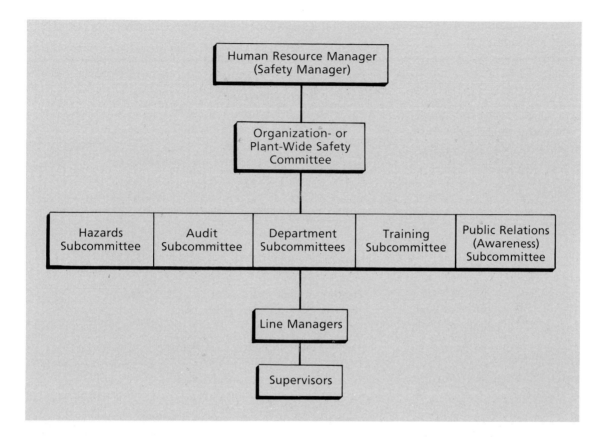

Figure 17.1. Sample Organizational System for Safety Programs.

Government Regulation

With the upward trend in accident rates, the federal governments of the United States and Canada have increased their efforts to protect the health of employees. The primary regulation in the United States is the **Occuptaional Safety and Health Act,** while in Canada it is **Part IV of the Canadian Labour Code** (Safety of Employees). Although these laws were enacted at different times and prescribe different administrative procedures, basically they serve the same purpose — protection of the worker while on the job. In both instances these laws were passed to ensure uniformity of safety standards and correction of safety hazards, and to provide for enforcement and penalties where violations occur.

Incidence Rates

Part of an organization's responsibility is reporting injuries and occupational diseases to an agency that enforces these regulations. The data are generally reported according to a formula that computes the number of

Table 17.1. Sample of Activities, Goals, and Responsibilities for Five Functional Areas of Safety Management.

Goal	Action step	Responsibility
Committee Administration		
Improve awareness of committee; goals, authority and objectives.		
Organization-wide committee		
Review area hazards; determine they are being repaired or removed	Send report to top-level managers	Organization-Wide Committee
Communicate serious accidents to the subcommittees	Post accident reports in conspicuous places in organization. Designate copies to managers and supervisors and discuss with employees	Safety Administrator
Ensure all subcommittees are meeting on a monthy basis	Audit committee to ensure meetings are actually taking place	Audit Subcommittee
Department Committee		
Make employees aware of their representative	Post on bulletin boards — have representatives wear badges	Awareness Subcommittee
Ensure that hazards are dealt with immediately	Define authority of individuals to deal with hazards and report hazards to the supervisor responsible	Hazards Subcommittee
	Training	
	Program Management	
Develop a comprehensive, effective training plan applicable to all employees	Designate full-time training coordinator	Training Subcommittee
	Provide special safety-related training for subcommittee members	
	Establish specific selection criteria for potential members	
	Content Information	
	Standardize safety rules	
	Structure training program	
	Train employees by worker classification	
	Training Techniques	
	Video techniques	
	Closed circuit television	
	Learning center concept	
	Outside training resources	

Goal	Action step	Responsibility
	Committee Administration	
	Hazard Identification	
Recognize that supervisors and employees have primary responsibility for reporting, acting upon, and correcting hazardous conditions	During committee meetings, discuss new procedures, hazards, and review problem areas	Department Safety Committee
Develop criteria for severity index for reporting hazards	Develop different categories for hazards identification	Supervisors
Special training in hazards identification	Attend seminars; bring in outside trainers	Organization-Wide Committee
	Awareness	
Establish better communication	Develop guidelines and time frames for reporting and publicizing	Organization-Wide Committee
Publish: Organization-wide Committee minutes Department Committee minutes Monthly hazards report Monthly injury summary		
Create individual interest and personal involvement in safety Create a new recognition program	Develop awareness team	Public Relations Committee (Awareness)
	Accountability	
Establish and implement safety education program to define to all employees responsibilities in the safety program	Review accountability, standards, and existing safety procedures Define responsibilities of each employee	Department Committee
Create environment that stimulates acceptance of safety program	Establish new techniques a. Buddy system b. DuPont system c. Accident review system	
Establish a realistic and equitable policy on safety compliance	Top/Down Accountability Superintendent--→ Manager Manager --------→ Supervisor Supervisor ------→ Employee	

Table 17.2. Summary of Accident Data.

Type of Accident	Number		
	1980	*1981*	*1982*
Hand, finger or thumb	25	35	36
Leg, ankle, or foot	15	8	8
Head, face, or neck	6	4	2
Chest, stomach, or back	12	14	10
TOTAL	58	61	56

Number of employees: 100
Available hours/100 employees: 2000
Total hours worked: 185,000

accidents per man-hour worked, or the **incident rate.** A generalized version of this formula is as follows:

Incidence rate = (Total number of injuries and diseases × base)/(Total number of hours worked)

The base is an index of the available hours an established number of employees will work in one year's time. Even though this generalized formula represents an organization's incidence rate, it can be utilized by a supervisor to keep records on the accident rates within his or her own department. Once the rate is calculated, the supervisor will be able to compare the current rate with historical records, and thus obtain an indication of any trends in the accident rate.

An example of how the incidence rate can be utilized will demonstrate how useful this tool can be. Assume that a supervisor suspects he or she has some problems in accidents, but does not know how to develop the data to analyze the problem. After talking it over with the manager, he or she decides to use the incidence rate formula the company utilizes to report accidents. Table 17.2 shows the areas and number of accidents that occurred in the department over the previous year.

At first glance it does not appear that there is a problem. The total number of accidents in the department has dropped from the previous year. Only the hand injuries could be a possible problem area since the frequency has increased. If we calculate each of the incidence rates for 1982 we find:

Misleading Incidence Rates

Recall that in Chapter 16 the concept of error rate was discussed with regard to grievances filed. It was noted that some level of error is expected in organizations and the error rate is the measurement of those errors. The incidence rate for accidents is a similar concept and can be used in the same way.

I was talking with a personnel manager once about his company's safety program. He commented on how poor their safety record had been, and then showed me the data for the previous six months. I was amazed! Only two accidents had been reported during that period, compared to over 20 during the same period a year ago. I asked him how he managed to achieve such impressive results. "It was easy," he said, "all we did was institute a disciplinary program for safety. Anyone involved in an accident was automatically laid off for three days without pay."

What do you think happened to their accidents?

Incidence Rate (Hand injuries) $= 36 \times 100 \times 2000/185{,}000 = 38.92$

Calculating the rates for the remaining categories shows that leg injuries $= 8.65$, head injuries $= 2.6$, and chest injuries $= 10.81$. If he or she looks at the industry averages for these three types of accidents, he or she finds that hand injuries $= 30.01$, leg injuries $= 8.7$, head injuries $= 2.9$, and chest injuries $= 9.2$. This indicates two problem areas, hand injuries and chest injuries. The supervisor's efforts can now be concentrated on finding out why the incidence rate in each of these areas is higher than average.

Behavioral Science in Safety Programs

Because good safety programs depend heavily upon the motivation of employees to adhere to sound safety procedures, behavioral science provides assistance in improving the effectiveness of safety programs. This section analyzes the role of the supervisor in these programs and shows how theories of motivation can be applied to safety management.

Supervisory Responsibilities

Even though supervisors may be actively involved in all levels of the safety program, their primary responsibility is still execution of the program. They are in the best position to increase awareness and enforcement of a good program. Table 17.3 shows the roles that the safety administrator, personnel manager, line manager, and supervisor occupy in safety programs, and indicates that the supervisor is most often the individual responsible for training and enforcement. To execute these responsibilities properly, there are several things supervisors can do.

Table 17.3. Distribution of Safety Responsibilities

Function	Safety Administrator	Personnel Manager	Line Manager	Supervisor
	Person Assigned Responsibility			
Inspection	52%	—	10%	38%
Training	5%	5%	20%	70%
Enforcement	11%	4%	10%	75%
Policy	37%	55%	5%	3%
Publicity	54%	12%	24%	18%
Administration	42%	46%	7%	5%

Source: Harry Schneider, Unpublished study, Southeastern Oklahoma State University.

1. *Set a good example.* It is difficult to convince employees of the value of good safety practices if the supervisor doesn't adhere to rules and regulations as well.

2. *Enforce consistently.* Once safety rules and regulations have been established, they should be enforced consistently for all employees. Inconsistency not only encourages bad safety habits, but also creates poor attitudes toward safety programs.

3. *Recognize good safety behavior.* Enforcement means not only catching employees doing something wrong, but catching them doing things right as well. Supervisors should always be looking for good behavior as well as bad. This gives the safety program a good image.

4. *Follow the learning curve.* Learning about safe work behavior is the same as learning anything else. A proper learning climate must be established. Supervisors should not expect too much too soon, and should encourage employee progression through the learning curve.

5. *Integrate the safety function.* Safety programs work best if they are integrated into the rest of the management system. If it is seen by employees as tacked on to their jobs, or something that is the subject of a big campaign once a year, it will not be effective. The supervisor can assist in this by making safety a regular part of the supervisory role.

Employee Response to Safety Programs

The primary concern of supervisors should be the employee response to safety programs. Regardless of how much time is spent in the design, execution, and monitoring of safety programs, if the response of employees is poor, the program will not be effective. Many employees elect not to participate in safety programs for a variety of reasons. Others not only do not participate, but actively try to inhibit the program's progress.

Identifying Safety Hazards at Work

As the text has noted, some occupations are more hazardous than others, but all jobs have an element of danger in them somewhere. Form into groups of three to five individuals, and make a list of the safety violations you have observed in your work experience. Do not worry about whether the acts were official violations or not; just that they endangered either the employee or others in the work area. Share your list with others in the class. This will give you a feeling for the wide variety of unsafe practices that can be found everywhere.

They accomplish this by complaining about safety hazards, filing grievances every time they find a safety hazard, and generally obstructing positive attempts to improve safety practices.

As a supervisor, how do you cope with these attitudes toward safety? It is difficult enough to handle the problems with safety procedures, violations, and related activities, but trying to manage employees with a poor attitude toward safety compounds the problem. Many times employees do not view safety as an activity which will lead to any benefit. They usually ask themselves questions like those on the next page.

Why Should We?

I had occasion to work with a supervisor who had problems in the area of employee response to the safety program. He related the following story: "I received a memo from my boss stating that the company safety administrator was going to tour all the company facilities and make a surprise safety inspection during the next month. That afternoon I met with my employees, read the memo, and went over some things we needed to do before the safety administrator's visit. Some of them started grumbling and a few wondered aloud why the company was worried about safety now when it didn't show any concern during the year. I ignored these comments and gave out the assignments.

"Everyone did his job and I felt sure that we were in good shape for our inspection. I even double-checked some of the practices to make sure we were within standard. The day of the inspection arrived and I was touring our department with my boss and the company safety administrator. When we walked around a corner, there stood two of my best employees violating basic safety rules of the company! One was smoking a cigarette in a no-smoking area and the other was holding a drink which could have created a hazardous spill. I questioned the two later about their behavior, and they replied, 'The company doesn't worry about safety, so why should we?' "

- Will I actually receive a reward if I become involved in the program?
- Will I receive better rewards for doing other jobs?
- Is this really important to management or are there other areas more important?
- With no effective standards, how can management measure my performance?
- Can I slide my performance without management really noticing the drop in performance?[3]

These questions explain something about the attitude of many employees toward safety and why they do not want to participate. The next step, of course, is to change their attitudes so that safety becomes an important function in their daily activities. Since this is largely a motivation problem, we can utilize the discussion in Chapter 7 on expectancy theory to provide some answers.

Application of Expectancy Theory

Expectancy theory proposes that employees will be motivated to exhibit behaviors which they see as leading to a desirable outcome (goal). The model presented in Chapter 7 can be adapted to safety management and is shown in Figure 17.2, which indicates that the employee expects that through his or her effort, safety performance can be affected. However, whether or not the employee exerts this effort will be a function of the relationship perceived between safety performance and the outcomes (goals). If the relationship is strong (i.e., positive) and leads to an outcome that is positively valent for the employee, there will be motivation to practice good safety. Figure 17.2 is constructed to show how a poor relationship between safety performance and employee outcomes can lead to a lack of interest in safety. This lack of interest will not produce dissatisfaction in most employees, but it will not reinforce the desirable safety behaviors. Therefore, employees develop poor attitudes toward safety.

In the example on page 444, Mr. Brown destroyed any attempt at keeping the employees interested in the safety committee. In essence, he did not consider the application of expectancy theory to the safety program.

Steps in Application

The first step in the application of expectancy theory is for the supervisor to know the goals of the employees. What is it they want from the safety program? What are they after? How will the safety program satisfy

3. Herbert J. Chruden and Arthur W. Sherman Jr., *Personnel Management: The Utilization of Human Resources.* (Dallas, TX: Southeastern), p. 520.

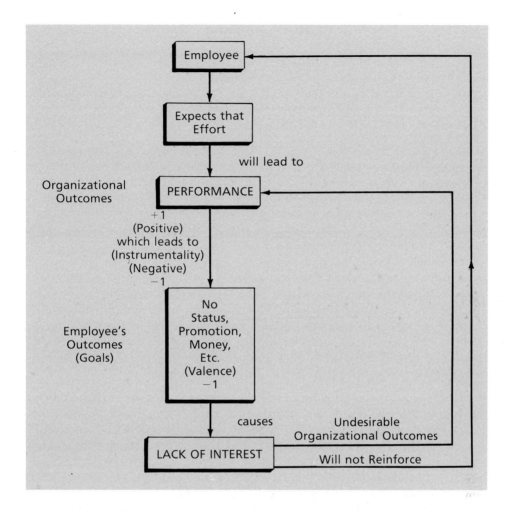

Figure 17.2. Applying Expectancy Theory to Safety Management.

their needs? Then the supervisor must clarify the relationship between the behaviors desired by management and the employees' goals. For example, being active in the safety program could lead to a desired goal the employee wants and the company wants. In the case of Mr. Brown (page 444), he clarified the relationship between *his* desired behaviors and *his* desired goals without receiving feedback from the committee itself. Since everything was decided by the boss, the employees felt that their efforts toward a desired performance would not lead to any perceived rewards. A smarter approach by the manager would have been to listen to the ideas of the committee and determine what they wanted, then relate their wants to an outcome the manager desired. Clarifying their

Not This Time

Remember the supervisor from the previous example who took his lumps in the safety inspection? I had occason to talk with him several months later and found that he had talked his two problem employees into participating in the safety program. He said things were going fine until the first safety committee meeting with the manager, Mr. Brown. Mr. Brown walked into the meeting and immediately began listing the topics he wanted the comittee to develop for the safety program. Once he had finished, one of the employees stood up and said, "Mr. Brown, this is the same way all our committees are run. No input comes from the committee members themselves. You dictate the rules, then leave. Not this time."

With this, the employee and several other committee members walked out of the conference room and went back to work. My friend the supervisor just groaned. It took a month to convince his two employees to join the committee again.

goals and explaining what they needed to do to achieve these goals would have provided the manager with a productive safety committee.

The next step in application of the expectancy theory is for the supervisor to remove any barriers which would cause the instrumentality to change. The employees must be shown that good safety performance is worth the effort. How does the supervisor accomplish this? What barriers must be removed? Here are some suggestions.

1. *Make your expectations clear.* Too many times supervisors do not tell employees the exact results desired. Proper standards must be set with participation of employees, but the supervisor's expectations should be clear to all. These expectations should also be consistent with overall organizational objectives.

2. *Find out what employees want.* Let the employees establish what they want out of the program, and then tie the organization's goals into the employees' goals. Most supervisors find that there generally are enough similarities between the two that little modification is needed.

3. *Delineate specific rewards for good performance.* Tell the employees that if an excellent job is done certain rewards will result. Once specific objectives are established and the employees know a positive reward is associated with the performance, the perceived reward is understood and performance can improve. Here again, ask the employees what they want for superior accomplishments. Supervisors will find that different rewards will affect people in different ways. Rewards will be discussed in greater detail later in this chapter.

4. *Give personal attention to safety.* If employees know the supervisor has a sincere interest in safety and takes time to help employees who are involved in the safety program, they will find the work more rewarding. Not taking a personal interest in the employees' efforts or delay in

processing a request made by a safety representative are the quickest ways of destroying positive attitudes toward safety.

  5. *Involve employees.* Supervisors must actively involve as many employees in the safety program as possible. At first probably only a few will want to participate. Once the proper recognition is given to these few, more employees will want to participate and should be encouraged to do so.

  6. *Make safety a joint effort.* Make the safety program a cooperative program between management and employees. One suggestion is to appoint an employee as cochairman of the safety committee along with a member of management. Employees could also be named as chairmen of subcommittees, as well as assist the supervisor in doing a safety audit. Any type of cooperative effort will enhance the employees' desire to become involved if they know that they are part of the problem-solving process. This strategy is also useful for the chronic complainer or the habitual grievance filer. Most of the time, these people do this as a defense mechanism to attract attention. Positive attention in safety practices can reverse this process.

  7. *Work through the informal group leader.* The importance of the informal leader has been mentioned on several occasions, and this is yet another time that person can be helpful. If the informal leader is in agreement on the need for good safety management, his or her influence can be used with the rest of the group. He or she may even be a likely candidate for the cochairmanship of your safety committee.

These are only a few examples of methods to help remove barriers to employee cooperation. The application of sound behavioral science principles can enhance the effectiveness of any safety management program.

Using Role Theory to Improve Safety

Chapter 5 described the importance of social role as a determinant of behavior, and it was noted that changing roles can have a significant impact upon people's behavior. One company used this concept to its advantage and solved a sticky problem in safety.

It seems that one employee was a chronic complainer about safety requirements and frequently violated safety regulations. After a while, he developed an image as a safety violator and tended to react to the expectations of his co-workers. The problem became so serious that it was thought that he purposely violated safety regulations that he actually thought were necessary.

To solve the problem, the safety director made the employee a safety training instructor. This formal change in role allowed him to change his behavior (after all, an instructor couldn't be seen violating regulations) and take advantage of his years of experience in the organization.

Applying Rewards
in Safety Management

Part of the expectancy theory centers around reward systems. Unless employees feel there are rewards equal to their output they will never develop interest in the safety program. Understanding how rewards affect the expectancy relationship is a valuable tool for supervisors. Chapter 8 discussed the basic concepts of reward systems and how a supervisor might apply them as effective tools to increase employee morale and motivation toward the desired goal. We can also apply them to our discussion of safety. The basic principles are contingency, awareness, timing, consistency, and type.

✓ **CONTINGENCY PRINCIPLE.** Rewards and punishments should depend upon the desired behavior. In safety, the supervisor must ensure that the employees know safe practices and that performance in the safety program will lead to rewards. Occasional reinforcement on the possible outcomes of good behavior will encourage employees to do more. As noted in Chapter 8, supervisors should be wary of using punishment to motivate performance. Disciplining an employee for an accident is like punishing a person twice for the same offence. Most people will feel that the accident victim has already suffered enough. If the supervisor disciplines the accident victim, the resentment incurred among employees may jeopardize the entire safety program.

√ **AWARENESS PRINCIPLE.** If the supervisor wants to establish rewards associated with the safety program, the program itself must be communicated to the employees. They must be told what is expected, what the desired results are, and what they will receive for their efforts.

TIMING PRINCIPLE. The effectiveness of a reward is related to how soon after the behavior the reward is given. Since it is often difficult to instill enthusiasm for safety management, this principle becomes very important. The reward system for safety should be designed so the rewards come as soon as possible after the task or behavior occurs. This not only ensures continued involvement by participating members, but can also be a positive incentive for more employees to join in the safety effort.

CONSISTENCY PRINCIPLE. Rewards should be consistent over time and among individuals. If this principle is not followed closely, it could be a key area of dissatisfaction with the employees. The supervisor must ensure that all employees exhibiting the same desired behavior are rewarded as equitably as possible. If it is perceived by employees that

Exercise 17.2

Designing a Reward System for Safety

Assume that you are the safety manager for a construction company that builds roads, and you want to implement a reward system to encourage safety on the job. Design the system by specifying (a) a standard by which safe behavior can be measured, (b) the types of reward you will offer, and (c) how and when the rewards will be applied. You may make any reasonable assumptions you think necessary.

---

one person receives a reward greater than another person, their motivation toward safety may diminish. Some employees could conceivably attempt to undermine the safety program if they feel that the rewards are inequitable.

TYPE PRINCIPLE. The type of reward may be one of the most difficult decisions the supervisor will have to make. Different types of rewards will motivate different employees. If a supervisor sees that a particular reward does not work well for one individual, another type should be tried. Chapter 8 described four types of rewards that can be used to recognize good performance: tangible-external, intangible-external, intangible-internal, and tangible-internal. Supervisors might use these same categories of rewards to motivate better safety practices.

1. Tangible-External: Present a plaque or recognition letter to the employee. Effective rewards have also included banquets honoring safety participants, company or department picnics, safety gifts, and gift certificates. Money can be used as a reward, providing that the reward system is well designed. However, since money is such a complex reward, other rewards should be tried first.

2. Intangible-External: Simple recognition is an effective reward for many employees. Some examples of recognition could include supervisors and managers telling employees they are doing a good job, placing recognition displays on bulletin boards and other prominent locations, and articles in the company newsletter about safety achievements of employees.

3. Intangible-Internal: Some employees enjoy the pleasure of accomplishing a difficult task safely and feeling good about it. Supervisors should, therefore, strive to make the safety program challenging to their employees. Providing recognition for good performance assists in stimulating this type of reward.

4. Tangible-Internal: This would be the most difficult for a supervi-

sor to apply. However, discovering what types of tangible rewards an employee wants and providing the means for the employee to obtain the reward would be the method to use.

These are a few suggestions to enhance the reward system for employees. Once they feel the effort is worth the reward, the safety program will run more effectively. Eventually, employees will claim ownership for their efforts and will work hard to help management establish an effective safety management program.

Accident Prevention

The objective of a safety management program is **accident prevention.** Although employees are ultimately responsible for their own behavior, supervisors play an important role in accident prevention. This section describes the causes of accidents, accident investigation, and some guidelines supervisors can use to help prevent accidents.

Causes of Accidents

Accidents are caused by two major factors: the physical environment and employee inattentiveness. The relationship between these two factors is illustrated in Figure 17.3. This shows that inattentiveness is caused largely by stress and unrewarding work, and that unsafe conditions are caused by the physical environment. Both can lead to accidents.

Examples of items that are classified as causes for accidents in the physical environment are:

- Unguarded or improperly guarded machinery,
- Poor housekeeping,
- Poor lighting,
- Defective equipment,
- Loose-fitting clothing or jewelry, and
- Slippery floors or blocked aisles.

Although this list is just an example of possible hazards, it shows the areas that supervisors should examine in the performance of their regular safety inspections.

Inattentiveness accounts for 70 percent of all accidents that occur within a facility. Inattentiveness is caused primarily by two factors, unrewarding work and stress. Workers generally adapt to unrewarding jobs by finding a way to get along or being absent from the job. Finding a way to adapt to a boring job takes many, and often ingenious, forms. The

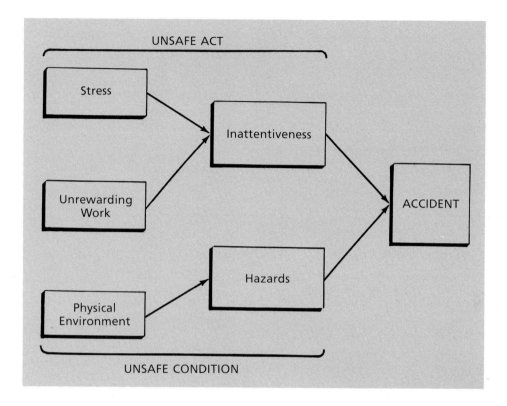

Figure 17.3. Causes of Accidents.

problem with these ingenious forms, more often than not, is that they are hazardous to the employee. Adaptation may take the form of day-dreaming, alcohol and drug abuse, trading jobs, or intentionally getting behind, then rushing to catch up. In all these examples, the potential for accidents increases when employees try to adapt to the boring job. Not only could they injure themselves, but others as well.

Another cause of accidents is stress. Stress generally has two sources, stress from the job and stress due to personal problems. A quarrel at home or an argument with the boss can cause enough stress to distract the employee from the close concentration needed to perform the job. As a direct result, the employee could be seriously injured. Supervisors must be watchful for signs of stress in employees. In some cases, the supervisor may be able to help with job-related stress (as described in Chapter 18), and in other situations, refer the employee to professional help. In either case, the supervisor must first make a judgment regarding the employee's ability to perform the job properly and safely.

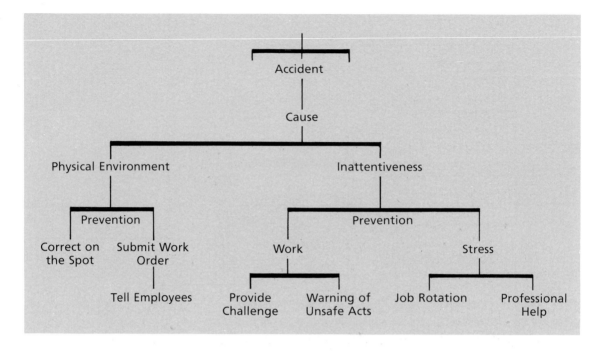

Figure 17.4. Guide for Accident Investigation and Prevention.

Investigation, Diagnosis, and Prevention

Once an accident occurs, the supervisor must determine not only how the accident happened, but the causes behind it as well. Organizations usually have their own procedures for reporting and investigating the causes of accidents, so we shall concentrate on diagnosis and prevention. Figure 17.4 illustrates a model for the prevention and investigation functions.

If the accident is caused by the physical environment, a correction on the spot should be made if possible. If the condition cannot be fixed, a work order to fix the condition should be submitted and meanwhile the hazardous area should be conspicuously marked and employees informed.

Accidents that are caused by inattentiveness are more difficult to prevent. Some guidelines to assist supervisors in preventing them are:

For Unrewarding Jobs

1. *Provide challenging work.* The supervisor must try to create an environment so that employees feel there is an important goal to be met. Many employees want to view their jobs as a means of self-expression or

growth. Giving employees different tasks on a periodic basis could change the parameters of their jobs and challenge their talents.

2. *Warn of unsafe acts.* If an employee is performing the job incorrectly or intentionally falls behind, the supervisor must warn the individual of the impending dangers. Do not avoid or ignore the situation; it probably will not go away. In giving the warning, respect the individual and concentrate on the unsafe act. Warnings should always occur as soon as a violation is noticed.

3. *Provide professional help.* For the employee who suffers from alchohol or drug abuse, the supervisor should offer to refer him or her for professional help. By no means should the supervisor try to be counsellor for this type of problem. Many organizations provide this service. Or the personnel department generally has references to professional counsellors qualified in these areas. If these problems persist or the employee becomes a constant threat to himself or others, the supervisor may have to remove him or her from the job.

For Stress

1. *Know your Employees.* Supervisors must be acquainted with their employees so they can detect changes in their behavior. Without knowing the basic nature, character, and behavior of the employee, you cannot know if the employee is under any stress.

2. *Rotate Jobs.* Rotating a person to a less hazardous job is a possible solution in these circumstances, provided the employee is trained in the other job. An employee worried about a spouse's health problem will not pay much attention to his or her job, and could be a danger to others.

3. *Obtain professional help.* If the employee's stress persists, offer to obtain professional counselling for him or her. Be as helpful as possible and try to understand the employee's situation. Sometimes patience can do more for the employee than anything else.

As we have stated, the supervisor's main concern should be prevention, not investigation, It may require more time to prevent accidents but it will be well worth the effort.

Key to Success

Getting employees to use good safety behaviors on the job is not difficult. Strong punishments for ignoring safety regulations, close supervision of employees, and rigid enforcement of all safety regulations are all methods of minimizing accidents on the job. The difficult part is getting employees to *voluntarily* observe safety regulations so that good safety management becomes the accepted way of doing things. In other words, it is the difference between wanting to versus having to. In the ideal situation employees want to observe good safety practices.

Having employees who voluntarily practice safe behaviors is basic to the motivation process itself. If employees see that safety is related to their personal goals at work, they will be motivated to avoid unsafe behaviors. If they do not perceive the personal relevance of safety, they will not be motivated.

How, then, might this positive motivation be created? It will be established only through the meaningful experiences of employees that reinforce the importance of safety on the job. These experiences can be either positive (such as a reward or recognition for safe behaviors) or negative (such as experiencing an accident or seeing the effects of accidents upon others). Since few would recommend creating an accident on purpose to use as an example, the positive approach is better.

Also important to the success of any safety program is the support of senior management. Employees tend not to identify with goals and objectives that are seen as low priority. At the supervisory level, this priority is most often exemplified by the supervisor setting the example. While this by itself will not cause improved attitudes toward safety, the absence of it will cause problems.

We can also look to reward systems to show how supervisors can encourage safety on the job on a one-to-one basis. Many supervisors are quite adept at catching employess violating safety regulations. In fact, some may consider this a major part of their job. What about the employees who are doing things right? Are they ignored? In many cases, they are. Supervisors should spend *more* time recognizing employees who are abiding by regulations and less time catching the violators. The positive approach encourages internal motivation for safety; the negative method only discourages employees from getting caught. A wise manager once said, "It doesn't matter so much what employees do when you're around. What really matters is what they do when you're *not* around!"

Summary

This chapter has described the various functional areas of safety programs: training and development, hazard prevention, employee accountability and acceptability, safety awareness, and committee administration. The personnel department usually has primary responsibility for the safety program, with an organization-wide committee serving as the main controlling structure for the program.

Employees often view formal safety programs as unimportant. Expectancy theory can be a useful tool in management, as it helps the supervisor to understand, predict, and possibly change employee attitudes. Two important functions of the supervisor in safety management are to remove attitudinal barriers of the employees, and to provide a reward system for the safety program. To remove attitudinal barriers, supervisors should make expectations clear, delineate specific performances, give personal attention, involve employees, make the progam a joint effort, and work through informal group leaders.

Once the barriers are removed, a reward must be provided that will make employees feel their efforts are worthwhile. Supervisors should apply the contingency, type, consistency, timing, and awareness principles of effective reward systems.

Supervisors should also be aware of the two primary sources of accidents: the physical environment and inattentiveness. Hazards associated with the physical environment are relatively obvious, but supervisors must ensure that they are kept to a bare minimum. Two major causes of acidents due to inattentiveness are unrewarding work and stress. These conditions are more difficult to recognize and the supervisor needs to be aware of stress symptoms in employees.

Supervisors' efforts should be centered around the prevention of accidents. Some alternative methods of minimizing accidents are to provide challenging work, give proper warnings, rotate jobs, or refer to professional help if necessary. In any case, supervisors must make the safety program meaningful for the employees. If they are not involved in the program, they will not be interested. Their lack of interest may cause accidents that cost the organization and themselves time and money.

Opening Incident Revisited

Harry's problem is common to many supervisors who have concerns about safety. They know accidents are a serious problem, but are not really sure how to work through the situation.

Harry must decide how to set up the program for implementation. Should he use the committee arrangement, or only have one person in charge of safety? The best approach may be to set up a department safety committe, with one of the employees serving as cochairperson with the distribution manager. Perhaps this employee should be given the same authority as the manager to make decisions about the safety program. If Harry could enlist the help of an informal group leader, this would be quite effective. The group leader may be a logical choice as cochairperson.

Safety programs should revolve around a central theme to instill enthusiasm. Harry might utilize the theme, "Driving for Safety." He could have a rodeo for the lift truck drivers, a publicity campaign such as a small department fair, or a lift truck parade with signs on the trucks advertising safety slogans and facts about the distribution department. The parade could drive through the other parts of the facility, if possible, showing the other departments their achievements. Simple recognition of the safe drivers, or in the case of the parade, recognition of the whole department, will help increase employee interest in Harry's program and promote enough awareness that accidents will decrease.

Review Questions

1.   What are the five functional areas in a safety program?
2.   Who has primary responsibility for a safety program?
3.   What is the supervisor's responsibility in safety managment?
4.   How does a supervisor apply expectancy theory to safety?
5.   Describe how a supervisor could remove attitudinal barriers to a safety program.
6.   What are five principles utilized to enhance a reward system for safety?
7.   What are the two major causes of accidents?
8.   What actions can a supervisor take to prevent accidents?

Chapter Glossary

Safety management.	A program designed to encourage positive attitudes toward safety, prevent accidents, identify hazards, diagnose causes of accidents, and motivate safe work behavior.
Functional areas of safety management.	The five major areas of safety covered by safety management programs: training and development, hazard prevention, employee accountability and acceptability, safety awareness, and committee administration.
Occupational Safety and Health Act.	United States law that provides for the protection of employees while on the job.
Canadian Labour Code Part IV.	Canadian law that provides for protection of employees.
Incidence rate.	The index utilized to compute the number of accidents per man-hour worked that occur in an organization.
Accident prevention.	Major safety responsibility of the supervisor. Accidents are due to either inattentiveness on the job or physical conditions.

Case Problem

Viking General Hospital

Terry Hall has been employed as a central supply technician at the Viking General Hospital since 1975. Most of Terry's job entails filling orders for the different nursing stations, sterilizing surgery trays, ordering supplies, and resupplying the stockroom when necessary.

This morning Dick Jordon, Terry's supervisor, told Terry to start stacking the I.V. solution six cases high in the stockroom.

On receiving this instruction, Terry replied, "Dick, I don't think we should stack the cases six high. It's a safety hazard for two reasons. The cases are not sturdy enough to be stacked that high and anyone stacking the cases that high could strain his back."

Dick answered, "I don't think it will be a problem, go ahead and stack them six high. I have stacked them six high before without any problem."

Terry retorted, "I know they will fall and I will not stack them six high, no matter what you tell me. I know if this is a safety hazard hospital rules state I do not have to follow your instructions!"

Dick became very angry and yelled, "You better start stacking those cases now! I will be back in ten minutes and you better have the job completed!"

Dick stormed out of Central Supply furious about Terry's refusal to do the work he was assigned. Twenty minutes later Dick returned and found Terry still sitting down and the cases lying on the floor.

Angered, Dick said, "All right, Mr. Wise Guy, let's go see Mr. Dickinson about this situation!"

Ten minutes later Terry and Dick were in Mr. Dickinson's office arguing about stacking the cases six high in the stockroom.

Questions for Discussion

1. Did Terry, in fact, raise a safety issue when he refused to do the work?
2. Is sincerity of belief of danger sufficient to excuse Terry's refusal, or must the condition be proven?
3. Does the nature of a perceived danger matter?
4. Does Mr. Dickinson have the right to discipline Terry? Should he investigate the possible hazard?
5. If you were Mr. Dickinson, how would you resolve the problem?

Interviewing, Counselling, and Performance Appraisal

18

Chapter Learning Objectives

After reading and studying this chapter you should be able to:

1. Define directive and nondirective interviewing and describe when the supervisor might use each method.

2. Define the funnel approach and describe why it is used.

3. Explain why nondirective interviewing is useful in selection, exit, and investigative interviews.

4. Explain the role of the supervisor in counselling.

5. List and explain the requirements for being an effective counsellor.

6. Explain why being an effective counsellor is important for supervisors.

7. Explain how interviewing techniques can improve performance appraisal interviews.

8. Define the three types of performance appraisal interviews.

9. List and explain the general principles of conducting performance appraisal interviews.

Key Terms

Directive interview
Nondirective interview
Funnel approach
Selective interview
Exit interview
Investigative interview
Counselling

Performance appraisal
  (Formal)
Performance appraisal
  (Informal)
Tell-and-Sell method
Tell-and-Listen method
Problem-solving method

457

The Uptight Employee

Sam Johnson is the supervisor of the billing department in the financial division of a city government. He supervises twenty-five clerks, analysts, and secretaries, one of whom is Brian Furman. Furman joined the unit about six months ago and Johnson has noticed that he seems to have difficulty fitting in with the rest of the group. Furman usually has little to say to the other workers, and they generally ignore him during the day. Furman usually eats lunch by himself or leaves the premises entirely during lunch hour. Although his work is generally satisfactory, Johnson thinks that the group would work better as a team if Furman were a part of the group.

This afternoon, Johnson looked up to see Furman standing in his office doorway. This was the first time that Johnson could recall that Furman had ever come to see him. He didn't say anything, but just stood in the doorway and stared at the floor. Finally, Johnson opened the conversation:

JOHNSON: Well, Furman, what is it?

FURMAN: Oh, nothing really . . . I thought I might . . . well, if you're busy I can come back later. . . .

JOHNSON: No, might as well see me now as later. But I do have to get busy on these reports, so make it snappy. What is it?

FURMAN: Well . . . I just wanted to talk with you about . . . well, about me and the rest of the department. . . .

JOHNSON: Oh, that. Well, I'm glad you came to see me. I've noticed that you haven't done much to fit in since you've been here. I thought it strange that you kept to yourself all the time. I don't mind saying that it bothers me, since if you worked better with the other people we would have better coordination around here. You're going to have to decide what you're going to do. You'll have to take it upon yourself to get to know these people better. Talk to them . . . you'll find they're really a good bunch. Just go out there and jump in. You'll do OK. You've just got to give it a try.

At first glance it may seem unusual to include the topics of interviewing, counselling, and performance appraisal in the same chapter. They may seem like very different subjects. In fact, however, they have much in common. All are based on the effective use of communication skills, and the principles discussed in Chapter 10 are all relevant to these three topics.

Another way of looking at the relationship is illustrated in Figure 18.1. The common denominator among the three is communication. Communication is a major tool used in interviewing, and counselling and performance appraisal are simply two specific applications of the

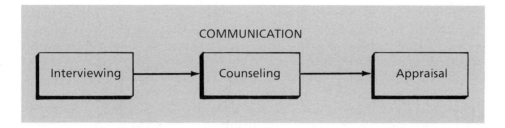

Figure 18.1. Relationship Among Interviewing, Counselling, and Performance Appraisal.

interviewing process. Also, the relationship between counselling and performance appraisal is such that the skills necessary for good counselling are also pertinent to conducting a good performance appraisal interview.

This chapter gives an overview of each topic and shows how an understanding of the interviewing process can lead to better counselling and performance appraisals.

Interviewing

The opportunities for conducting interviews are many: selection interviews for new employees, performance appraisal interviews for current employees, exit interviews for employees who are leaving, counselling interviews for those who are having problems on the job, or general purpose interviews that attempt to gather information on something pertaining to the supervisor's work unit. Depending upon the situation, different interviewing strategies should be used. In Chapter 13 the concepts of directive and nondirective interviewing were briefly introduced in connection with selection interviewing. This section develops the two interview styles in greater depth. We shall first explore the alternative interviewing methods available, and then show how they can be used by supervisors.

Directive Interviewing

The **directive interview** is the most basic type of interview. Often referred to as the structured or patterned interview, its major feature is that the interviewer (in this case, the supervisor), directs the interview. By directing, we mean that the supervisor determines the purpose, timing, content, and direction of the interview. The supervisor plays a dominant role and the interviewee a relatively passive role.

In this type of interview the supervisor asks relatively direct questions of the interviewee. This approach tends to confine the interviewee to a structured answer and the information provided seldom goes beyond the specific question asked.

When supervisors use the directive method, they are assuming (a) that they know exactly what information is needed, and (b) that the subordinate is willing to provide the information. If either of these two conditions is not met, the directive interview will not result in good communication. It may seem strange that a supervisor would initiate an interview not knowing what information is needed, but this is often the case. In a problem-solving situation, for example, the supervisor would know a problem exists, but may not know why, so the directive interview may not be appropriate. Even if the supervisor asked direct questions, if the subordinate felt threatened by the situation he or she might not be willing to give direct answers.

As a general rule, the directive approach is most suitable for situations that have little or no emotional (i.e., psychological) implications for either party. When problems or situations arise that can be dealt with by logic, reason, or other types of rational information, the directive approach is faster and more effective.

The Nondirective Approach

As we well know, organizational life is seldom logical or rational. Many things that normally occur have emotional and psychological implications for everyone. For these situations, the nondirective approach is generally recommended.

In the **nondirective interview**, the interviewer — or supervisor — plays a relatively passive role. Questions are phrased in very general terms to allow the interviewee — or employee — freedom to express feelings and emotions that may not come out under directive methods. The supervisor directs only to the extent that the general topic may be mentioned so that the employee knows the interview has a purpose. Beyond this, the supervisor only guides, suggests, or makes understanding and supportive comments to encourage the person to express his or her true feelings.

The primary role of the supervisor in nondirective situations is that of listener who listens not only for factual information, but also for the more subtle and underlying feelings that may be expressed. As we noted in Chapter 10, being a good listener requires sensitivity to what other people are really saying and knowing when they are being open with their feelings.

As Figure 18.2 illustrates, directive and nondirective methods can be viewed as two extremes of an interviewing continuum. As one moves

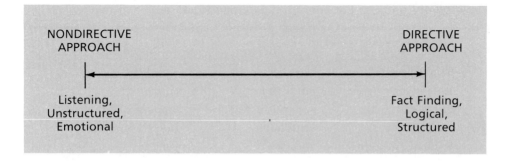

Figure 18.2. Directive and Nondirective Interviewing Style Continuum.

from one extreme to the other, various mixes of the two approaches are possible. Supervisors will seldom operate at either extreme; most situations require either a middle-of-the-road style or a mixture of styles that avoids the extremes.

When we use the nondirective method, the major assumption is that feelings, perceptions, attitudes, and values are more important than whatever facts may be present. It is also assumed that only in a nonthreatening, supportive climate will a subordinate talk freely about personal feelings. Finally, it is assumed that the major barrier to improved behavior is an individual's emotional state. That is, until employees have the opportunity to get things off their chest, their psychological and emotional state will hinder any improvement in performance.

Testing the New Supervisor

The importance of having good nondirective skills became apparent on one occasion when I was able to watch a new supervisor the first day on the job. He had been hired from outside and had been chosen over several internal candidates. No one in the work group knew him and there was a lot of talk over what he would be like. The morning of his first day was normal, but in the afternoon, several of the group members approached him about "something that bothered them." The new supervisor immediately led them to his office and closed the door.

About an hour later, they all emerged apparently in good spirits. I went to one of the men and asked what had happened. He said, "He listened to us. He's the first supervisor we've ever had who took the time to really listen to us instead of lecturing us on why he couldn't give us what we wanted." Of course I don't know for sure, but I suspect that the group chose that particular moment to confront the supervisor because it was a very good method of quickly finding out what kind of supervisor they had.

Table 18.1. Contrasts Between Directive and Nondirective Interviewing

Comparison factor	Directive	Nondirective
Time spent talking	most	very little
Role of supervisor	authoritative	supportive
End result	supervisor decides	employee decides
Atmosphere	structured	loose
Type of questions	specific	general
Supervisory response	evaluative	supportive
Training required	technical knowledge	listening skills
Time required	little	a lot
Efficiency rating	very efficient	relatively inefficient

The differences between directive and nondirective interviewing are summarized in Table 18.1.

Using Directive and Nondirective Methods

This section will give examples of how these two techniques can be applied to specific situations. The examples will have to be general, since every situation will be different. However, understanding the basic principles will assist you in deciding which technique in what proportion works best.

Two Basic Principles

There are two basic principles that underlie all interviews. The first is that interviews tend to follow a particular pattern, as is illustrated in Figure 18.3. This diagram indicates that most interviews follow a **funnel approach**. In other words, the interview begins in a relatively nondirective fashion and as it progresses, the supervisor adopts a more directive style. This can happen because the nondirective approach establishes a supportive climate between the supervisor and subordinate; once this is done, directive questions are perceived as less threatening than they would have been otherwise. Another reason the funnel approach can be used is because the nondirective method draws off any emotions that may be inhibiting responses from the employee so that subsequent directive questions can be answered more openly.

The second principle is that if you are unsure whether the situation you face requires directive or nondirective methods, it is best to begin

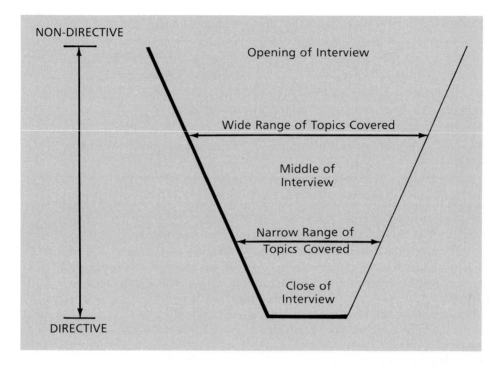

NON-DIRECTIVE

Opening of Interview

Wide Range of Topics Covered

Middle of
Interview

Narrow Range of
Topics Covered

Close of
Interview

DIRECTIVE

Figure 18.3. The Funnel Approach to Interviewing.

with the nondirective approach. This is because there is less risk of affecting the emotional state of the employee if, in fact, the situation is potentially emotional. If it turns out that nondirective methods are not needed, you can quickly switch to more directive means. However, if you are unknowingly facing a situation that has strong emotional and psychological implications and you begin with the directive approach, it is more difficult to change back to nondirective because damage may have already been done. More importantly, using the directive method may itself keep you from discovering that the nondirective method should have been used. The employee may withdraw and become very agreeable, leaving you with the impression that the interview was a success.

Applying the Two Methods

Table 18.1 shows that the skills required are very different. Basically, the directive method requires that you (a) know what information you want, and (b) be able to phrase questions in such a way that the interviewee

Table 18.2. Examples of Directive and Nondirective Questions

Directive	Nondirective
What is your work experience?	Tell me about your career.
Did you and your last supervisor get along?	How have you found your previous supervision?
Are you handling your job OK?	How are things going?
Are you having difficulty with your co-workers?	Tell me about your co-workers.

understands what you want. In other words, technical competence and clarity of communication are of paramount importance.

For the nondirective method, good listening skills and the ability to ask nonthreatening questions, to communicate understanding and empathy, and to interpret information are important. Questions in a nondirective interview are on the pattern of those in Table 18.2. In terms of implementing the two approaches, often it is only a matter of how questions are phrased, as the examples show. Table 18.2 shows several examples of how simply phrasing a question differently changes it from directive to nondirective.

Given these general principles of interviewing, we can now proceed to analyze which methods might be used in various types of situations.

Selection Interviews

As noted in Chapter 13, selection interviews are usually characterized by the need for factual information, at least in the initial stages. Later interviews can be used for different purposes and therefore would require different methods. If the supervisor needs factual information, the directive approach is usually best. For example, the supervisor may need to know an applicant's training, so it would be quite appropriate to ask directly for that information. Other items such as an applicant's experience and education can also be learned by the directive approach.

At later stages in the selection process, it might be advisable to change to more nondirective methods. Once the supervisor has decided that the factual information gained qualifies the applicant for the technical aspects of the job, it would be appropriate to learn more about the applicant's feelings and attitudes. If the supervisor attempts to use nondirective methods at the outset, the applicant may become suspicious and be very careful in his or her responses. But after the selection process has proceeded to a satisfactory point, the nondirective approach would be appropriate.

Exit interviews

Exit interviews present an interesting example of why it is impossible to state exactly which method should be used. Exit interviews are conducted just before an employee leaves the organization and are designed to gather information from the employee about his or her experiences with the organization. Often they are done by the personnel department, but there is no reason why the supervisor could not do them as well.

Since the employee has already decided to leave, he or she may be relatively uninhibited in responding to direct questions. If so, the directive approach would be the more appropriate. However, being interviewed by the supervisor would probably have a negative effect upon the employee's openness, so the nondirective method should be used. Establishing a nonthreatening supportive climate would encourage the employee to talk openly about his or her feelings.

It should be noted that exit interviews should never be used by a supervisor to solicit information about other employees. This type of spying would certainly threaten any remnants of a positive interviewing climate, and reports of underhanded methods would no doubt get back to the employees, seriously jeopardizing the trust and respect that is necessary between supervisor and subordinates.

The Investigative Interview

The term *investigative* here is not meant to describe an FBI type of inquiry. It simply means there are times when supervisors must interview employees for the purpose of gathering information about a decision, a proposal, or a past event. For example, suppose a particular shipment of finished goods did not get shipped on time and the supervisor wants to know why. This would call for an investigative interview. The supervisor is usually the initiator of the investigative interview, a fact that suggests that the approach should be directive.

During the course of the interview, however, the supervisor may perceive that there are feelings and attitudes that should come out as well. The supervisor may then switch to a more nondirective approach, but only after it appears the interviewee is not being open with the directive approach. Starting off an investigative interview with a nondirective approach may arouse the suspicions of the employee.

Concluding Remarks

Later in this chapter we will deal with two more types of interviews, the counselling interview and the performance appraisal interview. On the basis of the material already presented, however, we offer a few concluding remarks.

First, although directive and nondirective methods have been described as very different, one seldom uses the extremes of either. Most supervisors find that moderate degrees of each are more appropriate.

Second, most interviews will involve a combination of each method. This could be either the funnel approach mentioned earlier, or one in which the supervisor switches from directive to nondirective and back again as the situation warrants.

Third, the climate of any interview cannot be divorced from the rest of the organizational climate established by the supervisor. If the overall climate is punitive and negative, then no amount of effort at the nondirective technique will result in open and honest communication. Similarly, if a supervisor has established a warm supportive climate in which to work, directive interviewing methods may be more effective than in other environments.

Finally, although the theoretical descriptions of directive and nondirective interviewing are easy to understand, putting them into practice can be a different matter, indeed. Like any skill, effective interviewing requires practice before one feels comfortable with it. Through practice, one becomes more effective at deciding which approach is more appropriate, as well as more skillful at using the approach itself.

Supervision and Counselling

The counselling process is fundamental to every supervisor's job. It may involve a disgruntled employee, one who is experiencing difficulties on the job, or an individual who has a problem with alcoholism or drugs. Supervisors need the sensitivity and skill to deal with these problems.

The Need for Counselling

We often underestimate the need for counselling in organizations. There are many employees who have no one to turn to when they have problems. To help with this situation, many organizations employ people whose job is mainly to listen to the concerns, fears, and emotions of others. The problems they deal with range all the way fom alcoholism and drug abuse to parental anxieties. As one example of the need for such counselling, one branch of the Canadian Post Office employing approximately seven hundred employees recently established a Help Center that is available to all employees. In its first year of operation, it handled over eight hundred referrals. This means that some employees visited the center more than once, but we may still conclude that a large number of the employees needed some type of counselling assistance during the year.

What is Counselling?

Counselling is a process that establishes a climate in which people can deal with their problems. Oftentimes employees experience emotional and psychological problems that affect job performance. The origins of these problems are such that only the persons themselves can decide if and how they will deal with them. The role of the counsellor in these situations is to create an environment that will allow the individual to confront and deal with his or her problems.

Counselling is also a therapeutic process. Professional counsellors are experienced in dealing with numbers of clients with similar problems so they can provide advice as well as support and understanding. This type of therapy often takes long periods of time and in some instances, individuals are never able to overcome their problems.

The Role of the Supervisor

The specific role of the supervisor in counselling is a critical point in this discussion, for if it is misunderstood, supervisors could get themselves into areas in which they are not qualified. It is not the intent of this chapter to teach supervisors to be professional counsellors, but rather to develop an appreciation of what basic counselling skills can do and to recognize when and to what degree counselling is necessary.

The basic question often asked is, Should supervisors get involved with their employees' personal problems? The answer is a qualified "yes." If it becomes obvious that an individual's emotional or physical health is affecting his or her job performance, it becomes the supervisor's responsibility to deal with it. However, in many instances, dealing with it may mean only that the supervisor refers the employee to professional help. It does not mean that supervisors should attempt to counsel the employee themselves.

Similarly, it is a good rule of thumb that if an employee's personal situation is *not* affecting his or her job performance, the supervisor has no business getting involved. Of course each situation must be judged on its own merits. For example, a supervisor might know that an employee drinks too much, even though it doesn't affect job performance. The supervisor could decide to intervene on the grounds that the drinking may get worse and eventually affect performance. These are individual decisions that supervisors must make on their own. Strictly speaking, however, supervisors have no business getting involved in matters that are not job related.

In general, then, supervisors should not attempt to counsel employees in the professional sense. What is described in this section is the general application of counselling skills to situations in which the emotional state of the employee is interfering with his or her job performance. Some example are:

- an upset employee who has been passed over for promotion,
- an employee who feels neglected by the supervisor,
- an employee who doesn't agree with a supervisor's decision, or
- an employee who feels his or her importance in the work unit is not appreciated.

HOW MUCH COUNSELLING? In some cases supervisors may find that their counselling skills are so renowned that they become a dumping ground for everyone who has some personal problem. On the one hand, this has to be seen as good because it means that the supervisor is perceived as a sympathetic, understanding person. On the other hand, a supervisor could easily spend hours each day just listening to other people's problems.

At some point, you as a supervisor must decide when people are taking advantage of your listening skills (rather than your managerial skills) and nip the process in the bud. If their problems are truly serious, you can do them a favor by directing them to a professional counsellor, but in any case they must be informed that you cannot spend inordinate amounts of time in counselling sessions. So supervisors basically have two decisions to make, one on their own qualifications for counselling in specific situations and the other on the amount of time they can afford to spend in dealing with the emotional side of employees' work lives. While counselling is an important supervisory function, it should never take priority over the regular managerial duties that must be performed.

SHOULD YOU COUNSEL OTHERS' SUBORDINATES? This is a difficult issue because the strong people orientation in some of us causes us to lend a sympathetic ear to most people, whether they work for us or not. Clearly, one would not want to be seen as undermining the influence of other supervisors. At the same time, however, many supervisors would like to help others' subordinates, within their own time limits. Generally speaking, this would not cause problems if all you did was listen to someone's problems (note, however, that because you listened, you may be *seen* to be doing something more). The difficulty usually arises if you take action (or are perceived as taking action) as a result of your counselling. Other supervisors will resent not only the attention you are getting from their subordinates, but also the influence you apparently have with them.

So to the extent you have the desire and time to listen to the problems of people working for other supervisors, no serious danger exists. But beware of being tabbed the company social worker or being suspected of going behind the backs of your fellow supervisors. If someone else's subordinate asks that you do something as a result of your interview, either request that they tell their supervisor what they just told you, or inform them that you will have to talk with their supervisor before any action can be taken. The decision is theirs.

SHOULD YOU MAKE DECISIONS?   Experience suggests that the greatest fear that most supervisors have in counselling situations is that of having to make a difficult decision. They often feel that when a subordinate comes to them with a personal problem or concern, they will be placed in a position of having to take some form of action they don't want to.

Usually this happens when supervisors don't fully appreciate what counselling is all about. They fail to realize that in true counselling situations, the supervisor *cannot* solve the problem because the problem exists within the individual, not the supervisor or the organization. They do not understand the importance of listening to people and drawing off their emotions so they can deal with their concerns themselves.

So if supervisors aren't to make decisions in these situations, what can they do? If the counselling interview has proceeded satisfactorily and the employee's emotions have been released, the supervisor may begin to suggest alternative courses of action, or ask more directive questions that will prompt the employee to begin thinking about solutions. If the supervisor tells the employee what to do and the solution does not work, the employee may blame the supervisor.

Requirements for Effective Counselling

Certain characteristics are necessary to be an effective counsellor. They are very difficult to develop, but having an awareness of them will suggest what your chances are of performing the counselling function effectively.

First, you must be sensitive to other people's feelings. This is an obvious requirement since counselling is almost totally concerned with feelings. Supervisors who are insensitive to the feelings of others will not be able to interpret the data gathered and are likely to spend most of their time evaluating what the employee has said. It was noted in Chapter 10 that our tendency to evaluate is a significant barrier to good communication.

You must also be able to approach counselling situations with an open mind. If you believe you already have all the facts, then you will not be willing to listen sensitively to what the other person says. By definition, counselling interviews have little to do with facts or logic.

It is also necessary to have a basic belief in other peoples' ability to solve their own problems. This does not mean you are unwilling to help, but if you believe the other person is totally incapable of coping with the problem, you will not have much patience with him or her.

For instance, one of the areas in which many supervisors have difficulty is in dealing with problems of alcoholism, especially if the supervisor is a nondrinker. Nondrinkers often cannot understand why people ruin their lives with alcohol abuse when the negative effects are so obvious. Also, it appears to be such an easy problem to solve — they should simply stop drinking! The problem, of course, is that these supervisors are seeing the problem logically, and alcoholism is not a logical problem. It usually has strong emotional and psychological roots that must be dealt with before the problem can be solved. Not realizing this, some supervisors have little patience with alcoholics. It is no accident, of course, that the most effective counsellors in this field are former alcoholics.

Another characteristic of effective counsellors is that they accept people for what they are rather than what they should be. If we have some perfect model in our mind as to how employees should behave, we will continually be disappointed. Our disappointment will invariably show in our communication with them. When people feel that their behavior is understood rather than judged, they are more likely to be stimulated to initiate improvement.

Finally, effective counsellors are able to reflect feelings. Reflecting feelings shows the employee that he or she is being understood and accepted. This helps to establish the positive interview climate that is nec-

Understanding Can Cause Trouble

Though most of you will never encounter this situation, it does have a useful lesson for counselling. Several years ago during final examination week, a student came to me and I could tell he was upset about something. He looked tired, haggard, and generally distraught. After he sat down, he told me he had a serious problem. When asked what it was he replied, "I've missed two final exams this week." When I asked why, he said, "My father died three days ago."

Without really thinking, but trying to show sympathy and understanding, I replied, "Oh, I understand." He raised his head and asked, "Why? Is your father dead?" It was then I had to admit that my father was not dead, whereupon he said, "If your father is still living, there's no way you can understand how I feel."

At the time, the significance of his statement bypassed me as I thought he was just being a smart aleck. But as I thought about it later, I saw that what the student meant was that when I decided what was to happen to him as a result of missing two final exams, he wanted me to know that I really couldn't understand what he was going through. The lesson? be careful in using the words "I understand."

Exercise 18.1

Both of the exercises in this section allow you to do some role playing. The specifics of the roles will be given to you by your instructor, but here are the ground rules for playing roles:

1. Although you can play the role any way you like, you cannot change the facts given to you;
2. Act as you normally would under the circumstances given you;
3. You may interject any new information into the role provided it does not conflict with what you have been given;
4. The role play will have a time limit given by your instructor.

At the end of the role play, your interview will be debriefed by an observer.

---

essary for counselling to be effective. Feelings can be reflected either through the spoken word, such as "Yes, I understand," or through facial or other physical expressions.

The Counselling Process

Being an effective counsellor requires the application of nondirective interviewing methods. This means the role of the supervisor is primarily that of a listener. In some situations, it is conceivable that the employee would do 90 percent of the talking. The supervisor would guide the interview by asking questions of clarification or interpretation, and by communicating interest, empathy, and understanding to the employee. The principles outlined in Chapter 10 on communication are also useful guidelines for counselling interviews and should be reviewed.

To give you a flavor of how counselling interviews progress, below is an excerpt from an actual counselling session between an employee and his manager. The employee has come to his supervisor's office and opened with the classic line, "Boss, do you have a minute?"

EMPLOYEE: Boss, do you have a minute?
BOSS: Of course. Have a seat.
EMPLOYEE: It's about this whole place . . . (pauses)
BOSS: This whole place?
EMPLOYEE: Well, you know . . . what's going on and everything . . . (pauses)
BOSS: Un-huh.

EMPLOYEE: I'm just not satisfied with . . . well, you know . . . with where I'm going and everything.

BOSS: Un-huh.

EMPLOYEE: I've really felt that I've been doing good work lately and particularly proud of that last project I completed.

BOSS: Yes, I know. I'm glad you're proud.

EMPLOYEE: Well, that's just it. I'm happy about that job but I still feel frustrated about this place.

BOSS: How do you mean?

EMPLOYEE: Oh, I don't know . . . it's difficult to say sometimes . . . but I just don't feel right.

BOSS: Un-huh.

EMPLOYEE: Like yesterday for example. I know I did a good job on that special order for the Shipping Department, but after it was all done, I got a phone call from the supervisor over there bawling me out for taking so long. That really frosted me! After busting my buns to get their job done, all I get back is a bunch of complaints!

BOSS: You really got mad.

EMPLOYEE: You're damn right I did! I get so tired of busting my rear end around here and having no one appreciate it. Sometimes I feel like telling this whole place to go to hell!

BOSS: I can understand that.

Space prevents us from reporting the entire interview, but the outcome was that after talking over his feelings with his supervisor, the employee felt much better and went back to work. The supervisor did not have to take any action as a result of the interview because apparently all the employee wanted was to tell someone how he felt. Of course this would not always be the case.

Even in this brief excerpt it is possible to see the general pattern of the interview and draw some conclusions. First, it should be noted that this is a relatively common situation. In other words, the supervisor made use of counselling skills, even though this was not a case of alcoholism, drug abuse, or marital problems. This shows the wide applicability of counselling skills.

Second, the behavior of the supervisor deserves comment. Note that he never judged the employee's feelings or attempted to argue with him. He simply listened and reflected back his feelings of understanding. The climate created caused the employee to open up about his feelings (note that he was very hesitant at the outset) and begin discussing his problem. The employee dominated the conversation and the supervisor merely served as a catalyst in the process.

Finally, notice that the supervisor helped the employee deal with his own problem. There was nothing the supervisor could do to change his feelings except to listen to them. Imagine the effect of the statement, "Aw, don't get mad about a little thing like that." Trying to reason with someone who is emotional will probably make the situation worse.

Concluding Remarks

Using nondirective interviewing skills in counselling situations can be an effective technique, provided that you recognize your own limitations as a counsellor. Many employee problems you encounter will need professional help and you should not try to deal with these yourself. However, there are a great many situations in which counseling skills can be useful, as in dealing with employees who are angry, afraid, insecure, jealous, frustrated, or with customers or clients who are upset. Generally speaking, the principles of counselling can be used in any interpersonal situation in which emotions are involved.

Perhaps the main difference between effective and ineffective counsellors is how they see their own role. People who see themselves primarily as problem solvers tend to become frustrated at counselling techniques because they are not action oriented. Their tendency is to "get on with it" and get the problem solved. People who are more process oriented are less concerned with action and more concerned with the process by which results are achieved. For them counselling is an important process in the achievement of results. Your own orientation along these lines may affect how well you can utilize counselling skills.

Performance Appraisal Interviews

Experience suggests that the interview which is often conducted poorly is the performance appraisal interview. Both supervisors and subordinates dislike them; supervisors dislike them because they know the subordinate will rarely be totally satisfied with the appraisal, and subordinates dislike them because they resent being judged by someone who never sees them as they see themselves. The result is a situation in which both parties enter the interview uptight and, frequently, both leave in a worse state of mind than when they began. It seems that if this is generally the case, we would probably be better off not having performance appraisal interviews at all.

To address these problems we approach the appraisal process from two different perspectives: the philosophy behind performance appraisal, and the interview itself. The philosophy part is concerned with the objectives of performance appraisal, why we do it, when it should be done, and how it should be done. The interview part of the process is concerned with applying the concepts developed in this chapter to communicating the appraisal to the employee.

Purpose of Performance Appraisal

The primary purpose of performance appraisal is to provide feedback to employees regarding their performance. Unless employees know what they are doing right and wrong, they will probably not improve. Within this broad objective, performance appraisal is designed to improve poor performance and maintain good performance. The key, therefore, to effective performance appraisal is not to let the supervisor's concern with poor performance affect those areas in which an employee is performing well.

The basic purpose can be compromised by including other objectives in with performance appraisal. For example, some companies use performance appraisals to determine salary increases or promotions. While this may seem logical, it can negatively affect the basic purpose of conducting performance appraisals — which is to talk about *performance*, not salary or promotion.

When It Should Be Done

Many companies schedule annual or semiannual **formal performance appraisals,** usually for administrative convenience. The supervisor is required to complete an evaluation form and interview the employee within a specific period. In most cases, supervisors will have to stay with this schedule for *formal* appraisals.

However, it is possible to do an *informal* appraisal at any time. In Chapter 8 we noted the importance of quick feedback systems and how these can affect behavior, and it is because of this principle that informal appraisal systems can be more effective than formal ones. More importantly, unlike the formal appraisal, supervisors have complete control over informal appraisals so they can do them in addition to whatever the formal system requires.

The guiding principle for **informal performance appraisals** is that *performance should be appraised when it occurs.* This means that when employees do something good, they should be told, and when they do something bad they should be told that as well. These mini-appraisals provide the quick feedback that employees need and communicate in no uncertain terms what their supervisor thinks of their performance.

There is an added benefit from using the informal method. Part of the problem with the annual performance review is that for an entire year, the employee may have no feedback on his or her performance, and significant anxiety can build up by the time the employee enters the formal appraisal interview. If the informal method is used, the annual appraisal becomes more routine, the anxiety of each party is reduced, and better communication can result.

How to Do It

Before getting into the specifics of performance appraisal interviews, we list some general principles of conducting performance appraisals that are consistent with any interview format.

1. *Avoid reference to attitudes.* Attitudes are personal to each individual and may or may not have anything to do with the employee's work. Attitudes cannot be observed by other people and therefore it is risky to try to talk about them. The same purpose can be accomplished by making reference to behavior. For example, instead of saying, "I don't like your attitude around here," one can say, "I don't like your behavior around here." Unfortunately, many company appraisal forms require supervisors to evaluate the employee's attitude. This is a no-win situation for supervisors.

2. *Avoid criticizing the individual personally.* Separate the individual (who is good) from his or her behavior (which can be bad). People can accept the fact that they have done something wrong, but resent being told they are a bad person.

3. *Emphasize positive as well as negative factors.* Part of establishing a positive climate for effective performance appraisal is recognition of the positive behaviors as well as the negative ones. If employees receive only criticism and never any praise, they will view performance appraisals as a threatening and punitive event.

4. *Emphasize specifics.* Employees resent generalities if they cannot be backed up with specifics. Also, unless they know what events or actions you are using to make your appraisal, they have no benchmarks to use in making improvements.

5. *Set specific targets.* An appraisal should not end with just a general handshake and "thanks a lot." The employee should leave with a clear understanding of how his supervisor sees his performance, and some clear targets to shoot for in the future. Avoid generalities like, "I want you to improve in the future." In what specific ways should the employee improve? How long should it take? Follow-up by the supervisor at the appropriate time is also necessary.

6. *Avoid comparing employees.* People resent being compared unfavorably to other people. While we may admit to ourselves that others can do certain things better, we don't like to have this pointed out by a third person — especially our supervisor. Even worse is when the supervisor implies that a particular individual is a better person than we are. If you are going to compare, compare behaviors not individuals.

Exercise 18.2

This is another role-playing exercise which will be given to you by your instructor. The same ground rules apply as before. This will be a role play in performance appraisal, which will allow you to again use the principles of nondirective interviewing.

Types of Appraisal Interviews

Each of the preceding prescriptions is relevant for all appraisal interviews. However, different interview formats are necessary, depending upon the situation facing the supervisor. This section will present three alternative appraisal interview methods: tell and sell, tell and listen, and problem solving.[1]

Table 18.3 describes the basic characteristics of these three approaches to performance appraisal. In terms of the thrust of this chapter, two of the approaches — tell and listen and problem solving — use nondirective interviewing principles. Nondirective techniques are not relevant for the tell-and-sell method as this format has a different purpose than most appraisal interviews.

The Tell-and-Sell Method

As the name implies, in a **tell-and-sell** interview the supervisor informs the employee of the evaluation and attempts to convince him or her of the validity of the evaluation. Communication is primarily one way from supervisor to employee and the supervisor dominates the interview. The success of this approach depends heavily upon the supervisor's ability to communicate the facts about the employee's performance and, of course, the employee's willingness to accept the supervisor's evaluation.

As noted in Table 18.3, this approach is most likely to be successful when the employee has a great deal of respect for the supervisor. Otherwise, the interview will probably end in an argument. It would also be successful when the supervisor holds considerable power over the subordinate, although it could be that the subordinate would only withhold argument and merely give the impression that he or she agreed.

---

1. Norman R.F. Maier, *The Appraisal Interview* (La Jolla, CA: University Associates, 1976).

Table 18.3. Comparisons Among Three Types of Appraisal Interviews

Method	Tell and Sell	Tell and Listen	Problem Solving
Objectives	To communicate evaluation To persuade employee to improve	To communicate evaluation To release defensive feelings	To stimulate growth and development in employee
Psychological Assumptions	Employee desires to correct weaknesses if he knows them Any person can improve if he so chooses A superior is qualified to evaluate a subordinate	People will change if defensive feelings are removed	Growth can occur without correcting faults Discussing job problems leads to improved performance
Role of Interviewer	Judge	Judge	Helper
Attitude of Interviewer	People profit from criticism and appreciate help	One can respect the feelings of others if one understands them	Discussion develops new ideas and mutual interests
Skills of Interviewer	Salesmanship Patience	Listening and reflecting feelings Summarizing	Listening and reflecting feelings Reflecting ideas Using exploratory questions Summarizing
Reactions of Employee	Suppresses defensive behavior Attempts to cover hostility	Expresses defensive behavior Feels accepted	Problem-solving behavior
Employee's Motivation for Change	Use of positive or negative incentives or both Extrinsic: motivation is added to the job itself	Resistance to change reduced Positive incentive Extrinsic and some intrinsic motivation	Increased freedom Increased responsibility Intrinsic motivation — interest is inherent in the task
Possible Gains	Success most probable when employee respects interviewer	Employee develops favorable attitude toward superior, which increases probability of success	Almost assured of improvement in some respect
Risks of Interview	Loss of loyalty Inhibition of independent judgment Face-saving problems created	Need for change may not be developed	Employee may lack ideas Change may be other than what superior had in mind

Method	Tell and Sell	Tell and Listen	Problem Solving
Probable Results	Perpetuates existing practices and values	Permits interviewer to change his views in light of employee's responses Some upward communication	Both learn, because experience and views are pooled Change is facilitated

Source: Reprinted from: Norman R. F. Maier, *The Appraisal Interview: Three Basic Approaches*, San Diego, CA: University Associates, Inc., 1976. Used with permission.

The information in Table 18.3 gives a pretty dim picture of the tell-and-sell method. This is because the information in that table does not consider the circumstances of the subordinate. There are some instances in which this method is the best approach for performance appraisal. The most appropriate situation is for new employees. New employees are not in a position to share in problem solving or to give feedback on their own perceptions. Their immediate need is for concrete feedback on what their supervisor thinks of their performance. These people are still learning and the information they need to continue their learning is vastly different from that needed by senior, experienced employees.

The tell-and-sell method might also be used for extremely difficult performance problems. Imagine an employee, new or otherwise, who is performing extremely poorly. As a last step before dismissal, a good tell-and-sell interview may make an improvement, since it will leave the employee in no doubt as to what the supervisor has in mind.

Other than these specific cases, the tell-and-sell method is not generally recommended, because the negative outcomes as described in Table 18.3 usually result. Unfortunately, many supervisors do use the tell-and-sell method, probably because it is the quickest way out of a potentially unpleasant situation. Mature and responsible adults resent being told how they are doing. This violates all we know about effective communication and participation on the job.

The Tell-and-Listen Method

Tell and listen differs from tell and sell primarily in the quantity and direction of communication that occurs. Here the supervisor informs the subordinate of the evaluation, but is willing to listen to the subordinate's opinions as well. Listening skills are important in this method because subordinates must feel that their supervisor is appreciative and understanding of their feelings.

The opportunity for feedback makes the employee feel more a part of the interview. Two-way communication with a supervisor who understands the subordinate's opinions can increase the subordinate's motivation to improve. This method also allows for the supervisor to change the evaluation based upon information provided by the subordinate.

Tell and listen could be used for employees who are still learning, but are not new employees. People experiencing a new job or task need some fairly directive feedback on how well they are doing, and would welcome the supervisor's opinion, as well as the opportunity to express their feelings about it.

The Problem-Solving Method

It is with **problem solving** that the nondirective technique is used extensively. The two parties to the interview share influence, with the supervisor playing the role of supporter and helper rather than evaluator. Performance problems are viewed as just that — problems — and each party is willing to share in the responsibility for solving the problem.

Given the nondirective approach of the problem-solving method, change is more likely to occur because the subordinate will be less defensive during the interview. With defenses and anxiety reduced, efforts can be concentrated on joint problem solving and strategies for improvement. In each of the other methods, defensive reactions of the subordinate are both possible and probable.

The problem-solving approach would likely start out with a probing, but nonthreatening question by the supervisor. Playing a nondirective role by listening, supporting, and understanding, the supervisor will learn how the subordinate perceives his or her own performance, and what barriers to improvement are present. The supervisor seldom has to tell employees what their performance is like in these circumstances; the climate created will be such that the employee will freely talk about his or her concerns.

The problem-solving approach is not for everyone. It would be nice if it could be used with all employees, but this is not practical. As we noted previously, some employees need to be told in no uncertain terms how they stack up. But other employees, and possibly the majority, can responsibly participate in a joint problem-solving session with their supervisor. This method is most often recommended for experienced employees who have the maturity to accept responsibility for their own behavior. It is these same employees who resent both the tell-and-sell and tell-and-listen methods.

Perhaps the best way to view these three methods is not as separate interviews themselves, but different strategies that can be used within the same interview. One method may dominate the interview, but the supervisor might change from one to the other as the situation requires.

Nor do the interview methods normally fall into the discrete categories suggested here. Moving from tell and sell to problem solving can involve some very subtle changes. The key to using the three methods is to be sensitive to the requirements of the situation and be able to use each interview method as the situation demands. You should emphasize your tell-and-sell skills as much as your problem-solving skills because you will eventually need both.

Key to Success

Many occasions arise in which supervisors must interview others. These could be subordinates, fellow supervisors, customers, or higher-level managers. Effective interviewing consists of (a) clearly identifying the purpose of the interview, (b) knowing what type of skills the interviewer should use in those circumstances, and (c) being able to practice those skills effectively.

To make maximum use of these skills, you should remember that interviewing skills can be used in situations other than formal interviews. Daily face-to-face communications are subject to the same influences that affect interviews. Therefore, the concepts and skills presented in this chapter can have far-reaching effects. The more you appreciate the skills involved in interviewing, counselling, and performance appraisal, the better you will be in all types of communication.

Summary

Interviewing skills are important to every supervisor. Two instances in which these skills are useful are in counselling situations and performance appraisals. The two primary interviewing styles are the directive and the nondirective. The directive style is best used for situations in which specific factual information is desired, and the nondirective style is best used when dealing with situations in which there are strong psychological or emotional implications. Most interviews will be a combination of the two.

The nondirective style tends to generate more information than the directive one. This is why the technique is useful in selection, exit, investigative, counselling, and performance appraisal interviews. However, the supervisor must have the skill to sort out all the information and interpret its meaning.

One of the important roles of supervisors is that of counsellor. Supervisors should be cautious not to probe into areas in which they are not qualified, but there are some important counselling functions that they can and should perform. Supervisors should also recognize the problems associated with being an effective counsellor and be careful to keep the counselling function in proper perspective. Supervisors cannot solve emotional problems for employees, but they can set a climate in which the employees can deal with problems themselves. In order to be effective counsellors, supervisors must be sensitive to other people's feelings, have an open mind, have a basic belief in other people's abilities to cope with their problems, and be able to accept people for what they are rather than what they should be.

Performance appraisal interviews are often difficult because supervisors lack the proper interviewing skills. There are three basic ways of doing a performance appraisal interview: the tell-and-sell method, the tell-and-listen method, and the problem-solving method. Each is an appropriate strategy for specific situations. The tell-and-sell method is primarily directive, the problem-solving method is primarily nondirective, and the tell-and-listen method is a little of both.

Opening Incident Revisited

Johnson's behavior represents an example of a supervisor who is an insensitive listener. Although he is trying to be helpful to Furman, Johnson has failed to realize that Furman's problem is not as easy as "go ahead and jump in there."

If we go back to the beginning of the incident, we can see that Johnson doesn't even take the time to find out what Furman really wants. He *thinks* he knows what Furman wants to talk about, but he doesn't really know for sure. It could be that Furman actually wants to talk about a totally different matter than what Johnson has brought up.

Knowing when nondirective skills should be used requires a degree of sensitivity on the part of the supervisor. Johnson did not have the sensitivity to read Furman's behavior. To the sensitive individual, it would appear that Furman is overly hesitant to speak his mind and is choosing his words very cautiously. Seeing this, a sensitive supervisor would have used nondirective methods to draw Furman out and learn how he feels. Instead, Johnson plays a very directive and evaluative role and instructs Furman on what he should be doing. Even if he is talking about the correct matter, it is still unlikely that Furman will rush out and change his behavior. It is possible that Furman has a deep, personal concern that is bothering him and needs to talk to someone about it. If Johnson reacts in a supportive manner, Furman may open up about his feelings. But in the circumstances described here, it is unlikely that will happen.

Should Johnson even get involved in this matter? Yes, inasmuch as he feels that Furman's behavior is affecting the work of the department. But if he does try to get to the source of the problem, he may find that the problem is deeper than what he can handle. In that case, it will be Johnson's responsibility to see that Furman gets whatever help he needs.

Review Questions

1. What is directive and nondirective interviewing and how are they different?
2. Why should supervisors have good interviewing skills?
3. What are the major assumptions underlying the directive method of interviewing?
4. What is the primary role of the supervisor in nondirective interviewing?
5. What is the funnel approach and how is it used?
6. What are the major assumptions underlying the nondirective interviewing method?
7. What are the major skills required in directive and nondirective interviewing methods?
8. In which types of interviews could nondirective skills be used?
9. What is counselling and what is the supervisor's role in it?
10. What are the requirements for being an effective counsellor?
11. Why are performance appraisals often difficult for supervisors?
12. What can a supervisor do to improve the performance appraisal process?
13. What are the general principles of conducting performance appraisal interviews?
14. What are the three basic types of appraisal interviews, and when should each be used?

Chapter Glossary

Directive interviewing	An approach to interviewing in which the interviewer decides the direction and content of the interview. Consists of asking the proper questions and obtaining factual information. Interviewee plays a passive role in the interview.
Nondirective interviewing	An approach to interviewing in which the interviewer sets a positive, nonthreatening climate which encourages the interviewee to talk about his or her feelings and emotions. Interviewer plays a passive role in the interview and poses questions that will encourage interviewee to discuss his or her feelings.
Funnel approach	An approach to interviewing in which the interviewer uses a combination of directive and nondirective methods. Usually begins with nondirective approach and then becomes more directive after interviewee releases emotions.
Selection interview	An interview in the preemployment process in which the supervisor attempts to gain information which will assist in selection decision.
Exit interview	An interview conducted after an employee gives notice of terminating employment. Objective is to gather in-

formation that will assist the supervisor to manage more effectively.

Investigative interview	A general-purpose interview conducted to gather information. May be directive or nondirective.
Counselling	A process of setting a climate in which an individual feels free to speak about his or her feelings, attitudes, or beliefs. Objective is the removal of the emotional barrier(s) that prevents clear thinking.
Performance appraisal (formal)	Required evaluation by a supervisor of the performance of subordinates. Usually consists of completion of a written form and an interview with the employee to communicate the supervisor's evaluation
Performance appraisal (informal)	The practice of communicating an evaluation as performance occurs rather than on a regularly scheduled basis.
Tell-and-sell method	A directive approach to conducting a performance appraisal. Supervisor communicates the evaluation to employee and then attempts to convince the employee of its validity.
Tell-and-listen method	Combination of directive and nondirective methods in performance appraisals. Supervisor communicates evaluation to subordinate, but also listens to employee's perceptions about performance.
Problem-solving method	Nondirective method of conducting performance appraisal. Supervisor and subordinate share in the communication process and work together to maintain or improve performance.

Case Problem

Whiting Textiles, Inc.

Marie Grissom supervises ten designers in the product development division of Whiting Textiles, Inc. All of the designers are graduates of textile design programs and have been with Whiting for several years. The company requires supervisors to conduct performance appraisals of all their employees once each year. It is now that time of year, and Marie prepared her evaluations last week. She decided that on Friday of this week she would conduct all the interviews in one day. She sent a brief memo to all her employees telling them that she would have the performance appraisal interviews that day.

One of the designers is Ginger Cortez who has been with Whiting for seven years. After reviewing her file over the past year, Marie jotted down a few notes and called Ginger in for the first interview.

MARIE: Hi, Ginger. Come in and have a seat.
GINGER: Thanks.
MARIE: Ginger, I've been thinking about your performance over the past year and

I've jotted a few things down here we can talk about. I've filled out the evaluation form and you can have a copy for yourself if you'd like. Basically, I think your performance has been OK. You've very dependable and I know that when I give you a job I don't have to worry. You're a good person to have around here because you get along well with the other people.

GINGER: Thanks.

MARIE: That's ok. you know how much I value cooperation between all the staff.

GINGER: Yes, I know that.

MARIE: There are a few things, though, that I am concerned about. You have been taking longer coffee breaks than you should. I noticed that began happening several months ago when you started having coffee with those people over in data processing. So I'm going to have to rate you lower on our punctuality criteria than I did last year.

GINGER: But I've been working late several evenings to get those rush designs out, so I figured I was due a couple of extra minutes or so.

MARIE: Well, that may be, but it looks bad for the rest of the staff if you break the rules. Also, I noticed that on several occasions you refused to help some of the other people when they asked for it. With your experience and talent, I expect you to help some of the newer ones.

GINGER: I used to help them. But then I discovered they were unloading all their work on me . . . and I was already swamped. So now I just figure they can do their own.

MARIE: But that's not a very cooperative attitude. If everybody did that we would really have problems. Don't you see?

GINGER: Well, I don't see why I should carry everyone else in the department.

MARIE: I don't expect you to. Just do your fair share and help the others when you can.

Questions for Discussion

1. Comment on how this interview is progressing?
2. What style of interviewing is Marie using?
3. What do you think will be the probable result of the interview?

Managing Change

19

Chapter Learning Objectives

After reading and studying this chapter you should be able to:

1. List and describe the reasons why employees resist change.

2. Describe the difference between rational and emotional resistance to change.

3. List some types of changes that employees are likely to resist.

4. List and describe methods for overcoming resistance to change.

5. Describe the conditions under which change should be implemented quickly and when it should be implemented slowly.

Key Terms

Rational resistance to change

Participation

Emotional resistance to change

Quid pro quo

487

Opening Incident

Changing Spaces

The Allied Printing Company recently purchased new facilities to accommodate the growth in its business. The new facilities are larger than the old, but the space is not divided in the same way. Some units end up with more space, and some with less. One of the units that has more space is the accounting department. Their previous quarters were cramped and poorly lighted, and they were isolated from the rest of the company, but morale was high and the unit had no difficulty keeping up with its workload.

The planning for the move went on for six months. Although the employees were not directly involved in the planning, supervisors were kept informed about progress. When the move finally took place, employees left the old building on Friday and came to work at the new one on Monday. The new environment appeared to be much better. There was more room, the lighting was good, and all of the clerical employees were placed in a single large room.

After only one week in the new location, the complaints began to surface. Some complained that the lighting was too bright, others that there was too much glare on their desks. Others said the work area was too noisy and it was hard to concentrate on what they were doing. The employees in the accounting department appear to be the most upset. It seems that their practice of bringing in morning and afternoon snacks was stopped after the office manager complained to the accounting supervisor that it was causing difficulty with the rest of the workers. Now, at the end of the first month, the accounting supervisor is surprised that the department is ten days behind in its billing.

Managing change is a phrase that probably comes closest to describing the essence of a supervisor's job. Practically everything a supervisor does is concerned in some way with implementing change. Hiring a new employee (changing the work group), purchasing a new piece of equipment (changing work methods), rearranging the work stations (changing workflow), all require knowledge of how to manage change effectively.

Being able to manage change requires a large part of the knowledge and many of the skills discussed in previous chapters. Knowledge about motivation, leadership, group dynamics, causes of behavior, and communication are all important in understanding how change processes can be managed effectively. It is useful, therefore, to view this chapter as the integration and application of much of what has been presented in the previous chapters.

This chapter is divided into two parts: the first part analyzes the reasons why people resist change; the second discusses some of the strategies available to supervisors to overcome this resistance.

The Positive Side of Change

Although resistance to change is frequently encountered by supervisors, not all changes are resisted. In fact, if we looked at any organization closely we would probably find that far more changes are accepted than resisted. It is only because the instances of resistance are the notable exceptions that resistance to change gains so much attention. Although we tend to characterize employees as "antichange," in fact, human beings are the most adaptable creatures on earth. It is probably this singular characteristic that has allowed our survival thus far and will continue to do so in the future.

Accepting the fact that people have a natural instinct to adapt to their environment is the first step towards effective management of change. It not only has the advantage of placing people in a more positive light, but it also suggests that resistance to change is an *unnatural* behavior and is probably a result of the situation in question rather than any built-in response to change. If supervisors first accept this premise, they can then proceed to analyze the situation to find the cause of resistance.

An Example of Change

As a means of illustrating the fact that adapting to change is a natural process for people, let us begin with a common belief about change, that is, that the bigger the change, the greater the resistance. This belief is an outgrowth of the theory that small changes can be implemented with little difficulty, but larger ones usually meet resistance — if for no other reason than because more people are affected. We begin our analysis with an example.

> My place of residence — Winnipeg, Canada — has many positive features and only one negative one: the winter. Our winters are long and cold, temperatures occasionally reaching 40 below zero. Winnipeggers are noted for their tendency to take winter vacations and any winter day will see hundreds — perhaps thousands — of people at the airport waiting to board airplanes to the south. When you stop to think about it, these people are going through a major change process: they are changing physical location (and often this means a totally different culture), their daily habits, their manner of dress, and their social contacts. In short, they are going to experience a major change in their total environment. And yet, rather than showing resistance to the change, they are eager to experience it and are even willing to pay large sums of money for the privilege! So much for resistance to change.

This example has some important lessons for supervisors. It illustrates that people do not necessarily resist change, even large ones. If we can discover why a change such as a winter vacation is readily accepted, we can apply what we learn to changes in organizations. Therefore, we will analyze our example to develop principles relating to why people accept change. These principles will then form the basis for our discussion of resistance to change.

Reasons for Accepting Change

The major reasons why people accepted the changes described in the example are:

1. *It is their choice.* All of the people are taking a winter vacation because they want to, not because they have to. No one is forcing the change upon them. The opportunity to determine one's own destiny is an important one and resistance is often met when change is forced.

2. *The change is for the better.* Each of the vacationers anticipates a positive experience. This outcome is practically assured because (a) they have done it before, or (b) they have talked with others who have. For those who do not like warm weather, this change would not be positive — and they are therefore not going.

3. *The change satisfies a need.* If you interviewed everyone on a plane, you would find a variety of motivations for his or her trip, although the warm weather would probably be common to all. But regardless of the individual reasons, you would find that the trip is satisfying each individual's needs to some degree.

4. *Everyone is fully informed.* Each person has been involved in the change from the start. He or she has talked with travel agents, read literature, and interacted with others who have had similar experiences. All information needed to make the trip was acquired, thus reducing the anxiety associated with the change.

5. *The change is planned.* It is unlikely that anyone taking the trip is doing it on the spur of the moment. Most have planned months ahead so that when the change occurs, they will be ready — both physically and psychologically — for it.

Given this analysis of why the travelers are accepting such a drastic change, it follows that if the same conditions can be created on the job, employees might accept change just as readily. Of course it is well known that they do not, so it must be that many changes implemented in organizations lack the characteristics of the change just described.

Analyzing Resistance to Change

Each of the foregoing points suggests ways in which resistance to change can be decreased. Later in this chapter we shall explore in detail specific strategies for reducing resistance to change. For the present, however, we must first understand the reasons why people resist change, still keeping in mind that many changes are not resisted.

Economic Reasons

Many people see change as a threat to their economic well-being and security. Technological changes in particular can have this effect, as they tend to displace people from jobs. For example, post office workers have traditionally resisted technological changes such as automated letter sorting because these are a threat to job security. Resistance to change can also occur simply because the employee doesn't know or understand the effect of a change on his or her economic position. Uncertainty in these situations usually has negative efects. In other words, the no-news-is-good-news philosophy is definitely not true when it comes to economic and job security.

As is the case with all sources of resistance, the important factor is the *perception* of the individual. There may not be any actual threat to economic security in a proposed change, but if people perceive that there is, they will behave accordingly. This can be frustrating for the supervisor who knows that the change holds no economic threat, but supervisors must deal with the problem as perceived by the employees, not by themselves.

Social Reasons

Chapter 9 dealt with the problems supervisors face in managing groups of employees, and noted that the social relationships established within groups can be important determinants of behavior. For the same reasons, groups will resist change if the change is seen to be threatening to the group's norms of behavior. For example, many changes proposed by supervisors affect the work flow in the unit, which therefore changes the social relationships that have been established. A rearrangement of desks in an office may have severe repercussions on the way the group is used to conducting its business. We also know that group norms can be major influences on employee behavior and any change that violates a group norm will be resisted.

Status Reasons

Changes almost always affect the social status of employees. Over a period of time, the status system within a group becomes firmly established and any change that touches this system is likely to meet with resistance. Again, technological changes can be a major cause of status problems because they may alter job skill requirements and responsibility levels. A common example today is the introduction of word processors in offices. Former typists suddenly become operators of high-technology equipment, and this often has adverse effects on the status of others. Automation generally has the opposite effect because it reduces the skill level needed in jobs and so lowers the status of those occupying the jobs.

It is difficult to conceive of any organizational change that will not affect someone's status. Physical change in a unit's layout or space allocation, implementation of a new work procedure, insertion of a new employee into the work group, or purchase of a new piece of equipment will have effects, not only upon the specific employees, but also upon others in the system.

Security Reasons

One of the things we all strive for in our lives is some degree of security and predictability in our environment. The strength of this need varies from person to person, but we all have a need for some degree of security. The preservation of this security blanket requires that we resist changes that create uncertainty. Many changes are designed at the upper levels of the organization, and are then passed down to supervisors for implementation. These types of changes create uncertainty in employees because they had no role in designing them. It is only the changes that we control ourselves that minimize the negative effects of uncertainty.

Ego Reasons

Resistance caused by the ego is closely related to the status problem. Examining resistance from this perspective, however, provides a different focus upon a problem that is common in many organizations but is seldom understood. Many changes have the net effect of making competent employees feel incompetent. Again, changes of a technological nature seem to fit this category most often, although they are not the only ones.

The New Truck Problem

One of the classic cases in implementing change is a case referred to as the "new truck problem." The supervisor of a repair crew for a public utility is faced with the problem of introducing one new truck into a crew of ten employees, all of whom drive older trucks of various ages, mileages, and models. To complicate the situation, the seniority of employees varies considerably and the requirements of their jobs differ somewhat (some drivers have to drive farther than others). The problem the supervisor faces is to introduce this one new truck into the group with a minimum of bad feelings, and also remove the worst truck for trade-in. The status implications of this decision are quite complicated because assigning the new truck to any one driver will affect the status of all the others.

Making Good People Incompetent

A good example of this unintentional creation of incompetent employees was given to me in a supervisory training program. A particular company dealt in buying and shipping grain and for years had used standard weights and measures for calculating prices, volumes, and shipping rates. A change in the federal regulations made it necessary to begin using the metric system, which is a major change for anyone not educated in it. One supervisor could not adapt. She resisted the change for as long as possible, despite the company's attempts to train her in metric measurements. It was finally determined that she simply could not understand the metric system and felt frustrated as a supervisor since all of her subordinates had adapted with little trouble. Her feelings of inadequacy were finally so great that she had to be transferred to a different department that was not directly involved with metric calculations.

Consider an employee who has been performing a job in a certain way for a long time. The supervisor institutes a change in the job that alters the way the employee must do it. Depending upon the magnitude of the change, the employee could now feel incompetent because he or she is not as efficient at the new job as in the old one. If the change is a major one, the employee could easily experience considerable frustration since he or she is not used to feeling inadequate. For individuals with strong ego needs, these feelings could be devastating, as illustrated above.

Most of the changes that normally occur in organizations do not evoke the strong reaction described in the metric example above. Nevertheless, it is a fact that any change in job design, job content, or job procedures will, temporarily at least, turn a competent employee into an incompetent one.

The Path-of-Least-Resistance Reason

A general source of resistance to change is often called the path-of-least-resistance phenomenon. This is really a way of saying that many times people resist change simply because they have no compelling reason to go along with it. It's not that they don't want it, it's just that it is far easier (both psychologically and physically) to stay with the status quo. For example, if I like soft drink X and you want me to switch to soft drink Y, you must give me a reason to switch; otherwise, I will stay with brand X. Since I like brand X now, to switch to brand Y will cause all sorts of mental anguish that I would prefer to avoid if possible (the psychologists call this "dissonance," that is, the uncertainty associated with two satisfactory alternatives). This, of course, is why soft drink companies devise all sorts of incentives to get us to try their brands, such as prizes, price discounts, and so forth.

Exercise 19.1

Why Do You Resist Change?

We often think of resistance to change as something characteristic of other people. Yet, if we are to consider ourselves as normal individuals, it must be that we also resist change from time to time. Using your own work experience, think of a change that you resisted in your organization. After thinking through the experience thoroughly, list the reasons why you resisted the change — and be honest with yourself! Share your example with others and see if they understand why you resisted. Do they agree that your resistance was reasonable? Why or why not?

The same phenomenon occurs in organizations. The inertia of the present situation, the satisfaction with the present state of affairs, and the lack of a good reason to change, all serve to create resistance to many proposed changes. This tends to happen more frequently with the smaller changes; larger changes will be seen to have greater costs and rewards and therefore evoke strong feelings one way or another. The resistance may still be present, but for one or more of the other reasons listed above.

Emotional Versus Rational Resistance to Change

As the previous analysis suggests, people resist change for a variety of reasons. When a change we must implement is met with resistance, we must first find out if the reasons are rational or emotional. Depending upon which they are, different strategies would be used to overcome the resistance.

The distinction between emotional and rational resistance to change is sometimes difficult to make in practice. The supervisor cannot ask subordinates if their resistance is emotional or rational because we always see ourselves as rational people. Some would even be upset if it was suggested they were resisting because of emotional reasons. In the final analysis, the judgment must be made by the supervisor. The best test is usually to provide all the *facts* and the *reasons* for a change, which should satisfy **rational resistance**. If this has no effect upon the resistance, then it is probably emotional.

In **emotional resistance to change** feelings of fear, anxiety, and suspicion are evoked because of the individual's *perception* of how the change will affect him or her. Because of the personal nature of emotional resistance, it is often difficult for others to understand. The supervisor can easily see how a proposed change will benefit an employee, but often the employee cannot understand because of emotional blocks. Change is viewed from an individual frame of reference, and to understand properly how a change looks to another person, you must put yourself in his or her shoes.

The bank example below shows how the perceptions of employees can affect the implementation of change. The supervisor was equipped with the facts relevant to the change; what was overlooked was how the change would be viewed by those most affected — the operators themselves. The example also illustrates another important aspect of the change process. There is no such thing as a good or bad reason for resistance to change — there is only resistance. Supervisors who make value judgments regarding reasons for resistance will reveal their lack of understanding of the problem, and thus probably increase the resistance. For example, it is tempting to think of the resistance described in (d) of the bank example as stupid and childish, but the fact remains that these are very real feelings that must be dealt with. Failure to do so will only aggravate the situation.

The complicating factor in this process is that, unfortunately, employees are not always frank with the supervisor. You may ask subordinates how they feel about a proposed change and they may express

Dealing with Resistance to Change

I once observed a change process in a bank that illustrated the difference between emotional and logical resistance to change quite well. The bank had decided to replace some older check processing equipment with newer and more sophisticated electronic data processing equipment. Working with the supervisor of the group, the manufacturer spent considerable time with the operators showing them how much more efficient the new machines were, as well as how easy they were to operate. Studies had proved that the new machines were 50 percent faster than the old ones.

Resistance to the new machines was strong, and the supervisor was having difficulty getting the operators to accept them. The resistance was also frustrating to the supervisor and hard to understand because the machines offered so many benefits to the employees. The supervisor then decided to initiate more discussions with employees regarding the resistance. These discussions revealed that (a) because the new machines were so much faster, employees were afraid of layoffs; (b) the new machines reduced the skill required in the jobs so the status associated with mastery of the job would be reduced; (c) the more experienced operators (who were offered the first machines) resented having to learn a new job in the presence of their peers; and (d) some of the operators had formed emotional attachments to their old machines (some had given them names such as "Tessie" and "Clyde") and did not want to give them up.

agreement, but the sensitive supervisor will be able to detect the less than enthusiastic reaction. The key is for supervisors to know their subordinates well so they can detect when a reaction is abnormal — as it is likely to be for a change they really are not enthusiastic about. Only under ideal circumstances will a subordinate be totally honest with his or her supervisor, and therefore supervisors must constantly be on the watch for the differences between what subordinates *say* and what they *feel.*

The principal lesson to be learned from this section is that supervisors who have the sensitivity to understand emotional reactions to organizational changes will have more success in implementing these changes than will a supervisor who sees everything as logical, factual, and in black-and-white terms. This latter type of supervisor tends to ramrod changes through with little feeling for how the change affects the employees. Resistance is dealt with as a problem that can be solved by providing more factual information about the change. If lack of information is a problem, this solution will reduce resistance. Unfortunately, the experience of many supervisors suggests that resistance to change is seldom due to lack of adequate information.

Types of Changes
That Arouse Resistance

In addition to the general sources of resistance to change, there are specific types of events that may cause resistance. These events occur as a result of many different change processes and are therefore likely to be encountered by supervisors. The mere fact that they are resisted does not mean that supervisors should avoid them, but understanding the potential dangers can assist in reducing the resistance. It should also be understood that these types of changes *generally* are resisted, but by no means is it always true.

Changes frequently resisted are changes that:

- reduce the skill required in jobs,
- reduce status,
- disrupt established social relationships,
- threaten psychological or job security,
- are not fully understood,
- violate norms of behavior,
- affect accepted ways of doing things,
- are forced upon people,
- reduce the information flowing to people,
- reduce social interaction opportunities,

- make people feel ineffective or incompetent,
- reduce the power and influence of people,
- ✓ reduce personal privacy,
- reduce personal authority,
- expose personal weaknesses, or
- cost employees more than they benefit.

From the length of this list it would almost appear that it is impossible for a supervisor to implement any changes at all. To some extent, this is true. Most changes proposed by management are designed to reduce costs and/or improve efficiency, and often they have negative effects on the work experiences of the employees. But with our better understanding of *why* the changes are resisted, we can now begin to examine ways of reducing the resistance.

⚡ Overcoming Resistance to Change

Overcoming resistance to change is seldom a matter of only a single strategy. Because change itself is a complex process with many potential ramifications, the supervisor must usually use several strategies simultaneously. Even this is sometimes not enough to overcome extremely strong resistance.

As in other problem-solving situations, anticipation of the problem is superior to attempting to deal with it after it has occurred. With some idea of the types of events most likely to arouse resistance, you are better equipped to take preventive measures. But there will always be situations in which this is neither possible nor probable, so this section also includes strategies for dealing with change after the resistance arises.

As we noted in the earlier chapters on the role of the supervisor, the uniqueness of the supervisory role presents some problems in itself, and these can severely limit your alternatives. Therefore, we have tried to concentrate on those strategies that are likely to be available to most supervisors. Some of the changes that supervisors must implement are handed down from higher levels. The same principles will operate, but the supervisor will still be at a disadvantage because much of the planning for the change will be done before the supervisor is involved. An unfortunate situation, to say the least, but nevertheless quite common.

Participation in the Change

One of the methods most often used to overcome resistance to change is to arrange **participation,** involvement in the change of those affected by it. There is an old saying: "The people in the boat with you never bore a hole in it." If employees participate in the change, they are provided with more information about it, and they have the opportunity to exert influence with their own ideas. Participation serves to reduce (though not eliminate) some of the anxiety associated with the change and gives the participants some ownership of the change itself. Commitment is also increased so that the actual implementation tends to be easier.

Participation, however, is not without some potential problems. When you decide to involve your employees in the change, you must be prepared to accept their ideas. If participation is used as a manipulative process simply to get the participants to agree with your proposal, the process will backfire and create resentment. Participation must be real.

There is also the question of at *what stage* in the change process the employees should become involved. If they are invited in during the early planning stages, not only will they probably not have the necessary information to make adequate suggestions, but they also may resist the very idea of change. For example, management might want to implement a new production process that will affect many of the jobs in the work unit; if the employees are presented with the initial idea of the change, they may resist it. However, once the *fact* of change is decided by management, employee participation could be invited at the level where it is determined how and in what form the change could be implemented. The fundamental principle here is that the supervisor must decide those

Participating In Change

The problem of the level of participation is illustrated by a situation faced by a company regarding the choice of a new uniform for employees. Management had decided that it was in the best interests of the company for new uniforms to be purchased. The company wanted to build a new image for itself and the new uniforms were an important part of that strategy. The problem they faced was trying to find a new style that would be accepted by the employees — the ones who had to wear the uniforms. The decision to purchase the new uniforms, therefore, did not involve the employees. The second part of the problem — the acceptance of the specific uniform — was the more difficult one, so it was decided to get employee participation in choosing the new uniform. But even more problems were anticipated here, since it was unlikely that all employees would agree on one uniform. If the choice was put to a vote, the losers would resent having to wear a uniform they didn't like, and if a committee of employees made the decision, they would unfairly bear the wrath of their colleagues. Management didn't want to make the decision because they knew that not everyone would like their choice. The outcome of this dilemma was that the company selected three different styles of uniforms as alternatives (to control uniform costs), and then passed the decision of which of the three would be purchased to the union executive. In this way, the company satisfied its objective, and any dissatisfaction with the choice would be directed toward the union, not the management.

items that from the managerial perspective are nondebatable, those that the supervisor cannot compromise on. For the aspects of the change that are a matter of preference to the employees and do not alter the objective of the decision itself, participation can be invited.

Involving employees in change is not a guarantee that there will be no resistance. However, since resistance is sometimes caused by lack of information and anxiety associated with uncertainty, participation can be a useful tool if used properly. It should not, however, be used as a method of getting employees to agree with the supervisor's ideas. Participation is a method of getting input into change, not just agreement.

Often what is important to subordinates is not participation itself, but the opportunity for it. If the opportunity is offered, this alone may reduce the anxiety normally associated with change and the subordinates may be quite willing for the supervisor to proceed with the change. The potential trap is that the supervisor may conclude that subordinates don't care about participation and may not give them the opportunity in the future.

✓ Providing Incentives for Change

Most changes in organizations are initiated and planned by the upper levels of management, but the major effects of the changes are experienced by the employees at the lowest levels. In addition, the benefits of change usually accrue to the planners, not the doers. We have learned, however, that change can be implemented more effectively if *everyone* affected by the change receives something positive from it.

From another perspective, resistance to change is simply a function of the fact that subordinates have no reason to change. From their point of view, the change causes them nothing but anxiety and discomfort and

---

Exercise 19.2

Problems With Participation in Change

Although participation by subordinates in the change process is generally recommended as a method of reducing resistance, it is not without its problems. Before inviting participation, you should be aware of the problems you might encounter. The class should form into small groups of three to five people. Each person should think of three problems that the supervisor might encounter by inviting participation in a proposed change. Share your three with the others in your group. At the close of the exercise the class should have a useful list of potential problems caused by participation.

Management Giveth and Management Taketh Away

One method of introducing change is called the **quid pro quo** approach, a Latin phrase meaning "this for that." In managing change, it means that each party to the change is willing to give the other a benefit if it can have something it wants. A good example of this is a change planned by a company to improve the office layout for efficiency reasons. The management realized that employees would likely resist their plan to remove the private offices and change to an open area office. Since the employees' privacy was being taken away, it had to be replaced with something else that would be seen as a benefit by the employees. With the participation of employees, it was decided that the new work area would be more luxuriously furnished, each employee would have a private telephone line (they previously shared a central switchboard), and a private lounge was constructed to give them a place to socialize and eat lunch. In this way, everyone received a benefit from the change they didn't have before.

there is no positive incentive to change, that is, there is nothing in the change for them.

For organizational changes to be successful they should have built-in incentives for everyone. This is a tall order and usually requires a degree of compromise on the part of the planners. Most changes are designed with a theoretical ideal objective in mind and with little attention to concerns of those affected by the change. If the objective is broadened to include the needs and desires of subordinates, the change is more likely to include positive incentives for them.

One of the reasons the quid pro quo strategy is effective is that the items in the trade are often not comparable. In our example, completely different items were traded, making it difficult for employees to feel if they had lost in the change. Also, by including a variety of changes, the chances of making improvements for employees are increased. The major caution to observe in this approach is to make sure that the benefits you are providing to employees are seen as a benefit by them, and this can be accomplished through inviting their participation.

To sum up, supervisors should always make sure that a change has something positive in it for everyone. If one person or group suffers unduly, the change will be resisted. If you take something away, it must be replaced with something else — and participation by those affected will help you find out what that "something" might be.

Using Communications

To understand how this strategy can reduce resistance to change, we must first realize — and this is difficult for many people to realize — that very few things are truly secret in any organization. Our discussion of informal groups and the grapevine in Chapters 9 and 10 in this book suggests that information, especially the really important stuff, runs rampant. This means that any change contemplated by any level of management, including the supervisor, is not likely to be confidential.

If this is true, withholding information about change will only serve to increase anxiety about it and therefore increase resistance. At some point in the planning of change (and I recommend as early in the planning as possible) employees should be informed of the change and be allowed to participate in it if that is feasible. But even if participation is not possible, providing information about the change *may* reduce anxiety.

Admittedly, this is not always easy. There are times when providing only part of the information (because that is all that you have) can aggravate tensions needlessly. For this reason, some supervisors prefer to wait until all information is available before communicating to subordinates. For example, a supervisor may be contemplating a change in the work schedules of subordinates. Open communication about this may upset people as they worry about how the change might affect them. If the supervisor invites participation in a change, this alone will communicate to employees that something is in the wind, thus causing anxiety. Unfortunately, there is no clear-cut rule on when communication should begin in the change process. There are advantages and disadvantages both ways and each supervisor must make the decision based upon his or her particular situation and past experiences. As a general rule, however, open communications about changes does reduce resistance, especially resistance caused by uncertainty. Secretive, confidential planning may be necessary in some situations, but it can also have serious negative consequences.

Making Change the Norm

One reason employees resist change is simply because they aren't used to it. Anything different can be threatening to us because we are unfamiliar with it. If changes are always taking place, the unusual soon will be seen as normal. This is not to say that supervisors should make changes merely for the sake of making changes, but a conscious effort to keep the work unit from getting stale will help reduce resistance to those changes that are implemented by management.

Introducing Multiple Changes

This is a variation and combination of several strategies already mentioned. The logic of the multiple-change strategy is that as long as you are going to encounter resistance to change, the additional resistance to multiple changes is marginally lower than if each were introduced separately. This is because a portion of all resistance is due to the initial anxiety produced by the fact of change. Therefore, if several changes are introduced at once, the initial resistance is spread over them all.

Another reason why this strategy can be useful is because it gives more opportunities to build in positive incentives for the whole change process. A single change offers limited opportunities and therefore increased chances of resistance.

Working Through Informal leaders

Chapter 9 discussed the importance of informal work groups and their leaders. Because of the influence of these informal leaders, they can play an important role in implementing change. If the supervisor can gain the cooperation and commitment of the informal leader(s), resistance to change by the work group may be substantially reduced.

The important question here is how to get the cooperation of these informal leaders. The best method is to involve them in the planning of the change. If the informal leader becomes involved, then his or her commitment to the change will be greater. The informal leader can also anticipate problems that may be encountered, and the plans can be revised accordingly before resistance arises. Managed properly, the informal leader can play an important role in getting change introduced successfully.

However, using informal leaders can also be dangerous. If the informal leader feels that the supervisor is attempting to manipulate him or her, resistance will increase. To avoid this situation, the supervisor should always view the informal leader as a resource, a person who has ideas that can only be obtained through participation in the change. If the supervisor is able to gain the commitment of the informal

Working with Informal Leaders to Implement Change

In one case, a supervisor of nurses was encountering resistance to change from the nursing staff. The resistance was directed toward the introduction of disposable syringes to replace ones that needed sterilizing after each use. The nurses resisted the new product because they didn't trust the disposable syringes to be as sterile as the ones they sterilized themselves. To overcome the resistance, the supervisor invited the informal leader of the group to accompany her on a visit to the firm that made the syringes. After seeing how they were made and the sterilization process used, the informal leader convinced the others that the new product was superior to the old.

leader, then — and only then — can the supervisor utilize the leader's influence.

Using the Natural Motivators in People

As noted at the beginning of this chapter, people do not naturally resist change. They do so because many of the changes they experience are counter to their natural motivations. Resistance will be lessened if planned changes take advantage of these natural motivations rather than run counter to them. For example, employees who have a natural desire to feel important will resist any change which makes them feel less important. A better strategy would be to design the change such that it increases their feelings of importance, or at worst, doesn't reduce them.

Forcing the Change

Sooner or later, every supervisor will encounter a situation in which a change must be forced upon employees. It could be because of deep-seated feelings against the change, or because the change has been sprung on the supervisor and there is no time to use the participative and communication processes that would normally be available. In any case, forcing change upon employees is a fact of supervisory life, so it is important that you know how to do it properly.

First, if circumstances are appropriate, employees should be told why the change is occurring and, if possible, why they have not been involved in the planning of the change. This, of course, is appealing to the logic in people and therefore may not have much effect if their resistance is emotional — which it probably is. Nevertheless, the step is usually necessary.

The next step is the most crucial one. Once the change is implemented, *it is the responsibility of the supervisor to make sure that employees have a positive experience with the change.* Positive experiences, as we know, tend to have positive effects upon behavior and if the supervisor can provide these, resistance will be reduced. Depending upon the specific reasons for the resistance, most employees will need a lot of support, attention, and reinforcement during this difficult period. For example, if it is a change in job design, the employee may feel insecure and inadequate in the new job, and afraid of making mistakes. Understanding and positive reinforcement by the supervisor are necessary to reduce these negative feelings. As a general rule, the bigger the change, the more support employees will need.

You may have noticed that the forcing method is a variation of the "try it — you'll like it!" technique. People refuse to do something because they think they won't like it, but once they do it, they find it was not so bad after all. The supervisor's job is to make sure they like it, and this is done through a conscious effort to provide positive experiences.

The Fast Versus Slow Issue

One of the most difficult decisions supervisors must make is whether to implement change quickly or slowly. A good case can be made either way, which is why it is a difficult decision. Since there is no definite answer, we will present the advantages and disadvantages of each strategy, and the factors that must be considered in deciding which to choose.

The Case for Fast

The case for fast rests primarily on the premise that, while the initial shock of change may be great, the fact that the change has occurred forces people to adapt more quickly. If the change is implemented slowly, people are more likely to retain old behaviors than to adopt the new ones. Since the shock will occur either way, it is best to get all the pain out of the way at once rather than drag it on for long periods of time. This approach also recognizes that the longer the implementation process, the greater opportunity people have for sabotaging the change.

Of course some changes have to be implemented quickly by their very nature. In Sweden, for example, when they changed from driving on the left side of the road to the right, implementing the change slowly would have been disastrous. And when England changed its monetary system to decimal from pounds and shillings, confusion would have resulted if the change had been made slowly (although even here the educational part of the change occurred over a long period of time).

The Case for Slow

The case for implementing change slowly is based upon the premise that people have difficulty adapting to changes, and therefore a slow implementation process gives them a chance to adapt in small stages rather than having to make large changes all at once. If a staging process is used, less anxiety about the change is aroused and additional stages are not implemented until mastery of the initial stages have been achieved.

Another advantage of the slow method is that it gives opportunities for making improvements in the change along the way. After several stages have been implemented, the supervisor may see additional improvements that are needed, something that would have occurred too late had the change been made quickly. Also, the slow method allows the

Introducing Change Slowly

An excellent example of the slow method is the introduction of the metric system in Canada. When the change was announced, there was considerable resistance. Most claimed they couldn't understand it and since they had gotten by fine for two hundred years with the old system, there was no reason for them to change now. Citizens even organized groups to formally protest the change. The government decided to implement the change slowly. It was decided to change the least important measures first, then proceed to the others. Consequently, the first metric measures were for weather forecasting. But even here, the change was made slowly. For example, in the first stage, radio and television stations were allowed to give both the metric and standard weather information. In the second stage, the standard measures were dropped. The entire change process will take about ten years. The easier changes, such as the weather and distance, have now been accomplished. The more difficult ones are slowly being implemented, such as weights and measures. Interestingly, the resistance to metric measures of weather and distance has largely faded, as it probably will for the other measures once they are introduced.

supervisor to test the waters. If resistance seems to be insurmountable, then the change can be withdrawn or modified.

This method is often recommended because it allows people to retain most of what is familiar while experiencing a little of what is new. Resistance tends to be less if people have the opportunity to revert back to something they are more familiar with. Eventually, as they become more familiar with the new situation, they have less need for the old.

Many of the principles of managing change illustrated in the metric example above can be applied by supervisors. The example also illustrates the need for the supervisor to play a supportive role in situations that require major shifts in employees' attitudes or behaviors. Otherwise, organized resistance can make a supervisor's life difficult.

Deciding to Go Fast or Slow

The choice between the fast and slow method is based upon a preference for acceptance versus the need for quick implementation. Generally speaking, the greater the anticipated resistance to the change, the greater the need for a slow implementation process. Implementing slowly gives the supervisor more time for educating and preparing people for the change, and greater opportunity for providing factual and emotional support during the difficult times of adjustment. There are, however, situations in which only a minimal amount of acceptance is required and the most important factor is getting the change implemented because the cost of implementing slowly is too great.

There are many factors that ultimately affect the decision to implement change slowly or quickly. Supervisors must examine each situation on its own merits to reach the best decision. Recognizing that a decision can seldom be reached on the basis of a single factor, we list several factors that can be considered.

Change should be implemented quickly when:

- The change is a small one;
- There is a high level of agreement on the need for change;
- The cost of implementing slowly negates the value of the change itself; or
- No one affected by the change cares one way or the other.

Change should be implemented slowly when:

- The change requires major changes in attitudes and behaviors;
- Resistance to the change will be high;
- It is anticipated that changes to the original plan will probably be needed; or
- There is little agreement on the need for change.

Key to Success

As this chapter has indicated, one of the reasons why managing change can be difficult is because there are very few hard and fast answers on how to do it. Whether to invite participation or not, whether to implement change quickly or slowly, as well as other important questions, all serve to place the supervisor in a complex situation which requires sensitivity and judgment that cannot be taught in a single chapter on managing change. In the final analysis, each supervisor must rely on experience and intuition as a complement to the principles and concepts presented here.

On the behavioral science side of the subject, this chapter has presented some proven techniques for implementing change effectively. A major part of the process is to understand why people resist change. With this understanding, the supervisor can anticipate resistance and attempt to avoid it where possible. Techniques such as participation, communication, and supportive supervision can be useful in dealing with resistance.

The supervisor who will be effective in managing change will be one who can (a) diagnose and anticipate resistance to change, (b) understand what techniques can be useful in dealing with resistance, and (c) have the necessary skills to use the techniques properly.

Summary

Managing change is a central part of every supervisor's job. It involves the application of all the behavioral science concepts in this book. While resistance to change is very common, people often accept change readily. The key is to understand why some changes are accepted and some are not. People will accept change when (a) it is their choice to change, (b) the change is for the better, (c) the change satisfies a need, (d) they are fully informed about the change, and (e) the change is planned.

There are many sources of resistance to change: economic, social, status, security, ego, and a general resistance due to the inertia to the present situation. Resistance can also be characterized as either rational or emotional. Rational resistance occurs when people lack factual information about a change. Emotional resistance arises in situations in which change has psychological implications for the individual.

An important part of a supervisor's job is overcoming resistance to change. Several strategies have proven useful: getting employees to participate in the planning of the change, providing incentives to encourage acceptance of change, using communication to keep employees informed about change, making change the norm rather than the exception, introducing more than one change at a time to spread the effects, working through informal leaders, using the natural motivators in people, and, finally, forcing change. Supervisors must also decide if a change should be implemented slowly or quickly, and this chapter has described the criteria to be used in making this decision.

Opening Incident Revisited

The problems experienced by Allied Printing are quite common in change situations such as this. What appeared to be a well-planned change has now caused problems that are apparently affecting productivity.

Probably the main cause of this problem is that the management of Allied viewed the change largely as a logical process involving the physical moving of people and equipment. Therefore, the change was logically planned. However, as we now see, changes also have behavioral implications and these were not analyzed prior to the move.

The company has also failed to understand that perceptions of improvement will vary from employee to employee. While improved lighting would normally be welcomed by employees, it is apparently resented in this instance. One reason may be that employees see that to get the lighting they had to give up something more important to them, such as their snack breaks.

Furthermore, there has been little participation in the change by the employees. However, we will never know if getting them involved would have solved the problems that are occurring now. The cost of participation could be quite high, and it is unlikely that all employees would agree on how the new physical arrangement should look.

It may be appropriate to view their complaints as only a symptom of some other source of dissatisfaction (possibly a method of compensating for lack of participation) rather than the real problem. If this is the case, management will have to delve much deeper in order to solve the problem.

So what should management do? As it happens, their best strategy could be to do nothing. In other words, the present decline in morale and productivity could be a normal reaction to a major change. If this is the case, the employees will adjust to the new conditions over time. It might be wise to lend a sympathetic ear to their complaints and make as many adjustments as possible to accommodate their needs, but in the end they will probably all adapt. One of the most serious errors management could make would be to overreact to the problem, which would probably only serve to prolong it.

Review Questions

1. Do people naturally resist change? Why or why not?
2. What are the conditions under which people usually accept change?
3. What are the reasons why employees resist change?
4. What is the difference between rational resistance to change and emotional resistance to change?
5. What are some changes that are frequently resisted?
6. What are the strategies for overcoming resistance to change?
7. What factors determine whether change should be implemented fast or slow?

Chapter Glossary

Rational resistance to change	Resistance that arises because of lack of information about the change. Providing information usually reduces resistance.
Emotional resistance to change	Resistance that arises because of a perception that the change will have a negative effect. Resistance is not logical and can have strong psychological sources. Usually cannot be overcome with facts or additional information.
Participation	A technique for involving employees in decision making and planning changes.
Quid pro quo	Latin phrase meaning "this for that." Applied to change strategies, it suggests that resistance to change can be reduced if those affected by the change are given a benefit to offset the negative effects of a change.

Case Problem

General Manufacturing Company

Claude Grate is the new manager of the purchasing department at General Manufacturing Company. He had several years experience as a purchasing agent with another company and was hired by General to reorganize the purchasing function in accordance with an overall corporate plan to improve efficiency and reduce costs.

After several weeks, Claude recognized that the purchasing department performs little more than a clerical function. There are no purchasing policies, no central buying, and no control over who is buying what. His first step was to centralize certain purchases in his department. He decided to start with a dollar amount, and wrote up a procedure that requires that all purchase requisitions over $500 be approved by him before they can be sent to suppliers. He submitted his plan to his manager, who approved it.

Claude then drafted a memo to all the other managers which read as follows:

TO: All management personnel
FROM: Claude Grate, Purchasing Manager

I'm sure all of you understand the importance of getting the most value for our purchasing dollar. In the past the company has been very inefficient in its purchasing activities, and I am beginning a strategy to improve the purchasing function.

As an initial change, I am creating a new procedure whereby every purchase over $500 must come to the purchasing department first for approval. This will provide us with the opportunity to review the purchase and see if we are getting the most for our dollar. Attached is a copy of the new form to be used for this purpose.

I am sure all of you agree on the necessity for getting the most for our money, and I look forward to your cooperation on this matter.

During the past several weeks, Claude has received only two completed forms, yet there is every indication that the company is operating at its usual level of activity.

Questions for Discussion

1. Comment on Grate's method of implementing this change.
2. Is his new system working?
3. How should the change have been handled?

Index